WORLDS TOGETHER, WORLDS APART

VOLUME 2

A Companion Reader

WORLDS TOGETHER, WORLDS APART

VOLUME 2

A Companion Reader

EDITED BY

KENNETH L. POMERANZ
JAMES B. GIVEN
LAURA J. MITCHELL

W · W · NORTON & COMPANY
NEW YORK · LONDON

W. W. Norton & Company has been independent since its founding in 1923, when William Warder Norton and Mary D. Herter Norton first published lectures delivered at the People's Institute, the adult education division of New York City's Cooper Union. The firm soon expanded its program beyond the Institute, publishing books by celebrated academics from America and abroad. By midcentury, the two major pillars of Norton's publishing program—trade books and college texts—were firmly established. In the 1950s, the Norton family transferred control of the company to its employees, and today—with a staff of four hundred and a comparable number of trade, college, and professional titles published each year—W. W. Norton & Company stands as the largest and oldest publishing house owned wholly by its employees.

Copyright © 2011 by W. W. Norton & Company, Inc.

All rights reserved
Printed in the United States of America
Book design and composition by Westchester Book Group
Production manager: Ben Reynolds

Library of Congress Cataloging-in-Publication Data

Worlds together, worlds apart : a companion reader / edited by Kenneth L. Pomeranz, James B. Given, Laura J. Mitchell.
     p. cm.
     Companion to: Worlds together, worlds apart : a history of the world from the beginnings of humankind to the present / Robert Tignor . . . [et al.].
     Includes bibliographical references and index.
     ISBN 978-0-393-91160-2 (v. 1)—ISBN 978-0-393-91161-9 (v. 2)
1. World history—Sources.   I. Pomeranz, Kenneth.   II. Given, James Buchanan.   III. Mitchell, Laura Jane, 1963–   IV. Tignor, Robert L.
     D21.W939   2011
     909—dc22

                                                                2010038550

W. W. Norton & Company, Inc., 500 Fifth Avenue, New York, NY 10110
     wwnorton.com

W. W. Norton & Company Ltd., Castle House, 75/76 Wells Street,
London W1T 3QT

1 2 3 4 5 6 7 8 9 0

About the Editors

KENNETH L. POMERANZ (Ph.D. Yale University) is Chancellor's Professor of History at the University of California, Irvine. His publications include *The Great Divergence: China, Europe, and the Making of the Modern World Economy*; *The Making of a Hinterland: State, Society and Economy in Inland North China, 1853–1937*; and numerous other works. He is a Fellow of the American Academy of Arts and Sciences.

JAMES B. GIVEN (Ph.D. Stanford University) is professor of medieval history at the University of California, Irvine. His principal interests are the social and religious history of Europe in the thirteenth and fourteenth centuries. His works include *Society and Homicide in Thirteenth-Century England*, *State and Society in Medieval Europe: Gwynedd and Languedoc under Outside Rule*, and *Inquisition and Medieval Society: Power, Discipline, and Resistance in Languedoc*.

LAURA J. MITCHELL (Ph.D. University of California, Los Angeles) is associate professor of African history at UC Irvine. She has served on the World History Association Executive Council and is co-chair of the AP World History Curriculum Assessment and Development Committee. Her book *Belongings: Property, Family, and Identity in Colonial South Africa* (Columbia University Press, 2009) is available online at www.gutenberg-e.org/mitchell.

To our students, graduate and undergraduate,
in world history

CONTENTS

*Visual Source

CHAPTER 11 | CRISES AND RECOVERY IN AFRO-EURASIA 1300s–1500s

CHAPTER 12 | CONTACT, COMMERCE, AND COLONIZATION, 1450s–1600

CHAPTER 13 | WORLDS ENTANGLED, 1600–1750

CASEBOOK | COERCED LABOR IN THE EARLY MODERN WORLD

CHAPTER 14 | CULTURES OF SPLENDOR AND POWER, 1500–1780

CHAPTER 15 | REORDERING THE WORLD, 1750–1850

CHAPTER 16 | ALTERNATIVE VISIONS OF THE NINETEENTH CENTURY

CHAPTER 17 | NATIONS AND EMPIRES, 1850–1914

CHAPTER 18 | AN UNSETTLED WORLD, 1890–1914

CHAPTER 21 | GLOBALIZATION, 1970–2000

TEXT PERMISSIONS

PREFACE

An all-news radio station used to promise, "You give us 22 minutes, we give you the world." This book, however, will not "give" you world history. Nearly one hundred and fifty documents cannot be comprehensive, or even representative. Some documents, of course, reveal a great deal about a particularly important moment. A classic example is Bishop Eusebius of Caesarea's account of the Roman emperor Constantine's early fourth-century conversion to Christianity. But most great events—not to mention long-term trends and transformations—cannot be captured in a single text.

This book, however, can help students learn how to read primary sources and enrich their studies. For years, the history faculty at the University of California–Irvine have made the teaching of primary sources a centerpiece of our world history survey course. Many of us have also used *Worlds Together, Worlds Apart* since its first publication because it reinforces many of our course objectives. This document collection reflects our best effort to provide you with a diverse range of primary sources that we know to work well in class, and ones that will complement the main themes and existing primary sources in *Worlds Together, Worlds Apart*.

A number of factors influenced our document selection process. We have chosen items we know work well in the classroom, sometimes passing over more famous texts. For example, instead of including Newton's laws of gravity and universal motion (the foundation of modern physics), we have chosen a map that shows how the sources from which he gathered information for his work corresponded to early modern trade routes. Not only is the map easier to discuss outside the context of a physics class; it provides insights about how one set of specifically global *historical* transformations, in this case the expansion of information networks as maritime trade boomed, influenced science. This document also reflects our attention to a range of visual sources. We have included paintings, representations of objects, photographs, maps, and charts for the obvious reason that not all historical evidence is textual, but more importantly because in our experience, studying a wide range of sources and types of material is the best way to foster new ways of thinking about historical problems.

We selected documents that help the reader see "how," in Charles Tilly's phrase, "the little people lived the big changes." We have tried to cover major events, and provide documents for each period from various parts of the world, but we have been more concerned to present documents that start and sustain conversations about important *themes* which turn up, with variations, in many times and places. For example, Xu Jie's commentary (see Chapter 14) describes how relations between landlords and tenants changed in sixteenth-century China as the economy commercialized, the rich moved to towns, free tenants resisted being treated like servants, and the renting of land became a set of cash transactions between near-strangers. These trends did not occur together only in sixteenth-century Songjiang, nor were the results the same wherever and whenever they occurred. This document cannot stand for the individual experiences of Yorkshire, Anatolia, or Morelos. But considering what happened in sixteenth-century Songjiang should stimulate questions about how these same themes played out in other times and places.

We have also chosen documents that are particularly useful for learning *how* to analyze historical sources. Some documents are most useful for what their creators tell us about their topics: for example, a graph of trends in human energy consumption. In other documents we learn more by looking for what their creators reveal (often inadvertently) about their own assumptions, biases, and preoccupations. To take an extreme example, Adolf Hitler's writings (see *Mein Kampf* in Volume 2, Chapter 20) on Russia, Germany, and Jews tell us very little about the reality of any of those topics, but much about the obsessions of one very influential person. This document also reveals Hitler's preoccupations with struggles among empires and racially defined "nations," as it exemplifies some ideas of the day that were not unique to the writer, and help account for his influence.

Most documents tell us something about both their topics and their creators, so that readers must get used to looking at them with more than one goal in mind. For example, Robert Walsh's description of a Brazilian slave market (in the casebook on coerced labor) provides a physical description of the market conditions, but it also lets readers make inferences about how Walsh understood the extent of shared humanity (through his sympathy for the wretchedness of the slaves) and about European expectations of elite women's behavior.

The documents' genres also vary; they include letters, diaries, public proclamations, advertisements, paintings, photos, poems, scientific reports, statistical graphs, and so on. We did not aim for a particular balance among types of sources, but for diversity and a distribution of visual materials. Historians try to relate different aspects of an era to each other, showing how economics, religion, technology, literature, and family life fit together in ways that specialists in these fields might not recognize. Students need experience in seeing how historians extract both factual information and points of view from a wide variety of materials and relate them to each other. They will get that here.

We include four casebooks that combine documents that are thematically related to each other but come from different places and belong to different genres. The casebooks address women and rulership in ancient times, mobilizing for war in the age of the Mongols, coerced labor in the early modern world, and rubber and commodity chains. Historians often emphasize that they read documents in context. While philosophers might care only about whether the arguments in a text are logical, historians also want to know the circumstances in which it was written. They also ask how a text's insights, errors, habitual references, and so on tell us about that document's world, and how knowing that world helps us in turn understand the document. But we do not receive the context in which to read a document ready-made; we have to build it by reading other documents. Moreover, and this is especially important in the study of *world* history, a document often yields new insights when it is placed in different contexts. An account of seventeenth-century Caribbean slavery (coerced labor casebook) can be read in a strictly Caribbean context, or in the context of an Atlantic world that included Africa, Europe, and the Americas. But it yields other insights when juxtaposed with an account of forced labor in eighteenth-century Siberia. Similarly, knowing that William Dampier, who wrote about "slavery" in Aceh (in present-day Indonesia), was familiar with Atlantic slavery can help us understand why he viewed Acehnese bound labor in certain ways.

We hope that these documents will help readers learn to do for themselves some of what we do in our headnotes and questions: provide context for thinking about these sources as evidence for world historical questions, and suggest some ways to begin exploring what they can tell us. Interpreting in context is, after all, how people navigate both the past and the present.

Acknowledgments

We would like to thank our colleagues in Irvine and elsewhere whose conversations, suggestions, and replies to our questions have improved this book. We are grateful to Maura Cunningham, whose unflagging research and organizational skills helped the project stay on track, and to Jennifer Liu, whose administrative help got us started. The team at W. W. Norton was a pleasure to work with. Jon Durbin provided valuable guidance on the project, while Jason Spears and Becky Homiski contributed research and legwork to track down elusive original sources and secure permission to reprint the documents we selected.

WORLDS TOGETHER, WORLDS APART

VOLUME 2

A Companion Reader

Chapter 10

BECOMING "THE WORLD," 1000–1300 CE

The Rise of Chinggis Khan (c. 1206)

Chinggis Khan (c. 1162–1227) was the founder of the Mongol Empire, which ultimately became the largest contiguous land empire ever known. The construction of this empire began in Chinggis's reign, with successful military campaigns in China, central Asia, and Persia. Despite these successes, Chinggis's early life was beset with troubles. Fatherless, deserted by his kinsmen, at times a fugitive from his enemies in the wilderness, he nevertheless managed by 1206 to make himself master of the peoples of the East Asia steppe. The first text below comes from *The Secret History of the Mongols*, probably composed sometime between 1228 and 1252. This is the best source we have for Chinggis's early life. The excerpt describes the capture and execution of one of Chinggis's greatest rivals, Jamuqa, in 1206. Before he turned against Chinggis, Jamuqa had been the Khan's blood brother. The second text comes from Rashid-al-Din's *Jami' al-tawarikh* (Compendium of Chronicles), which he was commissioned to write by Ghazan Khan (1271–1304), the Mongol ruler of Persia. Rashid, a Jewish convert to Islam, and his sons were Ghazan Khan's most trusted advisers. However, he fell out with one of Ghazan's successors and was executed in 1318. Spelling has been updated in the following excerpts to reflect modern orthography.

THE SECRET HISTORY OF THE MONGOLS

When Chingis Khan defeated the Naiman army
Jamugha had been with the Naiman
and in the battle all of his people were taken away.
He had escaped with only five followers
and become a bandit in the Tangnu Mountains.
One day he and his companions were lucky enough to kill a great
    mountain sheep,
and as they sat around the fire roasting the mutton

* * *

his five followers seized him,
and binding Jamugha they brought him to Chingis Khan.
Because he'd been captured this way, Jamugha said:
"Tell my anda, the Khan,
'Black crows have captured a beautiful duck.
Peasants and slaves have laid hands on their lord.
My anda the Khan will see this and know what to do.
Brown vultures have captured a mandarin duck.
Slaves and servants have conspired against their lord.
Surely my holy anda will know how to respond to this.'"
When he heard Jamugha's words Chingis Khan made a decree:
"How can we allow men who lay hands on their own lord to live?
Who could trust people like this?
Such people should be killed
along with all their descendants!"
He brought before Jamugha the men who had seized him,
these men who had betrayed their own lord,
and in their lord's presence their heads were cut off.
Then Chingis Khan said:
"Tell Jamugha this.

SOURCE: "The Secret History of the Mongols": from *The Secret History of the Mongols*, trans. Francis Woodman Cleaves. "A maxim of Chinggis Khan": from Timothy May, *The Mongol Art of War: Chinggis Khan and the Mongol Military System* (Yardley, PA: Westholme, 2007), p. 77.

'Now we two are together.
Let's be allies.
Once we moved together like the two shafts of a cart,
but you thought about separating from me and you left.
Now that we're together again in one place
let's each be the one to remind the other of what he forgot;
let's each be the one to awaken the other's judgment whenever it
     sleeps.
Though you left me you were always my anda.
On the day when we met on the battlefield
the thought of trying to kill me brought pain to your heart.

*　*　*

Jamugha answered him:
"Long ago when we were children in the Khorkhonagh Valley
I declared myself to be your anda.
Together we ate the food which is never digested
and spoke words to each other which are never forgotten,
and at night we shared one blanket to cover us both.
Then it was as if people came between us with knives,
slashing our legs and stabbing our sides,
and we were separated from each other.
I thought to myself,
'We've made solemn promises to each other'
and my face was so blackened by the winds of shame
that I couldn't bring myself to show my face,
this shameful windburned face,
before the warm face of my anda, the Khan.

*　*　*

And now my anda, the Khan wants to favor me,
and says to me, 'Let's be allies.'
When I should have been his ally I deserted him.
Now, my anda, you've pacified every nation;
you've united every tribe in the world.
The Great Khan's throne has given itself to you.
Now that the world is ready for you

what good would I be as your ally?
I'd only invade your dreams in the dark night
and trouble your thoughts in the day.
I'd be like a louse on your collar,
like a thorn under your shirt.

* * *

Having been born a great hero,
he has skillful young brothers.
Having many fine men by his side,
he's always been greater than I am.
As for me,
since I lost both my parents when I was young,
I have no younger brothers.
My wife is a babbling fool.
I can't trust the men at my side.
Because of all this
my anda, whose destiny is Heaven's will,
has surpassed me in everything.
My anda, if you want to favor me,
then let me die quickly and you'll be at peace with your heart.
When you have me killed, my anda,
see that it's done without shedding my blood.
Once I am dead and my bones have been buried high on a cliff
I will protect your seed and the seed of your seed.
I will become a prayer to protect you."

* * *

Hearing this Chingis Khan spoke:
"Though my anda deserted me
and said many things against me,
I've never heard that he ever wanted me dead.
He's a man we all might learn from
but he's not willing to stay with us.
If I simply ordered him to be killed
there isn't a diviner in the world who could justify it.
If I harmed this man's life without good reason
it would bring a curse on us.

*   *   *

Now I say 'Let's be allies' but you refuse me.
When I try to spare your life you won't allow it.
So speak to Jamugha and tell him,
'Allow this man to kill you
according to your own wishes,
without shedding your blood.'"
And Chingis Khan made a decree, saying:
"Execute Jamugha without shedding his blood
and bury his bones with all due honor."
He had Jamugha killed and his bones properly buried.

[A maxim of Chinggis Khan:] Just as *ortaqs* [merchants engaged in commerce with capital supplied by the imperial treasury] come with gold spun fabrics and are confident of making profits on those goods and textiles, military commanders should teach their sons archery, horsemanship, and wrestling well. They should test them in these arts and make them audacious and brave to the same degree that *ortaqs* are confident of their own skill.

Questions

1. How important is loyalty to one's master in *The Secret History*?

2. What is Chinggis Khan's opinion of merchants? What status does he ascribe to them?

3. How can you account for the differences in the description of Chinggis Khan between *The Secret History* and Rashid's text?

Yuan Cai, The Problems of Women (twelfth century)

Yuan Cai (c. 1140–c. 1195) was an official and scholar best known for writing an advice book on how members of the scholar-gentry class should manage family matters. Such books had already appeared in China many centuries before, but with the boom in woodblock printing during the Song dynasty (960–1279 CE) and a marked increase in literacy rates, they became far more popular and influential. Increased social mobility also made such books more important, as successful people found themselves occupying roles that they had not had the opportunity to observe their parents handling.

The passages selected here deal with various aspects of the lives of women (though the presumed reader is a male household head). The Song dynasty was a period of major changes in the status of women, with most modern scholars concluding that the choices available to at least elite women narrowed considerably. (One formulation has it that in the Tang dynasty a young female aristocrat might be out horseback riding when her suitor came to call; by the Song dynasty she would not have learned to ride horses, would not have gone out on her own, and would not have seen her suitor prior to marriage.) But recent scholarship has suggested a more complex picture, with women losing ground in some areas but gaining in others.

WOMEN SHOULD NOT TAKE PART IN AFFAIRS OUTSIDE THE HOME

Women do not take part in extrafamilial affairs. The reason is that worthy husbands and sons take care of everything for them, while unworthy ones can always find ways to hide their deeds from the women.

Many men today indulge in pleasure and gambling; some end up mortgaging their lands, and even go so far as to mortgage their houses without their wives' knowledge. Therefore, when husbands are bad, even if wives try to handle outside matters, it is of no use. Sons must have their mothers' signatures to mortgage their family properties, but there are sons who falsify papers and forge signatures, sometimes borrowing money at high interest from people who would not hesitate to bring their claim to court.

* * * Therefore, when sons are bad, it is useless for mothers to try to handle matters relating to the outside world.

SOURCE: *Chinese Civilization: A Sourcebook*, 2nd ed., edited by Patricia Buckley Ebrey (New York: The Free Press, 1993), pp. 166–68.

* * * If husbands and sons could only remember that their wives and mothers are helpless and suddenly repent, wouldn't that be best?

WOMEN'S SYMPATHIES SHOULD BE INDULGED

Without going overboard, people should marry their daughters with dowries appropriate to their family's wealth. Rich families should not consider their daughters outsiders but should give them a share of the property. Sometimes people have incapable sons and so have to entrust their affairs to their daughters' families; even after their deaths, their burials and sacrifices are performed by their daughters. So how can people say that daughters are not as good as sons?

Generally speaking, a woman's heart is very sympathetic. If her parents' family is wealthy and her husband's family is poor, she wants to take her parents' wealth to help her husband's family prosper. If her husband's family is wealthy but her parents' family is poor, then she wants to take from her husband's family to enable her parents to prosper. Her parents and husband should be sympathetic toward her feelings and indulge some of her wishes. When her own sons and daughters are grown and married, if either her son's family or her daughter's family is wealthy while the other is poor, she wishes to take from the wealthy one to give to the poor one. Her sons and daughters should understand her feelings and be somewhat indulgent. But taking from the poor to make the rich richer is unacceptable, and no one should ever go along with it.

ORPHANED GIRLS SHOULD HAVE THEIR MARRIAGES ARRANGED EARLY

When a widow remarries she sometimes has an orphaned daughter not yet engaged. In such cases she should try to get a respectable relative to arrange a marriage for her daughter. She should also seek to have her daughter reared in the house of her future in-laws, with the marriage to take place after the girl has grown up. If the girl were to go along with the mother to her stepfather's house, she would not be able to clear herself if she were subjected to any humiliations.

For Women Old Age Is Particularly Hard to Bear

* * * For women who live a long life, old age is especially hard to bear, because most women must rely on others for their existence. * * * For this reason women often enjoy comfort in their youth but find their old age difficult to endure. It would be well for their relatives to keep this in mind.

It Is Difficult for Widows to Entrust Their Financial Affairs to Others

Some wives with stupid husbands are able to manage the family's finances, calculating the outlays and receipts of money and grain, without being cheated by anyone. Of those with degenerate husbands, there are also some who are able to manage the finances with the help of their sons without ending in bankruptcy. Even among those whose husbands have died and whose sons are young, there are occasionally women able to raise and educate their sons, keep the affection of all their relatives, manage the family business, and even prosper. All of these are wise and worthy women. But the most remarkable are the women who manage a household after their husbands have died leaving them with young children. Such women could entrust their finances to their husbands' kinsmen or their own kinsmen, but not all relatives are honorable, and the honorable ones are not necessarily willing to look after other people's business.

When wives themselves can read and do arithmetic, and those they entrust with their affairs have some sense of fairness and duty with regard to food, clothing, and support, then things will usually work out all right. But in most of the rest of the cases, bankruptcy is what happens.

Before Buying a Servant Girl or Concubine, Make Sure of the Legality

When buying a female servant or concubine, inquire whether it is legal for her to be indentured or sold before closing the deal. If the girl is impoverished and has no one to rely on, then she should be brought before the authorities to give an account of her past.

After guarantors have been secured and an investigation conducted, the transaction can be completed. But if she is not able to give an account of her past, then the agent who offered her for sale should be questioned. Temporarily she may be hired on a salaried basis. If she is ever recognized by her relatives, she should be returned to them.

HIRED WOMEN SHOULD BE SENT BACK WHEN THEIR PERIOD OF SERVICE IS OVER

If you hire a man's wife or daughter as a servant, you should return her to her husband or father on completion of her period of service. If she comes from another district, you should send her back to it after her term is over. These practices are the most humane and are widely carried out by the gentry in the Southeast. Yet there are people who do not return their hired women to their husbands but wed them to others instead; others do not return them to their parents but marry them off themselves. Such actions are the source of many lawsuits.

How can one not have sympathy for those separated from their relatives, removed from their hometowns, who stay in service for their entire lives with neither husbands nor sons. Even in death these women's spirits are left to wander all alone. How pitiful they are!

Questions

1. Which kinds of women seem to have the most control over their lives? Which ones have the least? What circumstances create openings for women to make their own choices?

2. The Song dynasty was a period in which commercial activity increased rapidly. What role do markets and money play in these documents?

3. What differences does Yuan Cai see between men and women? What capacities do they share? What moral significance, if any, does he attach to the differences?

Two Views of the Fall of Jerusalem (1099 CE)

In 1095 the Byzantine emperor, hard-pressed by the Seljuk Turks, wrote to Pope Urban II to request military aid. What he got was the First Crusade. Urban's call for an armed pilgrimage, full of stories of Muslim atrocities against Christians and promises of remission of sins for those who took part, touched off a wave of enthusiasm in western Europe. In 1096 large numbers of nobles and crowds of enthusiastic peasants set off to liberate Jerusalem from Muslim control. The three-year journey to Jerusalem was frightful, accompanied by massacres of Jews and Muslims, starvation, cannibalism, and near defeat and destruction. On July 15, 1099, those crusaders who had survived the frightful three-year long journey captured Jerusalem. They then proceeded to massacre the Muslim population of the city, an atrocity whose memory is still alive in Muslim consciousness. The following excerpts give two different perspectives on this event: one Christian, the other Muslim. The first is from the cleric Raymond d'Aguilers, who appears to have been a chaplain of Raymond, count of Toulouse, one of the leaders of the crusade. He was present at the siege and final storming of Jerusalem. The second is a lament for the destruction of Jerusalem written by the Arab poet, Abu l-Musaffar al-Abiwardi (1064–1113), who held important administrative positions in Baghdad under the Seljuks.

THE FIRST CRUSADE

When our efforts were ended and the machines completed, the princes held a council and announced: "Let all prepare themselves for a battle on Thursday; in the meantime, let us pray, fast, and give alms. Hand over your animals and your boys to the artisans and carpenters, that they may bring in beams, poles, stakes, and branches to make mantlets [movable shelters designed to protect

SOURCE: August C. Krey, *The First Crusade: The Accounts of Eye-Witnesses and Participants* (Princeton: Princeton University Press, 1921), pp. 258–61, and *Arab Historians of the Crusades*, translated from Arabic by Francesco Gabrieli, translated from Italian by E. J. Costello (Berkeley: University of California Press, 1969), p. 12.

soldiers assaulting a fortress]. Two knights should make one mantlet and one scaling ladder. Do not hesitate to work for the Lord, for your labors will soon be ended." This was willingly done by all. * * *

Meanwhile, the Saracens in the city, noting the great number of machines that we had constructed, strengthened the weaker parts of the wall, so that it seemed that they could be taken only by the most desperate efforts. Because the Saracens had made so many and such strong fortifications to oppose our machines, the * * * [leaders] spent the night before the day set for the attack moving their machines, mantlets, and platforms to that side of the city which is between the church of St. Stephen and the valley of Josaphat. You who read this must not think that this was a light undertaking, for the machines were carried in parts almost a mile to the place where they were to be set up. When morning came and the Saracens saw that all the machinery and tents had been moved during the night, they were amazed. Not only the Saracens were astonished, but our people as well, for they recognized that the hand of the Lord was with us. * * *

* * * But why delay the story? The appointed day arrived and the attack began. However, I want to say this first, that, according to our estimate and that of many others, there were sixty thousand fighting men within the city. * * * At the most we did not have more than twelve thousand able to bear arms, for there were many poor people and many sick. There were twelve or thirteen hundred knights in our army, as I reckon it, not more. I say this that you may realize that nothing, whether great or small, which is undertaken in the name of the Lord can fail. * * *

Our men began to undermine the towers and walls. From every side stones were hurled from the *tormenti* and the *petrariae* [that is, catapults] and so many arrows that they fell like hail. The servants of God bore this patiently, sustained by the premises of their faith, whether they should be killed or should presently prevail over their enemies. The battle showed no indication of victory, but when the machines were drawn nearer to the walls, they hurled not only stones and arrows, but also burning wood and straw. * * * Thus the fight continued from the rising to the setting sun in such splendid fashion that it is difficult to believe anything more glorious was ever done.

Then we called on Almighty God, our Leader and Guide, confident in His mercy. Night brought fear to both sides. * * * [O]n both sides it was a night of watchfulness, labor, and sleepless caution: on one side, most certain hope, on the other doubtful fear. We gladly labored to capture the city for the glory of God, they less willingly strove to resist our efforts for the sake of the laws of Mohammed. * * *

When the morning came, our men eagerly rushed to the walls and dragged the machines forward, but the Saracens had constructed so many machines that for each one of ours they now had nine or ten. * * *

By noon our men were greatly discouraged. They were weary and at the end of their resources. There were still many of the enemy opposing each one of our men; the walls were very high and strong, and the great resources and skill that the enemy exhibited in repairing their defenses seemed too great for us to overcome. But, while we hesitated, irresolute, and the enemy exulted in our discomfiture, the healing mercy of God inspired us and turned our sorrow into joy, for the Lord did not forsake us. * * * [A] knight on the Mount of Olives began to wave his shield to those who were with the Count and others, signalling them to advance. Who this knight was we have been unable to find out. At this signal our men began to take heart, and some began to batter down the wall, while others began to ascend by means of scaling ladders and ropes. Our archers shot burning firebrands, and in this way checked the attack that the Saracens were making upon the wooden towers of the Duke and the two Counts. * * * This shower of fire drove the defenders from the walls. Then the Count quickly released the long drawbridge which had protected the side of the wooden tower next to the wall, and it swung down from the top, being fastened to the middle of the tower, making a bridge over which the men began to enter Jerusalem bravely and fearlessly. * * *

[N]ow that our men had possession of the walls and towers, wonderful sights were to be seen. Some of our men (and this was more merciful) cut off the heads of their enemies; others shot them with arrows, so that they fell from the towers; others tortured them longer by casting them into the flames. Piles of heads, hands, and feet were to be seen in the streets of the city. It was necessary to pick one's way over the bodies of men and horses. But these were small matters compared to what happened at the Temple of Solomon, a place where religious services are ordinarily chanted. What happened there? If I tell the truth, it will exceed your powers of belief. So let it suffice to say this much, at least, that in the Temple and porch of Solomon, men rode in blood up to their knees and bridle reins. Indeed, it was a just and splendid judgment of God that this place should be filled with the blood of the unbelievers, since it had suffered so long from their blasphemies. * * *

Now that the city was taken, it was well worth all our previous labors and hardships to see the devotion of the pilgrims at the Holy Sepulchre. How they rejoiced and exulted and sang a new song to the Lord! For their hearts offered prayers of praise to God, victorious and triumphant, which cannot be told in words. A new day, new joy, new and perpetual gladness, the consummation of our labor and devotion, drew forth from all new words and new songs. This day, I say, will be famous in all future ages, for it turned our labors and sorrows into joy and exultation; this day, I say, marks the justification of all Christianity, the humiliation of paganism, and the renewal of our faith. "This is the day which the Lord hath made, let us rejoice and be glad in it," for on this day the Lord revevealed Himself to His people and blessed them.

Abu l-Muzaffar al-Abiwardi, [Destruction of Jerusalem]

We have mingled blood with flowing tears, and there is no room
    left in us for pity
To shed tears is a man's worst weapon when the swords stir up the
    embers of war.
Sons of Islām, behind you are battles in which heads rolled at your
    feet.
Dare you slumber in the blessed shade of safety, where life is as soft
    as an orchard flower?
How can the eye sleep between the lids at a time of disasters that
    would waken any sleeper?
While your Syrian brothers can only sleep on the backs of their
    chargers, or in vultures' bellies!

Must the foreigners feed on our ignominy, while you trail behind
you the train of a pleasant life, like men whose world is at peace?

When blood has been spilt, when sweet girls must for shame hide
their lovely faces in their hands!

When the white swords' points are red with blood, and the iron of
the brown lances is stained with gore!

At the sound of sword hammering on lance young children's hair
turns white.

This is war, and the man who shuns the whirlpool to save his life
shall grind his teeth in penitence.

This is war, and the infidel's sword is naked in his hand, ready to
be sheathed again in men's necks and skulls.

This is war, and he who lies in the tomb at Medina seems to raise
his voice and cry: "O sons of Hashim [an ancestor of the
prophet Muhammad]!

I see my people slow to raise the lance against the enemy: I see
the Faith resting on feeble pillars.

For fear of death the Muslims are evading the fire of battle,
refusing to believe that death will surely strike them."

Must the Arab champions then suffer with resignation, while the
gallant Persians shut their eyes to their dishonour?

Questions

1. What is Raymond's attitude toward the massacre of the inhabitants of
   Jerusalem?

2. To what does Raymond attribute the success of the crusaders?

3. What is al-Abiwardi's purpose in writing his poem? How does he try to
   motivate his fellow Muslims to take action?

Joseph Ben Abraham, Letter from Aden to Abraham Yijū (c. 1130)

Dispersed communities of merchants who shared language, religion, or
ethnic identity facilitated thriving long-distance trade in the twelfth

century. Many records of Jewish merchants working in Mediterranean and Indian Ocean networks were preserved in the Cairo Geniza. According to Jewish custom, text inscribed with the name of God should not be destroyed. So writings—from small scraps to complex documents—were stored in a dedicated room in a synagogue. Since God's blessing was frequently invoked in letters and commercial contracts, many of these ordinary documents connecting individual merchants were preserved. The synagogue in old Cairo accumulated documents and fragments from about 800 CE through the nineteenth century, at which point scholars began to work with this unparalleled collection of medieval sources to investigate aspects of Jewish life and the thick web of connections that linked communities across great distances.

Partnerships, many of them life-long, cemented connections between ports and served to spread the risks of long-distance trade. Ongoing correspondence, the exchange of presents, and sometimes the exchange of slaves or dependents created bonds between traders who might never have met in person. The following letter is a glimpse into one such relationship between Joseph ben Abraham in Aden, on the Arabian Peninsula, and Abraham Yijū in Mangalore, in southwestern India.

A. Losses and arrivals

In (Your) name, O Merci(ful).

The letter of your excellency, the illustrious elder, my master, has arrived. It was the most pleasant letter that came and the most delightful message that reached me. I read and understood it, etc. (another three lines).

You, my master, may God make your honored position permanent, wrote that you kindly sold the silk and sent goods for its proceeds and that you sent them in the ships of *Rāshmit*. I learned, however, that *Rāshmit's* two ships were lost completely. May *the H(oly one, be) he b(lessed)*, compensate me and you. Do not ask me, my master, how much I was affected by the loss of the cargo belonging

---

SOURCE: *Letters of Medieval Jewish Traders*, translated by S. D. Goitein (Princeton: Princeton University Press, 1973), pp. 192–96.

to you. But the Creator will compensate you soon. In any case, there is no counsel against the decree of God.

All the "copper" (vessels, *naḥās*), which you sent with Abū 'Alī, arrived, and the "table-bowl" also arrived. It was exactly as I wished— may God give you a good reward and undertake your recompensation (for only he is able to do it adequately).

B. Excommunication of a tardy debtor

You, my master, mentioned that you approached the *kārdāl* gently in order to get something for us back from him. Perhaps you should threaten him that here in Aden we excommunicate anyone that owes us something and does not fulfill his commitments. Maybe he will be afraid of the excommunication. If he does not pay, we shall issue an official letter of excommunication and send it to him, so that he will become aware of his crime.

C. Various orders, especially for bronze vessels

The re(d) betel-nuts arrived, as well as the two washbasins— may God give you a good reward. Please do not send me any more red betel-nuts, for they are not good. If there are any white, fresh betel-nuts to be had, it will be all right.

Please do not send me anything either betel-nuts or any other goods you acquire for me, in partnership with anyone, but specify each person and every item of merchandise.

I am sending you a broken ewer and a deep washbasin, weighing seven pounds less a quarter. Please make me a ewer of the same measure from its copper (or bronze, *ṣufr*) for it is good copper. The weight of the ewer should be five pounds exactly.

I am also sending 18¼ pounds of good yellow copper (*ṣufr asfar*, hardly "brass") in bars and five pounds of Qal'ī "lead" in a big mold and a piece of Egyptian "lead" (in the form of) a shell. Please put the bars, the "lead," and what remains from the manufacture of the ewer together and have two table-bowls for two dishes made for your servant, each table-bowl being of seventeen *fil(l)*, of the same form as the table-bowl you sent me; they should be of good workmanship.

D. DETAILED DESCRIPTION OF A LAMP ORDERED

Make me a nice lamp from the rest of all the copper (*ṣufr*). Its column should be octagonal and stout, its base should be in the form of a lampstand with strong feet. On its head there should be a copper (*naḥās*) lamp with two ends for two wicks, which should be set on the end of the column so that it could move up and down. The three parts, the column, the stand and the lamp, should be separate from one another. If they could make the feet in spirals, then let it be so; for this is more beautiful. The late *Abu 'l-Faraj al-Jubaylī* made a lamp of such a description. Perhaps this will be like it.

E. ADDITIONAL ORDERS

This year, I did not succeed in sending gold or silk. Instead, I am sending currency, 20 Malikī dinars, old dinars of good gold. Please pay with it the price of the labor of the coppersmith and for the rest buy me a quantity of "eggs" (a kind of cardamom) and cardamom, and if this is not to be had, anything else which God, be he praised, makes available. And, please, send everything with the first ship sailing.

Please buy me two washbasins of middle size, somewhat larger than those you previously sent me, and a large washbasin, which holds two waterskins of water, measuring two *siqāyas*.

F. PRESENTS SENT

I am sending you some things of no importance or value, namely two ruba'iyyas of white sugar; a bottle, in a tight basket, entirely filled with raisins; and in a *mazza* a pound of Maghrebi kohl, a pound of costus, a pound of vitriol, half a pound of litharge, three ounces of *'ilk* gum, and five sets of Egyptian paper; furthermore, in a little basket seven molds of "kosher" cheese; five packages altogether. Furthermore, all the copper (*naḥās*) sent by me is in a canvas. This makes six packages. I wrote on each: "*Abraham Yijū*, shipment of Joseph," and sent the whole together with the 20 dinars with the Sheikh Aḥmad, *the captain, son of Abu 'l-Faraj.*

Furthermore, in a bag there are two linen *fūṭas* for the children and two network veils dyed with carthamus. Please accept delivery and forward them to the Sheikh *Abu 'l-Surūr b. Khallūf al-Ṭalḥī*, as well as the letter destined for him. His name is on the bag.

My lord mentioned that there remained from last year copper to manufacture two bowls for drinking water. Kindly send them with the other copper.

Altogether there are seven packages with the bag of *Abu 'l-Surūr al-Ṭalḥī*.

May my master receive for his honored self the best greetings. And *upon you be peace!*

Questions

1. Which passages in this letter suggest to you that Ben Abraham and Yijū have an ongoing business relationship? What can you infer about twelfth-century Indian Ocean trade from the specificity of Ben Abraham's requests?

2. What kinds of trade goods are moving between Mangalore and Aden? How do these items compare to the trade goods mentioned in *The Periplus of the Erythraean Sea* (see Chapter 6)? What does this suggest to you about change or continuity in long-distance trade over centuries?

3. What does this letter tell us about production in Yijū's bronze factory? What does the letter tell us about the relationship between the value of the materials, the utility of the items produced, their workmanship, and aesthetics?

Letters between Pope Innocent IV and Güyük Khan (1245–1246)

In 1236 Batu, a grandson of Chinggis Khan, embarked on the conquest of Russia. By late 1240 the Mongols had subdued all of Russia and pressed on into eastern Europe. Separate columns destroyed an army of Germans and Poles at Liegnitz on April 9 and the army of the kingdom of Hungary at Mohi on April 11, 1241. For the next year the Mongols occupied Hungary. One of their armies reached the Adriatic on the coast of what is today Montenegro. Panic spread through central and western Europe. But Batu, in order to influence the impending election of a new Great Khan in Mongolia, withdrew his forces to the Volga. In 1245 Pope Innocent IV sent two Franciscan friars, John of Plano Carpini and Benedict the Pole, east to evaluate the situation. After an exhausting journey they reached Karakorum, the Mongol capital, in time to be present at the election of Güyük as Great Khan in August 1246. After delivering two letters from the pope and meeting with Güyük, they made a return journey to the Volga in the dead of winter. The first two selections below are excerpts from Innocent's letters to the Great Khan; the third is the message Güyük sent back with the Franciscans.

THE MONGOL MISSION

Wherefore we, * * * turn our keen attention, before all else incumbent on us in virtue of our office, to your salvation and that of other men, and on this matter especially do we fix our mind, sedulously keeping watch over it with diligent zeal and zealous diligence, so that we may be able, with the help of God's grace, to lead those in error into the way of truth and gain all men for Him. But since we are unable to be present in person in different places at one and the same time * * * in order that we may not appear to neglect in any way those absent from us we send to them in our stead prudent and discreet men by whose ministry we carry out the obligation of our apostolic mission to them. It is for this reason that we have thought fit to send to you our beloved son Friar Laurence of Portugal and his companions of the Order of Friars Minor, the bearers of this letter, men remarkable for their religious spirit, comely in their virtue and gifted with a knowledge of Holy Scripture, so that following their salutary instructions you may acknowledge Jesus Christ the very Son of God and worship His glorious name by practising the Christian religion. * * * We have thought fit to send to you the

SOURCE: *The Mongol Mission: Narratives and Letters of the Franciscan Missionaries in Mongolia and China in the Thirteenth and Fourteenth Centuries*, edited by Christopher Dawson (New York: Sheed and Ward, 1955), pp. 74–76, 85–86.

above-mentioned Friars, whom we specially chose out from among others as being men proved by years of regular observance and well versed in Holy Scripture, for we believed they would be of greater help to you, seeing that they follow the humility of our Saviour: if we had thought that ecclesiastical prelates or other powerful men would be more profitable and more acceptable to you we would have sent them.

Lyons, 5th March 1245

Seeing that not only men but even irrational animals, nay, the very elements which go to make up the world machine, are united by a certain innate law after the manner of the celestial spirits, * * * it is not without cause that we are driven to express in strong terms our amazement that you, as we have heard, have invaded many countries belonging both to Christians and to others and are laying them waste in a horrible desolation, and with a fury still unabated you do not cease from stretching out your destroying hand to more distant lands, but, breaking the bond of natural ties, sparing neither sex nor age, you rage against all indiscriminately with the sword of chastisement. We, therefore, following the example of the King of Peace, and desiring that all men should live united in concord in the fear of God, do admonish, beg and earnestly beseech all of you that for the future you desist entirely from assaults of this kind and especially from the persecution of Christians, and that after so many and such grievous offences you conciliate by a fitting penance the wrath of Divine Majesty, which without doubt you have seriously aroused by such provocation; nor should you be emboldened to commit further savagery by the fact that when the sword of your might has raged against other men Almighty God has up to the present allowed various nations to fall before your face; for sometimes He refrains from chastising the proud in this world for the moment, for this reason, that if they neglect to humble themselves of their own accord He may not only no longer put off the punishment of their wickedness in this life but may also take greater vengeance in the world to come. * * *

Lyons, 13th March 1245

GUYUK KHAN'S LETTER TO POPE INNOCENT IV (1246)

We, by the power of the eternal heaven,

Khan of the great Ulus [Community]

Our command:—

This is a version sent to the great Pope, that he may know and understand in the [Persian] tongue, what has been written. The petition of the assembly held in the lands of the Emperor [for our support], has been heard from your emissaries.

If he reaches [you] with his own report, Thou, who art the great Pope, together with all the Princes, come in person to serve us. At that time I shall make known all the commands of the *Yasa* [Mongol laws and statutes].

You have also said that supplication and prayer have been offered by you, that I might find a good entry into baptism. This prayer of thine I have not understood. Other words which thou hast sent me: "I am surprised that thou hast seized all the lands of the Magyar and the Christians. Tell us what their fault is." These words of thine I have also not understood. The eternal God has slain and annihilated these lands and peoples, because they have neither adhered to Chingis Khan, nor to the Khagan [supreme ruler], both of whom have been sent to make known God's command, nor to the command of God. Like thy words, they also were impudent, they were proud and they slew our messenger-emissaries. How could anybody seize or kill by his own power contrary to the command of God?

Though thou likewise sayest that I should become a trembling Nestorian Christian, worship God and be an ascetic, how knowest thou whom God absolves, in truth to whom He shows mercy? How dost thou know that such words as thou speakest are with God's sanction? From the rising of the sun to its setting, all the lands have been made subject to me. Who could do this contrary to the command of God?

Now you should say with a sincere heart: "I will submit and serve you." Thou thyself, at the head of all the Princes, come at once to serve and wait upon us! At that time I shall recognize your submission.

If you do not observe God's command, and if you ignore my command, I shall know you as my enemy. Likewise I shall make you understand. If you do otherwise, God knows what I know.

At the end of Jumada the second in the year 644 [November 1246].

Questions

1. What does Innocent IV want the Khan to do? Why might he think the Khan would actually do what he wants?

2. Why does Güyük refuse to accede to the pope's requests?

3. How does each party understand heavenly favor and how it manifests itself in politics?

Francesco Pegolotti, Advice to Merchants Bound for Cathay (c. 1340)

The rise of the Mongol Empire in the thirteenth century greatly facilitated contacts across Eurasia. For a long time the Mongols were able to maintain good order along the Silk Route that ran from China to the Mediterranean. Indeed, under their rule a new branch of the Silk Road opened that ran north of the Caspian Sea to the Black Sea, where the Italian cities of Genoa and Venice had trading colonies. European envoys visited the court of the Great Khan in Mongolia. Catholic missionaries reached China; for a time there was even a Franciscan archbishop in Beijing. Dominican missionaries were even allowed into Muslim Iran. Merchants, the most famous of whom were the Polos, traveled to China. The following document (c. 1340) comes from a commercial handbook titled the *Book of Descriptions of Countries and of Measures of Merchandise*, written by the Florentine merchant Francesco Balducci Pegolotti (c. 1310–c. 1340). Among other things it describes markets, trade goods, exchange rates, and customs duties from the Atlantic to China.

This book is called the Book of Descriptions of Countries and of measures employed in business, and of other things needful to be known by merchants of different parts of the world, and by all who have to do with merchandise and exchanges; showing also what relation the merchandise of one country or of one city bears to that of others; and how one kind of goods is better than another kind; and where the various wares come from, and how they may be kept as long as possible.

*   *   *

In the first place, you must let your beard grow long and not shave. And at Tana [at the mouth of the Don River on the Sea of Azov in modern Russia] you should furnish yourself with a dragoman [translator]. And you must not try to save money in the matter of dragomen by taking a bad one instead of a good one. For the additional wages of the good one will not cost you so much as you will save by having him. And besides the dragoman it will be well to take at least two good menservants, who are acquainted with the Cumanian tongue. And if the merchant likes to take a woman with him from Tana, he can do so; if he does not like to take one there is no obligation, only if he does take one he will be kept much more comfortably than if he does not take one. Howbeit, if he do take one, it will be well that she be acquainted with the Cumanian tongue as well as the men.

And from Tana travelling to Gittarchan [Astrakhan on the Caspian Sea] you should take with you twenty-five days' provisions, that is to say, flour and salt fish, for as to meat you will find enough of it at all the places along the road. And so also at all the chief stations noted in going from one country to another in the route, according to the number of days set down above, you should furnish yourself with flour and salt fish; other things you will find in sufficiency, and especially meat.

SOURCE: *Cathay and the Way Thither*, H. Yule, ed., 2nd ed. H. Cordier (London: Hakluyt Society, 1916).

The road you travel from Tana to Cathay is perfectly safe, whether by day or by night, according to what the merchants say who have used it. Only if the merchant, in going or coming, should die upon the road, everything belonging to him will become the perquisite of the lord of the country in which he dies, and the officers of the lord will take possession of all. And in like manner if he die in Cathay. But if his brother be with him, or an intimate friend and comrade calling himself his brother, then to such an one they will surrender the property of the deceased, and so it will be rescued.

And there is another danger: this is when the lord of the country dies, and before the new lord who is to have the lordship is proclaimed; during such intervals there have sometimes been irregularities practised on the Franks, and other foreigners. (They call "Franks" all the Christians of these parts from Romania [the Byzantine empire] westward.) And neither will the roads be safe to travel until the other lord be proclaimed who is to reign in room of him who is deceased.

Cathay is a province which contains a multitude of cities and towns. Among others there is one in particular, that is to say the capital city, to which is great resort of merchants, and in which there is a vast amount of trade; and this city is called Cambalec [Beijing]. And the said city hath a circuit of one hundred miles, and is all full of people and houses and of dwellers in the said city.

You may calculate that a merchant with a dragoman, and with two menservants, and with goods to the value of twenty-five thousand golden florins, should spend on his way to Cathay from sixty to eighty sommi of silver, and not more if he manage well; and for all the road back again from Cathay to Tana, including the expenses of living and the pay of servants, and all other charges, the cost will be about five sommi per head of pack animals, or something less. And you may reckon the sommo to be worth five golden florins. You may reckon also that each ox-waggon will require one ox, and will carry ten cantars Genoese weight; and the camel-waggon will require three camels, and will carry thirty cantars Genoese weight; and the horse-waggon will require one horse, and will commonly carry six and a half cantars of silk, at two hundred and fifty Genoese pounds to the cantar. And a bale of silk may be reckoned at between one hundred and ten and one hundred and fifteen Genoese pounds.

You may reckon also that from Tana to Sara[i] the road is less safe than on any other part of the journey; and yet even when this part of the road is at its worst, if you are some sixty men in the company you will go as safely as if you were in your own house.

Anyone from Genoa or from Venice, wishing to go to the places above-named, and to make the journey to Cathay, should carry linens with him, and if he visit Organci [Urgench in modern Turkmenistan] he will dispose of these well. In Organci he should purchase sommi of silver, and with these he should proceed without making any further investment, unless it be some bales of the very finest stuffs which go in small bulk, and cost no more for carriage than coarser stuffs would do.

Merchants who travel this road can ride on horseback or on asses, or mounted in any way that they list to be mounted.

Whatever silver the merchants may carry with them as far as Cathay the lord of Cathay will take from them and put into his treasury. And to merchants who thus bring silver they give that paper money of theirs in exchange. This is of yellow paper, stamped with the seal of the lord aforesaid. And this money is called balishi; and with this money you can readily buy silk and all other merchandise that you have a desire to buy. And all the people of the country are bound to receive it. And yet you shall not pay a higher price for your goods because your money is of paper. And of the said paper money there are three kinds, one being worth more than another, according to the value which has been established for each by that lord.

And you may reckon that you can buy for one sommo of silver nineteen or twenty pounds of Cathay silk, when reduced to Genoese weight, and that the sommo should weigh eight and a half ounces of Genoa, and should be of the alloy of eleven ounces and seventeen deniers to the pound.

You may reckon also that in Cathay you should get three or three and a half pieces of damasked silk for a sommo; and from three and a half to five pieces of nacchetti [cloths] of silk and gold, likewise for a sommo of silver.

Questions

1. What does Pegolotti see as the chief dangers for merchants traveling to China?

2. What role does the city of Urgench play in the flow of trade across Eurasia as it is described by Pegolotti?

3. How well informed does Pegolotti seem to be about mercantile affairs in the lands he discusses?

Mobilizing for War in the Age of the Mongols

Although military technology did not differ dramatically across
Afro-Eurasia in the eleventh through the fourteenth centuries, there
were significant differences in the ways armies were conscripted,
organized, and fielded. Moreover, armies related to their societies
differently. For example, in settled societies military training is a
distraction from the pursuit of other forms of economic productivity,
but in a nomadic society, a horseman is more integral to general social
and economic pursuits, so there can be less differentiation between
martial and other goals. In most societies, the elites saw themselves as
participants in military culture, and many hunted and rode horses as
leisure—Chinese elites were a notable exception. Nevertheless, China
wanted a skilled cavalry and at times recruited horsemen from central
Asia.

Regardless of differences, all societies had to find ways of feeding
and equipping the military, and motivating and disciplining the troops.
As you will see from the following documents, various societies found
different approaches to these problems. Another commonality across
most of Afro-Eurasia was the influence of the Mongols. The painting of
Sir Geoffrey Luttrell is the only source in this group that comes from the
period after the Mongol threat had been eclipsed. The other sources are
all either about Mongols or people who were worried about central Asian
nomads.

These documents show multiple adaptations to shared sets of
problems. As you read, pay attention both to questions of military

effectiveness as well as to the material and cultural consequences of mobilization on society at large.

Images of Mongol Horsemen and a Medieval European Knight (fourteenth and fifteenth centuries)

The two images below show different ways of depicting, and perhaps conceptualizing, warriors in the fourteenth century. The first comes from the Luttrell Psalter (a psalter is a book containing psalms from the Old Testament). This was commissioned by an English knight, Sir Geoffrey Luttrell, and produced sometime between 1320 and 1340. The image shows Sir Geoffrey mounted on his war horse with his wife handing him his great helm and lance, while his daughter-in-law holds his shield. Both the shield and the horse's trapper (the cloth placed over the horse) bear the Luttrell family's coat of arms, a diagonal silver line between six silver swifts. The second image is from a fifteenth-century manuscript copy of the *Jami' al-tawarikh* (Compendium of Chronicles) by Rashid al-Din (1247–1318). He was commissioned to write this by Ghazan Khan (1271–1304), the Mongol ruler of Persia (see The Rise of Chinggis Khan, in Chapter 10). It shows dismounted Mongol warriors with their recurved bows fighting mounted opponents with small round shields.

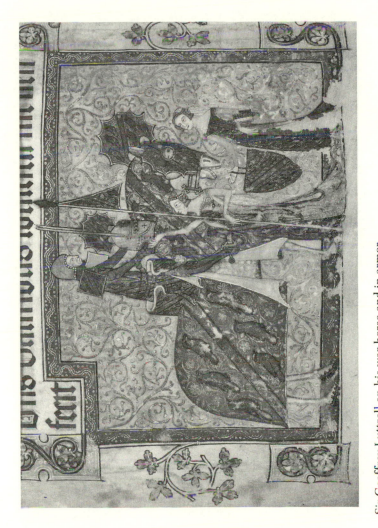

Sir Geoffrey Luttrell on his war horse and in armor

SOURCE: Luttrell Psalter, in the collection of the British Library. HIP/Art Resource, NY.

Mongolian warriors

Questions

1. Compare the equipment shown in the Luttrell Psalter illustration with that in the illustration from the *Jami' al-tawarikh*. What differences or similarities do you see?

2. Which of these warriors would have cost more to equip? Which could move faster? Which would have an advantage in close-range fighting?

Source: Rashid-al-din, *Jami' al-tawarikh*. AKG Images.

3. What makes Luttrell more identifiable as an individual than the Mongol soldiers? How does this reflect different ideas about warfare in medieval Afro-Eurasia?

'Ala-ad-Din 'Ata-Malik Juvaini, Genghis Khan: The History of the World Conqueror (mid-thirteenth century)

The Mongol army that carried out the great conquests of the thirteenth century was organized very differently from those of the settled peoples of Afro-Eurasia. In Afro-Eurasia armies were recruited in a great variety of ways. Some men served for pay; some received land in return for military service; and in some Muslim countries slaves were used as soldiers. When these armies assembled, their members often differed greatly in armament, training, and organization. Discipline, both on and off the battlefield, was often not very good. The following description of the Mongol military is from 'Ala-ad-Din 'Ata-Malik Juvaini's *History of the World Conqueror*. Juvaini (1226–1283) was a Persian historian and administrator. In the 1240s and 1250s he made two trips to Mongolia, where he began writing his history. In 1256 he entered the service of the Mongol Hülügü and accompanied him on the conquests of Persia and Iraq, which culminated with the destruction of Baghdad and the death of the last Abbasid caliph in 1258. Thereafter he became a provincial governor for the Mongols.

What army in the whole world can equal the Mongol army? In time of action, when attacking and assaulting, they are like trained wild beasts out after game, and in the days of peace and security they are like sheep, yielding milk, and wool, and many other useful things. In misfortune and adversity they are free from dissension and opposition. It is an army after the fashion of a peasantry, being

---

SOURCE: 'Ala-ad-Din 'Ata-Malik Juvaini, *Genghis Khan: The History of the World Conqueror,* translated from the text of Mizra Muhammad Qazvini by J. A. Boyle (Seattle: University of Washington Press, 1997), pp. 30–32.

liable to all manner of contributions *(mu'an)* and rendering without complaint whatever is enjoined upon it, whether *qupchur*, occasional taxes *('avāriẓāt)*, the maintenance *(ikhrājāt)* of travellers or the upkeep of post stations *(yam)* with the provision of mounts *(ulagh)* and food *('ulūfāt)* therefor. It is also a peasantry in the guise of an army, all of them, great and small, noble and base, in time of battle becoming swordsmen, archers and lancers and advancing in whatever manner the occasion requires. Whenever the slaying of foes and the attacking of rebels is purposed, they specify all that will be of service for that business, from the various arms and implements down to banners, needles, ropes, mounts and pack animals such as donkeys and camels; and every man must provide his share according to his ten or hundred. On the day of review, also, they display their equipment, and if only a little be missing, those responsible are severely punished. Even when they are actually engaged in fighting, there is exacted from them as much of the various taxes as is expedient, while any service which they used to perform when present devolves upon their wives and those of them that remain behind. Thus if work be afoot in which a man has his share of forced labour *(bīgār)*, and if the man himself be absent, his wife goes forth in person and performs that duty in his stead.

The reviewing and mustering of the army has been so arranged that they have abolished the registry of inspection *(daftar-i-'arẓ)* and dismissed the officials and clerks. For they have divided all the people into companies of ten, appointing one of the ten to be the commander of the nine others; while from among each ten commanders one has been given the title of "commander of the hundred," all the hundred having been placed under his command. And so it is with each thousand men and so also with each ten thousand, over whom they have appointed a commander whom they call "commander of the *tümen*." In accordance with this arrangement, if in an emergency any man or thing be required, they apply to the commanders of *tümen*; who in turn apply to the commanders of thousands, and so on down to the commanders of tens. There is a true equality in this; each man toils as much as the next, and no difference is made between them, no attention being paid to wealth or power. If there is a sudden call for soldiers an order is issued that so many thousand men must present themselves in such and such a place at such and such an hour of that day or night. *"They shall not retard it* (their appointed time) *an hour; and they shall not advance it."* And they arrive not a twinkling of an eye before or after the appointed hour. Their obedience and submissiveness is such that if there be a commander of a hundred thousand between whom and the Khan there is a distance of sunrise and sunset, and if he but commit some fault, the Khan dispatches a single horseman to punish him after the manner prescribed: if his head has been demanded, he cuts it off, and if gold be required, he takes it from him.

How different it is with other kings who must speak cautiously to their own slave, bought with their own money, as soon as he has ten horses in his stable, to say nothing of when they place an army under his command and he attains to wealth and power; then they cannot displace him, and more often than not he actually rises in rebellion and insurrection! Whenever these kings prepare to attack an enemy or are themselves attacked by an enemy, months and years are required to equip an army and it takes a brimful treasury to meet the expense of salaries and allotments of land. When they draw their pay and allowances the soldiers' numbers increase by hundreds and thousands, but on the day of combat their ranks are everywhere vague and uncertain, and none presents himself on the battle-field. A shepherd was once called to render an account of his office. Said the accountant: "How many sheep remain?" "Where?" asked the shepherd. "In the register." "That," replied the shepherd, "is why I asked: there are none in the flock." This is a parable to be applied to their armies; wherein each commander, in order to increase the appropriation for his men's pay, declares, "I have so and so many men," and at the time of inspection they impersonate one another in order to make up their full strength.

Another *yasa* is that no man may depart to another unit than the hundred, thousand or ten to which he has been assigned, nor may he seek refuge elsewhere. And if this order be transgressed the man who transferred is executed in the presence of the troops, while he that received him is severely punished. For this reason no man can give refuge to another; if (for example) the commander be a prince, he does not permit the meanest person to take refuge in his company and so avoids a breach of the *yasa*. Therefore no man can take liberties with his commander or leader, nor can another commander entice him away.

Questions

1. What strikes Juvaini as most remarkable about the Mongol army?

2. What does he mean by the comments that "it is an army after the fashion of a peasantry" and "a peasantry in the guise of an army"?

3. How does Juvaini compare the Mongol military organization to those he was familiar with in Persia and Iraq?

Ouyang Xiu and Fan Zhen, Conscription and Professional Soldiers in Song China (960–1127 CE)

The northern Song dynasty (960–1127 CE) was the largest empire on earth, and also the richest; its army often had well over 1 million men—far more than any other state of that era. But most of the time it was on the defensive against nomadic invaders from the north, to whom it succumbed in 1127.

The Song could not raise enough high quality horses themselves, and had to import them from central Asian pastoralists. The large infantry forces they could raise were not fast enough to contend with nomadic cavalry, and were prohibitively expensive to feed if stationed along the semi-arid northern frontier. Moreover, after a mutiny had nearly destroyed the previous (Tang) dynasty, the Song had strengthened civilian control of its armies—but at the cost of weakening them. Defense and defense costs were central issues in debates that ran throughout the dynasty's life.

The two brief texts excerpted here come from high-ranking, reform-minded civilian politicians who favored reducing reliance on professional soldiers and relying more on conscription. There had been a universal draft in the Qin and early Han dynasties, and various modified draft systems in other periods. Although farmers could quickly learn the skills needed for local self-defense tasks, or serve the army as porters, learning the sophisticated horsemanship and archery needed on the northern frontiers would have required a long, very burdensome service period. The professional army, however, attracted many of the "wrong" people, and cost a great deal even during peacetime. Spelling has been updated in the following excerpts to reflect modern orthography.

FROM A MEMORIAL BY OUYANG XIU, C. 1040

The weakness of our forces has been exposed recently by the defeat sustained on the western frontier by our troops under Qi Zongju. If only the troops were hardy and efficient it might be considered justifiable to expend the resources of the farming class upon their maintenance. But what reason have we for maintaining the mere pretence of an army, composed as it is of such proud, lazy, and useless men?

The ancient practice was to give the strong and robust fellows of the farming class military drill and instruction in the intervals between the agricultural seasons, keeping them free for their farming work at other times. But this practice no longer obtains. The recruiting officers go out in times of dearth, measuring the height of the men, testing their strength, and enrolling them in the standing army. Those of better physique are drafted into the Imperial Army, while those of inferior standard are allocated to the Provincial Corps. The recruiting officers are rewarded according to the number of recruits they enrol. In times of dearth and poverty it is only natural that there should be competition to enter the army. So it has come about that after every period of famine, the strong and robust have been found in the army, while the older and feebler folk have been left on the fields.

I am not unaware of the criticism that if such men were not received into the army at such times they might turn to banditry for a living. But the pity is that while such critics are conscious of

---

SOURCE: H. R. Williamson, *Wang An-shih: A Chinese Statesman and Educationalist of the Song Dynasty* (London: Arthur Probsthain, 1935), vol. 1, pp. 187, 189–90.

the danger that these men might become robbers for a short period, they seem completely to overlook the fact that once they are enrolled in the regular army they become robbers for practically the whole of their lives.

FROM A MEMORIAL BY FAN ZHEN, C. 1260

Though taxation is heavy the revenue remains insufficient. The chief cause for this is to be found in the size of our standing army. It is said that this is essential to our frontier policy, as we must be prepared for the Qitans. But, as a matter of fact, the Qitans have made no incursion southwards for over fifty years. Why? Because it is much more to their advantage to go on receiving our handsome tribute gifts of money and silk, and to maintain the peace. But supposing they were to decide to launch an attack. In that case I venture to predict that the only defenders of our cities north of the Yellow River would be found to be composed of women and girls. For the soldiery who are stationed in the districts, and who engage in no farming or other productive work, would be found quite useless.

And yet we continue to maintain them at the expense of the people. The policy of creating and maintaining a standing army leads to a great decrease in the numbers of those engaged in agriculture. This, of course, means that great areas of arable land lie fallow. This in its turn involves the people in heavier taxation and an increase of the burden of public services. So the loyalty of the people gets strained, and cannot be relied upon.

On the contrary, the policy of raising Militia or People's Corps, making soldiers of them while they continue their work of farming, tends to eliminate these evils. The number engaged in farming operations is not decreased, more land gets tilled, taxation is lighter, and the loyalty of the people remains staunch and true.

It is surely preferable to prepare to meet the Qitans by a policy which ensures the loyalty of the people than by pressing a policy which tends to deprive the State of such an asset. I am convinced that if we pursue our present policy our resources both in money and men will be exhausted before the enemy appears. Whereas our revenue will be sufficient and our military strength more than adequate, if we adopt a policy of making soldier-farmers of our people.

Questions

1. What do each of these officials object to about the professional standing army?

2. What advantages do they see in training and mobilizing farmer-soldiers?

3. What assumptions do these writers make about how people think and act? What assumptions are made about the sources of their state's strength and weakness?

Ziya' al-Din Barani, The Challenges of Raising an Army (1357)

Alauddin Khilji (ruled 1296–1316), part of the second Muslim dynasty to rule the Delhi Sultanate, is best remembered for his attack on Chittor. Legend has it that Alauddin seized the city in order to posses the beautiful queen Rani Padmini, a story recounted in the epic poem *Padmavat*—though more recent scholarship emphasizes the strategic importance of the city. The sultanate was always vulnerable to attacks from central Asia, and the Khilji dynasty was engaged in territorial conquest of the south, so the military was an important part of the dynasty's success.

The following passage makes explicit some of the challenges of maintaining political power in a turbulent era. Like the Mongols and the Song, Alauddin had to worry about the caliber of his soldiers. Also like the Song, the sultanate faced real financial constraints to support the large army necessary to protect itself from the threat of Mongol invasion.

Ziya' al-Din Barani (1285–1357) was a Muslim political thinker from an aristocratic family that served the Delhi Sultanate. He wrote a history of thirteenth- and early fourteenth-century India and an important tract on Muslim social hierarchies in South Asia. Spelling has been updated in the following excerpt to reflect modern orthography.

After Sultan Alauddin had taken care to make these preparations against another inroad of the Mongols, he used to have discussions with his councillors both by day and night as to the means of effectually resisting and annihilating these marauders. * * *

The Sultan then took counsel with his advisers, everyone of whom was unequalled and eminently distinguished, saying: "To maintain an immense picked and chosen force well mounted, so that they may be fully equipped and efficient at all times, is impossible, without the expenditure of vast treasures; for one must give regularly every year whatever sum is fixed upon at first; and if I settle a high rate of pay upon the soldiery, and continue to disburse money to them at that rate annually, at the end of a few years, not withstanding all the treasure I possess, nothing will be left, and without treasure it is of course impossible to govern or deliberate.

"I am accordingly desirous of having a large force, well mounted, of picked and chosen men, expert archers, and well armed that will remain embodied for years; and I will give 234 *tankahs* to a *Murattab* and 78 *tankahs* to a *Du-aspah*; from the former of whom I shall require two horses with their corresponding equipments, and from the latter one with its usual gear. Consider now and inform me how this idea that has entered into my mind about raising a large force, and maintaining it permanently, may be carried into execution."

The councillors, endowed with abilities like those of Āsaf, exercised their brilliant intellects, and after some reflection unanimously expressed the following opinion before the throne: "As it has entered into your Majesty's heart, and become implanted there, to raise a large force and permanently maintained on small allowances such can never be accomplished unless horses, arms and all the equipments of a soldier, as well as subsistence for his wife and family, become excessively cheap, and are reduced to the price of water; for if your Majesty can succeed in lowering the price of pro-

SOURCE: Ziya al-Din Barani, *The Reign of Alauddin Khilji*, translated by A. R. Fuller and A. Khallaque (Calcutta: Pilgrim Publishers, 1967), pp. 100–103, 128–29.

visions beyond measure, a large force can be raised and permanently maintained according to the idea that has entered your august mind; and by the aid of this vast force all fear of danger from the Mongols will be averted."

The Sultan then consulted with his trusty and experienced councillors and ministers, as to what he should do, in order that the means of livelihood might be made exceedingly cheap and moderate, without introducing capital punishment, torture, or severe [coercion]. The Sultan's ministers and advisers represented, that until fixed rules were established, and permanent regulations introduced for lowering prices, the means of livelihood would never get exceedingly cheap. First then, for the cheapening of grain, the benefit of which is common to all, they proposed certain measures, and by the adoption of these measures, grain became cheap, and remained so for years.

* * *

As soon then the cheapness of all necessaries of life had been secured, and a large standing army could be entertained, the Mongols were defeated each time they invaded Delhi or the Delhi territory, and were slain, or captured, and the standard of Islam obtained one signal victory after the other over them. Several thousand Mongols with ropes on their necks were brought to Delhi and trampled to death by elephants. Of their heads, they formed a large platform or made turrets of the Mongol skulls, and the stench in the city of the dead bodies of such as had been killed in battle or had been executed in Delhi, was very great. The army of Islam gained in fact such victories over the Mongols that a *Duaspah* would bring in ten Mongols with ropes on their necks, or a single Muslim trooper would drive one hundred Mongols before himself.

Questions

1. What was Alauddin's biggest constraint in fielding an army adequate to defend against the Mongols?

2. What strategy did Alauddin and his advisers pursue to address this

challenge? Whom else would this policy have benefited? Who might have opposed it?

3. What differences do you note between the concerns of Mongol, Chinese, and Indian rulers in this period? What can account for the similarities and the differences you note?

Chapter 11

CRISES AND RECOVERY IN AFRO-EURASIA, 1300s–1500s

Giovanni Boccaccio, The Decameron (1353)

The establishment of the Mongol Empire in the thirteenth century greatly promoted trade across Afro-Eurasia. The Black Death, known to the Europeans who lived through it as the Great Pestilence, was transmitted westward from the empire into Afro-Eurasia. It entered Sicily in September 1347. In the next five years it spread across Europe. The most common estimates are that it killed one-third to one-half of the population of Europe, a demographic catastrophe without parallel in European history. One of the most vivid descriptions of it was written by Giovanni Boccaccio (1313–1375) as an introduction to his *Decameron*, a collection of one hundred short stories which he portrays as being told by ten people who have fled the city of Florence to the countryside to escape the plague.

[In 1348] when in the illustrious city of Florence, there made its appearance that deadly pestilence, which, whether disesminated by the influence of the celestial bodies, or sent upon us mortals by God in His just wrath by way of retribution for our iniquities, had had its origin some years before in the East. * * *

SOURCE: Giovanni Boccaccio, *The Decameron*, translated by J. M. Rigg (London, 1903), pp. 5–11.

In Florence, despite all that human wisdom and forethought could devise to avert it, as the cleansing of the city from many impurities by officials appointed for the purpose, the refusal of entrance to all sick folk, and the adoption of many precautions for the preservation of health; despite also humble supplications addressed to God, and often repeated both in public procession and otherwise, by the devout; towards the beginning of the spring of the said year the doleful effects of the pestilence began to be horribly apparent by symptoms that [showed] as if miraculous.

* * * [I]n men and women alike it first betrayed itself by the emergence of certain tumours in the groin or the armpits, some of which grew as large as a common apple, others as an egg, some more, some less, which the common folk called gavoccioli. From the two said parts of the body this deadly gavocciolo soon began to propagate and spread itself in all directions indifferently; after which the form of the malady began to change, black spots or livid making their appearance in many cases on the arm or the thigh or elsewhere, now few and large, now minute and numerous. And as the gavocciolo had been and still was an infallible token of approaching death, such also were these spots on whomsoever they [showed] themselves. * * * [N]ot merely were those that recovered few, but almost all within three days from the appearance of the said symptoms, sooner or later, died, and in most cases without any fever or other attendant malady.

Moreover, * * * not merely by speech or association with the sick was the malady communicated to the healthy with consequent peril of common death; but any that touched the clothes of the sick or aught else that had been touched or used by them, seemed thereby to contract the disease.

* * *

In which circumstances, * * * divers[e] apprehensions and imaginations were engendered in the minds of such as were left alive, inclining almost all of them to the same harsh resolution, to wit, to shun and abhor all contact with the sick and all that belonged to them, thinking thereby to make each his own health secure. Among whom there were those who thought that to live temperately and avoid all excess would count for much as a preservative against sei-zures of this kind. Wherefore they banded together, and, dissociat-ing themselves from all others, formed communities in houses where there were no sick, and lived a separate and secluded life, which they regulated with the utmost care, avoiding every kind of luxury, but eating and drinking very moderately of the most delicate viands and the finest wines, holding converse with none but one another, lest tidings of sickness or death should reach them, and diverting their minds with music and such other delights as they could devise. Others, the bias of whose minds was in the opposite direction, maintained, that to drink freely, frequent places of public resort, and take their pleasure with song and revel, sparing to satisfy no appe-tite, and to laugh and mock at no event, was the sovereign remedy for so great an evil: and that which they affirmed they also put in practice, so far as they were able, resorting day and night, now to this tavern, now to that, drinking with an entire disregard of rule or measure, and by preference making the houses of others, as it were, their inns, if they but saw in them aught that was particu-larly to their taste or liking. * * * Thus, adhering ever to their inhuman determination to shun the sick, as far as possible, they ordered their life. In this extremity of our city's suffering and tribula-tion the venerable authority of laws, human and divine, was abased and all but totally dissolved, for lack of those who should have administered and enforced them, most of whom, like the rest of the citizens, were either dead or sick, or so hard bested for servants that they were unable to execute any office; whereby every man was free to do what was right in his own eyes.

Not a few there were who belonged to neither of the two said par-ties, but kept a middle course between them, neither laying the same restraint upon their diet as the former, nor allowing themselves the same license in drinking and other dissipations as the latter, but living with a degree of freedom sufficient to satisfy their appetites, and not as recluses. They therefore walked abroad, carrying in their hands flowers or fragrant herbs or divers[e] sorts of spices, which they frequently raised to their noses * * * because the air seemed to be everywhere laden and reeking with the stench emitted by the dead and the dying. * * *

Some again, the most sound, perhaps, in judgment, as they were also the most harsh in temper, of all, affirmed that there was no medicine for the disease superior or equal in efficacy to flight; following which prescription a multitude of men and women, negligent of all but themselves, deserted their city, their houses, their estates, their kinsfolk, their goods, and went into voluntary exile, or migrated to the country parts, as if God in visiting men with this pestilence in requital of their iniquities would not pursue them with His wrath wherever they might be, but intended the destruction of such alone as remained within the circuit of the walls of the city; or deeming, perchance, that it was now time for all to flee from it, and that its last hour was come.

* * * Tedious were it to recount, how citizen avoided citizen, how among neighbours was scarce found any that [showed] fellow-feeling for another, how kinsfolk held aloof, and never met, or but rarely; enough that this sore affliction entered so deep into the minds of men and women, that in the horror thereof brother was forsaken by brother, nephew by uncle, brother by sister, and oftentimes husband by wife; nay, what is more, and scarcely to be believed, fathers and mothers were found to abandon their own children, untended, unvisited, to their fate, as if they had been strangers. Wherefore the sick of both sexes, whose number could not be estimated, were left without resource but in the charity of friends (and few such there were), or the interest of servants. * * *

It had been, as to-day it still is, the custom for the women that were neighbours and of kin to the deceased to gather in his house with the women that were most closely connected with him, to wail with them in common, while on the other hand his male kins-folk and neighbours, with not a few of the other citizens, and a due proportion of the clergy according to his quality, assembled without, in front of the house, to receive the corpse; and so the dead man was borne on the shoulders of his peers, with funeral pomp of taper and dirge, to the church selected by him before his death. Which rites, as the pestilence waxed in fury, were either in whole or in great part disused, and gave way to others of a novel order. For not only did no crowd of women surround the bed of the dying, but many passed from this life unregarded, and few indeed were they to whom were accorded the lamentations and bitter tears of sorrowing relations; nay, for the most part, their place was taken by the laugh, the jest, the festal gathering; observances which the women, domestic piety in large measure set aside, had adopted with very great advantage to their health. Few also there were whose bodies were attended to the church by more than ten or twelve of their neighbours, and those not the honourable and respected citizens; but a sort of corpse-carriers drawn from the baser ranks, who called themselves becchini and performed such offices for hire, would shoulder the bier, and with hurried steps carry it, not to the church of the dead man's choice, but to that which was nearest at hand, with four or six priests in front and a candle or two, or, perhaps, none; nor did the priests distress themselves with too long and solemn an office, but with the aid of the becchini hastily consigned the corpse to the first tomb which they found untenanted. The condition of the lower, and, perhaps, in great measure of the middle ranks, of the people [showed] even worse and more deplorable; for, deluded by hope or constrained by poverty, they stayed in their quarters, in their houses, where they sickened by thousands a day, and, being without service or help of any kind, were, so to speak, irredeemably devoted to the death which overtook them. Many died daily or nightly in the public streets; of many others, who died at home, the departure was hardly observed by their neighbours, until the stench of their putrefying bodies carried the tidings; and what with their corpses and the corpses of others who died on every hand the whole place was a sepulchre.

It was the common practice of most of the neighbours, moved no less by fear of contamination by the putrefying bodies than by charity towards the deceased, to drag the corpses out of the houses with their own hands, aided, perhaps, by a porter, if a porter was to be had, and to lay them in front of the doors, where any one who made the round might have seen, especially in the morning, more of them than he could count; afterwards they would have biers brought up, or, in default, planks, whereon they laid them. * * * And times without number it happened, that, as two priests, bearing the cross, were on their way to perform the last office for some one, three or four biers were brought up by the porters in rear of them, so that, whereas the priests supposed that they had but one corpse to bury, they discovered that there were six or eight, or sometimes more. Nor, for all their number, were their obsequies honoured by either tears or lights or crowds of mourners; rather, it was come to this, that a dead man was then of no more account than a dead goat would be to-day.

Questions

1. What are the physical symptoms of the plague as described by Boccaccio? What possible causes does he give for its outbreak?

2. How do the people of Florence try to deal with the outbreak in their city? How effective are their efforts?

3. What is the impact of the plague on the behavior of the people of Florence?

Jean Froissart, On the Jacquerie (1358)

The fourteenth and fifteenth centuries saw major peasant revolts in Europe. The population collapse following the Black Death forced down rents and drove up wages. The peasantry deeply resented efforts by the nobility to halt these processes. At the same time large-scale warfare became a fixture of European politics, often resulting in destruction of peasant property. One of the bloodiest revolts was the Jacquerie (whose name comes from "Jacques," or in English "Jack" or "John," a slang term for peasant used by the upper classes). This took place in May and June 1358. It followed a massive defeat of the French and the capture of their king by the English at the Battle of Poitiers in 1356, which left in its wake quarrels among the French ruling elite, a revolt by the people of Paris, the ravaging of the countryside by mercenary bands, and heavy war taxation. All these factors sparked a revolt of the peasants living north of Paris. Jean Froissart (c. 1337–c. 1404) describes the revolt in his *Chronicles*. From a merchant background, Froissart became a cleric and writer catering to the interests of the nobility. His *Chronicles*, despite its imprecision, is one of the best sources for the first part of the Hundred Years War between France and England.

Anon after the deliverance of the king of Navarre there began a marvellous tribulation in the realm of France, as in Beauvoisin, in Brie, on the river of Marne, in Laonnois, and about Soissons. For certain people of the common villages, without any head or ruler, assembled together in Beauvoisin. In the beginning they passed not a hundred in number: they said how the noblemen of the realm of France, knights and squires, shamed the realm, and that it should be a great wealth to destroy them all; and each of them said it was true, and said all with one voice: "Shame have he that doth not his power to destroy all the gentlemen of the realm!"

Thus they gathered together without any other counsel, and without any armour saving with staves and knives, and so went to the house of a knight dwelling thereby, and [broke] up his house and slew the knight and the lady and all his children great and small and [burned] his house. And then they went to another castle, and took the knight thereof and bound him fast to a stake, and then violated his wife and his daughter before his face and then slew the lady and his daughter and all his other children, and then slew the knight by great torment and [burned] and beat down the castle. And so they did to divers[e] other castles and good houses; and they multiplied so that they were a six thousand, and ever as they went forward they increased, for such like as they were fell ever to them, so that every gentleman fled from them and took their wives and children with them, and fled ten or twenty leagues off to be in surety, and left their houses void and their goods therein.

These mischievous people thus assembled without captain or armour robbed, [burned] and slew all gentlemen that they could lay hands on, and forced and ravished ladies and damosels, and did such shameful deeds that no human creature ought to think on any such, and he that did most mischief was most praised with them and greatest master. I dare not write the horrible deeds that they did to ladies and damosels: among other they slew a knight and after did

SOURCE: *The Chronicles of Froissart*, translated by John Bourchier and Lord Berners, edited by G. C. Macaulay (London: Macmillan and Co., 1895), pp. 136–37.

put him on a broach and roasted him at the fire in the sight of the lady his wife and his children; and after the lady had been enforced and ravished with a ten or twelve, they made her perforce to eat of her husband and after made her to die an evil death and all her children. They made among them a king, one of Clermont in Beauvoisin: they chose him that was the most ungraciousest of all other and they called him king Jaques Goodman, and so thereby they were called companions of the Jacquerie. They destroyed and [burned] in the country of Beauvoisin about Corbie, Amiens and Montdidier more than threescore good houses and strong castles. In like manner these unhappy people were in Brie and Artois, so that all the ladies, knights and squires of that country were fain [compelled] to fly away to Meaux in Brie, as well the duchess of Normandy and the duchess of Orleans as divers[e] other ladies and damosels, or else they had been violated and after murdered. Also there were a certain of the same ungracious people between Paris and Noyon and between Paris and Soissons, and all about in the land of Coucy, in the county of Valois, in the bishopric of Laon, Noyon and Soissons. There were [burned] and destroyed more than a hundred castles and good houses of knights and squires in that country.

Questions

1. What does Froissart identify as the causes of the peasant uprising?

2. How organized do the peasants appear to be?

3. How does Froissart characterize the rebellious peasants' behavior?

Chihab Al-ʿUmari, The Pilgrimage of Mansa Musa (1342–1349)

The following account of Mansa Musa's 1324 visit to Cairo has circulated widely since the fourteenth century. The author, Chihab Al-ʿUmari (1300–1384), was born in Damascus and visited Cairo shortly after Mansa Musa's highly visible stay. Mansa Musa, king of Mali, traveled with a large, well-supplied caravan to perform the *hajj*—the pilgrimage to Mecca incumbent upon all Muslims who can afford the journey. When Al-ʿUmari arrived in Cairo, people were still talking about the extraordinary visit of a monarch who brought so much wealth that his spending and alms-giving undermined the price of gold in Egypt for the next decade. The following selections provide descriptions of the Malian kingdom, the tribute system that provided abundant gold for the Malian king, Mansa Musa's piety, and the effect of his retinue's presence on the Cairene economy. As you read, remember that Al-ʿUmari, writing at least two decades later, relied on what people who met Mansa Musa had to say. The fact that he was not a direct witness does not make his account unreliable, but it does raise questions about how information was relayed from one person to the next in the fourteenth century.

[S]ultan Mūsā the king of [Mali] * * * came to Egypt on the Pilgrimage. He was staying in [the] Qarāfa [district of Cairo] and Ibn Amīr Ḥājib was governor of Old Cairo and Qarāfa at that time. A friendship grew up between them and this sultan Mūsā told him a great deal about himself and his country and the people of the Sūdān who were his neighbours. One of the things which he told him was that his country was very extensive and contiguous with the Ocean. By his sword and his armies he had conquered 24 cities each with its surrounding district with villages and estates. * * * He has a truce with the gold-plant people, who pay him tribute.

Ibn Amīr Ḥājib said that he asked him about the gold-plant, and he said: "It is found in two forms. One is found in the spring and blossoms after the rains in open country. It has leaves like grass and its roots are gold. The other kind is found all the year round at known sites on the banks of the Nīl and is dug up. There are holes there and roots of gold are found like stones or gravel and gathered up." * * * Sultan Mūsā told Ibn Amīr Ḥājib that gold was his prerogative and he collected the crop as a tribute except for what the people of that country took by theft.

SOURCE: *Corpus of Early Arabic Sources for West African History,* translated by J. F. P. Hopkins, edited by V. Levtzion and J. F. P. Hopkins (Cambridge: Cambridge University Press, 1981), pp. 267–71.

But * * * in fact he is given only a part of it as a present by way of gaining his favour, and he makes a profit on the sale of it, for they have none in their country. * * *

[I]t is a custom of his people that if one of them should have reared a beautiful daughter he offers her to the king as a concubine and he possesses her without a marriage ceremony as slaves are possessed, and this in spite of the fact that Islam has triumphed among them and that * * * this sultan Mūsā was pious and assiduous in prayer, [Quran] reading, and mentioning God.

"I said to him (said Ibn Amīr Ḥājib) that this was not permissible for a Muslim, whether in law or reason and he said: 'Not even for kings?' and I replied: 'No! not even for kings! Ask the scholars!' He said: 'By God, I did not know that. I hereby leave it and abandon it utterly!'

"I saw that this sultan Mūsā loved virtue and people of virtue. He left his kingdom and appointed as his deputy there his son Muḥammad and emigrated to God and His Messenger. He accomplished the obligations of the Pilgrimage, visited [the tomb of] the Prophet [at Medina] (God's blessing and peace be upon him!) and returned to his country with the intention of handing over his sovereignty to his son and abandoning it entirely to him and returning to Mecca the Venerated to remain there as a dweller near the sanctuary; but death overtook him, may God (who is great) have mercy upon him.

* * *

"This sultan Mūsā, during his stay in Egypt both before and after his journey to the Noble Ḥijāz, maintained a uniform attitude of worship and turning towards God. It was as though he were standing before Him because of His continual presence in his mind. He and all those with him behaved in the same manner and were well-dressed, grave, and dignified. He was noble and generous and performed many acts of charity and kindness. He had left his country with 100 loads of gold which he spent during his Pilgrimage on the tribes who lay along his route from his country to Egypt, while he was in Egypt, and again from Egypt to the Noble Ḥijāz and back. As a consequence he needed to borrow money in Egypt and pledged his credit with the merchants at a very high rate of gain so that they made 700 dinars profit on 300. Later he paid them back amply. He sent to me 500 mithqals of gold by way of honorarium.

* * *

"This man flooded Cairo with his benefactions. He left no court emir nor holder of a royal office without the gift of a load of gold. The Cairenes made incalculable profits out of him and his suite in buying and selling and giving and taking. They exchanged gold until they depressed its value in Egypt and caused its price to fall."

* * *

[W]hen he made the Pilgrimage * * * the sultan was very open-handed towards the pilgrims and the inhabitants of the Holy Places. He and his companions maintained great pomp and dressed magnifi-cently during the journey. He gave away much wealth in alms. * * *

Gold was at a high price in Egypt until they came in that year. The mithqal did not go below 25 *dirhams* and was generally above, but from that time its value fell and it cheapened in price and has remained cheap till now. The mithqal does not exceed 22 *dirhams* or less. This has been the state of affairs for about twelve years until this day by reason of the large amount of gold which they brought into Egypt and spent there.

Questions

1. How does Al-'Umari choose to document Mansa Musa's piety?

2. What is Al-'Umari's attitude toward Mansa Musa's incredible wealth?

3. Al-'Umari's retelling of a conversation between Mansa Musa and the governor of Cairo suggests that gold was the product of plants. Does this fanciful description undermine the reliability of other aspects of this account? Why or why not?

Galileo Galilei, Letter to Madame Cristina di Lorena, Grand Duchess of Tuscany (1615)

Galileo Galilei (1564–1642) was born to a relatively poor noble family. Sent to the University of Pisa to study medicine, he instead became interested in physics and mathematics. He became a professor of mathematics at Padua in 1592. He made important discoveries about falling objects that called Aristotelian physics into question, about the motion of the pendulum, and in several other areas. He also developed an improved water pump and other practical implements. He is best known, however, for inventing a telescope. The observations he made with it in 1610 confirmed the arguments of Copernicus (1473–1543) that the sun is the center of the solar system, and the earth and other planets move around it.

This position conflicted with the doctrine of the Catholic Church; Galileo was denounced in 1614, tried by the Inquisition in 1616, and warned against publicly advocating Copernicanism. Still, he persisted. Various powerful people, including the Pope, tried to arrange a compromise in which Galileo would be protected so long as he was relatively quiet in his support of heliocentrism; Galileo, however, continued to publish. In 1632 he was tried and convicted of heresy, and spent the rest of his life under house arrest.

In the letter excerpted below, Galileo addresses Cristina di Lorena (1565–1636), Grand Duchess of Tuscany—a descendant of French royalty who married into the Medici family, which had patronized Galileo. Although Galileo had not yet been condemned by the Inquisition, and this letter was not made public until much later, it represents a forceful statement of views on the relationship between science and religious authority that the Catholic Church of his time was unwilling to accept. The Catholic Church stopped prohibiting books advocating heliocentrism in 1758, but it did not formally absolve Galileo until 1992.

Some years ago, as your Serene Highness well knows, I discovered many things in the heavens that had remained unseen until our own era. Perhaps because of their novelty, perhaps because of certain consequences which followed from them, these discoveries conflicted with certain propositions concerning nature which were commonly accepted by the philosophical schools. Hence no small number of professors became stirred up against me—almost as though I, with my own hand, had placed these things in heaven in order to disturb and obscure nature and the sciences. Displaying greater affection for their own opinions than for true ones, and, at the same time, forgetting that the multitude of truths contribute to inquiry by augmenting and establishing science, and not by diminishing and destroying it, these professors set about trying to deny and abolish these new discoveries. Although their very senses, had they seen fit to heed them attentively, would have rendered these things as certain, they nonetheless alleged various things and published various writings full of empty reasoning and containing—a still graver error—scattered testimonies from Holy Scripture. The latter were not only cited out of context, but had little to do with the matter at hand. * * *

Thus it is that these men persist in their primary objective, which is to try, by every means imaginable, to destroy me and all that is mine. They know that, in my astronomical and philosophical studies concerning the structure of the world, I maintain that the Sun, without moving, remains stationary in the center of the revolution of celestial orbs; and that the Earth, turning about its own axis, revolves around the Sun as well. They are aware, moreover, that I proceed to confirm the above hypothesis (*posizione*), not simply by condemning the account of Ptolemy and Aristotle, but by bringing forward much conflicting evidence—in particular, certain natural effects, the causes of which cannot be explained in any other manner, and certain celestial effects, determined by the concordance of many new astronomical discoveries, which clearly confute the Ptolemaic system, and which admirably agree with and support the other hypothesis. Now, perhaps they are confused by the fact that certain other propositions, contrary to common opinion but affirmed by me, have been recognized as true. And thus unsure of their defenses on the battlefield of philosophy, they have sought to make a shield

SOURCE: *Introduction to Contemporary Civilization in the West*, 2nd ed., edited by the Contemporary Civilization Staff of Columbia College, Columbia University (New York: Columbia University Press, 1954), vol. 1, pp. 724–27.

for their fallacious arguments out of the mantle of simulated piety and the authority of Scripture, applied by them with little intelligence to combat arguments which they have neither thought about nor understood. * * *

But who could with all certainty insist that the Scripture has chosen rigorously to confine itself to the strict and literal meaning of words when it speaks incidentally of the Earth, water, the Sun, and other creatures? And above all when it asserts something about these creatures which in no way touches upon the primary purpose of Holy Writ, which has to do with the service of God, the salvation of souls, and things far removed indeed from vulgar apprehension? Considering this, then, it seems to me that, when discussing natural problems, we ought to begin with sensory experience and logical demonstrations, and not with the authority of passages in Scripture. For both Nature and the Holy Scripture proceed alike from the Word of God, the latter being the dictate of the Holy Spirit, and the former being the utterly obedient executrix of Divine Law. Now, it is the case that Scripture finds it convenient, in order to accommodate itself to the understanding of everyone, to say many things which, from the bare meaning of the words it employs, differ in aspect from the absolute truth. But in just the opposite way, Nature is inexorable and immutable, never transcending the limits imposed upon her by law; and it is as though she feels no concern whether her deep reasons and hidden modes of operation shall ever be revealed to the understanding of humankind or not. From this it would seem that natural effects, either those which sensory experience sets before our eyes or those which are established by logical demonstration, ought never on any account to be called into question, much less condemned, on the basis of Scriptural passages whose words may appear to support a conflicting opinion. For not every Scriptural dictum is connected to conditions as severe as those which hold with respect to effects of Nature; nor does God reveal Himself less excellently to us in the effects of Nature than He does in the sacred utterances of Scripture. It is this, perchance, that Tertullian meant when he wrote: *We conclude that God is first cognized in Nature, then recognized in Doctrine: in Nature through His works; in Doctrine through His word preached.* * * *

I should judge that the authority of Scripture was intended principally to persuade men of certain articles and propositions which transcend the powers of human reason, and which could be made credible by no other science and by no means other than the very voice of the Holy Spirit. * * * But I do not feel it necessary to believe that God, Who gave us senses, reason, and intellect, should have wished us to postpone using these gifts; that He has somehow given us, by other means, the information which we can obtain with our own senses, reason, and intellect; nor that He should want us to deny the senses and reason when sensory experience and logical demonstration have revealed something to our eyes and minds! And above all I do not feel it necessary to believe this where a science [like astronomy] is concerned, only a tiny part of which is written about (and then in contradictory ways) in Scripture. * * *

Experience plainly indicated that, concerning the rest and motion of Sun and Earth, it was necessary for Scripture to assert what it did, in order that the popular capacity [for understanding] should be satisfied. For even in our own day, individuals far less rude still persist in the same opinion for reasons which, if they were well weighed and examined, would be found to be completely specious, and which experiment would show to be wholly false or altogether beside the point. Nor can we attempt to remove their ignorance, for they are incapable of grasping the contrary reasons, which depend upon the most delicate observations and the most subtle demonstrations, involving abstractions the comprehension of which demands a more vigorous imagination than they possess. And though the stability of the Sun and the motion of the Earth are more than certain and demonstrated to the wise, it is nonetheless necessary, in order to maintain belief amongst the innumerable vulgar, to assert the contrary. If a thousand ordinary men were interrogated on this matter, perhaps not a single one would be found who would not respond by saying that he thinks, and firmly believes, that the Sun moves and the Earth stands still. But such common popular assent must in no way be taken as an argument for the truth of what is being affirmed. For if we were to question the same men about the causes and motives which provide the basis for their belief, and then to contrast what they say with the experiments and reasons which lead a few to believe otherwise, we would find the former to have been persuaded by simple appearances and the shallowest and silliest objections, and the latter to have been persuaded by the most substantial reasons. It is obvious, then, how necessary it was [for Scripture] to attribute motion to the Sun and stability to the Earth. It was necessary in order not to confuse the limited understanding of the vulgar, and in order not to render them obstinate and antagonistic, and in order that they should have faith in the principal doctrines which have altogether to do with Faith. And if this had to be done, it is not at all to be wondered at that it was done with such consummate wisdom in divine Scripture.

Questions

1. How does Galileo think people should read the Bible? What should they do when it appears to conflict with evidence observed in nature?

2. Does Galileo believe that his position is consistent with Christian faith and church authority? Why or why not?

3. What do you think Galileo was trying to accomplish with this letter?

Ibn Battuta, Visit to Mombassa and Kilwa, Rhila (c. 1358)

Ibn Battuta (1304–c. 1368) was born in Tangier, Morocco. He studied Islamic law and in 1325 embarked on his first *hajj* to Mecca. The pilgrimage should have taken about a year and half—but Ibn Battuta traveled for twenty-four years, moving through the extensive *Dar-al-Islam* (areas ruled by Muslims) including Africa, Southwest Asia, central Asia, and India. His travels took him to places as diverse as Constantinople, Baghdad, and the Maldive Islands. He supported himself as a *qadi* (jurist) and so found work in numerous places. When he finally returned to Morocco, the sultan asked him to dictate his adventures. Whether due to the faulty memories of an aging man or deliberate fabrication, some segments of the *Rhila* (travels) do not correlate with other sources. Nevertheless, the work as a whole sheds light on the extensive world of educated, urbane elites connected through a shared belief in Islam. The following selections describe Ibn Battuta's visit to the Swahili coastal towns of East Africa.

Manbasā [Mombasa] is a large island with two days' journey by sea between it and the land of the Sawāḥil. It has no mainland. Its trees are the banana, the lemon, and the citron. They have fruit which they call the jammūn, which is similar to the olive and its stone is like its stone except that it is extremely sweet. There is no cultivation of grain among the people of this island: food is brought to them from the Sawāḥil. The greater part of their food is bananas and fish. They are Shāfiʿī [a practice within Sunni Islam] by rite, they are a religious people, trustworthy and righteous. Their mosques are made of wood, expertly built. At every door of the mosques there are one or two wells. The depth of their wells is a cubit or two. They take water from them in a wooden container into which a thin stick of a cubit's length has been fixed. The ground around the well and the mosque is level. He who wants to enter the mosque washes his feet and enters. There is at its gate a piece of thick matting upon which he rubs his two feet. He who wants to make the ablution holds the pot between his thighs and pours water upon his hands and carries out the ablutions. All the people walk barefoot. We spent the night on this island and travelled by sea to the city of Kulwā [Kilwa]. [Kilwa is] a great coastal city. Most of its people are Zunūj, extremely black. They have cuttings on their faces like those on the faces of the Līmiyyīn of Janāda. * * * The city of Kulwā is amongst the most beautiful of cities and most elegantly built. All of it is of wood, and the ceiling of its houses are of al-dīs [reeds]. The rains there are great. They are a people devoted to the Holy War because they are on one continuous mainland with unbelieving Zunūj. Their uppermost virtue is religion and righteousness and they are Shāfiʿī in rite.

* * *

SOURCE: Said Hamdun and Noël King, *Ibn Battuta in Black Africa* (Princeton, N.J.: Markus Weiner, 1975), pp. 21–22, 24–25.

DESCRIPTION OF THE SULTAN OF KULWĀ

Its sultan at the time of my entry into Kulwā was Abū al-Muẓaffar Ḥasan whose *kunya* [honorific title] was Abū al-Mawāhib [father of gifts] because of his many gifts and deeds of generosity. He was much given to razzias upon the land of the Zunūj; he raided them and captured booty. He used to set aside one fifth of it, which he spent in the ways indicated in the book of God the Exalted. He put the share of the kindred [of the prophet, the *sharīfs*] in a treasury by itself. When the *sharīfs* came to him he gave it to them. The *sharīfs* used to come to him from 'Irāq and Ḥijāz and other places. * * * This sultan is a very humble man. He sits with the poor people [*faqīrs*] and eats with them, and gives respect to people of religion and of prophetic descent.

A STORY CONCERNING THE SULTAN OF KULWĀ'S DEEDS OF GENEROSITY

I was present with him on a Friday when he came out from the prayer and was returning to his house. He was confronted on the road by one of the Yemeni *faqīrs*. He said to him, "O father of gifts." He replied, "At your service, O *faqīr*, what is your need?" He said, "Give me these clothes which you are wearing." He replied, "Yes, I will give them to you." He said to him, "This very moment." He said, "Yes, this very moment." He went back to the mosque and went into the house of the preacher [*khaṭīb*]. He put on other clothes and took off those clothes. He said to the *faqīr*, "Enter and take them." So the *faqīr* went in, tied them in a piece of cloth and put them on his head and went away. The gratitude of the people to the sultan increased at the evidence of his humility and graciousness. His son and heir-apparent took that suit of clothes from the *faqīr* and compensated him for it with ten slaves. When the news reached the sultan of the gratitude of the people to him for that deed he ordered the *faqīr* to be given in addition ten head of fine slaves and two loads of ivory. (The greater part of their gifts are ivory and seldom do they give gold.) When this honourable and generous sultan was gathered to God (may God have mercy on him), his brother Dā'ūd succeeded him. He was the opposite from him. When a beggar came to him he said to him, "He who used to give has died, and he did not leave anything after him to be given."

Questions

1. This description of the sultan of Kilwa presents a ruler both belligerent and generous. How does Ibn Battuta reconcile these two different facets of a ruler?

2. As in many other passages of the book, Ibn Battuta's description of Mombassa is disjointed, with little apparent connection between the elements he chooses to mention. What captures his attention in Mombassa? Why might Ibn Battuta want to tell readers about these features of Mombassa and emphasize different things about Kilwa?

3. What social and religious values does this passage emphasize?

Kabir, Three Poems (fifteenth century)

Kabir (1398–1448) was probably illiterate, and his mysticism earned him passionate enemies among both Muslims and Hindus during much of his lifetime. He was born to a family of Muslim weavers, but lived an itinerant life. By the end of his life, however, he was renowned as one of India's great religious poets and teachers; Hindus and Muslims both attempted to claim him, and still do. There is also a Kabir sect of people who revere him as a holy man.

In part, Kabir made enemies during his lifetime by an uncompromising insistence on what he considered to be honesty, and scathing criticisms of those whom he thought robbed religion of its deep, ecstatic meaning. Scholars and clergy whom he felt focused on the details of textual and ritual correctness and missed the physical experience and intense emotions that went with true insight were one of his favorite targets; priestly sacrifices and attempts to picture gods in physical forms were another; rules and customs that restricted women in particular were a third. He often went out of his way to behave publicly in ways that religious and political authorities would find scandalous.

54

She went with her husband to the in-laws' house
but didn't sleep with him,
didn't enjoy him.
Her youth slipped away like a dream.
Four met and fixed the marriage date,
five came and fixed the canopy,
girlfriends sang the wedding songs
and rubbed on her brow the yellow paste
of joy and sorrow.
Through many forms her mind turned
as she circled the fire.
The knot was tied, the pledge was made,
the married women poured the water.
Yet with her husband on the wedding square
she became a widow.
She left her marriage without the groom.
On the road the father-in-law explained.
Kabir says, I'm off to my real marriage now.
I'll play the trumpet
when I cross with my lord.

84

Qazi, what book are you lecturing on?
Yak yak yak, day and night.
You never had an original thought.
Feeling your power, you circumcise—
I can't go along with that, brother.
If your God favored circumcision,
why didn't you come out cut?

SOURCE: *The Bijak of Kabir*, translated by Linda Hess and Shukdev Singh (San Francisco: North Point Press, 1983), pp. 59, 69–70, and *Songs of Saints of India*, translated by J. S. Hawley and Mark Juergensmeyer (Oxford: Oxford University Press, 2004), pp. 50–51.

If circumcision makes you a Muslim,
what do you call your women?
Since women are called man's other half,
you might as well be Hindus.
If putting on the thread makes you Brahmin,
what does the wife put on?
That Shudra's touching your food, pandit!
How can you eat it?
Hindu, Muslim—where did they come from?
Who started this road?
Look hard in your heart, send out scouts:
where is heaven?
Now you get your way by force,
but when it's time for dying,
without Ram's refuge, says Kabir,
brother, you'll go out crying.

[*Untitled*]

Go naked if you want,
Put on animal skins.
    What does it matter till you see the inward Ram?

If the union yogis seek
Came from roaming about in the buff,
    every deer in the forest would be saved.

If shaving your head
Spelled spiritual success,
    heaven would be filled with sheep.

And brother, if holding back your seed
Earned you a place in paradise,
    eunuchs would be the first to arrive.

Kabir says: Listen brother,
Without the name of Ram

who has ever won the spirit's prize?

Pundit, how can you be so dumb?
You're going to drown, along with all your kin,
    unless you start speaking of Ram.

Vedas, Puranas—why read them?
    It's like loading an ass with sandalwood!
Unless you catch on and learn how Ram's name goes,
    how will you reach the end of the road?

You slaughter living beings and call it religion:
    hey brother, what would irreligion be?
"Great Saint"—that's how you love to greet each other:
    Who then would you call a murderer?

Your mind is blind. You've no knowledge of yourselves.
    Tell me, brother, how can you teach anyone else?
Wisdom is a thing you sell for worldly gain,
    so there goes your human birth—in vain.

You say: "It's Narad's command."
    "It's what Vyas says to do."
    "Go and ask Sukdev, the sage."
Kabir says: you'd better go and lose yourself in Ram
    for without him, brother, you drown.

Questions

1. What does the first poem suggest about what is and is not important in marriage? How can you tell?

2. What complaints against both Muslims and Hindus can you find in the second poem? How does the third poem extend those complaints?

3. What hints do you get in these poems of what Kabir thinks would constitute genuine religious experience? What might some Hindus find particularly objectionable about this? What might some Muslims object to?

Leo Africanus, On Timbuktu (1526)

Leo Africanus (c. 1494–c. 1554) was born al-Hasan ibn Muhammad al-Wazzan al-Fasi in Granada. Given the difficulties for Muslims in Spain after the expulsion of the Moors, his family joined relatives in Fez, where al-Hasan grew up and studied at the university. As a young man he traveled with his uncle throughout the Maghreb, going as far south as Timbuktu, then part of the Songhai Empire. He later performed the *hajj* to Mecca, and traveled across the Mediterranean to Istanbul. In 1518 his ship was captured by pirates; he was eventually taken to Rome and presented to Pope Leo X. As a man of letters with extensive diplomatic knowledge, he was welcomed at the papal court. He was baptized as Leo Africanus in 1520.

The historical geography of Africa is Africanus' best known scholarly work. It was quickly translated from Italian and had several printings in the sixteenth century. Although he was well-traveled, it is unlikely that Africanus visited all the places he described. Like other early modern writers, he probably relied on relayed oral descriptions from other travelers. When Leo Africanus visited Timbuktu, it was a vibrant commercial city famous for its wealth and learning.

This name was in our times (as some think) imposed upon this kingdom from the name of a certain town, so called, which (they say) king Mansa Suleiman founded in the year of the Hegira 610 [1213 CE] and it is situated within twelve miles of a certain branch of the Niger. All the houses are now changed into cottages built of chalk, and covered with thatch. Howbeit there is a most stately temple [mosque] to be seen, the walls whereof are made of stone and lime; and a princely palace also built by a most excellent workman of Granada. Here are many shops of artificers [craftspersons], and merchants, and especially of such as weave linen and cotton cloth.

SOURCE: Leo Africanus, *The History and Description of Africa and of the Notable Things Therein Contained*, translated by Robert Brown (London: Hakluyt Society, 1896), vol. 3, pp. 824–26. Text modernized by Norton authors for this edition.

And hither do the Barbary [North African] merchants bring cloth of Europe.

All women of this region go with their faces covered, except maid-servants who sell all necessary victuals. The inhabitants and especially strangers there residing, are exceedingly rich, insomuch as the king that now is, married both his daughters to two rich merchants. Here are many wells containing most sweet water; and so often as the river Niger overflows, they convey the water thereof by certain sluices into the town. Grain, cattle, milk, and butter this region yields in great abundance, but salt is very scarce here. It is brought hither by land from Taghaza [also in modern-day Mali], which is five hundred miles distant. When I myself was here, I saw one camel load of salt sold for 80 ducats.

The rich king of Timbuktu has many plates and scepters of gold, some whereof weigh 1300 pounds. He keeps a magnificent and well furnished court. When he travels he rides upon a camel which is led by some of his noblemen. He does likewise when he goes to war, and all his soldiers ride upon horses. Whosoever will speak to this king must first fall down before his feet, and then taking up earth must sprinkle it upon his own head and shoulders. This custom is ordinarily observed by them that never saluted the king before, or come as ambassadors from other princes. He always has three thousand horsemen, and a great number of footmen that shoot poisoned arrows, attending on him. They often have skirmishes with those that refuse to pay tribute, and so many [prisoners] as they take they sell to the merchants of Timbuktu.

Very few horses are bred here. The merchants and courtiers keep certain little nags which they use to travel upon, but their best horses are brought out of Barbary. As soon as the king hears that any merchants are come to town with horses, he commands a certain number to be brought before him. Choosing the best for himself, he pays a most liberal price for them.

He so deadly hates all Jews that he will not admit any into his city. Any merchants he understands have dealings with Jews, he presently causes their goods to be confiscated.

Here are a great store of doctors, judges, priests, and other learned men that are bountifully maintained by the king's cost and charge.

And hither are brought diverse manuscripts or written books out of Barbary; they are sold for more money than any other merchandise.

The coin of Timbuktu is of gold without any stamps or superscription. In matters of small value they use certain shells brought out of Persia, four hundred of which shells are worth a ducat. Six pieces of their golden coin with two thirds parts weigh an ounce.

The inhabitants are people of a gentle and cheerful disposition, and spend a great part of the night in singing and dancing through all the streets of the city. They keep a great store of men and women slaves. Their town is in much danger of fire; at my second visit, half the town was almost burned in five hours time. Without the suburbs there are no gardens or orchards at all.

Questions

1. What features of a sophisticated economy are evident in this description of Timbuktu?

2. What connection did Timbuktu have to other regions?

3. Both Leo Africanus and Ibn Battuta (see Ibn Battuta, Visit to Mombassa and Kilwa, in this chapter) left records of their visits to Muslim cities in Africa. Compare their descriptions. What explains the similarities and differences in their accounts?

Chapter 12

CONTACT, COMMERCE, AND COLONIZATION, 1450s–1600

Christopher Columbus, On World Geography (late fifteenth century)

Christopher Columbus (c. 1451–1506) was born in Genoa, but achieved his fame sailing for Spain after several other kingdoms declined to back his venture. By the late fifteenth century, the spice routes eastward to Asia were dominated by Muslims and by Genoa's rival, Venice. Columbus was convinced that one could also reach Asia by sailing west across the uncharted Atlantic, thus bypassing these hostile powers. Contrary to a common belief today, Columbus was not unusual—at least among educated people—in realizing that the earth was round; note in the excerpt below that he takes this as obvious. While he failed to find a westward sea route to Asia, the bringing of the Americas into contact with Europe was one of the most consequential events in recorded history.

In all, Columbus made four voyages in search of a passage to Asia. He also served as a colonial governor in Hispaniola, but was removed and arrested for committing various abuses. He was returned to Spain as a prisoner, but freed after about six weeks.

I have always read that the world, land and water, was spherical, and authoritative accounts and the experiments which Ptolemy [ancient Greek geographer] and all the others have recorded

66

concerning this matter, so describe it and hold it to be, by the eclipses of the moon and by other demonstrations made from east to west, as well as from the elevation of the pole star from north to south. Now, as I have already said, I have seen so great irregularity that, as a result, I have been led to hold this concerning the world, and I find that it is not round as they describe it, but that it is the shape of a pear which is everywhere very round except where the stalk is, for there it is very prominent, or that it is like a very round ball, and on one part of it is placed something like a woman's nipple, and that this part, where this protuberance is found, is the highest and nearest to the sky, and it is beneath the equinoctial line and in this Ocean sea at the end of the East. I call that "the end of the East," where end all the land and islands.

clueless

not quite right

* * *

Holy Scripture testifies that Our Lord made the earthly paradise and in it placed the tree of life, and from it issues a fountain from which flow four of the chief rivers of this world, the Ganges in India, the Tigris and Euphrates in * * *, which cut through a mountain range and form Mesopotamia and flow into Persia, and the Nile which rises in Ethiopia and enters the sea at Alexandria.

I do not find and I have never found any writing of the Romans or of the Greeks which gives definitely the position in the world of the earthly paradise, nor have I seen it in any world map, placed with authority based upon proof. Some placed it there where are the sources of the Nile in Ethiopia, but others traversed all these lands and found no similarity to it in the climate or in elevation towards the sky, to make it comprehensible that it was there, nor that the rising waters of the deluge had reached that place, &c [etc.]. Some Gentiles wished to show by arguments that it was in the Fortunate islands, which are the Canaries, &c. St. Isidore [of Seville] and Bede and [Walafridus] Strabo and the Master of Scholastic History [Petrus Comestor] and St. Ambrose and [Duns] Scotus and

biblical conception. eden 11

SOURCE: *The Four Voyages of Columbus*, translated and edited by Cecil Jane. Originally published by the Hakluyt Society.

all the learned theologians agree that the earthly paradise is in the East, &c.

I have already said that which I hold concerning this hemisphere and its shape, and I believe that if I were to pass beneath the equinoctial line, then, arriving there at the highest point, I should find an even more temperate climate and difference in the stars and waters. Not that I believe that to the summit of the extreme point is navigable, or water, or that it is possible to ascend there, for I believe that the earthly paradise is there and to it, save by the will of God, no man can come.

Questions

1. What sources of geographic knowledge does Columbus draw on in this text? How does he decide among them?

2. Columbus does not believe that anyone can sail to the earthly paradise. Why do you think he discusses it in the context of navigation?

3. What does this document suggest to you about faith and reason in Columbus's thinking?

The Broken Spears: The Aztec Account of the Conquest of Mexico (1519)

The Broken Spears is a Spanish translation of several accounts in Nahuatl of the Spanish conquest of the Aztecs in 1519. (A more accurate translation would actually be "The Broken Bones.") The earliest of these accounts seems to have been written in 1528, nine years after Cortés landed at Veracruz and seven years after the Aztec capital at Tenochtitán fell.

The arrival of the Spanish on the coast led to intense debates about how to deal with them. Aztec society was far from united; in fact, indigenous allies were of great help to the vastly outnumbered Spanish. There was also disagreement over who the Spanish were. As this passage shows, some people thought Cortés was the fulfillment of a prophecy about an ancient god who would return to rule someday. In the passage just before this (not reprinted here), Emperor Moctezuma decides—against the will of many of his advisers—to welcome him as such. Spelling has been updated in the following excerpt to reflect modern orthography.

When Moctezuma had given necklaces to each one, Cortés asked him: "Are you Moctezuma? Are you the king? Is it true that you are the king Moctezuma?"

And the king said: "Yes, I am Moctezuma." Then he stood up to welcome Cortés; he came forward, bowed his head low and addressed him in these words: "Our lord, you are weary. The journey has tired you, but now you have arrived on the earth. You have come to your city, Mexico. You have come here to sit on your throne, to sit under its canopy.

"The kings who have gone before, your representatives, guarded it and preserved it for your coming. The kings Itzcoatl, Moctezuma the Elder, Axayacatl, Tizoc and Ahuitzol ruled for you in the City of Mexico. The people were protected by their swords and sheltered by their shields.

"Do the kings know the destiny of those they left behind, their posterity? If only they are watching! If only they can see what I see!

"No, it is not a dream. I am not walking in my sleep. I am not seeing you in my dreams. * * * I have seen you at last! I have met you face to face! I was in agony for five days, for ten days, with my eyes fixed on the Region of the Mystery. And now you have come out of the clouds and mists to sit on your throne again.

"This was foretold by the kings who governed your city, and now it has taken place. You have come back to us; you have come down from the sky. Rest now, and take possession of your royal houses. Welcome to your land, my lords!"

When Moctezuma had finished, La Malinche [a native woman who served as Cortés' translator, adviser, and mistress] translated his address into Spanish so that the Captain could understand it.

SOURCE: *The Broken Spears: The Aztec Account of the Conquest of Mexico*, edited by Miguel Leon-Portilla (Boston: Beacon Press, 1962), pp. 64–69, 71–73.

Cortés replied in his strange and savage tongue, speaking first to La Malinche: "Tell Moctezuma that we are his friends. There is nothing to fear. We have wanted to see him for a long time, and now we have seen his face and heard his words. Tell him that we love him well and that our hearts are contented."

Then he said to Moctezuma: "We have come to your house in Mexico as friends. There is nothing to fear."

La Malinche translated this speech and the Spaniards grasped Moctezuma's hands and patted his back to show their affection for him.

ATTITUDES OF THE SPANIARDS AND THE NATIVE LORDS

The Spaniards examined everything they saw. They dismounted from their horses, and mounted them again, and dismounted again, so as not to miss anything of interest.

* * *

When Moctezuma was imprisoned, they [the chiefs and princes who served him] all went into hiding. They ran away to hide and treacherously abandoned him!

THE SPANIARDS TAKE POSSESSION OF THE CITY

When the Spaniards entered the Royal House, they placed Moctezuma under guard and kept him under their vigilance. They also placed a guard over Itzcuauhtzin, but the other lords were permitted to depart.

Then the Spaniards fired one of their cannons, and this caused great confusion in the city. The people scattered in every direction; they fled without rhyme or reason; they ran off as if they were being pursued. It was as if they had eaten the mushrooms that confuse the mind, or had seen some dreadful apparition. They were all overcome by terror, as if their hearts had fainted. And when night fell, the panic spread through the city and their fears would not let them sleep.

In the morning the Spaniards told Moctezuma what they needed in the way of supplies: tortillas, fried chickens, hens' eggs, pure water, firewood and charcoal. Also: large, clean cooking pots, water jars, pitchers, dishes and other pottery. Moctezuma ordered that it be sent to them. The chiefs who received this order were angry with the king and no longer revered or respected him. But they furnished the Spaniards with all the provisions they needed—food, beverages and water, and fodder for the horses.

The Spaniards Reveal Their Greed

When the Spaniards were installed in the palace, they asked Moctezuma about the city's resources and reserves and the warriors' ensigns and shields. They questioned him closely and then demanded gold.

Moctezuma guided them to it. They surrounded him and crowded close with their weapons. He walked in the center, while they formed a circle around him.

When they arrived at the treasure house called Teucalco, the riches of gold and feathers were brought out to them: ornaments made of quetzal feathers, richly worked shields, disks of gold, the necklaces of the idols, gold nose plugs, gold greaves and bracelets and crowns.

The Spaniards immediately stripped the feathers from the gold shields and ensigns. They gathered all the gold into a great mound and set fire to everything else, regardless of its value. Then they melted down the gold into ingots. As for the precious green stones, they took only the best of them; the rest were snatched up by the Tlaxcaltecas. The Spaniards searched through the whole treasure house, questioning and quarreling, and seized every object they thought was beautiful.

The Seizure of Moctezuma's Treasures

Next they went to Moctezuma's storehouse, in the place called Totocalco [Place of the Palace of the Birds], where his personal treasures were kept. The Spaniards grinned like little beasts and patted each other with delight.

When they entered the hall of treasures, it was as if they had arrived in Paradise. They searched everywhere and coveted everything; they were slaves to their own greed. * * *

La Malinche called the nobles together. She climbed up to the palace roof and cried: "Mexicanos, come forward! The Spaniards need your help! Bring them food and pure water. They are tired and hungry; they are almost fainting from exhaustion! Why do you not come forward? Are you angry with them?"

The Mexicans were too frightened to approach. They were crushed by terror and would not risk coming forward. They shied away as if the Spaniards were wild beasts, as if the hour were midnight on the blackest night of the year. Yet they did not abandon the Spaniards to hunger and thirst. They brought them whatever they needed, but shook with fear as they did so. They delivered the supplies to the Spaniards with trembling hands, then turned and hurried away.

✳ ✳ ✳

THE PREPARATIONS FOR THE FIESTA

The Aztecs begged permission of their king to hold the fiesta of Huitzilopochtli. The Spaniards wanted to see this fiesta to learn how it was celebrated. A delegation of the celebrants came to the palace where Moctezuma was a prisoner, and when their spokesman asked his permission, he granted it to them.

As soon as the delegation returned, the women began to grind seeds of the chicalote. These women had fasted for a whole year. They ground the seeds in the patio of the temple.

The Spaniards came out of the palace together, dressed in armor and carrying their weapons with them. They stalked among the women and looked at them one by one; they stared into the faces of the women who were grinding seeds. After this cold inspection, they went back into the palace. It is said that they planned to kill the celebrants if the men entered the patio.

THE STATUE OF HUITZILOPOCHTLI

On the evening before the fiesta of Toxcatl, the celebrants began to model a statue of Huitzilopochtli. They gave it such a human appearance that it seemed the body of a living man. Yet they made the statue with nothing but a paste made of the ground seeds of the chicalote, which they shaped over an armature of sticks.

When the statue was finished, they dressed it in rich feathers, and they painted crossbars over and under its eyes. They also clipped on its earrings of turquoise mosaic; these were in the shape of serpents, with gold rings hanging from them. Its nose plug, in the shape of an arrow, was made of gold and was inlaid with fine stones.

They placed the magic headdress of hummingbird feathers on its head. They also adorned it with an *anecuyotl,* which was a belt made of feathers, with a cone at the back. Then they hung around its neck an ornament of yellow parrot feathers, fringed like the locks of a young boy. Over this they put its nettle-leaf cape, which was painted black and decorated with five clusters of eagle feathers.

Next they wrapped it in its cloak, which was painted with skulls and bones, and over this they fastened its vest. The vest was painted with dismembered human parts: skulls, ears, hearts, intestines, torsos, breasts, hands and feet. They also put on its *maxtlatl,* or loincloth, which was decorated with images of dissevered limbs and fringed with amate paper. This *maxtlatl* was painted with vertical stripes of bright blue.

* * *

Finally, they put the wristbands on its arms. These bands, made of coyote skin, were fringed with paper cut into little strips.

The Beginning of the Fiesta

Early the next morning, the statue's face was uncovered by those who had been chosen for that ceremony. They gathered in front of the idol in single file and offered it gifts of food, such as round seedcakes or perhaps human flesh. But they did not carry it up to its temple on top of the pyramid.

All the young warriors were eager for the fiesta to begin. They had sworn to dance and sing with all their hearts, so that the Spaniards would marvel at the beauty of the rituals.

Questions

1. What are the Spanish interested in? What does the narrator conclude from this?

2. What do you learn about Aztec society and culture from this passage?

3. What things seem to upset the narrator most about these events? How can you tell?

Arana Xajilá, Plague in Central America (1519–1560)

The Cakchiquels were one of four related indigenous groups living in part of what is today Guatemala. The excerpt below comes from a history of the tribe—*Annals of the Cakchiquels*—written by four members, including Arana Xajilá, also known as Francisco Hernández (c. 1502–c. 1581). We know very little of the history of the text; it was written in the Cakchiquel language and gives firsthand accounts of sixteenth- and early seventeenth-century events (the last one in 1621). It was first discovered in the archives of a Guatemalan convent in 1844. It appears to have been part of a complaint filed in a lawsuit, but we do not know what the suit was about, or what points this history was intended to prove.

Some of the events recorded go back to about 1380. From today's perspective we might assume that the Spanish conquest would be the most important event recorded in the chronicle, but the authors place much greater emphasis on a bloody revolt against the Cakchiquel rulers (who had recently conquered various other tribes) in 1495–1496. In fact, this event looms so large in the story that all subsequent events are dated with reference to it (so that 1519–1520, for instance, is the twenty-fifth year after the revolt). The plague, which forms the focus of this excerpt, reached the Cakchiquel in 1519, about five years before the Spanish themselves did.

---

127. In the course of the [twenty-]fifth year [1519] the pestilence began, O my children. First there was a cough, then the blood was corrupted, and the urine became yellow. The number of deaths at

this time was truly terrible. The Chief Vakaki Ahmak died, and we ourselves were plunged in great darkness and great grief, our fathers and ancestors having contracted the plague, O my children.

On the day 1 Ah [October 3, 1520] there were one cycle and 5 years [25 years] from the Revolt, and the pestilence spread.

128. In this year the pestilence spread, and then died our ancestor Diego Juan. On the day 5 Ah [March 12, 1521] war was carried to Panatacat by our ancestor, and then began the spread of the pestilence. Truly the number of deaths among the people was terrible, nor did the people escape from the pestilence.

129. Forty were seized with the sickness; then died our father and ancestor; on the day 14 Camey [April 14, 1521] died the king Hunyg, your grandfather.

130. But two days afterward died our father, the [Ahpop Achi] Balam, one of the ancients, O my children. The ancients and the fathers died alike, and the stench was such that men died of it alone. Then perished our fathers and ancestors. Half the people threw themselves into the ravines, and the dogs and foxes lived on the bodies of the men. The fear of death destroyed the old people, and the oldest son of the king died at the same time as his young brother. Thus did we become poor, O my children, and thus did we survive, being but a little child—and we were all that remained.

* * *

144. * * * On the day 1 Ganel [February 20, 1524] the Quiches [a related, rival people] were destroyed by the Castilians. [The chief,] Tunatiuh Avilantaro, as he was called, conquered all the towns. Their countenances were previously unknown and the people rendered homage to sticks and stones.

* * *

165. During this year [1530–1531] [heavy tribute was imposed]; they paid gold and silver before the face of Tunatiuh, and there were demanded as tribute five hundred men and five hundred women to

SOURCE: *The Annals of the Cakchiquels*, translated by Daniel G. Brinton (Philadelphia, 1885), pp. 171, 177, 188–91, 194.

go to the gold washings; all the people were busy seeking gold. Five hundred men and five hundred women were also demanded by Tunatiuh to aid in building Pangan for his princely residence. All that, yes, all that, we ourselves witnessed, O my children.

* * *

170. In the course of the year, on the 11th Noh [May 16, 1536], . . . the prince Mantunalo arrived to relieve the nation from its sufferings; the washing for gold and silver promptly ceased, and the tribute of young men and women ceased; the burnings alive and the hangings ceased, and, indeed, all the various acts of violence of the Castilians and the imposts which they had forcibly laid upon us. The roads were once more frequented by travelers when the Prince Mantunalo arrived, as they had been eight years before, when the imposts were first laid upon us, O my children.

* * *

* * * [T]here arrived at our house our fathers of St. Dominic, Brother Pedro [Angulo] and Brother Juan de Torres. They arrived from Mexico on the day 12 Batz [February 10, 1542], and we began to receive instruction from our fathers of St. Dominic. Then also appeared the Doctrin[e] in our language. Our fathers, Brother Pedro and Brother Juan were the first who taught us the word of God. Until that time the word and the commandments of God were unknown to us; we had lived in darkness, for no one had spoken to us of the doctrine of God.

* * *

Six months after the arrival of the [Lord] President at Pangan, began here again the pestilence which had formerly raged among the people. It came from a distance. It was truly terrible when this death was sent among us by the great God. Many families bowed their heads before it [succumbed to the plague]. The people were seized with a chill and then a fever; blood issued from the nose; there was a cough, and the throat and nose were swollen, both in the lesser and the greater pestilence. All here were soon attacked. These maladies began, O my children, on the day of the Circumcision, a

Monday [January 1, 1560], and as I was writing, we also were attacked with the disease.

Questions

1. Since the plague came from Europe to Mesoamerica, why might it have reached these people before they had ever seen a Spaniard?

2. What changes does the author connect with the coming of Spanish authority? With the church?

3. How does the author understand the significance of the plague?

Juan Sepúlveda, On the Causes of Just War with the Indians (1547)

Juan Ginés de Sepúlveda (1489–1573) was a Spanish philosopher and theologian. He vigorously defended the Spanish Empire's right of conquest, the moral justifications of colonization, and the necessity of evangelization in New Spain. Sepúlveda based his arguments in European ideas of natural law, which presume an inherent order in the world (an order that happens to be dominated by Christian Europeans). Bartolomé de las Casas, a Dominican priest and the first resident Bishop of Chiapas (Mexico) staunchly opposed Sepúlveda's views. Las Casas, who witnessed the brutality of colonial conquest, opposed violence toward indigenous people in New Spain. He returned to Europe to advocate for the rights of Native Americans before King Charles V.

In the following passage, Sepúlveda articulates a justification for the Spanish conquest of native societies.

In regard to those [of the Aztec and other Indian civilizations] who inhabit New Spain and the province of Mexico, I have already said that they consider themselves the most civilized people [in the

SOURCE: Frederick B. Pike, *Latin American History: Select Problems* (New York: Harcourt, Brace and World, 1969), pp. 50–51.

New World]. They boast of their political and social institutions, because they have rationally planned cities and nonhereditary kings who are elected by popular suffrage, and they carry on commerce among themselves in the manner of civilized people. But * * * I dissent from such an opinion. On the contrary, in those same institutions there is proof of the coarseness, barbarism, and innate servility of these men. Natural necessity encourages the building of houses, some rational manner of life, and some sort of commerce. Such an argument merely proves that they are neither bears nor monkeys and that they are not totally irrational. But on the other hand, they have established their commonwealth in such a manner that no one individually owns anything, neither a house nor a field that one may dispose of or leave to his heirs in his will, because everything is controlled by their lords, who are incorrectly called kings. They live more at the mercy of their king's will than of their own. They are the slaves of his will and caprice, and they are not the masters of their fate. The fact that this condition is not the result of coercion but is voluntary and spontaneous is a certain sign of the servile and base spirit of these barbarians. They had distributed their fields and farms in such a way that one third belonged to the king, another third belonged to the religious cult, and only a third part was reserved for the benefit of everyone; but all of this they did in such a way that they themselves cultivated the royal and religious lands. They lived as servants of the king and at his mercy, paying extremely large tributes. When a father died, all his inheritance, if the king did not decide otherwise, passed in its entirety to the oldest son, with the result that many of the younger sons would either die of starvation or subject themselves to an even more rigorous servitude. They would turn to the petty kings for help and would ask them for a field on the condition that they not only pay feudal tribute but also promise themselves as slave labor when it was necessary. And if this kind of servitude and barbaric commonwealth had not been suitable to their temperament and nature, it would have been easy for them to take advantage of the death of a king, since the monarchy was not hereditary, in order to establish a state that was freer and more favorable to their interests. Their failure to do so confirms that they were born for servitude and not for the civil and liberal life. * * * Such are, in short, the character and customs of these barbarous, uncultivated, and inhumane little men. We know that they were thus before the coming of the Spaniards. Until now we have not mentioned their impious religion and their abominable sacrifices, in which they worship the Devil as God, to whom they thought of offering no better tribute than human hearts. * * * Interpreting their religion in an ignorant and barbarous manner, they sacrificed human victims by removing the hearts from the chests. They placed these hearts on their abominable altars. With this ritual they believed that they had appeased their gods. They also ate the flesh of the sacrificed men. * * *

How are we to doubt that these people, so uncultivated, so barbarous, and so contaminated with such impiety and lewdness, have not been justly conquered by so excellent, pious, and supremely just a king as Ferdinand the Catholic was and the Emperor Charles now is, the kings of a most humane and excellent nation rich in all varieties of virtue?

Questions

1. According to Sepúlveda, what aspects of indigenous political structures demonstrate the barbarism of American natives?

2. What are Sepúlveda's criticisms of Native American property rights?

3. Why might Sepúlveda devote more space to criticisms of political structures and property rights than to differences in religious practice?

Cabeza de Vaca, Years as a Wandering Merchant (1542)

Álvar Núñez Cabeza de Vaca (c. 1507–c. 1557) was a Spanish explorer who arrived in North America with the Narváez expedition in 1527. The party of 300 men landed near present-day Tampa. They walked along the coast and made relatively little progress until they made rafts and sailed along the Gulf Coast toward Mexico. Strong currents at the Mississippi River mouth overturned some of the rafts. Survivors pressed on, until they were stranded near Galveston Island. There the remaining men were taken captive by indigenous groups including the Hans and the Capoques. Ultimately reduced to four survivors, the explorers managed to find support among the indigenous communities. Together with some Native Americans, they made it to Mexico City. Cabeza de Vaca returned to Europe in 1537 and later published *La Relacion* (The Report), which provides detailed descriptions of many American native groups and a firsthand perspective on early colonial encounters in the Americas. The following passage from *La Relacion* (1542) describes a period of time the survivors spent near present-day Galveston and Cabeza de Vaca's unique strategies for survival.

After Dorantes and Castillo had come back to the island, they gathered together all the Christians, who were somewhat scattered, and there were in all fourteen. I, [as I have said], was in another place, on the mainland, whither my Indians had taken me and where I suffered from such a severe illness that, although I might otherwise have entertained some hope for life, this was enough to take it away from me completely. When the Christians learned of it they gave an Indian the robe of marten we had taken from the cacique * * * in order that he should guide them to where I was, to see me. * * *

The names of those who came are: Alonso del Castillo, Andrés Dorantes and [his cousin] Diego Dorantes, [Pedro de] Valdivieso, Estrada, Tostado, Chaves, Gutierrez, an Asturian priest; Diego de Huelva, Estevanico, the negro Benitez, and as they reached the mainland they found still another of our men named Francisco de Léon, and the thirteen went along the coast. After they had gone by, the Indians with whom I was told me of it, and how [Jerónimo] de Alaniz and Lope de Oviedo had been left on the island.

My sickness prevented me from following or seeing them. I had to remain with those same Indians of the island for more than one

---

SOURCE: *The Journey of Alvar Nuñez Cabeza de Vaca*, translated by Fanny Bandelier (New York: A. S. Barnes and Co., 1905), pp. 72–76.

year, and as they made me work so much and treated me so badly
I determined to flee and go to those who live in the woods on the
mainland, and who are called those from * * * Charruco.

I could no longer stand the life I was compelled to lead. Among
many other troubles I had to pull the eatable roots out of the water
and from among the canes where they were buried in the ground,
and from this my fingers had become so tender that the mere touch
of a straw caused them to bleed. The reeds would cut me in many
places, because many were broken and I had to go in among them
with the clothing I had on. * * *

This is why I went to work and joined the other Indians. Among
these I improved my condition a little by becoming a trader, doing
the best in it I could, and they gave me food and treated me well.

[The Indians] entreated me to go about from one part to another
to get the things they needed, as on account of constant warfare
there is neither travel nor barter in the land.

So, trading along with my wares I penetrated inland as far as I
cared to go and along the coast as much as forty or fifty leagues.
My stock consisted mainly of pieces of seashells and cockles, and
shells with which they cut a fruit which is like a bean, used by
them for healing and in their dances and feasts. * * * These things
I carried inland, and in exchange brought back hides and red ochre
with which they rub and dye their faces and hair; flint for arrow
points, glue and hard canes wherewith to make them, and tassels
made of the hair of deer, which they dye red.

This trade suited me well because it gave me liberty to go wherever I pleased; I was not bound to do anything and no longer a
slave. Wherever I went they treated me well, and gave me to eat for
the sake of my wares. My principal object in doing it, however, was
to find out in what manner I might get further away. I became well
known among them; they rejoiced greatly when seeing me and I
would bring them what they needed, and those who did not know
me would desire and endeavor to meet me for the sake of my fame.

My sufferings, while trading thus, it would take long to tell; danger, hunger, storms and frost overtaking me often in the open field
and alone, and from which through the mercy of God, Our Lord, I
escaped. For this reason I did not go out trading in winter, it being

the time when the Indians themselves remain in their huts and abodes, unable to go out or assist each other.

Nearly six years I spent thus in the country, alone among them and naked, as they all were themselves.

The reason for remaining so long was that I wished to take with me a Christian called Lope de Oviedo, who still lingered on the island. The other companion, Alaniz, who remained with him after Alonso del Castillo and Andrés Dorantes and all the others had gone, soon died, and in order to get him (Oviedo) out of there, I went over to the island every year, entreating him to leave with me and go, as well as we could, in search of Christians. But year after year he put it off to the year that was to follow.

Questions

1. How does Cabeza de Vaca's status as a cultural outsider allow him to trade?

2. What is the range of relationships he has with different communities of American Indians?

3. What does Cabeza de Vaca's solitary mobility for a period of at least six years tell us?

William Bradford, Treaty with the Indians (c. 1650)

William Bradford (1590–1657) was a leader of the English settlers of Plymouth Colony in Massachusetts. He served as governor of the colony for thirty-five years and kept a regular journal of his activities between 1620, when the Pilgrims arrived in North America, and 1647. Published as *Of Plymouth Plantation*, the book remains an important source for the history of early settlement in the English colonies. The original manuscript copy of the text has an interesting history. Kept in the Bradford family for about a century, the manuscript was in Boston's Old South Meeting House when the building was occupied by British troops. After that, there was no trace of the document until it was discovered in the

Bishop of London's library in the 1850s. Legal arguments resulted in its return to the United States in 1857.

The following passage describes early relationships between settlers and Native Americans. Notice the difference in tone once the Pilgrims began to deal with individuals of high rank, including two Indians who could speak some English.

All this while the Indians came skulking about them, and would sometimes show themselves aloof of, but when any approached near them, they would run away. And once they stole away their tools where they had been at work, and were gone to dinner. But about the 16th of March a certain Indian came boldly amongst them, and spoke to them in broken English, which they could well understand, but marveled at it. At length they understood by discourse with him, that he was not of these parts, but belonged to the eastern parts, where some English ships came to fish, with whom he was acquainted, and could name sundry of them by their names, amongst whom he had got his language. He became profitable to them in acquainting them with many things concerning the state of the country in the east parts where he lived, which was afterwards profitable unto them; as also of the people here, of their names, number, and strength; of their situation and distance from this place, and who was chief amongst them. His name was Samoset; he told them also of another Indian whose name was Squanto, a native of this place, who had been in England and could speak better English than himself. Being, after some time of entertainment and gifts, dismissed, a while after he came again, and five more with him, and they brought again all the tools that were stolen away before, and made way for the coming of their great Sachem [chief], called Massasoit; who, about four or five days later, came with the chief of his

---

SOURCE: *Bradford's History of Plymouth Plantation*, edited by William T. Davis (New York: Charles Scribner's Sons, 1920), pp. 110–12. Text modernized by Norton authors for this edition.

friends and other attendance, with the aforesaid Squanto. With whom, after friendly entertainment and some gifts given him, they made a peace with him (which hath now continued this twenty-four years) in these terms:

1. That neither he nor any of his should injure or do hurt to any of theirs.

2. That if any of his did any hurt to any of theirs, he should send the offender, that they might punish him.

3. That if anything were taken away from any of theirs, he should cause it to be restored, and they should do the like to his.

4. If any did unjustly war against him, they would aid him; if any did war against them, he should aid them.

5. He should send to his neighbors confederates, to certify them of this, that they might not wrong them, but be likewise comprised in the conditions of peace.

6. That when their men came to them, they should leave their bows and arrows behind them.

After these things he returned to his place called Sowams, some forty miles from this place, but Squanto continued with them, and was their interpreter, and was a special instrument sent of God for their good beyond their expectation. He directed them how to set their corn, where to take fish, and to procure other commodities, and was also their pilot to bring them to unknown places for their profit, and never left them till he died. He was a native of this place, and scarce any left alive besides himself. He was carried away with diverse others by one Hunt, a master of a ship, who thought to sell them for slaves in Spain; but he got away for England, and was entertained by a merchant in London, and employed to Newfoundland and other parts, and lastly brought hither into these parts by one Mr. Dermer, a gentleman employed by Sir Fernando Gorges and others, for discovery, and other designs in these parts.

Questions

1. What kind of information is Bradford most interested in getting from Samoset? Does Bradford deal with what Samoset wanted from the settlers?

2. Describe the main terms of the agreement between Massasoit and the settlers. Is the agreement fairly equal, or does one side benefit more than the other?

3. Squanto is the central figure of these events, yet his brief biography comes at the end of the passage. Can you suggest a reason Bradford structured the passage in this order?

Colonel Benjamin Church, In the Nipmuck Country (1675–1676)

Burgeoning settlements in Massachusetts, Connecticut, and Rhode Island in the 1630s and 1640s increased tensions between colonists and Native American communities and among Indian groups. While some leaders like Massasoit made alliances with the Pilgrims, using access to trade goods (including firearms) to their advantage in local rivalries, other leaders, including Massasoit's son, Metacomet (called King Philip by the colonists), became increasingly suspicious of the settlers' intentions and tactics. Despite ongoing talks between the Indians and leaders of the Plymouth Colony, rumors of Metacomet's intention to attack scattered settlements and disputes over Indian sovereignty erupted in war. In proportion to the existing population, King Philip's War (1675–1676) was one of the bloodiest in North America: more than half of New England's ninety towns were assaulted; about 15 percent of the region's Indians died.

Benjamin Church (c. 1639–1718) was an aide to Governor Josiah Winslow. Church persuaded his commanders to let him recruit American natives, who proved to be skillful fighters. Church's account of the war was first published in 1716; it remains in print. The following excerpt illustrates the brutality of the conflict, the intimacy of hand-to-hand combat, and tensions common to many colonial encounters, such as the importance of personal relationships, and a sense of unfamiliarity with the enemy.

Nipmucks, along with Wampanoags, Podunks, and Mohegans, were among the belligerents. Metacomet died in battle; afterward his body was drawn and quartered, standard English punishment for treason in the seventeenth century. Spelling has been updated in the following excerpt to reflect modern orthography.

But the General's great importunity again persuaded him to accompany him in a long march into the Nipmuck country, though he had then tents in his wounds, and [was] so lame as not [to be] able to mount his horse without two men's assistance.

In this march the first thing remarkable was [that] they came to an Indian town where there were many wigwams in sight, but an icy swamp lying between them and the wigwams prevented their running at once upon it, as they intended. There was much firing upon each side before they passed the swamp. But, at length, the enemy all fled, and a certain Mohegan that was a friend-Indian, pursued and seized one of the enemy that had a small wound in his leg and brought him before the General, where he was examined. Some were for torturing of him to bring him to a more ample confession of what he knew concerning his countrymen. Mr. Church, verily believing he had been ingenuous in his confession, interceded and prevailed for his escaping torture. But the army being bound forward in their march, and the Indian's wound somewhat disenabling him for travelling, 'twas concluded he should be knocked on the head. Accordingly, he was brought before a great fire, and the Mohegan that took him was allowed, as he desired, to be the executioner.

Mr. Church, taking no delight in the sport, framed an errand at some distance among the baggage horses, and when he had got some ten rods or thereabouts from the fire, the executioner, fetching a blow with his hatchet at the head of the prisoner, he, being aware of the blow, dodged his aside, and the executioner, missing

---

SOURCE: Colonel Benjamin Church, *Diary of King Philip's War, 1675–76* (Chester, U.K.: Pequot Press, 1975), pp. 102–104. Originally published in 1716.

his stroke, the hatchet flew out of his hand and had like to have done execution where 'twas not designed.

The prisoner, upon his narrow escape, broke from them that held him and, notwithstanding his wound, made use of his legs and happened to run right upon Mr. Church, who laid hold on him. And a close scuffle they had; but the Indian, having no clothes on, slipped from him and ran again. And Mr. Church pursued the Indian, although, being lame, there was no great odds in the race, until the Indian stumbled and fell, and they closed again, scuffled, and fought pretty smartly until the Indian, by the advantage of his nakedness, slipped from his hold again and set out on his third race, with Mr. Church close at his heels, endeavoring to lay hold on the hair of his head, which was all the hold could be taken of him. And, running through a swamp that was covered with hollow ice, it made so loud a noise that Mr. Church expected (but in vain) that some of his English friends would follow the noise and come to his assistance.

But the Indian [happened] to run athwart a mighty tree that lay fallen near breast-high, where he stopped and cried out aloud for help. But Mr. Church, being soon upon him again, the Indian seized him fast by the hair of his head and, endeavored, by twisting, to break his neck. But, though Mr. Church's wounds had somewhat weakened him, and the Indian [was] a stout fellow, yet he held him well in play and twisted the Indian's neck as well and took the advantage of many opportunities while they hung by each other's hair, to give him notorious bunts in the face with his head.

But in the heat of this scuffle they heard the ice break with some bodies coming apace to them, which, when they heard, Church concluded there was help for one or other of them, but was doubtful which of them must now receive the fatal stroke. Anon, somebody comes up to them who proved to be the Indian that had first taken the prisoner. Without speaking a word, he felt them out (for 'twas so dark he could not distinguish them by sight), the one being clothed, and the other naked; he felt where Mr. Church's hands were fastened in the Netop's hair, and, with one blow, settled his hatchet in between them and ended the strife. He then spoke to Mr. Church and hugged him in his arms and thanked him abundantly for catching his prisoner; and cut off the head of his victim and carried it to the camp. And giving an account to the rest of the friend-Indians in the camp how Mr. Church had seized his prisoner, they all joined a mighty shout.

Proceeding in this march, they had the success of killing many of the enemy, until at length, their provision failing, they returned home.

Questions

1. How did the colonial forces decide whether or not to kill their Indian captive?

2. Although Church did not favor executing the captive, he nevertheless worked very hard to keep him from escaping. Why?

3. It was not Church's "English friends" who came to his aid in a frozen swamp, but a Mohegan ally. Is this significant? Why or why not?

Nzinga Mbemba, Letters to the King of Portugal (1526)

Portuguese navigators traveled as far as the mouth of the Congo River in 1483 and made contact there with peoples of the Kongo kingdom, the largest state at the time in west-central Africa. The Kongo king sent emissaries to Portugal, and they returned in 1491 with European goods and Catholic priests. That same year the king and his son, Nzinga Mbemba, converted to Christianity. Nzinga Mbemba, also known as Afonso I (ruled c. 1506–c.1543), actively encouraged conversion and sought education for elites. He envisioned even greater state expansion through partnership with the Portuguese. However, the dissemination of European goods, especially firearms, the changes that accompanied Christian conversion, and the demographic shifts caused by the Atlantic slave trade all served to destabilize the Kongo kingdom. Afonso and his Portuguese-educated courtiers sent at least twenty-four letters to João III, many asking for the king's help in limiting the damage caused by Portuguese merchants and missionaries. The excerpts from two different letters illustrate the challenges faced by Nzinga Mbemba (and other leaders) trying to control the terms of cross-cultural interaction that accompanied trade.

AFONSO OF CONGO: EVILS OF THE TRADE

[1526] Sir, Your Highness [of Portugal] should know how our Kingdom is being lost in so many ways that it is convenient to provide for the necessary remedy, since this is caused by the excessive freedom given by your factors and officials to the men and merchants who are allowed to come to this Kingdom to set up shops with goods and many things which have been prohibited by us, and which they spread throughout our Kingdoms and Domains in such an abundance that many of our vassals, whom we had in obedience, do not comply because they have the things in greater abundance than we ourselves; and it was with these things that we had them content and subjected under our vassalage and jurisdiction, so it is doing a great harm not only to the service of God, but the security and peace of our Kingdoms and State as well.

And we cannot reckon how great the damage is, since the mentioned merchants are taking every day our natives, sons of the land and the sons of our noblemen and vassals and our relatives, because the thieves and men of bad conscience grab them wishing to have the things and wares of this Kingdom which they are ambitious of; they grab them and get them to be sold; and so great, Sir, is the corruption and licentiousness that our country is being completely depopulated, and Your Highness should not agree with this nor accept it as in your service. And to avoid it we need from those [your] Kingdoms no more than some priests and a few people to teach in schools, and no other goods except wine and flour for the holy sacrament. That is why we beg of Your Highness to help and assist us in this matter, commanding your factors that they should

SOURCE: Basil Davidson, *The African Past: Chronicles from Antiquity to Modern Times* (Boston: Little, Brown and Co., 1964), pp. 191–92, and *Modern Asia and Africa*, edited by William H. McNeill and Mitsuko Iriye (New York: Oxford University Press, 1971), pp. 43, 56–57.

not send here either merchants or wares, because it is *our will that in these Kingdoms there should not be any trade of slaves nor outlet for them.* Concerning what is referred above, again we beg of Your Highness to agree with it, since otherwise we cannot remedy such an obvious damage. Pray Our Lord in His mercy to have Your Highness under His guard and let you do for ever the things of His service. * * *

AFONSO I: AN AFRICAN RESPONSE TO CHRISTIANITY

Now we wish to tell your Highness about a certain Rui do Rego whom your Highness sent here to teach us and set an example for us, but as soon as he arrived here he wished to be treated like a nobleman and never wanted to teach a single boy. During the Lenten season [when Catholics are prohibited from eating meat] he came to us and asked for an ox, and we ordered one to be given to him. Then he said he was dying of hunger, and we ordered two sheep to be given to him, but that he was to eat them secretly, so that our people would not see him. Yet he, disregarding this, went and killed the ox in the middle of Lent, in front of all our nobles, and even tempted us with the meat; so that when our people saw it, those who were young and had only been Christians a short time all fled to their lands, and the older ones who remained with us said things that are not to be repeated, stating that we had forbidden them to eat meat, while the white men had plenty of meat, and that we had deceived them and they wanted to kill us. Then we, with much patience and many gifts, were able to pacify them, telling them that they should save their souls and not look at what that man was doing, and that if he wished to go to Hell then they should let him go.

We were so disgusted with all this that we could not see Rui do Rego again and ordered him to go to Chela, so that he could board the first ship that arrived—for he had not taught as your Highness had ordered him to, but had caused to return to idols those whom we, with much fatigue, had converted. * * *

Questions

1. In the first letter, what does Nzinga Mbemba identify as the biggest problem with Portuguese trade? Why is it difficult for him to control what he sees as excesses?

2. Nzinga Mbemba explicitly requested priests and teachers, but individuals like Rui do Rego also posed problems. Describe the religious and political challenges that do Rego's behavior created for Nzinga Mbemba. What considerations might have constrained Nzinga Mbemba from imposing a harsher punishment?

3. In both letters, the Kongolese seem to be undone by their own hospitality, providing more consideration to foreigners than they received in return. Why might the Kongolese have found it difficult to impose greater control in their own territories?

Anonymous Journal of Vasco da Gama's Voyage around Africa to India (1499)

In 1497–1498 Vasco da Gama (c. 1460–1524) became the first European to find an all-water route to India. Following the path of another Portuguese sailor, Bartolomeo Diaz, who had become the first European to round the Cape of Good Hope from the Atlantic to the Indian Ocean in 1487, da Gama started up the East African coast, raiding Arab merchant ships along the way. But at Malindi, in present-day Kenya, da Gama was able to hire a navigator (according to some stories, a Muslim) who knew the monsoon winds and got him across the Indian Ocean to Calicut in twenty-three days. On the return trip, da Gama ignored what he had been told about the monsoon winds; that crossing took 132 days, and many sailors died.

As the document below shows, da Gama's time in Calicut was complicated by political and religious rivalries, by misunderstandings, and by what people in Calicut considered the inadequate gifts he had brought. But when two of his three ships made it back to Lisbon, the king was sufficiently encouraged to send other, much larger, missions, including two more led by da Gama. The result was the founding of several Portuguese colonies in Asia, important changes in the spice trade, and new patterns of rivalry and warfare in many parts of the world bordering the Indian

Ocean. The author of this journal is unknown, and it has sometimes been mistakenly attributed to da Gama himself. It was probably written by a clerk or officer on the ship, but we cannot be sure. It is fairly certain, however, that it is a contemporaneous account. Spelling has been updated in the following excerpt to reflect modern orthography.

[*Arrival.*] That night (May 20, [1498]) we anchored two leagues from the city of Calicut, and we did so because our pilot mistook *Capna*, a town at that place, for Calicut. Still further there is another town called *Pandarani*. We anchored about a league and a half from the shore. After we were at anchor, four boats (*almadias*) approached us from the land, who asked of what nation we were. We told them, and they then pointed out Calicut to us.

On the following day (May 21) these same boats came again alongside, when the captain-major [da Gama] sent one of the convicts to Calicut, and those with whom he went took him to two Moors from Tunis, who could speak Castilian and Genoese. The first greeting that he received was in these words: "May the Devil take thee! What brought you hither?" They asked what he sought so far away from home, and he told them that we came in search of Christians and of spices. * * * After this conversation they took him to their lodgings and gave him wheaten bread and honey. When he had eaten he returned to the ships, accompanied by one of the Moors, who was no sooner on board, than he said these words: "A lucky venture, a lucky venture! Plenty of rubies, plenty of emeralds! You owe great thanks to God, for having brought you to a country holding such riches!" We were greatly astonished to hear his talk, for we never expected to hear our language spoken so far away from Portugal.

The city of Calicut is inhabited by Christians. [The first voyagers to India mistook the Hindus for Christians.] They are of tawny complexion. Some of them have big beards and long hair, whilst others

---

SOURCE: *The Library of Original Sources*, edited by Oliver J. Thatcher (Milwaukee: University Research Extension Co., 1901), vol. 5, pp. 29–37.

clip their hair short or shave the head, merely allowing a tuft to remain on the crown as a sign that they are Christians. They also wear moustaches. They pierce the ears and wear much gold in them. They go naked down to the waist, covering their lower extremities with very fine cotton stuffs. But it is only the most respectable who do this, for the others manage as best they are able.

The women of this country, as a rule, are ugly and of small stature. They wear many jewels of gold round the neck, numerous bracelets on their arms, and rings set with precious stones on their toes. All these people are well-disposed and apparently of mild temper. At first sight they seem covetous and ignorant.

* * *

what are they looking for

When we were at anchor, a message arrived informing the captain-major that the king was already in the city. At the same time the king sent a *bale*, with other men of distinction, to Pandarani, to conduct the captain-major to where the king awaited him. This *bale* is like an *alcaide*, and is always attended by two hundred men armed with swords and bucklers. * * *

On the following morning, which was Monday, May 28th, the captain-major set out to speak to the king, and took with him thirteen men, of whom I was one. We put on our best attire, placed bombards in our boats, and took with us trumpets and many flags. On landing, the captain-major was received by the *alcaide*, with whom were many men, armed and unarmed. The reception was friendly, as if the people were pleased to see us, though at first appearances looked threatening, for they carried naked swords in their hands. A palanquin was provided for the captain-major, such as is used by men of distinction in that country, as also by some of the merchants, who pay something to the king for this privilege. * * *

* * *

After we had left that place, and had arrived at the entrance to the city (of Calicut) we were shown another church, where we saw things like those described above. Here the crowd grew so dense that progress along the street became next to impossible, and for this reason they put the captain into a house, and us with him.

The king sent a brother of the *bale*, who was a lord of this country, to accompany the captain, and he was attended by men beating drums, blowing *anafils* and bagpipes, and firing off matchlocks. In conducting the captain they showed us much respect, more than is shown in Spain to a king. The number of people was countless, for in addition to those who surrounded us, and among whom there were two thousand armed men, they crowded the roofs and houses.

The further we advanced in the direction of the king's palace, the more did they increase in number. * * * When we reached the palace we passed through a gate into a courtyard of great size, and before we arrived at where the king was, we passed four doors, through which we had to force our way, giving many blows to the people. * * * Several men were wounded at this [final] door, and we only got in by the use of much force.

* * *

[In a private audience, the king asks da Gama what he wants.] And the captain told him he was the ambassador of a King of Portugal, who was Lord of many countries and the possessor of great wealth of every description, exceeding that of any king of these parts; that for a period of sixty years his ancestors had annually sent out vessels to make discoveries in the direction of India, as they knew that there were Christian kings there like themselves. This, he said, was the reason which induced them to order this country to be discovered, not because they sought for gold or silver, for of this they had such abundance that they needed not what was to be found in this country. He further stated that the captains sent out travelled for a year or two, until their provisions were exhausted, and then returned to Portugal, without having succeeded in making the desired discovery. There reigned a king now whose name was Dom Manuel, who had ordered him to build three vessels, of which he had been appointed captain-major, and who had ordered him not to return to Portugal until he should have discovered this King of the Christians, on pain of having his head cut off. That two letters had been intrusted to him to be presented in case he succeeded in discovering him, and that he would do so on the ensuing day; and, finally, he had been instructed to say by word of mouth that he [the King of Portugal] desired to be his friend and brother.

In reply to this the king said that he was welcome; that, on his part, he held him as a friend and brother, and would send ambassadors with him to Portugal. This latter had been asked as a favour, the captain pretending that he would not dare to present himself before his king and master unless he was able to present at the same time, some men of this country.

* * *

On Tuesday [May 29] the captain got ready the following things to be sent to the king, viz., twelve pieces of *lambel*, four scarlet hoods, six hats, four strings of coral, a case containing six wash-hand basins, a case of sugar, two casks of oil, and two of honey. And as it is the custom not to send anything to the king without the knowledge of the Moor, his factor, and of the *bale*, the captain informed them of his intention. They came, and when they saw the present they laughed at it, saying that it was not a thing to offer to a king, that the poorest merchant from Mecca, or any other part of India, gave more, and that if he wanted to make a present it should be in gold, as the king would not accept such things. When the captain heard this he grew sad, and said that he had brought no gold, that, moreover, he was no merchant, but an ambassador; that he gave of that which he had, which was his own [private gift] and not the king's; that if the King of Portugal ordered him to return he would intrust him with far richer presents; and that if King Camolim would not accept these things he would send them back to the ships. Upon this they declared that they would not forward his presents, nor consent to his forwarding them himself. When they had gone there came certain Moorish merchants, and they all depreciated the present which the captain desired to be sent to the king.

* * *

↳ blame it on the muslim* interference

[Da Gama receives a second audience on May 30. He brings no presents, but promises that future ships will bring them.] The king then asked what it was he had come to discover: stones or men? If he came to discover men, as he said, why had he brought nothing? Moreover, he had been told that he carried with him the golden image of a Santa Maria. The captain said that the Santa Maria was not of gold, and that even if she were he would not part with her, as she had guided him across the ocean, and would guide him back to his own country. The king then asked for the letter. The captain said that he begged as a favour, that as the Moors wished him ill and might misinterpret him, a Christian able to speak Arabic should be sent for. The king said this was well, and at once sent for a young man, of small stature, whose name was Quaram. The captain then said that he had two letters, one written in his own language and the other in that of the Moors; that he was able to read the former, and knew that it contained nothing but what would prove acceptable; but that as to the other he was unable to read it, and it might be good, or contain something that was erroneous. As the Christian was unable to *read* Moorish, four Moors took the letter and read it between them, after which they translated it to the king, who was well satisfied with its contents.

The king then asked what kind of merchandise was to be found in his country. The captain said there was much corn, cloth, iron, bronze, and many other things. The king asked whether he had any merchandise with him. The captain replied that he had a little of each sort, as samples, and that if permitted to return to the ships he would order it to be landed, and that meantime four or five men would remain at the lodgings assigned them. The king said no! He might take all his people with him, securely moor his ships, land his merchandise, and sell it to the best advantage. Having taken leave of the king the captain returned to his lodgings, and we with him.

Questions

1. What examples of inter-religious hostility do you see here? What examples do you see of cooperation across religious lines?

2. What does da Gama say about who he is and what he wants out of his voyage? What do the people he encounters in Calicut seem to want from him?

3. How are the Portuguese received by the different groups they encounter in Calicut? What misunderstandings can you detect on either side of this encounter?

Galeota Pereira, A Portuguese Voyage to China (1561)

Even before the first Portuguese ships reached the South China coast in 1517, the sultan of Malacca, whom they had deposed, sent word to Ming China that these men were dangerous. When conflicts did ensue, the Ming banned trade with the Portuguese—but it was so profitable for both sides that it continued. In 1549 a local Chinese official decided to make an example of the Portuguese on two ships he captured. Ninety-six were executed; the others jailed. But members of the local elite (probably concerned that such repression might succeed in stopping trade) protested to the emperor, and an investigation concluded that these Portuguese were peaceful, though illegal traders. Those still in jail were released and deported. The responsible officials were punished for abusing their offices and carrying out executions without permission.

One of the freed prisoners was Galeota Pereira, the third son of a Portuguese nobleman who had been in Asia for fifteen years. His account of China was first published in 1561, and was soon translated into several European languages. It is generally very positive; his praise of "heathen" justice in particular struck many Europeans as so excessive that it was deleted or abridged in many published editions. Yet Pereira also had no doubt that the Chinese needed to be converted to Christianity. He thought their reasonableness made them ready for this; but if not, he recommended an invasion, since he also thought they were deficient in military valor.

———

They have moreover another sort of temples, wherein both upon the altars and also on the walls do stand many idols well propor-

SOURCE: Galeote Pereira, Gaspar Da Cruz, and Martin De Rada, *South China in the Sixteenth Century*, edited by C. R. Boxer (London: Hakluyt Society, 1953), pp. 16–17, 19–21.

tioned, but bare-headed. These bear name *Omithofom* [Amithaba or Buddha], accompted of them spirits, but such as in heaven do neither good nor evil, thought to be such men and women as have chastely lived in this world in abstinence from fish and flesh, fed only with rice and salads. Of that devil they make some accompt; for these spirits they care little or nothing at all. Again they hold opinion that if a man do well in this life, the heavens will give him many temporal blessings, but if he do evil, then shall he have infirmities, diseases, troubles, and penury, and all this without any knowledge of God. Finally, this people knoweth no other thing than to live and die, yet because they be reasonable creatures, all seemed good unto them we spake through our interpreter, though it were not very sufficient. Our manner of praying especially pleased them, and truly they are well enough disposed to receive the knowledge of the truth. Our Lord grant in his mercy all things so to be disposed, that it may some time be brought to pass, that so great a nation as this is, perish not for want of help.

* * *

Now will I speak of the manner the which the [Chinese] do observe in doing justice, that it may be known how far these Gentiles do herein exceed Christians, that be more bounden than they to deal justly and in truth.

* * *

The Louteas [magistrates] observe moreover this: when any man is brought before them to be examined, they ask him openly in the hearing of as many as be present, be the offence never so great. Thus did they also behave themselves with us. For this cause amongst them can there be no false witness, as daily amongst us it falleth out, whence it often happens that men's goods, lives and honours are imperilled by being placed in the hand of a dishonest notary. This good cometh thereof, that many being always about the judge to hear the evidence, and bear witness, the process cannot be falsified, as it happeneth sometimes with us. The Moors, Gentiles, and Jews, have all their sundry oaths; the Moors, do swear by their *moçafa*, the Brahmans by their sacred thread, the Jews by their

Torah, the rest likewise by the things they do worship. The [Chinese] though they be wont to swear by heaven, by the moon, by the sun, and by all their idols, in judgement nevertheless they swear not at all. If for some offence an oath be used of anyone, by and by with the least evidence he is tormented; so be the witnesses he bringeth, if they tell not the truth, or do in any point disagree, except they be men of worship and credit, who are believed without any further matter; the rest are made to confess the truth by force of torments and whips.

* * *

We poor strangers brought before them might say what we would, as all to be lies and fallacies that they did write, neither did we stand before them with the usual ceremonies of that country, yet did they bear with us so patiently, that they caused us to wonder, knowing specially how little any advocate or judge is wont in our country to bear with us. And if the wand of office were taken from any one of our judges they could very well serve any one of these [Chinese],—disregarding the fact that these are heathen, for it is obvious that a Christian cannot demean himself to serve a heathen; and as for their being heathen, I do not know a better proof of praising their justice than the fact that they respected ours, we being prisoners and foreigners. For wheresoever in any town of Christendom should be accused unknown men as we were, I know not what end the very Innocents' cause would have; but we in a heathen country, having for our great enemies two of the chiefest men in a whole town, wanting an interpreter, ignorant of that country's language, did in the end see our great adversaries cast into prison for our sake, and deprived of their offices and honour for not doing justice, yea not to escape death, for as the rumour goeth, they shall be beheaded,—now see if they do justice or no?

Questions

1. How does Pereira describe Chinese religious practice and belief? What does he make of the Chinese emphasis on actions and their consequences in this world?

2. What can you tell about Chinese judicial procedures from this document? In particular, how do they deal with the complexities of administering justice in a multicultural port community?

3. What does Pereira find particularly impressive about Chinese justice? How might his personal experience, and/or conditions in the society he came from, have influenced these opinions?

Martin Luther, To the Christian Nobility of the German Nation (1520)

One of the pivotal events of early modern European history was the Protestant Reformation, which permanently divided the Christian church into two rival branches: Protestantism and Catholicism. Central to this process was Martin Luther (1483–1546). Much against his father's wishes he joined a monastery. Ultimately he became a professor of biblical studies at the German University of Wittenberg. There he worked out a theology that held that people were saved from sin and granted eternal salvation by faith alone, rather than by performing good works. This conclusion led him eventually to a complete recasting of Christian theology. Luther's 1517 protest against the selling of indulgences to help rebuild St. Peter's in Rome led him into a dispute with the papal authorities and to his ultimate rejection of papal authority over the church. A prolific writer, Luther produced many works justifying his position. One of these was a pamphlet titled *To the Christian Nobility of the German Nation*, published in 1520. In this he questioned the church's claims to authority and called on the laity to reform the church.

I. THE THREE WALLS OF THE ROMANISTS

The Romanists, with great adroitness, have built three walls about them, behind which they have hitherto defended themselves [so]

SOURCE: Martin Luther, *An Open Letter to the Christian Nobility of the German Nation Concerning the Reform of the Christian Estate*, translated by Charles M. Jacobs (Philadelphia: A. J. Holman Co., 1915), pp. 65–72.

that no one has been able to reform them; and this has been the cause of terrible corruption throughout all Christendom.

First, when pressed by the temporal power, they have made decrees and said that the temporal power has no jurisdiction over them, but, on the other hand, that the spiritual is above the temporal power. Second, when the attempt is made to reprove them out of the Scriptures, they raise the objection that the interpretation of the Scriptures belongs to no one except the pope. Third, if threatened with a council, they answer with the fable that no one can call a council but the pope.

In this wise they have slyly stolen from us our three rods, that they may go unpunished, and have ensconced themselves within the safe stronghold of these three walls, that they may practise all the knavery and wickedness which we now see.

* * *

Against the first wall we will direct our first attack.

It is pure invention that pope, bishops, priests and monks are to be called the "spiritual estate"; princes, lords, artisans, and farmers the "temporal estate." That is indeed a fine bit of lying and hypocrisy. Yet no one should be frightened by it; and for this reason * * * : that all Christians are truly of the "spiritual estate," and there is among them no difference at all but that of office, as Paul says (I Corinthians xii), We are all one body, yet every member has its own work, whereby it serves every other, all because we have one baptism, one Gospel, one faith, and are all alike Christians; for baptism, Gospel and faith alone make us "spiritual" and a Christian people.

But that a pope or a bishop anoints, confers tonsures, ordains, consecrates, or prescribes dress unlike that of the laity,—this may make hypocrites and graven images, but it never makes a Christian or "spiritual" man. Through baptism all of us are consecrated to the priesthood, as St. Peter says (I Peter ii), "Ye are a royal priesthood, a priestly kingdom," and the book of Revelation says, "Thou hast made us by Thy blood to be priests and kings." * * *

To make it still clearer. If a little group of pious Christian laymen were taken captive and set down in a wilderness, and had among them no priest consecrated by a bishop, and if there in the wilderness they were to agree in choosing one of themselves, married or unmarried, and were to charge him with the office of baptising, saying mass, absolving and preaching, such a man would be as truly a priest as though all bishops and popes had consecrated him. That is why in cases of necessity any one can baptise and give absolution, which would be impossible unless we were all priests. This great grace and power of baptism and of the Christian Estate they have well-nigh destroyed and caused us to forget through the canon law. It was in the manner aforesaid that Christians in olden days chose from their number bishops and priests, who were afterwards confirmed by other bishops, without all the show which now obtains. It was thus that Sts. Augustine, Ambrose and Cyprian became bishops.

Since, then, the temporal authorities are baptised with the same baptism and have the same faith and Gospel as we, we must grant that they are priests and bishops, and count their office one which has a proper and a useful place in the Christian community. For whoever comes out of the water of baptism can boast that he is already consecrated priest, bishop and pope, though it is not seemly that every one should exercise the office. Nay, just because we are all in like manner priests, no one must put himself forward and undertake, without our consent and election, to do what is in the power of all of us. For what is common to all, no one dare take upon himself without the will and the command of the community; and should it happen that one chosen for such an office were deposed for malfeasance, he would then be just what he was before he held office. Therefore a priest in Christendom is nothing else than an office-holder. While he is in office, he has precedence; when deposed, he is a peasant or a townsman like the rest. * * *

From all this it follows that there is really no difference between laymen and priests, princes and bishops, "spirituals" and "temporals," as they call them, except that of office and work, but not of "estate"; for they are all of the same estate,—true priests, bishops and popes,—though they are not all engaged in the same work, just as all priests and monks have not the same work. This is the teaching of St. Paul in Romans xii and I Corinthians xii, and of St. Peter in I Peter ii, as I have said above, * * * that we are all one body of

Christ, the Head, all members one of another. Christ has not two different bodies, one "temporal," the other "spiritual." He is one Head, and He has one body.

Therefore, just as those who are now called "spiritual"—priests, bishops or popes—are neither different from other Christians nor superior to them, except that they are charged with the administration of the Word of God and the sacraments, which is their work and office, so it is with the temporal authorities,—they bear sword and rod with which to punish the evil and to protect the good. A cobbler, a smith, a farmer, each has the work and office of his trade, and yet they are all alike consecrated priests and bishops, and every one by means of his own work or office must benefit and serve every other, that in this way many kinds of work may be done for the bodily and spiritual welfare of the community, even as all the members of the body serve one another.

See, now, how Christian is the decree which says that the temporal power is not above the "spiritual estate" and may not punish it. That is as much as to say that the hand shall lend no aid when the eye is suffering. Is it not unnatural, not to say unchristian, that one member should not help another and prevent its destruction? Verily, the more honorable the member, the more should the others help. I say then, since the temporal power is ordained of God to punish evil-doers and to protect them that do well, it should therefore be left free to perform its office without hindrance through the whole body of Christendom without respect of persons, whether it affect pope, bishops, priests, monks, nuns or anybody else. * * *

On this account the Christian temporal power should exercise its office without let or hindrance, regardless whether it be pope, bishop or priest whom it affects; whoever is guilty, let him suffer. All that the canon law has said to the contrary is sheer invention of Roman presumption. For thus saith St. Paul to all Christians: "Let every soul (I take that to mean the pope's soul also) be subject unto the higher powers; for they bear not the sword in vain, but are the ministers of God for the punishment of evildoers, and for the praise of them that do well." St. Peter also says: "Submit yourselves unto every ordinance of man for the Lord's sake, for so is the will of God." He has also prophesied that such men shall come as will despise the temporal authorities; and this has come to pass through the canon law.

So then, I think this first paper-wall is overthrown, since the temporal power has become a member of the body of Christendom, and is of the "spiritual estate," though its work is of a temporal nature. Therefore its work should extend freely and without hindrance to all the members of the whole body; it should punish and use force whenever guilt deserves or necessity demands, without regard to pope, bishops and priests,—let them hurl threats and bans as much as they will.

This is why guilty priests, if they are surrendered to the temporal law, are first deprived of their priestly dignities, which would not be right unless the temporal sword had previously had authority over them by divine right.

Again, it is intolerable that in the canon law so much importance is attached to the freedom, life and property of the clergy, as though the laity were not also as spiritual and as good Christians as they, or did not belong to the Church. Why are your life and limb, your property and honor so free, and mine not? We are all alike Christians, and have baptism, faith, Spirit and all things alike. If a priest is killed, the land is laid under interdict,—why not when a peasant is killed? Whence comes this great distinction between those who are equally Christians? Only from human laws and inventions!

Moreover, it can be no good spirit who has invented such exceptions and granted to sin such license and impunity. For if we are bound to strive against the works and words of the evil spirit, and to drive him out in whatever way we can, as Christ commands and His Apostles, ought we, then, to suffer it in silence when the pope or his satellites are bent on devilish words and works? Ought we for the sake of men to allow the suppression of divine commandments and truths which we have sworn in baptism to support with life and limb? Of a truth we should then have to answer for all the souls that would thereby be abandoned and led astray.

It must therefore have been the very prince of devils who said what is written in the canon law: "If the pope were so scandalously bad as to lead souls in crowds to the devil, yet he could not be deposed." On this accursed and devilish foundation they build at

Rome, and think that we should let all the world go to the devil, rather than resist their knavery.

Questions

1. How does Luther conceive of relationships between members of the Christian church?

2. For Luther, what is the correct relationship between the spiritual and the temporal power? Is one of them superior to the other?

3. How does Luther try to substantiate his arguments? To what sources or authorities does he appeal?

Otto von Guericke, The Destruction of Magdeburg (1631)

Seventeenth-century Europe was marked by large-scale warfare. The most destructive was the Thirty Years War, devastating Germany from 1618 to 1648. It also drew in most of the other great European powers of the day. In part the war was a religious war between Catholics and Protestants, although leaders often changed sides without regard for their religious affiliations. In part it was an effort by the Habsburg emperors of Germany to enhance their power. The 1631 sack of the Protestant city of Magdeburg was one of the most notorious events of the war. In March 1630 the Catholic forces of the Habsburg emperor laid siege to the city. The city was largely defended by a small Swedish force. The city was finally taken by storm on May 20, 1631. As many as 25,000 of the town's 30,000 inhabitants died during the ensuing massacre. News of this massacre spread widely throughout Europe and gave rise to the use of the term "Magdeburg quarter" to designate merciless killing. The following account was written by Otto von Guericke, a distinguished scientist and mayor of the city at the time of the massacre.

So then General Pappenheim [one of the imperial commanders] collected a number of his people on the ramparts by the New Town, and brought them from there into the streets of the city. Von Falckenberg [commander of the Swedish defenders] was shot, and fires were kindled in different quarters; then indeed it was all over with the city, and further resistance was useless. Nevertheless some of the soldiers and citizens did try to make a stand here and there, but the imperial troops kept bringing on more and more forces—cavalry, too—to help them, and finally they got the Kröckenthor open and let in the whole imperial army and the forces of the Catholic League,—Hungarians, Croats, Poles, Walloons, Italians, Spaniards, French, North and South Germans.

Thus it came about that the city and all its inhabitants fell into the hands of the enemy, whose violence and cruelty were due in part to their common hatred of the adherents of the Augsburg Confession [a statement of Lutheran beliefs], and in part to their being imbittered by the chain shot which had been fired at them and by the derision and insults that the Magdeburgers had heaped upon them from the ramparts.

Then was there naught but beating and burning, plundering, torture, and murder. Most especially was every one of the enemy bent on securing much booty. When a marauding party entered a house, if its master had anything to give he might thereby purchase respite and protection for himself and his family till the next man, who also wanted something, should come along. It was only when everything had been brought forth and there was nothing left to give that the real trouble commenced. Then, what with blows and threats of shooting, stabbing, and hanging, the poor people were so terrified that if they had had anything left they would have brought it forth if it had been buried in the earth or hidden away in a thousand castles. In this frenzied rage, the great and splendid city that had stood like a fair princess in the land was now, in its hour of direst need and unutterable distress and woe, given over to the flames, and thousands of innocent men, women, and children, in the midst

Source: James Harvey Robinson, *Readings in European History* (Boston: Ginn and Co., 1906), vol. 2, pp. 211–12.

of a horrible din of heartrending shrieks and cries, were tortured and put to death in so cruel and shameful a manner that no words would suffice to describe, nor no tears to bewail it. * * *

Thus in a single day this noble and famous city, the pride of the whole country, went up in fire and smoke; and the remnant of its citizens, with their wives and children, were taken prisoners and driven away by the enemy with a noise of weeping and wailing that could be heard from afar, while the cinders and ashes from the town were carried by the wind to Wanzleben, Egeln, and still more distant places. * * *

In addition to all this, quantities of sumptuous and irreplaceable house furnishings and movable property of all kinds, such as books, manuscripts, paintings, memorials of all sorts, * * * which money could not buy, were either burned or carried away by the soldiers as booty. The most magnificent garments, hangings, silk stuffs, gold and silver lace, linen of all sorts, and other household goods were bought by the army sutlers for a mere song and peddled about by the cart load all through the archbishopric of Magdeburg and in Anhalt and Brunswick. Gold chains and rings, jewels, and every kind of gold and silver utensils were to be bought from the common soldiers for a tenth of their real value.

Questions

1. What does the presence of so many soldiers from outside Germany tell you about the nature of the Thirty Years War?

2. Why does von Guericke believe that the soldiers who took the city were so violent?

3. When and why did the sack of the city become so brutal? What does this tell you about the nature of seventeenth-century armies?

Chapter 13

WORLDS ENTANGLED, 1600–1750

Jean de Léry, History of a Voyage to the Land of Brazil (1578)

Jean de Léry (1536–1613) was a French Protestant who joined a group of his coreligionists in 1556 to found a colony in Brazil. They were initially promised religious toleration by their sponsor, a Catholic, but he reneged. De Léry and some others then took refuge living among the Tupinamba tribe as they waited for a ship to take them back to Europe, returning to France after roughly one year. The colony itself was destroyed by the Portuguese a few years later. De Léry published a memoir of his American journey in 1578.

De Léry was considerably more sympathetic to the natives he encountered than most Europeans of his era, though he still had no doubt that they were "savages." Here he describes how the Tupinamba, who accumulated very few possessions, were affected by European desire for the brazilwood trees that grew in their area, and how he and they attempted to make sense of each other's very different understandings of wealth, nature, labor, and the purpose of life.

OF THE TREES, HERBS, ROOTS, AND EXQUISITE FRUITS PRODUCED BY THE LAND OF BRAZIL

Having already treated the four-footed animals as well as the birds, fish, reptiles, and things having life, movement, and feeling, * * * I will continue by describing the trees, herbs, plants, fruits, roots—all the things commonly said to have a vegetative soul—which are to be found in that country.

First, since brazilwood (from which this land has taken the name that we use for it) is among the most famous trees, and now one of the best known to us and (because of the dye made from it) is the most valued, I will describe it here. This tree, which the savages call *araboutan*, ordinarily grows as high and branchy as the oaks in the forests of this country; some are so thick that three men could not embrace a single trunk. While we are speaking of big trees, the author of the *General History of the West Indies* says that * * * in the country of Nicaragua there is a tree called *cerba*, which grows so big that fifteen men could not embrace it.

To return to our brazilwood: it has a leaf like that of boxwood, but of a brighter green, and it bears no fruit. As for the manner of loading it on the ships, take note that both because of the hardness of this wood and the consequent difficulty of cutting it, and because, there being no horses, donkeys, or other beasts to carry, cart, or draw burdens in that country, it has to be men who do this work: if the foreigners who voyage over there were not helped by the savages, they could not load even a medium-sized ship in a year. In return for some frieze garments, linen shirts, hats, knives, and other merchandise, that they are given, the savages, not only cut, saw, split, quarter, and round off the brazilwood, with the hatchets, wedges, and other iron tools given to them by the French and by others from over here, but also carry it on their bare shoulders, often from a league [2.8 to 4.2 miles, depending on local usage] or two away, over mountains and difficult places, clear down to the

SOURCE: Jean de Léry, *History of a Voyage to the Land of Brazil, Otherwise Called America*, translated by Janet Whatley (Berkeley: University of California Press, 1990), pp. 100–103.

seashore by the vessels that lie at anchor, where the mariners, receive it. I say expressly that it is only since the French and Portuguese have been frequenting their country that the savages have been cutting their brazilwood; for before that time, as I have heard from the old men, they had almost no other way of taking down a tree than by setting fire to the base of it. * * *

During the time that we were in that country we made fine fires of this brazilwood; I have observed that since it is not at all damp, like most other wood, but rather is naturally dry, it gives off very little smoke as it burns. One day one of our company decided to bleach our shirts, and, without suspecting anything, put brazilwood ash in with the lye; instead of whitening them, he made them so red that although they were washed and soaped afterward, there was no means of getting rid of that tincture, so that we had to wear them that way.

If the gentlemen over here with their perfectly starched pleats— those who send to Flanders to have their shirts whitened—choose not to believe me, they have my permission to do the experiment for themselves. * * *

Our Tupinamba are astonished to see the French and others from distant countries go to so much trouble to get their *araboutan*, or brazilwood. On one occasion one of their old men questioned me about it: "What does it mean that you *Mairs* and *Peros* (that is, French and Portuguese) come from so far for wood to warm yourselves? Is there none in your own country?" I answered him yes, and in great quantity, but not of the same kinds as theirs; nor any brazilwood, which we did not burn as he thought, but rather carried away to make dye, just as they themselves did to redden their cotton cord, feathers, and other articles. He immediately came back at me: "Very well, but do you need so much of it?" "Yes," I said (trying to make him see the good of it), "for there is a merchant in our country who has more frieze and red cloth, and even" (and here I was choosing things that were familiar to him) "more knives, scissors, mirrors, and other merchandise than you have ever seen over here; one such merchant alone will buy all the wood that several ships bring back from your country." "Ha, ha!" said my savage, "you are telling me of wonders." Then, having thought over what I had said to him, he questioned me further, and said, "But this man of whom you speak, who is so rich, does he never die?" "Certainly he does," I said, "just as others do." At that (since they are great discoursers, and pursue a subject out to the end) he asked me, "And when he is dead, to whom belong all the goods that he leaves behind?" "To his children, if he has any, and if there are none, to his brothers, sisters, or nearest kinsmen." "Truly," said my elder (who, as you will judge, was no dullard), "I see now that you *Mairs* (that is, Frenchmen) are great fools; must you labor so hard to cross the sea, on which (as you told us) you endured so many hardships, just to amass riches for your children or for those who will survive you? Will not the earth that nourishes you suffice to nourish them? We have kinsmen and children, whom, as you see, we love and cherish; but because we are certain that after our death the earth which has nourished us will nourish them, we rest easy and do not trouble ourselves further about it."

And there you have a brief and true summary of the discourse that I have heard from the very mouth of a poor savage American. This nation, which we consider so barbarous, charitably mocks those who cross the sea at the risk of their lives to go seek brazil-wood in order to get rich; however blind this people may be in attributing more to nature and to the fertility of the earth than we do to the power and the providence of God, it will rise up in judgment against those despoilers who are as abundant over here, among those bearing the title of Christians, as they are scarce over there, among the native inhabitants. Therefore, to take up what I said elsewhere—that the Tupinamba mortally hate the avaricious—would to God that the latter might be imprisoned among them, so that they might even in this life serve as demons and furies to torment those whose maws are insatiable, who do nothing but suck the blood and marrow of others. To our great shame, and to justify our savages in the little care that they have for the things of this world, I had to make this digression in their favor.

I think it is appropriate to add here what the historian of the West Indies has written of a certain nation of savages living in Peru. When the Spanish were first roaming up and down that country, because they were bearded, and because they were so swaggering and so foppish, the savages did not want to receive them, fearing that they would corrupt and alter their ancient customs; they called them "seafoam," fatherless people, men without repose, who cannot stay in any one place to cultivate the land to provide themselves with food.

Questions

1. What services did the Tupinamba perform for European merchants, and what did they get in return? How did these exchanges affect their society?

2. Why does the "savage" de Léry talks with think the Europeans must be "madmen"? What differences in values does this reflect?

3. To what extent does de Léry see merit in the Tupinamba perspective and lifestyle? How can you tell?

Brother Luis Brandaon, Letter to Father Sandoval (1610)

This letter—part of correspondence between Catholic priests—illustrates the web of connections between colonies that were not mediated through imperial governments. Although distant, colonial outposts were not necessarily isolated. Equally important, this letter is further evidence that a range of participants in the Atlantic slave trade questioned its legitimacy, which led to debates both civil (as the tone of this letter suggests) and more hostile (such as the rivalry between Juan Sepúlveda and Bartolomé Las Casas (see Juan Sepúlveda, On the Causes of the Just War with the Indians, in Chapter 12). Luis Brandaon was the rector of the College of the Society of Jesus at St. Paul de Luanda in Angola when he wrote this letter in reply to an inquiry from a priest in Brazil.

_____

Your Reverence writes me that you would like to know whether the negroes who are sent to your parts have been legally captured.

SOURCE: Elizabeth Donnan, _Documents Illustrative of the History of the Slave Trade to America_ (New York: Octagon, 1965), vol. 1, pp. 123–24.

To this I reply that I think your Reverence should have no scruples on this point, because this is a matter which has been questioned by the Board of Conscience in Lisbon, and all its members are learned and conscientious men. Nor did the bishops who were in São Thomé, Cape Verde, and here in Loando [Luanda]—all learned and virtuous men—find fault with it. We have been here ourselves for forty years and there have been [among us] very learned Fathers; in the Province of Brazil as well, where there have always been Fathers of our order eminent in letters, never did they consider this trade as illicit. Therefore we and the fathers of Brazil buy these slaves for our service without any scruple. Furthermore, I declare that if any one could be excused from having scruples it is the inhabitants of those regions, for since the traders who bring those negroes bring them in good faith, those inhabitants can very well buy from such traders without any scruple, and the latter on their part can sell them, for it is a generally accepted opinion that the owner who owns anything in good faith can sell it and that it can be bought. Padre Sánchez thus expresses this point in his Book of Marriage, thus solving this doubt of your Reverence. Therefore, we here are the ones who could have greater scruple, for we buy these negroes from other negroes and from people who perhaps have stolen them; but the traders who take them away from here do not know of this fact, and so buy those negroes with a clear conscience and sell them out there with a clear conscience. Besides I found it true indeed that no negro will ever say he has been captured legally. Therefore your Reverence should not ask them whether they have been legally captured or not, because they will always say that they were stolen and captured illegally, in the hope that they will be given their liberty. I declare, moreover, that in the fairs where these negroes are bought there are always a few who have been captured illegally because they were stolen or because the rulers of the land order them to be sold for offenses so slight that they do not deserve captivity, but these are few in number and to seek among ten or twelve thousand who leave this port every year for a few who have been illegally captured is an impossibility, however careful investigation may be made. And to lose so many souls as sail from here—out of whom many are saved—because some, impossible to recognize, have been captured illegally does not seem to be doing much service to God, for these are few and those who find salvation are many and legally captured.

Questions

1. Describe the relationship between priests and slaves in this letter.

2. How does Brother Brandaon justify the sale of illegal captives as slaves?

3. Compare Brother Brandaon's attitude toward slaves to that of Thomas Phillips (see Thomas Phillips, Buying Slaves at Whydah, in this chapter), and Richard Ligon (see Richard Ligon, *A True and Exact History of the Island of Barbadoes*, in this chapter). How do you explain the differences among men who all had firsthand observations of the Atlantic slave trade and slave labor?

Richard Ligon, A True and Exact History of the Island of Barbadoes (1657)

In the seventeenth century Europeans discovered that the islands of the Caribbean were ideally suited for the production of sugar, which was then shipped to Europe. The English colony on the island of Barbados was one of the principal exporters and Englishman Richard Ligon (c. 1585–1662) went there to seek his fortune. During his two-year stay he was a careful observer of the island's entwined slave and sugar economy, describing the rigors of slave labor that awaited African captives who survived the Atlantic crossing in ships such as Phillips's *Hannibal* (see Thomas Phillips, Buying Slaves at Whydah, in this chapter). As early as 1650, Ligon was able to comment on the dangers of replacing diverse crops with fields of sugar cane; he was critical of choices that put profit ahead of basic foodstuffs, yet he admired the possibility of building great family wealth from sugar plantations. (He himself lost his family fortune when he backed the king in the English civil war of the 1640s.) He also described the grueling work of processing sugar cane, which during the harvest season ran without stopping from Monday at 1 A.M. through Saturday night, requiring a constant flow of rested slaves and draft animals. Although he was clearly aware of the dangerous, exhausting work performed by slaves, Ligon associated wealth with the sugar itself, not the labor necessary to grow, harvest, and process the cane. Ligon first published his work in 1657. The excerpt below, however, comes from the 1673 edition.

The island is divided into three sorts of men, *viz*. Masters, Servants, and Slaves. The slaves and their posterity, being subject to their masters forever, are kept and preserved with greater care than the servants, who are theirs but for five years, according to the law of the island. So that for the time, the servants have the worser lives, for they are put to very hard labour, ill lodging, and their diet very slight. When we first came on the island some planters themselves did not eat bone meat above twice a week. * * * But the servants no bone meat at all, unless an ox died and then they were feasted as long as that lasted. And till they had planted good store of plantains, the Negroes were fed with * * * food * * * which gave them much discontent. But when they had plantains enough to serve them they were heard no more to complain; for tis a food they take great delight in. * * * One bunch a week is a Negroe's allowance. To this, no bread nor drink, but water. Their lodging at night a board, with nothing under, nor anything a top of them. They are happy people, whom so little contents. Very good servants, if they be not spoiled by the English. * * *

As for the usage of the servants, it is much as the master is, merciful or cruel. Those that are merciful treat their servants well, both in their meat, drink and lodging, and give them work such as is not unfit for a Christian to do. But if the masters be cruel, the servants have very wearisome and miserable lives. * * * I have seen an overseer beat a servant with a cane about the head, till the blood has followed, for a fault that is not worth the speaking of; and yet he must have patience or worse will follow. Truly, I have seen such cruelty there done to servants as I did not think one Christian could have done to another.

SOURCE: Richard Ligon, *A True and Exact History of the Island of Barbadoes* (London: Peter Parker, 1673), pp. 43–47, 89, 96. Text modernized by Norton authors for this edition.

* * *

It has been accounted a strange thing, that the Negroes, being more than double the number of Christians that are there, and they accounted a bloody people * * * that they should not commit some horrid massacre upon the Christians thereby to enfranchise themselves and become masters of the island. But there are three reasons that take away this wonder: the one is, they are not suffered to touch or handle any weapons; the other, that they are held in such awe and slavery as they are fearful to appear in any daring act; and seeing the mustering of our men and hearing their gun shot (which nothing is more terrible to them) their spirits are subjugated to follow a condition, as they dare not look up to any bold attempt. Besides these, there is a third reason, which stops all designs of that kind, and that is they are fetched from several parts of Africa who speak several languages, and by that means one of them understands not another. For some of them are fetched from Guinea and Bonny * * * some from Angola, and some from the river of Gambia. And in some of these places where petty kingdoms are, they sell their subjects, as such they take in battle, whom they make slaves; and some mean men sell their servants, their children, or sometimes their wives; and think all good traffic for such commodities as our merchants feed them.

When they are brought to us, the planters buy them out of the ship, where they find them stark naked, and therefore cannot be deceived in any outward infirmity. They choose them as they do horses in a market; the strongest, youngest, and most beautiful yield the greatest prices. * * * And we buy them so as the sexes may be equal; for if they have more men than women the men who are unmarried will come to their masters and complain, that they cannot live without wives. And he tells them that the next ship that comes he will buy them wives, which satisfies them for the present; and so they expect the good time: which the master performing with them, the bravest fellow is to choose first, and so in order, as they are in place, and every one of them knows his better and gives him precedence, as cows do one another in passing through a narrow gate; for the most of them are as near beasts as may be, setting their souls aside. * * *

At the time the wife is to [give birth], her husband removes his board (which is his bed) to another room (for many several divisions they have, in their little houses, and none above six foot square) and leaves his wife to God, and her good fortune, in the room, and upon the board alone, and calls a neighbour to come to her, who gives little help to her delivery, but when the child is born (which she calls her Pickininny) she helps to make a little fire near her feet. * * * In a fortnight the woman is at work with her Pickininny at her back, as merry a soul as any there is. If the overseer be discreet, she is suffered to rest herself a little more than ordinary; but if not, she is compelled to do as others do. Times they have of suckling their children in the fields, and refreshing themselves; and good reason, for they carry burdens on their backs, and yet work too. * * * The work which the women do is most of it weeding, a stooping and painful work; at noon and night they are called home by the ring of a bell, where they have two hours time for their repast at noon; and at night, they rest from six till six a clock the next morning.

On Sunday they rest, and have the whole day at their pleasure; and the most of them use it as a day of rest and pleasure; but some of them who will make benefit of that day's liberty go where the mangrove trees grow and gather the bark, of which they make ropes, which they truck away for other commodities, as shirts and drawers.

* * *

The [sugar] canes with their tops or blades, do commonly grow to be eight foot high. * * * The manner of cutting them is with little hand bills, about six inches from the ground; at which time they divide the tops from the canes, which they do with the same bills, at one stroke; and then holding the canes by the upper end, they strip off all the blades that grow by the sides of the canes, which tops and blades are bound up in faggots, and put into carts, to carry home. * * * The place where they unload, is a little platform of ground, which is contiguous to the mill house * * * done about with a double rail to keep the canes from falling out of that room; where one, or two, or more * * * make a stop there, are ready to unload them, and so turning them back again, they go immediately to the field, and there to take in fresh loading; so that they may not unjustly be compared to bees. * * * We work them out clean, and leave none to grow stale, for if they should be more than two days old, the juice will grow sour, and * * * their sourness will infect the rest.

* * *

Colonel Thomas Modiford has often told me that he has taken a resolution to himself not to set his face for England till he had made his voyage and employment there worth him a hundred thousand pounds sterling; and all by this sugar plant. * * * Now if such estates as these may be raised by the well ordering of this plant, by industrious * * * men, why not such estates, by careful keeping and moderate expending, be preserved in their posterity to the tenth generation, and by all the sweet negotiation of sugar?

Questions

1. What was life like for slaves on Barbados in the 1640s? How were they treated by the English? How were they fed and clothed? What was family life like for them? Did they have any possibility for some independence from their owners?

2. Ligon describes slaves as "happy people," but later suggests that they have reason to rebel against cruel treatment by their masters. What accounts for this significant contradiction?

3. Ligon describes Africans as having various, somewhat contradictory characteristics. What are they? How does he resolve this tension?

Thomas Phillips, Buying Slaves at Whydah (1694)

Captain Thomas Phillips's account of his only voyage in command of a slave ship contributed to abolition and anti-slavery campaigns in the eighteenth century; it remains a significant source of information about conditions of the Atlantic trade. Phillips's voyage took him from England to West Africa and on to Barbados. The business was financed by the Royal Africa Company and Phillips himself had a share in the ship.

Phillips wrote prolifically with an eye for detail. His 1694 journal reveals human sympathy for the suffering of the slaves and raises liberal questions about the validity of racialized slavery, but also pays careful attention to the profitability of the voyage. He could acknowledge the slaves' humanity, but nevertheless calculated them as "cargo."

The following selection describes the process of purchasing slaves at the port of Whydah (Ouidah in current-day Benin). In a previous section of his journal (not reprinted here), Phillips's account of the formal, hierarchical reception at the royal court shows the power wielded by the king of Whydah over his own subjects and the European traders who came to call.

Our factory [at Whydah] lies about three miles from the seaside, where we were carry'd in hamocks, which the factor [agent] Mr. Joseph Peirson, sent to attend our landing, with several arm'd blacks that belong'd to him for our guard. * * *

Our factory * * * stands low near the marshes, which renders it a very unhealthy place to live in; the white men the African company send there, seldom returning to tell their tale: 'tis compass'd round with a mud-wall, about six foot high, and on the south-side is the gate; within is a large yard, a mud thatch'd house, where the factor lives, with the white men; also a store-house, a trunk [prisonlike holding area] for slaves, and a place where they bury their dead white men, call'd, very improperly, the hog-yard; there is also a good forge, and some other small houses.

* * *

As soon as the king understood of our landing, he sent two of his cappasheirs [caboceers], or noblemen, to compliment us at our factory, where we design'd to continue, that night, and pay our devoirs [respects] to his majesty next day, * * * whereupon he sent two more of his grandees to invite us there that night, saying he

SOURCE: Elizabeth Donnan, *Documents Illustrative of the History of the Slave Trade to America*, (New York: Octagon, 1965), vol. 1, pp. 399–408, 410.

waited for us, and that all former captains used to attend him the first night: whereupon being unwilling to infringe the custom, or give his majesty any offence, we took our hamocks, and Mr. Peirson, myself, Capt. Clay [captain of another English ship], our surgeons, pursers, and about 12 men, arm'd for our guard, were carry'd to the king's town, which contains about 50 houses. * * *

We returned him thanks by his interpreter, and assur'd him how great affection our masters, the royal African company of England, bore to him, for his civility and fair and just dealings with their captains; and that notwithstanding there were many other places, more plenty of negro slaves that begg'd their custom [business], yet they had rejected all the advantageous offers made them out of their good will to him, and therefore had sent us to trade with him, to supply his country with necessaries, and that we hop'd he would endeavour to continue their favour by his kind usage and fair dealing with us in our trade, that we may have our slaves with all expedition. * * * He answer'd that the African company was a very good brave man; that he lov'd him; that we should be fairly dealt with, and not impos'd upon; But he did not prove as good as his word; * * * so after having examin'd us about our cargoe, what sort of goods we had, and what quantity of slaves we wanted, etc., we took our leaves and return'd to the factory. * * *

According to our promise we attended his majesty [the next day] with samples of our goods, and made our agreement about the prices, tho' not without much difficulty; * * * then we had warehouses, a kitchen, and lodgings assign'd us * * * ; next day we paid our customs to the king and cappasheirs, as will appear hereafter; then the bell was order'd to go about to give notice to all people to bring their slaves to the trunk to sell [to] us. * * *

Capt. Clay and I had agreed to go to the trunk to buy the slaves by turns, each his day, that we might have no distraction or disagreement in our trade, as often happens when there are here more ships than one, and the commanders can't set their horses together, and go hand in hand in their traffick, whereby they have a check upon the blacks, whereas their disagreements create animosities, underminings, and out-bidding each other, whereby they enhance the prices to their general loss and detriment, the blacks well knowing how to make the best use of such opportunities, and as we found make it their business, and endeavour to create and foment misunderstandings and jealousies between commanders, it turning to their great account in the disposal of their slaves.

When we were at the trunk, the king's slaves, if he had any, were the first offer'd to sale, * * * and we must not refuse them, tho' as I observ'd they were generally the worst slaves in the trunk, and we paid more for them than any others, which we could not remedy, it being one of his majesty's prerogatives: then the cappasheirs each brought out his slaves according to his degree and quality, the greatest first, etc. and our surgeon examin'd them well in all kinds, to see that they were sound wind and limb, making them jump, stretch out their arms swiftly, looking in their mouths to judge of their age; for the cappasheirs are so cunning, that they shave them all close before we see them, so that let them be never so old we can see no grey hairs in their heads or beards; and then having liquor'd them well and sleek with palm oil, 'tis no easy matter to know an old one from a middle-age one. * * *

When we had selected from the rest such as we liked, we agreed in what goods to pay for them, the prices being already stated before the king, how much of each sort of merchandize we were to give for a man, woman, and child, which gave us much ease, and saved abundance of disputes and wranglings * * * ; then we mark'd the slaves we had bought in the breast, or shoulder, with a hot iron, having the letter of the ship's name on it, the place being before anointed with a little palm oil, which caus'd but little pain, the mark being usually well in four or five days, appearing very plain and white after.

*   *   *

When our slaves were come to the seaside, our canoes were ready to carry them off to the longboat, if the sea permitted, and she convey'd them aboard ship, where the men were all put in irons, two and two shackled together, to prevent their mutiny, or swimming ashore.

The negroes are so wilful and loth to leave their own country, that they have often leap'd out of the canoes, boat and ship, into the sea, and kept under water till they were drowned, to avoid being taken up and saved by our boats, which pursued them; they having a more dreadful apprehension of Barbadoes than we can have of hell, tho' in reality they live much better there than in their own country; but home is home, etc.

* * *

I have been inform'd that some commanders have cut off the legs and arms of the most wilful, to terrify the rest, for they believe if they lose a member, they cannot return home again: I was advis'd by some of my officers to do the same, but I could not be [persuaded] to entertain the least thought of it, much less put in practice such barbarity and cruelty to poor creatures, who, excepting their want of christianity and true religion (their misfortune more than fault) are as much the works of God's hands, and no doubt as dear to him as ourselves; nor can I imagine why they should be despis'd for their colour, being what they cannot help, and the effect of the climate it has pleas'd God to appoint them. I can't think there is any [intrinsic] value in one colour more than another, nor that white is better than black, only we think so because we are so, and are prone to judge favourably in our own case, as well as the blacks, who in odium of the colour, say, the devil is white, and so paint him.

* * *

After we are come to an agreement for the prices of our slaves, ere the bell goes round to order all people to bring their slaves to the trunk to be sold, we are oblig'd to pay our customs to the king and cappasheirs for leave to trade, protection and justice; which for every ship are as follow, *viz.*

To the king six slaves value in cowries, or what other goods we can [persuade] him to take, but cowries are most esteem'd and desir'd; all which are measur'd in his presence, and he would wrangle with us stoutly about heaping up the measure.

To the cappasheirs in all two slaves value, as above.

* * *

The best goods to purchase slaves here are cowries, the smaller the more esteem'd. * * *

The next in demand are brass neptunes or basons [plates], very large, thin, and flat; for after they have bought them they cut them in pieces to make anilias or bracelets, and collars for their arms legs and necks.

The other preferable goods are blue paper sletias, cambricks or lawns, caddy chints, broad ditto [various types of cloth], coral, large, smooth, and of a deep red, rangoes [beads] large and red, iron bars, [gun] powder, and brandy.

* * * [B]ut without the cowries and brass they will take none of the last goods, and but small quantities at best, especially if they can discover that you have good store of cowries and brass aboard, then no other goods will serve their turn, till they have got as much as you have; and after, for the rest of the goods they will be indifferent, and make you come to their own terms, or else lie [offshore] a long time for your slaves, so that those you have on board are dying while you are buying others ashore; therefore every man that comes here, ought to be very cautious in making his report to the king at first, of what sorts and quantities of goods he has, and be sure to say his cargo consists mostly in iron, coral, rangoes, chints, etc. so that he may dispose of those goods as soon as he can, and at last his cowries and brass will bring him slaves as fast as he can buy them; but this is to be understood of a single ship: or more, if the captains agree, which seldom happens; for where there are divers [several] ships, and of separate interests, about buying the same commodity they commonly undermine, betray, and out-bid one the other; and the [Guinea] commanders words and promises are the least to be depended upon of any I know use the sea; for they would deceive their fathers in their trade if they could.

* * *

When our slaves are aboard we shackle the men two and two, while we lie in port, and in sight of their own country, for 'tis then they attempt to make their escape, and mutiny; to prevent which we always keep centinels upon the hatchways, and have a chest full of small arms, ready [loaded] and prim'd, constantly lying at hand upon the quarter-deck. * * * Their chief diet is call'd dabbadabb, being Indian corn ground as small as oat-meal, in iron mills, which we carry for that purpose; and after mix'd with water, and boil'd well in a large copper furnace, till 'tis as thick as a pudding, about a peckful of which in vessels, call'd crews, is allow'd to 10 men, with a little salt, malagetta [pepper], and palm oil, to relish; they are divided into messes of ten each, for the easier and better order in serving them: Three days a week they have horse-beans boil'd for their dinner and supper, great quantities of which the African company do send aboard us for that purpose; these beans the negroes extremely love and desire, beating their breast, eating them, and crying Pram! Pram! which is Very good! they are indeed the best diet for them, having a binding quality, and consequently good to prevent the flux [diarrhea], which is the inveterate distemper that most affects them, and ruins our voyages by their mortality. * * *

We often at sea in the evenings would let the slaves come up into the sun to air themselves, and make them jump and dance for an hour or two to our bag-pipes, harp, and fiddle, by which exercise to preserve them in health; but notwithstanding all our endeavour, 'twas my hard fortune to have great sickness and mortality among them.

Having bought my compliment of 700 slaves, *viz.* 480 men and 220 women, and finish'd all my business at [Whydah], I took my leave of the old king, and his cappasheirs, and parted, with many affectionate expressions on both sides, being forced to promise him that I would return again the next year, with several things he desired me to bring him from England; and having sign'd bills of lading to Mr. Peirson, for the negroes aboard, I set sail the 27th of July in the morning.

* * *

I deliver'd alive at Barbadoes to the company's factors 372, which being sold, came out at about nineteen pounds per head one with another.

Questions

1. How did the king of Whydah exert his power in the mechanics of the slave trade?

2. Identify specific passages in which Phillips challenges the validity of race-based chattel slavery, and other passages that show evidence of Phillips thinking like a pragmatic merchant.

3. How can you account for Phillips's contradictory attitude toward the slave trade?

Alexander Hamilton, A New Account of the East Indies (1688–1723)

Alexander Hamilton was a Scottish ship captain who spent most of the years from 1688 to 1725 sailing in the Indian Ocean and South China Sea, both as an employee of the English East India Company and as a private trader.

This excerpt from his *New Account of the East Indies* describes temporary marriages contracted between European merchants and indigenous women, mostly of elite backgrounds, in Pegu, in present-day Burma. (Poorer European men, such as sailors, also sometimes made temporary marriages, but they didn't necessarily work the same way.) Similar arrangements existed in many other Southeast Asia ports, though not in all of them. Very few European women came to the tropics before about 1850.

Many of the women in these marriages came from aristocratic families; women often handled these families' business interests, since aristocratic men were supposed to focus on matters of honor and holiness rather than profit. Thus, their marriages with Europeans often strengthened trading networks. The combination of a relaxed attitude about repeated marriages, but great strictness about fidelity within marriage, also appears to have been a feature of many Southeast Asia societies at this time.

This fashion of petticoats, they say, is very ancient, and it was first contrived by a certain queen of that country, who was grieved to see the men so much addicted to sodomy, that they neglected the pretty ladies. She thought that by the sight of a pretty leg and a plump thigh, the men might be allured from that abominable custom, and place their affections on proper objects, and according to the ingenious queen's conjecture, that dress of the Lungee had its desired end, and now the name of sodomy is hardly known in that country.

The women are very courteous and kind to strangers, and are very fond of marrying with Europeans, and most part of the strangers who trade thither, marry a wife for the term they stay. The ceremony is, (after the parties are agreed) for the bride's parents or nearest friends or relations, to make a feast, and invite her friends and the bridegroom's, and at the end of the feast, the parent or bride-man, asketh them both before the company, if they are content to cohabit together as man and wife, and both declaring their consent, they are declared by the parent or friend to be lawfully married, and if the bridegroom has a house, he carries her thither, but if not, they have a bed provided in the house where they are married, and are left to their own discretion on how to pass away the night.

They prove obedient and obliging wives, and take the management of affairs within doors wholly in their own hands. She goes to market for food, and asks the cook in dressing his victuals, takes care of his clothes, in washing and mending them; if their husbands have any goods to sell, they set up a shop and sell them by retail, to a much better account than they could be sold for by wholesale, and some of them carry a cargo of goods to the inland towns, and barter for goods proper for the foreign markets that their husbands are bound to, and generally bring fair accounts of their negotiations. If she proves false to her husband's bed, and on fair proof convicted, her husband may carry her to the Rounday, and have her hair cut,

SOURCE: Alexander Hamilton, *A New Account of the East Indies* (Edinburgh: John Mosman, 1727), vol. 1, pp. 51–53. Text modernized by Norton authors for this edition.

and sold for a slave, and he may have the money; but if the husband goes astray, she'll be apt to give him a gentle dose [of poison], to send him into the other world a sacrifice to her resentment.

If she proves prolific, the children cannot be carried out of the kingdom without the king's permission, but that may be purchased for 40 or 50 pounds sterling and if an irreconcilable quarrel happen where there are children, the father is obliged to take care of the boys, and the mother of the girls. If a husband is content to continue the marriage, whilst he goes to foreign countries about his affairs, he must leave some fund to pay her about six shillings eight pence per month, otherwise at the year's end she may marry again, but if that sum is paid her on his account, she is obliged to stay the term of three years, and she is never the worse, but rather the better looked on, that she has been married to several European husbands.

Questions

1. What advantages did European men probably gain from these marriages? What might the women (who had other marriage options within their own society) have gained from them?

2. The women in these relationships had a high probability of surviving their temporary husbands (since Europeans died at high rates in the tropics), or of having them leave for another port after a relatively short time. What can you surmise about what their position might have been after the marriage ended in one of these ways?

3. What can you infer from this passage about Hamilton's attitudes toward racial and cultural differences? How does it resemble or differ from other colonial documents you have read?

Casebook

COERCED LABOR IN THE EARLY MODERN WORLD

Brutal forced labor historically has occurred in regions where, because of labor scarcity, modern economic logic might suggest that labor would have a lot of bargaining power. In fact, it often seems to be scarcity that engenders regimes of coercion. There is a surprising variety of forced labor regimes, which tend to differ in the ways that they extract surplus. Labor has been conscripted seasonally, in terms of head counts from villages or families, or in terms of specific production (an amount of precious metal, agricultural produce, or feet of wall). Some laborers were bonded for fixed periods and others indefinitely. The wide geographic distribution of forms of coerced labor and its tenacious persistence across time suggest that despite the tremendous human cost, this form of production proved attractive to those in power in diverse economies.

Consequently, it is important to consider very carefully the conditions of labor, the terms of impressment, social hierarchies, the basis of political legitimacy for those controlling production, population densities, and the availability of natural resources (or resource constraints) when trying to understand how one group of people forcibly extracted labor from another. Moreover, different forms of forced labor had specific consequences for family composition and patterns of migration. Were men or women preferred as laborers? Did entire families serve? Did laborers live at home, or were they transported to a distant work site? Were laborers able to return to their families after a period of service, or was their bondage life-long?

As you read the following documents, pay attention to the relationships between labor regimes and the environment. Can you make connections between the kinds of resources at stake and the forms of labor bondage? What role did climate, endemic diseases, and mortality rates (which were particularly high in the New World tropics) play in

128

shaping the terms of bondage? Overall, was New World chattel slavery markedly different from other forms of bonded labor? Did the plantation system in the Americas look different from other forms of bonded labor simply because of its scale, or are there other markers of difference that historians should pay attention to?

Also consider the kinds of sources available to historians who want to better understand the terms of labor bondage, the motivations of those in power, and the experience of those in bondage. Although the selection of documents here is by no means fully representative, globally there are relatively few sources of information that relate the experience directly from the perspective of the workers.

Robert Walsh, Description of a Slave Market in Rio de Janeiro (1831)

Between the sixteenth and nineteenth centuries Brazil imported at least 3 million African slaves, about one-quarter of all slaves who crossed the Atlantic, primarily to work on sugar and coffee plantations. Brazil was the last country in the Americas to abolish slavery, in 1888. The following excerpt is by Robert Walsh (1772–1852), an Irish cleric and physician. Attached to the British embassy in Constantinople, he traveled widely in Turkey, Asia, and Russia. In the late 1820s he accompanied a diplomatic delegation to Brazil. The book he later wrote about his visit to Brazil resulted in his appointment to the Royal Society for the Abolition of Slavery.

The place where the great slave mart is held is a long winding street called the Vallongo, which runs from the sea, at the northern extremity of the city. Almost every house in this place is a large

---

SOURCE: Reverand R. Walsh, *Notices of Brazil in 1828 and 1829* (Boston: Richardson, Lord & Holbrook, William Hyde, Crocker & Brewster, and Carter, Hendee & Babcock, 1835), vol. 2, pp. 179–81.

ware-room, where the slaves are deposited, and customers go to purchase. These ware-rooms stand at each side of the street, and the poor creatures are exposed for sale like any other commodity. When a customer comes in, they are turned up before him; such as he wishes are handled by the purchaser in different parts, exactly as I have seen butchers feeling a calf; and the whole examination is the mere animal capability, without the remotest inquiry as to the moral quality, which a man no more thinks of, than if he was buying a dog or a mule. I have frequently seen Brazilian ladies at these sales. They go dressed, sit down, handle and examine their purchases, and bring them away with the most perfect indifference. I sometimes saw groups of well-dressed females here, shopping for slaves, exactly as I have seen English ladies amusing themselves at our bazaars.

There was no circumstance which struck me with more melancholy reflections than this market, which I felt a kind of morbid curiosity in seeing, as a man looks at objects which excite his strongest interests, while they shock his best feelings. The ware-rooms are spacious apartments, where sometimes three or four hundred slaves, of all ages and sexes, are exhibited together. Round the room are benches on which the elder generally sit, and the middle is occupied by the younger, particularly females, who squat on the ground stowed close together, with their hands and chins resting on their knees. Their only covering is a small girdle of cross-barred cotton, tied round the waist.

The first time I passed through this street, I stood at the bars of the window looking through, when a cigano [gypsy] came and pressed me to enter. I was particularly attracted by a group of children, one of whom, a young girl, had something very pensive and engaging in her countenance. The cigano observing me look at her, whipped her up with a long rod, and bade her with a rough voice to come forward. It was quite affecting to see the poor timid shrinking child standing before me, in a state the most helpless and forlorn, that ever a being, endued, like myself, with a reasonable mind and an immortal soul, could be reduced to. Some of these girls have remarkably sweet and engaging countenances. Notwithstanding their dusky hue, they look so modest, gentle and sensible, that you could not for a moment hesitate to acknowledge, that they are endued with a like feeling a common nature with your own daughters. The seller was about to put the child into all the attitudes, and display her person in the same way, as he would a man; but I declined the exhibition, and she shrunk timidly back to her place, and seemed glad to hide herself in the group that surrounded her.

The men were generally less interesting objects than the women; their countenances and hues were very varied, according to the part of the African coast from which they came; some were soot black, having a certain ferocity of aspect that indicated strong and fierce passions, like men who were darkly brooding over some deep-felt wrongs, and meditating revenge. When any one was ordered, he came forward with a sullen indifference, threw his arms over his head, stamped with his feet, shouted to show the soundness of his lungs, ran up and down the room, and was treated exactly like a horse, put through his paces at a repository; and when done, he was whipped to his stall.

The heads of the slaves, both male and female, were generally half shaved; the hair being left only on the fore part. A few of the females had cotton handkerchiefs tied round their heads, which, with some little ornaments of native seed or shells, gave them a very engaging appearance. A number, particularly the males, were affected with eruptions of a white scurf which had a loathsome appearance, like a leprosy. It was considered, however, a wholesome effort of nature, to throw off the effects of the salt provisions used during the voyage; and, in fact, it resembles exactly a saline concretion.

Many of them were lying stretched on the bare boards; and among the rest, mothers with young children at their breasts, of which they seemed passionately fond. They were all doomed to remain on the spot, like sheep in a pen, till they were sold; they have no apartment to retire to, no bed to repose on, no covering to protect them; they sit naked all day, and lie naked all night, on the bare boards, or benches, where we saw them exhibited.

Among the objects that attracted my attention in this place were some young boys, who seemed to have formed a society together. I observed several times in passing by, that the same little group was collected near a barred window; they seemed very fond of each other, and their kindly feelings were never interrupted by peevishness; indeed, the temperament of a negro child is generally so sound, that he is not affected by those little morbid sensations, which are the frequent cause of crossness and ill-temper in our children. I do not remember, that I ever saw a young black fretful, or out of humor; certainly never displaying those ferocious fits of petty passion, in which the superior nature of infant whites indulges. I sometimes brought cakes and fruit in my pocket, and handed them in to the group. It was quite delightful to observe the generous and disinterested manner in which they distributed them. There was no scrambling with one another; no selfish reservation to themselves. The child to whom I happened to give them, took them so gently, looked so thankfully, and distributed them so generously, that I could not help thinking that God had compensated their dusky hue, by a more than usual human portion of amiable qualities.

A great number of those who arrive at Rio are sent up the country, and we every day met cofilas [convoys], such as Mungo Park [Scottish explorer, 1771–1806] describes in Africa, winding through the woods, as they travelled from place to place in the interior. They formed long processions, following one another in a file; the slave-merchant, distinguished by his large felt hat and puncho, bringing up the rear on a mule, with a long lash in his hand. It was another subject of pity, to see groups of these poor creatures cowering together at night in the open ranchos, drenched with cold rain, in a climate so much more frigid than their own.

Questions

1. What does Walsh find most distressing about the condition of slaves in Brazil?

2. Does Walsh have different feelings about male and female slaves? Why?

3. How does the slave market operate?

Heinrich von Füch, Notes on the Treatment of the Natives in Northeast Siberia (1744)

For three centuries, beginning in 1582, the Russian Empire gradually conquered millions of square miles in Siberia. Government sales of Siberian furs provided almost 10 percent of its growing revenue during the 1600s. (Private sales were even larger.) Sable populations and revenues declined thereafter.

The following selection comes from a 1744 report by Heinrich von Füch, a political exile who spent time among Iakut and Evenki peoples (von Füch calls these peoples Tungus) of northeastern Siberia. When he left Siberia, he promised that he would report the hardships he witnessed to imperial Russian authorities. His report shows that collecting government furs, transporting goods for soldiers and officials, and other projects often relied on forced labor by local populations. Native peoples also suffered from smallpox and other migrant-borne diseases to which they had no resistance. By 1790, their numbers had probably bounced back beyond 1582 levels, but Russians were in full control of their homelands.

Almost all the Iakuts, as well as many of the Russian farm peasants who live along the Lena River, and even those who live as far away as the Irkutsk and Ilimsk uezds [districts], have been ruined by the Kamchatka Expedition. * * *

1. Every year Russian peasants are required to transport provisions over a distance of 2,000 to 3,000 versts [obsolete Russian unit of length equal to 1.07 kilometers] to the town of Iakutsk for this expedition. If there are not enough persons who have been exiled into hard labor, others have to transport provisions even farther, all the way to the mouth of the Main River. Consequently, many of the peasants are away from their homes for as long as three years at a time. When they return they have to live on charity or by hiring themselves out.

SOURCE: *Russian Penetration of the North Pacific Ocean*, edited and translated by Basil Dmytryshn, E. A. P. Crownhart-Vaughn, and Thomas Vaughn (Portland: Oregon Historical Society Press, 1988), pp. 168–73.

Likewise the Iakuts are required to send several hundred fully equipped horses to Iakutsk in the spring, plus one man to care for every five horses. These horses are used to transport provisions and supplies overland to Okhotsk. Because the land between Iakutsk and Okhotsk is marshy and barren steppe, very few of the horses come back. The officials who are sent out to requisition these horses burden the Iakuts in every possible way in order to enrich themselves. They * * * reject many good horses so that the Iakuts will have to give them twice or three times the value in livestock or goods. * * * Furthermore, the officials do not look only to the wealthier Iakuts for the necessary number of horses, but levy the same requirement on each Iakut. One Iakut may own 50 or 100 horses [and thus be able to supply the required number], while another [may be so poor he] cannot buy either horse or wife; in order to fulfill his iasak requirement he has to become a servant to the Russians or to other Iakuts. To buy one horse he has to pay an amount which is usually equal to the value of his iasak assessment.

* * *

2. [A] new policy of iasak [levy] collection must be adopted for the Iakutsk Tungus and others. When they are stricken with small-pox they die like flies. Nine years ago I saw one nomadic settlement where only two out of ten men survived; the survivors had to pay the arrears for all those who had died, and not just for an entire uezd or district of some collector, but also for their relatives. I personally knew several wealthy Iakuts who had to pay for four or five of their dead relatives. They were so impoverished that before I left they had had to forfeit all their livestock and horses, and some-times pawn their wives and children [to Russian officials]. Some of them hang or drown themselves. This is a natural consequence because a local native works very hard in the forest all through the winter and suffers hunger and cold until he traps enough to pay his iasak and make a gift [of furs] to the iasak collector and his assis-tants. If in addition to this he is forced to pay the iasak for those who have died or who have run off, first he loses all his livestock, then his wives and children. He cannot hunt without horses, so he commits suicide or runs off. Then the collectors find his relatives

and force them to pay. The collectors take everything, until the natives are destitute.

3. The third principal reason the local natives are ruined is that from the time they first came under Russian control they have been forced to pay tribute. Some have paid in sables, others in red foxes, still others in cash. At first there were plenty of furbearing animals there, but now there are no sables and not many foxes in those Iakut lands, from the shores of the [Arctic] ocean all the way south to the great Lena River. Moreover, almost half the natives cannot hunt because they have no horses. The instructions to the collectors always imply that they are to collect for the Treasury on the basis of the [original] assessment of one sable from each person on whom one sable was originally levied, and one fox from each person on whom one fox was levied. But the collectors know ahead of time that the natives do not have these furs and so they bring out from town a number of sable and fox pelts to sell [to the natives]. Then, even if the natives manage to trap sables and foxes before the collectors arrive, the collectors do not accept them, but force the natives to purchase the furs they have brought out, paying double or treble the value. * * * The collector profits, the native loses, and there is no profit at all for the Imperial Treasury.

Twice during my eleven-year stay there, deputations of natives went to town with a petition to be allowed to pay their iasak obligations in squirrels and wolverines instead of sables and foxes. On the basis of their petition the office issued an ukaz [imperial order] that collectors were to accept 100 squirrels or 40 wolverines in place of one fox or sable. In that particular year the natives achieved some reduction of their burden, but the next year their suffering began again because the new official had to act on the basis of the original instructions unless the natives could obtain a new ukaz for relief in that year. As a result, these people experience great hardship.

* * *

It would be possible to halt all native complaints if Her Imperial Majesty would graciously order a stipulation [allowing the iasak to be paid with wolverines or squirrels] * * * [T]he Treasury would not lose and the natives would have a great reprieve. If Her Imperial Majesty were to allow the collectors to accept the substitution for sables and foxes to be paid into the Treasury, they would still make a considerable profit, which they justly deserve, because they are sent into designated places at their own expense.

4. The fourth factor that completely ruins poor natives and burdens all others is that every year a new official or collector is sent out to each ostrog or district with a scribe, an interpreter, a tselovalnik [sworn men] and four to eight servitors. Each of these expects a gift. The gift to the official often equals the iasak due the Treasury. * * * When the official takes his share before the others do, it often happens that the poor natives cannot satisfy the other servitors, who then take the natives' wives and grown children to work for them. They also take the nets, axes, tools, boats, bows and arrows. Sometimes they take the clothes right off the backs of the natives, and beat and torture them secretly in their iurts.

Finally, I do not know of any [other] land where native inhabitants live without any protection and representation. When the voevodas [count or duke] dispense justice in town, then although the natives have some satisfaction for their complaints, nevertheless it often happens that they do not obtain whatever it is they seek. * * * Furthermore, no native can petition [a Russian official] in town until he has secured a town interpreter, who is nearly always related to the official, or at least is of one mind with him. Consequently, instead of reporting their grievances, the interpreter will upbraid the natives viciously and threaten to beat them. Sometimes he actually does flog them and sends them back. And if the voevoda is a greedy scoundrel, he mistreats them even more viciously.

On the basis of such complaints, the governors sometimes appoint commissions from among local officers to provide the Iakuts and other natives with the justice they seek, in which case they come to the city in great numbers with their petitions. However the [greedy] officials and their associates watch the petitioners as they come along the roads and rivers, and seize them and take them home where they reach some agreement and make peace. The officials give back half of what they have taken, and in this way avoid petitions and punishment.

Questions

1. What are the different ways in which officials oppress the indigenous people?

2. How do disease and ecological change worsen these problems?

3. Could the Russian government have achieved its aims in this sparsely populated region while causing less suffering? What does von Füch think?

Antonio Vazquez de Espinosa, Mercury Mining in Huanacavelica and Silver Mining in Potosí (1620s)

Father Antonio Vazquez de Espinosa (died 1630) was a Spanish Carmelite monk who gave up a scholarly life in favor of missionary work in the New World. He traveled extensively in Peru and New Spain and had opportunities to observe and interact with many indigenous American communities. He returned to Spain in 1622. His written descriptions of what he saw in the Americas were not published in his lifetime, though the formal tone and level of detail he records suggest that he intended for the document to be read by those unfamiliar with conditions in the Americas. Vazquez describes labor conditions as well as the volume and value of silver mining in Potosí, where the rich 1545 silver discovery created the New World's first mining boom town. Potosí sits 13,500 feet above sea level, too high to grow its own food. At the peak of the mining boom, the settlement would have been as large as one of the half-dozen biggest cities in Europe; consequently even more labor—both voluntary and conscripted—was necessary to haul supplies up and silver ore down the mountain. Vazquez also describes the *mita* (forced labor according to quotas; see *Worlds Together Worlds Apart*, p. 468) and money allocated by the Spanish crown to mercury mining. After 1555 the mercury amalgamation process was vital to the more efficient extraction of silver ore from rocks mined at Potosí.

HUANACAVELICA

Huanacavelica has 400 Spanish residents, as well as many temporary shops of dealers in merchandise and groceries, heads of trading houses, and transients, for the town has a lively commerce. It has a parish church with vicar and curate, a Dominican convent, and a Royal Hospital under the Brethren of San Juan de Diós for the care of the sick, especially Indians on the range; it has a chaplain with a salary of 800 assay pesos contributed by His Majesty; he is curate of the parish of San Sebastián de Indios, for the Indians who have come to work in the mines and who have settled down there. * * *

Every 2 months His Majesty sends by the regular courier from Lima 60,000 pesos to pay for the mita of the Indians, for the crews are changed every 2 months, so that merely for the Indian mita payment 360,000 pesos are sent from Lima every year, [across the risky] cold and desolate mountain country which is the puna and has nothing on it but llama ranches.

Up on the range there are 3,000 or 4,000 Indians working in the mine; * * * When I was in that town the excavation so extensive that it held more than 3,000 Indians working away hard with picks and hammers, breaking up that flint ore; and when they have filled their little sacks, the poor fellows, loaded down with ore, climb up those ladders or rigging, some like masts and others like cables, and so trying and distressing that a man empty-handed can hardly get up them. That is the way they work in this mine, with many lights and the loud noise of the pounding and great confusion. Nor is that the greatest evil and difficulty; that is due to thievish and undisciplined superintendents.

* * *

SOURCE: Antonio Vazquez de Espinosa, *Compendium and Description of the West Indies*, translated by Charles Upson Clark (Washington, D.C.: Smithsonian Institution, 1942), vol. 102, 542–43, 623–24, 629.

POTOSÍ

* * * According to His Majesty's warrant, the mine owners on this massive range have a right to the mita of 13,300 Indians in the working and exploitation of the mines. * * * It is the duty of the Corregidor of Potosi to have them rounded up and to see that they come in from all the provinces * * * ; this Potosi Corregidor has power and authority over all the Corregidors in those provinces mentioned; for if they do not fill the Indian mita allotment assigned each one of them in accordance with the capacity of their provinces as indicated to them, * * * he can suspend them, notifying the Viceroy of the fact.

These Indians are sent out every year under a captain whom they choose in each village or tribe, for him to take them and oversee them for the year each has to serve; every year they have a new election, for as some go out, others come in. This works out very badly, with great losses and gaps in the quotas of Indians, the villages being depopulated; and this gives rise to great extortions and abuses on the part of the inspectors toward the poor Indians, ruining them * * * and carrying them off in chains because they do not fill out the mita assignment, which they cannot do, for the reasons given and for others which I do not bring forward.

* * * These 13,300 are divided up every 4 months into 3 mitas, each consisting of 4,433 Indians, to work in the mines on the range and in the 120 smelters. * * * These mita Indians earn each day * * * 4 reals. Besides these there are others not under obligation, who are mingados or hire themselves out voluntarily: these each get from 12 to 16 reals, and some up to 24, according to their reputation of wielding the pick and knowing how to get the ore out. These mingados will be over 4,000 in number. They and the mita Indians go up every Monday morning to the locality of Guayna Potosí which is at the foot of the range; * * * [there] the Indians are * * * turned over to these mine and smelter owners.

After each has eaten his ration, they climb up the hill, each to his mine, and go in, staying there from that hour until Saturday.

* * *

So huge is the wealth which has been taken out of this range since the year 1545, when it was discovered, up to the present year of 1628, which makes 83 years that they have been working and reducing its ores, that merely from the registered mines, as appears from an examination of most of the accounts in the royal records, 326,000,000 assay pesos have been taken out. At the beginning when the ore was richer and easier to get out, for then there were no mita Indians and no mercury process, in the 40 years between 1545 and 1585, they took out 111,000,000 of assay silver. From the year 1585 up to 1628, 43 years, although the mines are harder to work, for they are deeper down, with the assistance of 13,300 Indians whom His Majesty has granted to the mine owners on that range, and of other hired Indians, who come there freely and voluntarily to work at day's wages, and with the great advantage of the mercury process, in which none of the ore or the silver is wasted, and with the better knowledge of the technique which the miners now have, they have taken out 215,000,000 assay pesos. That, plus the 111 extracted in the 40 years previous to 1585, makes 326,000,000 assay pesos, not counting the great amount of silver secretly taken from these mines, * * * which is beyond all reckoning; but I should venture to imagine and even assert that what has been taken from the Potosí range must be as much again as what paid the 20 percent royal impost.

Questions

1. The *mita* system of corvée labor funneled American natives to both mercury and silver mines. What differences does Vazquez note between labor conditions in Huanacavelica and Potosí?

2. What challenges or obstacles to mining existed in the seventeenth century? What benefits were gained by facing those challenges, and by whom?

3. Is Vazquez trying to position himself as a neutral observer? Why or why not?

Captain William Dampier, The General Slavery at Achin (1697)

William Dampier (1651–1715) circumnavigated the globe three times in his life, sailing as a pirate, navigator, and keen observer of the natural world. In 1697 he published five volumes of travel accounts, all written to provide a source of income. The following passage is taken from his description of Achin (Aceh) in Sumatra, where he spent time in 1688 on his first voyage. Dampier is surprised by the ways in which he sees social hierarchies expressed, and by the multiple, often wage-earning and independent role of slaves, a labor and social category he describes as much more fluid in Ache than the chattel slavery he encountered in the Atlantic world.

This Country is governed by a Queen, under whom there are 12 Oronkeys, or great Lords. These act in their several Precincts with great Power and Authority. Under these there are other inferiour Officers, to keep the Peace in the several parts of the Queens Dominions. The present Shabander of Achin is one of the Oronkeys. He is a Man of greater knowledge than any of the rest, and supposed to be very rich. I have heard say, he had not less than 1000 Slaves, some of whom were topping Merchants, and had many Slaves under them. And even these, tho' they are Slaves to Slaves, yet have their Slaves also; neither can a stranger easily know who is a Slave and who not among them: for they are all, in a manner, Slaves to one another: and all in general to the Queen and Oronkeys; for their Government is very Arbitrary. Yet there is nothing of rigour used by the Master to his Slave, except it be the very meanest, such as do all sorts of servile Work: but those who can turn their hands to any thing besides Drudgery, live well enough by their industry. Nay, they are encouraged by their Masters, who often lend them Money to begin some trade or business withal: Whereby the Servant lives [easy], and with great content follows

Source: Captain William Dampier, *Dampier's Voyages*, edited by John Masefield (London: E. Grant Richards, 1906), vol. 2, pp. 67–68.

what his Inclination or Capacity fits him for; and the Master also, who has a share in the gains, reaps the more profit, yet without trouble. When one of these Slaves dies, his Master is Heir to what he leaves; and his Children, if he has any, become his Slaves also: unless the Father out of his own clear gains has in his life time had wherewithal to purchase their Freedom. The Markets are kept by these People, and you scarce trade with any other. The Money-changers also are Slaves, and in general all the Women that you see in the streets; not one of them being free. So are the Fisher-men, and others who fetch Firewood in Canoas from Pulo Gomez, for thence those of this City fetch most of their Wood, tho' there is scarce anything to be seen but Woods about the City. Yet tho' all these are Slaves, they have habitations or houses to themselves in several parts of the City, far from their Masters Houses, as if they were free People.

Questions

1. How many kinds of labor does Dampier describe slaves doing in Aceh? How are these occupations different from the role of slaves in the Atlantic economy in the same period?

2. How would you characterize Dampier's description of social hierar-chies among free people, and among slaves? What was the role of physical force in controlling slaves?

3. What motivations might Dampier have had for publishing this descrip-tion of a merchant-driven economy in Aceh?

Chapter 14

CULTURES OF SPLENDOR AND POWER, 1500–1780

Ogier Ghiselin de Busbecq, Turkish Letters (1589)

Under Suleiman I "the Magnificent" (ruled 1520–1566) the power of the Ottoman Empire was at its height. Suleiman's empire included modern Turkey, the Balkans, parts of Hungary, the Crimea and southern Russia, and most of Southwest Asia and North Africa. In large part the empire's power rested on the *devşhirme*. Every four or five years a levy of Christian boys from the Balkans and some other places was taken. These boys, slaves of the emperor, were usually converted to Islam, and educated in special schools. The brightest were recruited into the imperial palace, where they staffed the Ottoman bureaucracy, including the office of grand vizier, the highest in the state. Many went into the Ottoman infantry corps, the Janissaries, who were the best trained, disciplined, and equipped military of the day. Thus, though they were legally slaves, some of these men became very wealthy and powerful. The following passage was written by Ogier Ghiselin de Busbecq, a Flemish nobleman and servant of the Habsburg dynasty. In 1555 Ferdinand I, archduke of Austria, king of Hungary and Bohemia, and Holy Roman Emperor, sent de Busbecq to Istanbul on a diplomatic mission. During the six years he spent in the Ottoman Empire, he learned a great deal about Ottoman institutions. After returning to Vienna in 1562, de Busbecq spent many more years serving the Habsburgs in various capacities and pursuing various scholarly projects, including polishing his Ottoman notebooks. He published them as *Turkish Letters* in 1589. Spelling has been updated in the following excerpt to reflect modern orthography.

Suleiman had a son by a concubine, who came from the Crimea. * * * His name was Mustapha, and at the time of which I am speaking he was young, vigorous, and of high repute as a soldier. But Suleiman had also several other children by a Russian woman (Roxolana).

* * *

Mustapha's high qualities and matured years marked him out, to the soldiers who loved, and the people who supported him, as the successor of his father, who was now in the decline of life. On the other hand, his step-mother [Roxolana] by throwing the claim of a lawful wife into the scale was doing her utmost to counterbalance his personal merits and his rights as eldest son, with a view to obtaining the throne for her own children. In this intrigue she received the advice and assistance of Roostem, whose fortunes were inseparably linked with hers by his marriage with a daughter she had had by Suleiman.

* * *

Well, inasmuch as Roostem was chief Vizier, * * * he had no difficulty, seeing that he was the Sultan's adviser in everything, in influencing his master's mind. The Turks, accordingly, are convinced that it was by the calumnies of Roostem and the spells of Roxolana, who was in ill repute as a practiser of witchcraft, that the Sultan was so estranged from his son as to entertain the design of getting rid of him. * * * The sons of Turkish Sultans are in the most wretched position in the world, for, as soon as one of them succeeds his father, the rest are doomed to certain death. The Turk can endure no rival to the throne, and, indeed, the conduct of the Janissaries renders it impossible for the new Sultan to spare his brothers; for if one of them survives, the Janissaries are for ever asking largesses. If these are refused, forthwith the cry is heard,

SOURCE: Charles Thornton Forster and F. H. Blackburne Daniell, *The Life and Letters of Ogier Ghiselin de Busbecq* (London: C. Kegan Paul Co., 1881), vol. 1, pp. 111, 113–15, 117–18, 153–55, 242–43, 253, 255, 405–406.

"Long live the brother!" "God preserve the brother!"—a tolerably broad hint that they intend to place him on the throne. So that the Turkish Sultans are compelled to celebrate their succession by imbruing their hands in the blood of their nearest relatives. * * *

Being at war with Shah Tahmasp, King of the Persians, [Suleiman] had sent Roostem against him as commander-in-chief of his armies. Just as he was about to enter the Persian territory, Roostem suddenly halted, and hurried off despatches to Suleiman, informing him that affairs were in a very critical state; that treason was rife everywhere; that the soldiers had been tampered with, and cared for no one but Mustapha; * * * and he must come at once, if he wished to preserve his throne. Suleiman was seriously alarmed by these despatches. He immediately hurried to the army, and sent a letter to summon Mustapha to his presence, inviting him to clear himself of those crimes of which he was suspected.

* * *

There was great uneasiness among the soldiers, when Mustapha arrived in the camp. He was brought to his father's tent, and there everything betokened peace. * * * But there were in the tent certain mutes—a favourite kind of servant among the Turks—strong and sturdy fellows, who had been appointed as his executioners. As soon as he entered the inner tent, they threw themselves upon him, and endeavoured to put the fatal noose around his neck. Mustapha, being a man of considerable strength, made a stout defence, and fought—not only for his life, but also for the throne; there being no doubt that if he escaped from his executioners, and threw himself among the Janissaries, the news of this outrage on their beloved prince would cause such pity and indignation, that they would not only protect him, but also proclaim him Sultan. Suleiman felt how critical the matter was, being only separated by the linen hangings of his tent from the stage, on which this tragedy was being enacted. When he found that there was an unexpected delay in the execution of his scheme, he thrust out his head from the chamber of his tent, and glared on the mutes with fierce and threatening eyes; at the same time, with signs full of hideous meaning, he sternly rebuked their slackness. Hereon the mutes, gaining fresh strength from the terror he inspired, threw Mustapha down, got the bowstring round his neck, and strangled him.

* * *

The Sultan's hall was crowded with people, among whom were several officers of high rank. Besides these there were all the troopers of the Imperial guard, * * * and a large force of Janissaries; but there was not in all that great assembly a single man who owed his position to aught save his valour and his merit. No distinction is attached to birth among the Turks; the deference to be paid to a man is measured by the position he holds in the public service. There is no fighting for precedence; a man's place is marked out by the duties he discharges. * * * It is by merit that men rise in the service, a system which ensures that posts should only be assigned to the competent. * * * Those who receive the highest offices from the Sultan are for the most part the sons of shepherds or herdsmen, and so far from being ashamed of their parentage, they actually glory in it, and consider it a matter of boasting that they owe nothing to the accident of birth; for they do not believe that high qualities are either natural or hereditary, nor do they think that they can be handed down from father to son, but that they are partly the gift of God, and partly the result of good training, great industry, and unwearied zeal. * * * Among the Turks, therefore, honours, high posts, and judgeships are the rewards of great ability and good service.

* * *

[T]he Turks are much afraid of carbines and pistols, such as are used on horseback. The same, I hear, is the case with the Persians, on which account some one advised Roostem [the grand vizier] when he was setting out with the Sultan on a campaign against them, to raise from his household servants a troop of 200 horse and arm them with fire-arms, as they would cause much alarm and do great execution in the ranks of the enemy. Roostem, in accordance with this advice, raised a troop of dragoons, furnished them with fire-arms, and had them drilled. But they had not completed half the journey when their guns began to get out of order. Every day some essential part of their weapons was lost or broken, and it was not often that armourers could be found capable of repairing them. So, a large part of the fire-arms having been rendered unserviceable, the men took a dislike to the weapon; and this prejudice was increased by the dirt which its use entailed, the Turks being a very cleanly people; for the dragoons had their hands and clothes begrimed with gunpowder, and moreover presented such a sorry appearance, with their ugly boxes and pouches hanging about them, that their comrades laughed at them, and called them apothecaries. So, * * * they gathered round Roostem, and showing him their broken and useless fire-arms, asked what advantage he hoped to gain from them when they met the enemy, and demanded that he should relieve them of them, and give them their old arms again. Roostem, after considering their request carefully, thought there was no reason for refusing to comply with it, and so they got leave to resume their bows and arrows.

* * *

[P]eople here are marvellously expert [with bows and arrows]. From the eighth, or even the seventh, year of their age they begin to shoot at a mark, and practise archery ten or twelve years. This constant exercise strengthens the muscles of their arms, and gives them such skill that they can hit the smallest marks with their arrows. * * * So sure is their aim, that in battle they can hit a man in the eye or in any other exposed part they choose.

* * *

[N]o nation in the world has shown greater readiness than the Turks to avail themselves of the useful inventions of foreigners, as is proved by their employment of cannons and mortars, and many other things invented by Christians.

* * *

Against us stands Suleiman, that foe whom his own and his ancestors' exploits have made so terrible; he tramples the soil of Hungary with 200,000 horse, he is at the very gates of Austria, threatens the rest of Germany, and brings in his train all the nations that extend from our borders to those of Persia. The army he leads is equipped with the wealth of many kingdoms. Of the three regions, into which the world is divided, there is not one that does not contribute its share towards our destruction.

Questions

1. What is the Turkish attitude toward adopting foreign technology? What problems does doing so pose?

2. What does de Busbecq see as the strengths of the Ottoman Empire?

3. What does he perceive as problems with the Ottoman political system?

Xu Jie, Economic Change in China (sixteenth century)

The sixteenth century witnessed an enormous commercial boom in China, especially in the Lower Yangzi valley. Songjiang, the subject of the first document below, was one of the wealthiest and most commercialized prefectures, based in large part on booming rural production of cotton and cotton textiles.

Historians agree that a number of important social changes accompanied this economic growth, though they do not agree about how they were related. Great landed estates, often farmed by wage laborers and bondservants, gave way to small farms owned or rented by free peasants. These peasants became increasingly involved in the market, often buying their food to concentrate on producing cotton, silk, or other processed goods. More and more landlords moved to town, and became socially distant from villagers. Tenants and debtors resisted rent and debt collection more often and more forcefully, especially in bad harvest years. Meanwhile, prices rose and fell unpredictably, making both farmers and townspeople less secure even though they became richer on average.

In the first selection here, Xu Jie (1503–1583), a Confucian scholar-official who was also a large landlord, laments what he sees as moral decline and its economic consequences. The second selection describes the cotton market in neighboring Taicang. Spelling has been updated in the following excerpts to reflect modern orthography.

Xu Jie

It is customary in Songjiang that when a great house has fields but cannot cultivate them it must employ tenants, and when tenants wish to cultivate but have insufficient provisions they must rely on a great house. The situation in this relationship is no different from one of mutual assistance between master and servant or one of mutual nourishment between father and son, elder and younger brother. Under these circumstances the reason why the great families who cannot help but be cruel toward their tenants do not dare to be too cruel is that they fear no one will cultivate for them. And, the reason why the tenants who cannot help but turn their backs on the great house do not dare to turn them completely is that they fear no one will allow them credit. Before the reign of the last emperor [1506–1522] the fact that the people were well off in their livelihood and there were no evil habits in the countryside, that the state's provisions were up and the jails rarely contained prisoners, was due to this way of life. In more recent years officers of the government have repeatedly sent down restrictions on pressing for payment of debts, and more seriously, they have instituted the punishment of division and dispersal [of estates]. As a result tenants have indifferently activated the disloyal and unfaithful sides of their nature [*tong qi buyi bu xin zhi xin*] and great houses have become anxious, fearing to enter the government officer's snare. The mutual assistance and mutual nourishment of former days then began to transform into mutual suspicion and enmity. Not only is it now impossible to collect on loans, but rents also go largely unpaid. That loans could not be collected at first seemed only to cause trouble for the great houses; that when tenants have no one to rely on for provisions they cannot avoid meeting an untoward end was not understood. * * *

Taicang

[In Taicang] transactions in the marketplace begin before dawn. Every year when the cotton comes in, many brokers gather youths

SOURCE: Jerry Dennerline, *The Chia-ting Loyalists* (New Haven, Conn.: Yale University Press, 1981), pp. 82–83, 86.

about them as their wings. Toting lanterns, they go out to intercept the rural folk, who do not know which way to turn. Amidst the grabbing and snatching some even lose their goods.

When a country person approaches, bearing his produce, they don't even ask whether it is for the market or not but snatch it away saying they will take it to such-and-such a shop and get a price for it. The country folk have no alternative but to follow.

Questions

1. How does Xu Jie think Songjiang society worked in the past? What has changed since then?

2. Whom does Xu Jie blame for these changes? Why? Can you imagine how a peasant or a local official might narrate these same changes?

3. In the description of the Taicang cotton market, what seems to determine whom peasants sell to? If true, how might these practices affect who benefited from increased commercialization?

Zhang Han, Tales of the Strange (sixteenth century)

Studying for the Chinese civil service exams was expensive. Especially in Ming (1368–1644) and Qing (1644–1912) times, the family wealth behind successful candidates often came from commerce. Such was the case for Zhang Han (1511–1593), a very successful scholar-official (and in retirement, also a painter and poet) whose family ran a large-scale textile business based in Hangzhou, profiting from the same Lower Yangzi boom described for Songjiang and Taicang (Economic Change in China, in Chapter 14). Some, though not all, of Zhang Han's official posts took advantage of his business knowledge: he ran a government shipyard at one point, and supervised the shipment of tax grain along the Grand Canal at another.

But unlike many such officials, Zhang Han made no effort to hide his merchant origins. In contrast to orthodox neo-Confucian doctrine, he emphasized the contribution of merchants to the general welfare of society. In fact, he is best known today for the guide for merchant travelers he published, and for his writings arguing that in most cases free trade was good both for the people and for the government.

This brief excerpt, describing the initial commercial success of his great-grandfather, comes from Zhang Han's *Tales of the Strange* (Yiwen Ji), rather than his writings on commerce. Such collections, which were quite popular, often described what we would call supernatural events in very realistic social settings; their authors usually insisted they represented actual events, but some are clearly works of fiction.

Ancestor Yian was of a humble family and made liquor as his profession. In the closing years of Chenghua (1465–1487) there was a flood. At that time my great-grandfather was living beside a river, and when the water flooded it entered the building. All the liquor he was making was completely spoiled. For several evenings he went out to look at his spoiled liquor and inundated jugs. One evening as he was returning home, someone suddenly called him from behind. My great-grandfather turned to greet him, and was handed something warm. Suddenly the person was not to be seen. When he got home he lit the lamp and shone it on what turned out to be a small ingot of silver. With this he gave up making liquor and bought a loom. He wove ramie (*zhu*) and silk (*bi*) of several colours, and achieved a very high level of craftsmanship. Every time a roll of fabric came off the loom, people competed to buy it. He calculated his profit at 20%. After saving for twenty years he bought another loom. Later he increased his looms to over twenty. The merchants who dealt in textiles constantly thronged the house inside and out, and still he couldn't meet their orders. Hereafter, the family profession brought great wealth. The next four ancestors carried on the profession, each gaining wealth in the tens of thousands. The story of his receiving silver late that night is very strange, yet since the time of my great-grandfather it has been passed down. How is it that it should have started with a spirit's gift?

Source: Timothy Brook, "The Merchant Network in 16th Century China: A Discussion and Translation of Zhang Han's 'On Merchants,'" *Journal of the Economic and Social History of the Orient* 24 (1981): 173–74.

Questions

1. How did Zhang Han's ancestor become wealthy?

2. What role did luck, skill, and hard work play in his success?

3. Many accounts of commercial success—both in fiction and in biographies—involve some intervention by spirits, who provide either money or a very valuable piece of information. (For a much earlier non-Chinese example, see *The Jataka or Stories of the Buddha's Former Births*, in Chapter 6.) Why might this trope have been so common?

Roger Cotes, Preface to Newton's *Principia Mathematica* (1713)

Sir Isaac Newton (1643–1727), Lucasian Professor of Mathematics at Cambridge University, member of Parliament, and warden of Great Britain's Royal Mint, is regarded as one of the most important scientists, if not the most important, who ever lived. His principal work was the *Philosophiae Naturalis Principia Mathematica* (Mathematical Principles of Natural Philosophy), first published in 1697. In this Newton described universal gravitation and the three laws of motion. He demonstrated that the motions of objects on the earth and of celestial bodies are governed by the same set of natural laws. His work, which dominated the field of physics for more than 200 years, marked the culmination of the Scientific Revolution. The following document comes from the preface by Roger Cotes (1682–1716) to the second edition of the *Principia Mathematica*, published in 1713. Cotes, also a professor at Cambridge, was a significant astronomer and mathematician in his own right. When Cotes began editing the *Principia*, Newton had largely lost interest in science. However, Cotes revived his enthusiasm and the two spent three and a half years working on the revised edition.

But if several vortices are contained in the same space, and are supposed to penetrate each other, and to revolve with different motions, then, because these motions must agree with those of the bodies carried away by them, which are perfectly regular, and performed in conic sections which are sometimes very eccentric, and sometimes nearly circles, one may reasonably ask, how it comes to pass that these vortices remain entire, and have suffered no manner of perturbation in so many ages from the actions of the conflicting matter? Certainly, if these fictitious motions are more compounded and more hard to be accounted for than the true motions of the planets and comets, it seems to no purpose to admit them into philosophy, since every cause ought to be more simple than its effect. Allowing men to indulge their own fancies, suppose any man should affirm that the planets and comets are surrounded with atmospheres like our earth, which hypothesis seems more reasonable than that of vortices. Let him then affirm that these atmospheres, by their own nature, move about the sun, and describe conic sections, which motion is much more easily conceived than that of the vortices penetrating each other. Lastly, that the planets and comets are carried about the sun by these atmospheres of theirs; and then applaud his own sagacity in discovering the causes of the celestial motions. He that rejects this fable, must also reject the other; for two drops of water are not more like than this hypothesis of atmospheres, and that of vortices.

Galileo has shown, that when a stone projected moves in a parabola, its deflection into that curve from its rectilinear path is occasioned by the gravity of the stone towards the earth; that is, by an occult quality. But, now, somebody more cunning than he may come to explain the cause after this manner. He will suppose a certain subtle matter, not discernible by our sight, our touch, or any other of our senses, which fills the spaces which are near and contiguous to the superficies of the earth; and that this matter is carried with different directions, and various, and often contrary

SOURCE: Roger Cotes, Preface, in Isaac Newton, *Principia Mathematica* (London: H. D. Symods, 1803), vol. 1, pp. xxv–xxvii, xxx–xxxi. Text modernized by Norton authors for this edition.

motions describing parabolic curves. Then see how easily he may account for the deflection of the stone above spoken of. The stone, says he, floats in this subtle fluid, and, following its motion, cannot choose but describe the same figure. But the fluid moves in parabolic curves, and therefore the stone must move in a parabola of course. Would not the acuteness of this philosopher be thought very extraordinary, who could deduce the appearances of nature from mechanical causes, matter, and motion, so clearly that the meanest man may understand it? Or, indeed, should not we smile to see this new Galileo taking so much mathematical pains to introduce occult qualities into philosophy, from whence they have been so happily excluded? But I am ashamed to dwell so long upon trifles.

The sum of the matter is this: the number of comets is certainly very great; their motions are perfectly regular, and observe the same laws with those of the planets. The orbits in which they move are conic sections, and those very eccentric. They move every way towards all parts of the heavens, and pass through the planetary regions with all possible freedom; and their motion is often contrary to the order of the signs. These phenomena are most evidently confirmed by astronomical observations, and cannot be accounted for by vortices. Nay, indeed, they are utterly irreconcilable with the vortices of the planets. There can be no room for the motions of the comets, unless the celestial spaces be entirely cleared of that fictitious matter.

*   *   *

Without all doubt, this world, so diversified with that variety of forms and motions we find in it, could arise from nothing but the perfectly free will of God directing and presiding over all.

From this fountain it is that those laws, which we call the laws of nature, have flowed; in which there appear many traces, indeed, of the most wise contrivance, but not the least shadow of necessity. These, therefore, we must not seek from uncertain conjectures, but learn them from observations and experiments. He who thinks to find the true principles of physics and the laws of natural things by the force alone of his own mind, and the internal light of his reason, must either suppose that the world exists by necessity, and by the same necessity follows the laws proposed; or, if the order of nature was established by the will of God, that himself, a miserable reptile, can tell what was fittest to be done. All sound and true philosophy is founded on the appearances of things, which, if they draw us ever so much against our will to such principles as most clearly manifest to us the most excellent counsel and supreme dominion of the All-wise and Almighty Being, those principles are not therefore to be laid aside, because some men may perhaps dislike them. They may call them, if they please, miracles or occult qualities; but names maliciously given ought not to be a disadvantage to the things themselves; unless they will say, at last, that all philosophy ought to be founded in atheism. Philosophy must not be corrupted in compliance to these men; for the order of things will not be changed.

Fair and equal judges will therefore give sentence in favor of this most excellent method of philosophy, which is founded on experiments and observations. To this method it is hardly to be said or imagined what light, what splendor, hath accrued from this admirable work of our illustrious author, whose happy and sublime genius, resolving the most difficult problems, and reaching the discoveries of which the mind of man was thought incapable before, is deservedly admired by all those who are somewhat more than superficially versed in these matters. The gates are now set open; and by his means we may freely enter into the knowledge of the hidden secrets and wonders of natural things. He has so clearly laid open and set before our eyes the most beautiful frame of the System of the World, that, if King Alphonsus were now alive, he would not complain for want of the graces either of simplicity or of harmony in it. Therefore we may now more nearly behold the beauties of nature, and entertain ourselves with the delightful contemplation; and, which is the best and most valuable fruit of philosophy, be thence incited the more profoundly to reverence and adore the great Maker and Lord of all. He must be blind, who, from the most wise and excellent contrivances of things, cannot see the infinite wisdom and goodness of their Almighty Creator; and he must be mad and senseless who refuses to acknowledge them.

Questions

1. Why does Cotes argue that "all sound and true philosophy is founded on the appearances of things"? What is wrong with depending on reason alone?

2. Why is Newton's physics compatible with the idea that there is a "great Maker and Lord of all"?

3. What can physics tell us about the "Almighty Creator"?

Simon Schaffer, Information Sources for *Principia Mathematica* (2008)

Isaac Newton (1643–1727), who revolutionized mathematics and physics, lived his entire life within eighty miles of Cambridge. Yet he and his peers were part of global information networks. This map, based on one compiled by science historian Simon Schaffer, illustrates the origin of every piece of data cited in Newton's masterpiece, *Principia Mathematica*. Some of Newton's most celebrated and important calculations depended on seemingly esoteric data: for instance, his breakthrough in calculations of slow changes in the earth's and moon's rotational axes (which affect the accuracy of astronomical observations generally) relied on precise measurements of unusual tides off Vietnam, Taiwan, and Cape Horn. European mariners provided this information, often relying in turn on local informants. The English East India Company, in which Newton had large investments, was particularly helpful. Mariners, in turn, benefited when Newton made prediction of tides more accurate.

SOURCE: Redrawn from Simon Schaffer, "Newton on the Beach: The Information Order of *Principia Mathematica*," *History of Science* 47 (2009): 249.

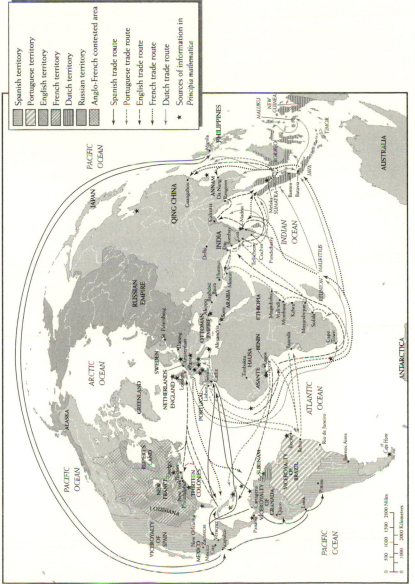

Legend

	Spanish territory
	Portuguese territory
	English territory
	French territory
	Dutch territory
	Russian territory
	Anglo-French contested area

→ Spanish trade route
→ Portuguese trade route
→ English trade route
→ French trade route
→ Dutch trade route
★ Sources of information in *Principia mathematica*

PACIFIC OCEAN

JAPAN

QING CHINA · Guangzhou

PHILIPPINES · Manila

ANNAM · Da Nang · Rangoon

RUSSIAN EMPIRE

Calcutta · Madras

SWEDEN · S. Petersburg · Danzig

INDIA · Delhi · Bombay · Goa

Melaka · SUMATRA · Banten · Batavia · JAVA

BORNEO

NEW GUINEA · MALUKU · TIMOR

AUSTRALIA

NETHERLANDS · Amsterdam · London · Paris

OTTOMAN EMPIRE · Istanbul · Alexandria · Smyrna · Jerusalem · Baghdad · Basra

ARABIA · Muscat · Hormuz

Tellicherry · Cochin · Pondicherry

INDIAN OCEAN

MAURITIUS · RÉUNION

ENGLAND · Lisbon · Cadiz · PORTUGAL

ETHIOPIA · Mogadishu · Malindi · Mombasa · Kilwa

Timbuktu · HAUSA · BENIN · Luanda · Mozambique · Sofala

ASANTE · Lagos

Cape Town

ARCTIC OCEAN

GREENLAND

ALASKA

PACIFIC OCEAN

RUPERT'S LAND

NEW FRANCE · Quebec · New York · THIRTEEN COLONIES

LOUISIANA

New Orleans · VICEROYALTY OF SPAIN · MEXICO · Mexico · Zacatecas · Veracruz · Acapulco

Panama · Cartagena · VICEROYALTY OF NEW GRANADA · Cusco · Lima · Potosí

SURINAM · Belém · Bahia · VICEROYALTY OF BRAZIL · Rio de Janeiro

Buenos Aires · Cape Horn

ATLANTIC OCEAN

ANTARCTICA

PACIFIC OCEAN

0 500 1000 1500 2000 Miles
0 1000 2000 Kilometers

Information sources for *Principia Mathematica* and the trade networks of early modern European empires

Questions

1. What is the earliest date at which any person could have had access to data from all these places? Where would such data have been available first?

2. What does this document suggest about relationships among early modern science, commerce, and empire?

Jahangir, Policy toward the Hindus (seventeenth century)

The Mughal Empire flourished in the seventeenth century. Its Muslim rulers actively supported Islam as they promulgated policies of religious tolerance. The official proclamation of tolerance—even if Islam was favored at the court—was important for the management of a multicultural empire that, at its height, encompassed most of South Asia (beyond the boundaries of modern India, Pakistan, and Bangladesh). Mughal courtly culture displayed a strong Persian influence; the elite cultivated the arts, music, literature, philosophy, and science. Jahangir (1569–1627) was the fourth emperor of the dynasty (ruled 1605–1627). A protector of Islam, he is also remembered for his personal piety, promotion of religious tolerance, attention to justice, and as a patron of the arts.

This passage comes from Jahangir's *Memoirs*, written for an audience in a culture in which only elites could read. His use of the first person and a conversational tone establishes an intimacy with the reader. He is frank in his disdain for Hindu beliefs, turning to the authority of his father to establish a rationale for a policy of tolerance.

I am here led to relate that at the city of Banaras [Benares, now Varanasi] a temple had been erected. * * * The principal idol in this temple had on its head a tiara or cap, enriched with jewels. * * *

SOURCE: Jahangueir, *Memoirs of the Emperor Jahangueir*, translated by David Price (London: Oriental Translation Committee, 1829), pp. 14–15, 28–29.

[Also] placed in this temple moreover, as the associates and minis-tering servants of the principal idol, [were] four other images of solid gold, each crowned with a tiara, in the like manner enriched with precious stones. It was the belief of these Jehennemites that a dead Hindu, provided when alive he had been a worshipper, when laid before this idol would be restored to life. As I could not possi-bly give credit to such a pretence, I employed a confidential person to ascertain the truth; and, as I justly supposed, the whole was detected to be an impudent [fraud]. * * *

On this subject I must however acknowledge, that having on one occasion asked my father the reason why he had forbidden any one to prevent or interfere with the building of these haunts of idolatry, his reply was in the following terms: "My dear child," said he, "I find myself a puissant monarch, the shadow of God upon earth. I have seen that he bestows the blessings of his gracious providence upon all his creatures without distinction. * * * With all of the human race, with all of God's creatures, I am at peace: why then should I permit myself, under any consideration, to be the cause of molestation or aggression to any one? Besides, are not five parts in six * * * either Hindus or aliens to the faith; and were I to be governed by motives of the kind suggested in your inquiry, what alternative can I have but to put them all to death! I have thought it therefore my wisest plan to let these men alone. Neither is it to be forgotten, that the class of whom we are speaking * * * are usefully engaged, either in the pursuits of science or the arts, or of improvements for the benefit of mankind, and have in numerous instances arrived at the highest distinctions in the state, there being, indeed, to be found in this city men of every description, and of every religion on the face of the earth."

* * *

In the practice of being burnt on the funeral pyre of their hus-bands, as sometimes exhibited among the widows of the Hindus, I had previously directed, that no woman who was the mother of children should be thus made a sacrifice, however willing to die; and I now further ordained, that in no case was the practice to be permitted, when compulsion was in the slightest degree employed, whatever might be the opinions of the people. In other respects they were in no [way] to be molested in the duties of their religion, nor exposed to oppression or violence in any manner whatever.

Questions

1. How did Akbar, Jahangir's father, justify his policy of religious tolerance?

2. What might Jahangir hope to gain by describing aspects of Hinduism as an "impudent fraud" but also arguing strongly for its protection?

3. What limits did Jahangir set on *sati* (widow burning)? How does he use this discussion of limits to further emphasize tolerance?

Abu'l Hasan, Jahangir's Dream (c. 1618–1622)

This painting is an example of the genre of Mughal miniatures and was among the many types of visual art commissioned by Jahangir, fourth emperor of the Mughal Empire, and other elites. The artist, Abu'l Hasan (born 1588), was a court painter. Jahangir described Abu'l Hasan's work as perfect, writing in his memoir that the artist had "no rival or equal." Mughal painting incorporated symbols from Persian, Indian, and other traditions—note the winged cherubs reminiscent of Italian paintings, for example. This borrowing can be understood as either adopting symbols of power in order to mimic a rival (implying inferiority), or the appropriation of symbols as a claim to dominance. Scholars have made both arguments about this painting.

The image shows Jahangir and Shah Abbas, the Safavid emperor, embracing. This visual representation emphasizes friendly relations between two major political powers that shared a religion and cultural heritage. It was intended as a counterweight to actual tensions between the two rulers, a very real political rivalry that involved direct military confrontation, such as the Safavid capture of Kandahar. The halo—which is common in Persian art—directs the viewer's eye to Jahangir at the center of the scene. He is also bigger than Shah Abbas, who struggles to get his arms all the way around Jahangir's imposing body. The lion and lamb together symbolize peace (as in Christian and Jewish thought). It's not a coincidence that Jahangir stands on the lion—also a symbol of kingship. The pair is together atop a globe—a representation of the world they've divided between them. The painting is now owned by the Smithsonian Museum in Washington, D.C.

SOURCE: *Jahangir's Dream,* Freer Gallery of Art, Smithsonian Institution, Washington, DC: Purchase F1945.9a.

Questions

1. The lamb lies with the lion, but each animal occupies specific geo-graphic space on the globe. What does the lion's position across central Asia and the lamb's in the Mediterranean imply to Mughal viewers?

2. Abu'l Hasan's depiction of world geography looks very much like European maps of the seventeenth century. What does this similarity tell us about the transmission of knowledge across Afro-Eurasia in this period?

3. How might a painting of this subject by a Safavid artist differ from Abu'l Hasan's work?

Voltaire, Sixth Philosophical Letter (1734)

François-Marie Arouet, known as Voltaire (1694–1778), was one of the major figures of the European Enlightenment. A polymath and prolific writer, he authored philosophical essays, poetry, history, satires, and plays. A critic of the French monarchy and its institutions and an exponent of reason and religious toleration, he was often in trouble with the authorities, frequently arrested or exiled. In 1726, after a period of imprisonment in the Bastille in Paris, he went into exile in Great Britain, where he remained for over two years. He became fluent in English, and moved in the highest literary and social circles. On his return to France he published, in English, *Letters Concerning the English Nation* (1733), which was later published in French as *Lettres philosophiques*. In this introduction to British politics, culture, literature, theater, and science, he presented Britain as a model of constitutional monarchy, liberty, tolerance, and prosperity.

The Anglican religion only extends to England and Ireland. Presbyterianism is the dominant religion in Scotland. This Presby-terianism is nothing more than pure Calvinism as it was estab-

---

SOURCE: Voltaire, *Letters on England*, translated by Leonard Tancock (New York: Penguin, 1980), pp. 40–41.

lished in France and survives in Geneva. As the priests in this sect receive very small stipends from their churches, and so cannot live in the same luxury as bishops, they have taken the natural course of decrying honours they cannot attain. Picture the proud Diogenes [an ancient Greek philosopher] trampling underfoot the pride of Plato: the Scottish Presbyterians are not unlike that proud and tattered reasoner. They treated Charles II [son of Charles I, executed during the English civil war, restored to the throne in 1660 after a long exile] with much less respect than Diogenes had treated Alexander. For when they took up arms on his behalf against Cromwell [a leader of the Parliamentary party during the civil war, and Lord Protector from 1653–1658 during the English republic known as the Commonwealth] who had deceived them, they made the poor King put up with four sermons per day, they forbade him to play cards, they sat him on the stool of repentance, with the result that Charles soon grew tired of being King of these pedants and escaped from their clutches like a schoolboy playing truant.

Compared with a young and lusty French student bawling in Theology Schools in the morning and singing with the ladies at night, an English theologian is a Cato [an ancient Roman statesman known for his severity], but this Cato looks like a gay young spark compared with a priest in Scotland. The latter affects a solemn gait and scowling expression, wears a huge hat, a long cloak over a short jacket, preaches through his nose and gives the name of Whore of Babylon to all Churches in which a few ecclesiastics are fortunate enough to have an income of fifty thousand *livres* and in which the people are good enough to put up with it and call them Monsignor, Your Lordship, Your Eminence.

These gentry, who also have a few churches in England, have brought solemn and austere airs into fashion in this country. It is to them that we owe the sanctification of Sunday in the three kingdoms [England, Scotland, and Ireland]. On that day both work and play are forbidden, which is double the severity of Catholic Churches. There are no operas, plays or concerts in London on Sunday, even cards are so expressly forbidden that only people of standing and what are called respectable people, play on that day. The rest of the nation goes to the sermon, the tavern and the ladies of the town.

Although the Episcopal and Presbyterian sects are the two dominant ones in Great Britain, all the others are perfectly acceptable and live quite harmoniously together, whilst most of their preachers hate each other with almost as much cordiality as a Jansenist [member of a Catholic religious movement condemned as a heresy] damns a Jesuit.

Go into the London Stock Exchange—a more respectable place than many a court—and you will see representatives from all nations gathered together for the utility of men. Here Jew, Mohammedan and Christian deal with each other as though they were all of the same faith, and only apply the word infidel to people who go bankrupt. Here the Presbyterian trusts the Anabaptist and the Anglican accepts a promise from the Quaker. On leaving these peaceful and free assemblies some go to the Synagogue and others for a drink, this one goes to be baptized in a great bath in the name of Father, Son and Holy Ghost, that one has his son's foreskin cut and has some Hebrew words he doesn't understand mumbled over the child, others go to their church and await the inspiration of God with their hats on, and everybody is happy.

If there were only one religion in England there would be danger of despotism, if there were two they would cut each other's throats, but there are thirty, and they live in peace and happiness.

Questions

1. Why is Voltaire's discussion of the Royal Exchange relevant to his discussion of religion in Great Britain?

2. What does Voltaire think of Presbyterian ministers? What motivates them? What effect have they had on the religious and social life of Britain? What do his comments in this passage suggest about his attitude toward religious belief in general?

3. Why does Voltaire believe that Britain enjoys religious peace?

Adam Smith, On Baubles and the Demise of Feudalism (1776)

Today, Adam Smith (1723–1790) is often called the father of modern economics, but this probably would have puzzled him: he was professor (at the University of Glasgow) of logic and of moral philosophy, and was at least as well known in his lifetime for his *Theory of Moral Sentiments* (1759) as for *Wealth of Nations* (1776), from which the excerpt below is taken. His economic vision focused on agriculture and commerce, with manufacturing and technological change playing relatively minor roles.

Yet in other ways, Smith did prophesy a new political and economic order. He insisted that people naturally pursued their rational self-interest, and that governments could best promote prosperity by accepting this rather than trying to change it. As long as people had to compete fairly, without force, collusion, or monopoly, self-interested competition would produce a good overall outcome. Moreover, he insisted that national wealth should be measured by the quantity of goods and services that people consumed, not, as the then-popular doctrine of mercantilism claimed, by the size of government gold and silver reserves.

In this passage, Smith argues that the temptations of exotic goods played a crucial role in dissolving western European feudalism, replacing it with a freer and more law-abiding society, and that markets could work a similar magic elsewhere. Few historians would accept this as a picture of how change actually occurred, but it provides a powerful example of Smith, the Enlightenment philosopher: relying on a few facts and supposed general truths, he reasons about how, under the right circumstances, a better world can emerge as an accidental by-product of people's vices.

In a country which has neither foreign commerce nor any of the finer manufactures, a great proprietor, having nothing for which he can exchange the greater part of the produce of his lands which is over and above the maintenance of the cultivators, consumes the whole in rustic hospitality at home. If this surplus produce is sufficient to maintain a hundred or a thousand men, he can make use of

SOURCE: Adam Smith, *Wealth of Nations* (London: T. Nelson and Sons, 1852), pp. 167–70.

it in no other way than by maintaining a hundred or a thousand men. He is at all times, therefore, surrounded with a multitude of retainers and dependents, who, having no equivalent to give in return for their maintenance, but being fed entirely by his bounty, must obey him, for the same reason that soldiers must obey the prince who pays them. Before the extension of commerce and manufactures in Europe, the hospitality of the rich and the great, from the sovereign down to the smallest baron, exceeded every thing which, in the present times, we can easily form a notion. * * * The great Earl of Warwick is said to have entertained every day, at his different manors, 30,000 people; and though the number here may have been exaggerated, it must, however, have been very great to admit of such exaggeration. A hospitality nearly of the same kind was exercised not many years ago in many different parts of the Highlands of Scotland. It seems to be common in all nations to whom commerce and manufactures are little known. I have seen, says Doctor Pocock, an Arabian chief dine in the streets of a town where he had come to sell his cattle, and invite all passengers, even common beggars, to sit down with him and partake of his banquet.

The occupiers of land were in every respect as dependent upon the great proprietor as his retainers. Even such of them as were not in a state of villanage [legal unfreedom], were tenants at will [whom the landlord could dismiss at any time] who paid a rent in no respect equivalent to the subsistence which the land afforded them. A crown, half a crown, a sheep, a lamb, was some years ago, in the Highlands of Scotland, a common rent for lands which maintained a family. In some places it is so at this day. * * * A tenant at will, who possesses land sufficient to maintain his family for little more than a quit-rent, is as dependent upon the proprietor as any servant or retainer whatever, and must obey him with as little reserve. * * *

Upon the authority which the great proprietors necessarily had, in such a state of things, over their tenants and retainers, was founded the power of the ancient barons. They necessarily became the judges in peace, and the leaders in war, of all who dwelt upon their estates. They could maintain order, and execute the law, within their respective demesnes, because each of them could there turn the whole force of all the inhabitants against the injustice of any one. No other person had sufficient authority to do this. The king, in particular, had not. * * * To have enforced payment of a small debt within the lands of a great proprietor, where all the inhabitants were armed, and accustomed to stand by one another, would have cost the king, had he attempted it by his own authority, almost the same effort as to extinguish a civil war. He was, therefore, obliged to abandon the administration of justice, through the greater part of the country, to those who were capable of administering it; and, for the same reason, to leave the command of the country militia to those whom that militia would obey.

* * *

But what all the violence of the feudal institutions could never have effected, the silent and insensible operation of foreign commerce and manufactures gradually brought about. These gradually furnished the great proprietors with something for which they could exchange the whole surplus produce of their lands, and which they could consume themselves, without sharing it either with tenants or retainers. All for ourselves, and nothing for other people, seems, in every age of the world, to have been the vile maxim of the masters of mankind. As soon, therefore, as they could find a method of consuming the whole value of their rents themselves, they had no disposition to share them with any other persons. For a pair of diamond buckles, perhaps, or for something as frivolous and useless, they exchanged the maintenance, or, what is the same thing, the price of the maintenance of 1000 men for a year, and with it the whole weight and authority which it could give them. The buckles, however, were to be all their own, and no other human creature was to have any share of them; whereas, in the more ancient method of expense, they must have shared with at least 1000 people. With the judges that were to determine the preference, this difference was perfectly decisive; and thus, for the gratification of the most childish, the meanest, and the most sordid of all vanities they gradually bartered their whole power and authority.

In a country where there is no foreign commerce, nor any of the finer manufactures, a man of L.10,000 a-year cannot well employ his revenue in any other way than in maintaining, perhaps, 1000 families, who are all of them necessarily at his command. In the present state of Europe, a man of L.10,000 a-year can spend his whole revenue, and he generally does so, without directly maintaining twenty people, or being able to command more than ten footmen, not worth the commanding. Indirectly, perhaps, he maintains as great, or even a greater number of people, than he could have done by the ancient method of expense. For though the quantity of precious productions for which he exchanges his whole revenue be very small, the number of workmen employed in collecting and preparing it must necessarily have been very great. * * * By paying [for his luxury goods], he indirectly contributes to the maintenance of all the workmen and their employers. He generally contributes, however, but a very small proportion to [the whole annual maintenance of any particular worker]. * * * Though he contributes, therefore, to the maintenance of them all, they are all more or less independent of him, because generally they can all be maintained without him.

* * *

The same cause gradually led [great landowners] to dismiss the unnecessary part of their tenants. Farms were enlarged, and the occupiers of land, not-withstanding the complaints of depopulation, reduced to the number necessary for cultivating it, according to the imperfect state of cultivation and improvement in those times. By the removal of the unnecessary mouths, and by exacting from the farmer the full value of the farm, a greater surplus, or, what is the same thing, the price of a greater surplus, was obtained for the proprietor, which the merchants and manufacturers soon furnished him with a method of spending upon his own person, in the same manner as he had done the rest. The cause continuing to operate, he was desirous to raise his rents above what his lands, in the actual state of their improvement, could afford. His tenants could agree to this upon one condition only, that they should be secured in their possession for such a term of years as might give them time to recover, with profit, whatever they should lay out in the further improvement of the land. The expensive vanity of the landlord made him willing to accept of this condition; and hence the origin of long leases.

* * *

The tenants having in this manner become independent, and the retainers being dismissed, the great proprietors were no longer capable of interrupting the regular execution of justice, or of disturbing the peace of the country. Having sold their birth-right, not like Esau, for a mess of pottage in time of hunger and necessity, but, in the wantonness of plenty, for trinkets and baubles, fitter to be the playthings of children than the serious pursuits of men, they became as insignificant as any substantial burgher or tradesmen in a city. A regular government was established in the country as well as in the city, nobody having sufficient power to disturb its operations in the one, any more than in the other.

Questions

1. How, according to Smith, did rich men with few attractive goods available to purchase use their wealth? How did this shape the social and political order?

2. Once such men began buying "baubles," how did their relations with poorer members of society change? How did this strengthen an emerging central government?

3. What does this version of history suggest about the likelihood and limits of human progress? About how such progress occurs?

Chapter 15

REORDERING THE WORLD, 1750–1850

Declaration of the Rights of Man (1789)

This foundational document of the French Revolution was adopted by the National Constituent Assembly after King Louis XVI had tried to curtail its activities and a Parisian crowd had stormed the Bastille prison—an important symbol of royal authority. Thus before the consolidation of a written document, French political leaders and popular sentiment had already made major challenges to the king's authority, which in ancien régime political philosophy was based on divine right. Although the *Declaration of the Rights of Man* (1789) refers to a divine being, it derives its authority from the inherent nature of man, rather than from revelation or religious theology.

The *Declaration* is based on Enlightenment ideas of universal natural rights—the idea that some rights are applicable to all people and are not dependent on local laws. The *Declaration* is evidence of the growing importance of the individual and the centrality of the social contract in eighteenth-century Europe and its colonies.

As a statement of individual and collective rights, the *Declaration* is the basis for subsequent modern international human rights law. But like other documents of the eighteenth century, the notion of "universal man" has some limits. For example, it does not address slavery or gender differences, despite significant legal restrictions for both slaves and women in France (and other European countries influenced by the Enlightenment).

DECLARATION OF THE RIGHTS OF MAN AND OF CITIZENS, BY THE
NATIONAL ASSEMBLY OF FRANCE

The representatives of the people of France, formed into a National
Assembly, considering that ignorance, neglect, or contempt of
human rights, are the sole causes of public misfortunes and corrup-
tions of Government, have resolved to set forth in a solemn declaration, these natural, imprescriptible, and inalienable rights; that this
declaration being constantly present to the minds of the members
of the body social, they may be forever kept attentive to their rights
and their duties; that the acts of the legislative and executive powers
of government, being capable of being every moment compared
with the end of political institutions, may be more respected; and
also, that the future claims of the citizens, being directed by simple
and incontestable principles, may always tend to the maintenance
of the constitution, and the general happiness.

For these reasons the National Assembly doth recognise and
declare, in the presence of the Supreme Being, * * * the following
sacred rights of men and of citizens:

I. *Men are born, and always continue, free and equal in respect of
their rights. Civil distinctions, therefore, can be founded only on public utility.*

II. *The end of all political associations is the preservation of the
natural and imprescriptible rights of man; and these rights are liberty, property, security, and resistance of oppression.*

III. *The nation is essentially the source of all sovereignty; nor can
ANY INDIVIDUAL, or ANY BODY OF MEN, be entitled to any authority
which is not expressly derived from it.*

IV. Political Liberty consists in the power of doing whatever
does not injure another. The exercise of the natural rights of every
man, has no other limits than those which are necessary to secure
to every *other* man the free exercise of the same rights; and these
limits are determinable only by the law.

SOURCE: Thomas Paine, *Rights of Man*, edited by Hypatia Bradlaugh
Bonner (London: Watts and Co., 1906), pp. 53–55.

V. The law ought to prohibit only actions hurtful to society. What is not prohibited by the law should not be hindered; nor should anyone be compelled to that which the law does not require.

VI. The law is an expression of the will of the community. All citizens have a right to concur, either personally or by their representatives, in its formation. It should be the same to all, whether it protects or punishes; and all being equal in its sight, are equally eligible to all honours, places, and employments, according to their different abilities, without any other distinction than that created by their virtues and talents.

VII. No man should be accused, arrested, or held in confinement, except in cases determined by the law, and according to the forms which it has prescribed. All who promote, solicit, execute, or cause to be executed, arbitrary orders, ought to be punished, and every citizen called upon, or apprehended by virtue of the law, ought immediately to obey, and renders himself culpable by resistance.

VIII. The law ought to impose no other penalties but such as are absolutely and evidently necessary; and no one ought to be punished, but in virtue of a law promulgated before the offence, and legally applied.

IX. Every man being presumed innocent till he has been convicted, whenever his detention becomes indispensable, all rigour to him, more than is necessary to secure his person, ought to be provided against by the law.

X. No man ought to be molested on account of his opinions, not even on account of his *religious* opinions, provided his avowal of them does not disturb the public order established by the law.

XI. The unrestrained communication of thoughts and opinions being one of the most precious rights of man, every citizen may speak, write, and publish freely, provided he is responsible for the abuse of this liberty, in cases determined by the law.

XII. A public force being necessary to give security to the rights of men and of citizens, that force is instituted for the benefit of the community and not for the particular benefit of the persons to whom it is intrusted.

XIII. A common contribution being necessary for the support of the public force, and for defraying the other expenses of government, it ought to be divided equally among the members of the community, according to their abilities.

XIV. Every citizen has a right, either by himself or his representative, to a free voice in determining the necessity of public contributions, the appropriation of them, and their amount, mode of assessment, and duration.

XV. Every community has a right to demand of all its agents an account of their conduct.

XVI. Every community in which a separation of powers and a security of rights is not provided for, wants a constitution.

XVII. The right to property being inviolable and sacred, no one ought to be deprived of it, except in cases of evident public necessity, legally ascertained, and on condition of a previous just indemnity.

Questions

1. What provisions of the *Declaration* challenge the divine rights of kings? Which provisions prescribe the rights of individuals?

2. Describe the relationship between an individual and the government as envisioned by the *Declaration*. Why was this significant in 1789?

3. Although the *Declaration* makes claims for the natural rights of individuals, it also establishes the need for specific legal constraints. What can explain this contradiction?

Olympe de Gouges, Declaration of the Rights of Women and the Female Citizen (September 1791)

Born to a provincial petit-bourgeois family in France, Marie Gouze (1748–1793) married in a match without love, great fortune, or title. Widowed soon thereafter, she moved to Paris, where she changed her name to Olympe de Gouges and became a playwright and political activist. From as early as 1788 she advocated ameliorating the conditions of slaves in French colonies. An early supporter of the French Revolution, she was nevertheless critical of the decision to execute the king.

The 1791 Constitution proclaimed equal suffrage, but did not extend the vote to women. De Gouges responded with a proposed declaration of the rights of women. In a postscript to this, playing off the title of the famous pamphlet *The Social Contract* by Jean-Jacques Rousseau (1762), she included a "Form for a Social Contract between Man and Woman." This envisaged marriage as based on gender equality.

De Gouges's *Declaration* echoes concerns with property claims and individual legal recognition typical of Enlightenment debates. Her work also anticipates later feminist arguments, such as the connection between the personal and political. Charged with treason for calling the Revolution into question, de Gouges was guillotined in 1793. While de Gouges called attention to the Revolution's failure to include women among those entitled to full natural rights, the Haitian Revolution (1791–1804) challenged the French Revolution's exclusion of blacks.

POSTSCRIPT

Women, wake up; the tocsin of reason is being heard throughout the whole universe; discover your rights. The powerful empire of nature is no longer surrounded by prejudice, fanaticism, superstition, and lies. The flame of truth has dispersed all the clouds of folly and usurpation. Enslaved man has multiplied his strength and needs recourse to yours to break his chains. Having become free, he has become unjust to his companion. Oh, women, women! When will you cease to be blind? What advantage have you received from the Revolution? A more pronounced scorn, a more marked disdain. In the centuries of corruption you ruled only over the weakness of men. The reclamation of your patrimony, based on the wise decrees of nature—what have you to dread from such a fine undertaking? The *bon mot* of the legislator of the marriage of Cana? Do you fear that our French legislator, correctors of that morality, long ensnared by political practices now out of date, will only say again to you: women, what is there in common between you and us? Everything, you will have to answer. If they persist in their weakness in putting

---

SOURCE: *Women in Revolutionary Paris, 1789–1795*, translated by Darline Gay Levy, Harriet Branson Applewhite, and Mary Durham Johnson (Champaign: University of Illinois Press, 1980), pp. 92–96.

this non sequitur in contradiction to their principles, courageously oppose the force of reason to the empty pretentions of superiority; unite yourselves beneath the standards of philosophy; deploy all the energy of your character, and you will soon see these haughty men, not groveling at your feet as servile adorers, but proud to share with you the treasures of the Supreme Being. Regardless of what barriers confront you, it is in your power to free yourselves; you have only to want to.

*   *   *

Marriage is the tomb of trust and love. The married woman can with impunity give bastards to her husband, and also give them the wealth which does not belong to them. The woman who is unmarried has only one feeble right; ancient and inhuman laws refuse to her for her children the right to the name and the wealth of their father; no new laws have been made in this matter. If it is considered a paradox and an impossibility on my part to try to give my sex an honorable and just consistency, I leave it to men to attain glory for dealing with this matter; but while we wait, the way can be prepared through national education, the restoration of morals, and conjugal conventions.

FORM FOR A SOCIAL CONTRACT BETWEEN MAN AND WOMAN

We, _____ and _____, moved by our own will, unite ourselves for the duration of our lives, and for the duration of our mutual inclinations, under the following conditions: We intend and wish to make our wealth communal, meanwhile reserving to ourselves the right to divide it in favor of our children and of those toward whom we might have a particular inclination, mutually recognizing that our property belongs directly to our children, from whatever bed they come, and that all of them without distinction have the right to bear the name of the fathers and mothers who have acknowledged them, and we are charged to subscribe to the law which punishes the renunciation of one's own blood. We likewise obligate ourselves, in case of separation, to divide our wealth and to set aside in advance the portion the law indicates for our children, and in the event of a perfect union, the one who dies will divest himself of half his property in his children's favor, and if one dies childless, the survivor will inherit by right, unless the dying person has disposed of half the common property in favor of one whom he judged deserving.

That is approximately the formula for the marriage act I propose for execution. Upon reading this strange document, I see rising up against me the hypocrites, the prudes, the clergy, and the whole infernal sequence. But . . . it [my proposal] offers to the wist the moral means of achieving the perfection of a happy government * * *

Moreover, I would like a law which would assist widows and young girls deceived by the false promises of a man to whom they were attached; I would like, I say, this law to force an inconstant man to hold to his obligations or at least [to pay] an indemnity equal to his wealth. Again, I would like this law to be rigorous against women, at least those who have the effrontery to have recourse to a law which they themselves had violated by their misconduct, if proof of that were given. At the same time, as I showed in *Le Bonheur primitif de l'homme*, in 1788, that prostitutes should be placed in designated quarters. It is not prostitutes who contribute the most to the depravity of morals, it is the women of society. In regenerating the latter, the former are changed. This link of fraternal union will first bring disorder, but in consequence it will produce at the end a perfect harmony.

I offer a foolproof way to elevate the soul of women; it is to join them to all the activities of man; if man persists in finding this way impractical, let him share his fortune with woman, not at his caprice, but by the wisdom of laws. Prejudice falls, morals are purified, and nature regains all her rights. Add to this the marriage of priests and the strengthening of the king on his throne, and the French government cannot fail.

Questions

1. What changes in property rights does de Gouges ask for? Why would inheritance and property rights be among the first claims de Gouges made in this document?

2. What other material needs of women does de Gouges identify? How does she connect these to ideas about natural rights?

3. Are de Gouges's assertions of necessary moral change comparable to the changes in political and property rights claimed by *the Declaration of the Rights of Man* (see previous selection)? Why or why not?

Maximilien Robespierre, Report on the Principles of a Revolutionary Government (1793)

When Maximilien Robespierre (1758–1794) gave this speech on December 25, 1793, the French Revolution had become increasingly radical. The monarchy had been abolished and a republic proclaimed in 1792. The republic had executed the king in 1793; it was at war with many European powers and facing internal rebellions. Feeling threatened by enemies both within and without, and facing a crisis in requisitioning supplies for the army, the National Convention (the republic's legislative body) established the Committee of Public Safety in 1793. Its dominant member was Robespierre. The committee became in effect the executive organ of the revolutionary government. To crush the presumed enemies of the republic, it launched "the Terror" (September 1793–July 1794). Several thousand people, many of them uninvolved in counter-revolutionary activity, were executed, often with only a semblance of a trial. Eventually the excesses of the Terror alienated enough people that Robespierre fell from power and was guillotined.

Citizens, members of the Convention! Success induces the weak to sleep, but fills the strong with even more powers of resistance.

* * *

The defenders of the Republic will be guided by Caesar's maxim, and believe that nothing has been accomplished so long as anything remains to be accomplished.

To judge by the power and the will of our republican soldiers, it will be easy to defeat the English and the traitors. But we have another task of no less importance, but unfortunately of greater difficulty. This task is the task of frustrating, by an uninterrupted excess of energy, the eternal intrigues of all enemies of freedom within the country, and of paving the way for the victory of the principles on which the general weal depends.

* * *

Let us first demonstrate the principles and the necessity of a revolutionary government, after which we shall describe those factors that aim to paralyze the birth of such a government.

The theory of the revolutionary government is as new as the Revolution itself, from which this government was born. This theory may not be found in the books of the political writers who were unable to predict the Revolution, nor in the law books of the tyrants. The revolutionary government is the cause of the fear of the aristocracy, or the pretext for its calumnies. For the tyrants this government is a scandal, for most people it is a miracle. It must be explained to all, so that at least all good citizens may be rallied around the principles of the general weal. * * *

The goal of a constitutional government is the protection of the Republic; that of a revolutionary government is the establishment of the Republic.

SOURCE: *Introduction to Contemporary Civilization in the West*, 2nd ed., edited by the Contemporary Civilization Staff of Columbia College, Columbia University (New York: Columbia University Press, 1954), vol. 1, pp. 51–56.

The Revolution is the war waged by liberty against its foes—but the Constitution is the régime of victorious and peaceful freedom.

The Revolutionary Government will need to put forth extraordinary activity, because it is at war. It is subject to no constant laws, since the circumstances under which it prevails are those of a storm, and change with every moment. This government is obliged unceasingly to disclose new sources of energy to oppose the rapidly changing face of danger.

Under constitutional rule, it is sufficient to protect individuals against the encroachments of the state power. Under a revolutionary régime, the state power itself must protect itself against all that attack it.

The revolutionary government owes a national protection to good citizens; to its foes it owes only death. * * *

Is the revolutionary government, by reason of the greater rapidity of its course and the greater freedom of its movements than are characteristic of an ordinary government, therefore less just and less legitimate? No, it is based on the most sacred of all laws, on the general weal and on the ironclad law of necessity!

This government has nothing in common with anarchy or with disorder; on the contrary, its goal requires the destruction of anarchy and disorder in order to realize a dominion of law. It has nothing in common with autocracy, for it is not inspired by personal passions.

The measure of its strength is the stubbornness and perfidy of its enemies; the more cruelly it proceeds against its enemies, the closer is its intimacy with the republicans; the greater the severities required from it by circumstances, the more must it recoil from unnecessary violations of private interests, unless the latter are demanded by the public necessity. * * *

If we were permitted a choice between an excess of patriotism and a base deficiency in public spirit, or even a morass of moderation, our choice should soon be made. A healthy body, tormented by an excess of strength, has better prospects than a corpse.

Let us beware of slaying patriotism in the delusion that we are healing and moderating it.

* * *

By virtue of five years of treason, by virtue of feeble precautions, and by virtue of our gullibility, Austria, England, Russia and Italy have had time to set up, as it were, a secret government in France, a government that competes with the French government. They have their secret committees, their treasures, their agents, they absorb men from us and appropriate them to themselves, they have the unity that we lack, they have the policy that we have often neglected, they have the consistency which we have so often failed to show.

Foreign courts have for some time been spewing out on French soil their well-paid criminals. Their agents still infect our armies. * * * All the bravery of our soldiers, all the devotion of our generals, and all the heroism of the members of this Assembly had to be put forth to defeat treason. These gentlemen still speak in our administrative bodies, in the various sections; they secure admission to the clubs; they sometimes may be found sitting among us; they lead the counter-revolution; they lurk about us, they eavesdrop on our secrets; they flatter our passions and seek even to influence our opinions and to turn our own decisions against us. When you are weak, they praise our caution. When you are cautious, they accuse us of weakness. Your courage they designate as audacity, your justice as cruelty. If we spare them, they will conspire publicly; if we threaten them, they will conspire secretly or under the mask of patriotism. Yesterday they murdered the defenders of liberty; to-day they mingle in the procession of mourners and weep for their own victims. Blood has flowed all over the country on their account, but we need this blood in the struggle against the tyrants of Europe. The foreigners have set themselves up as the arbitrators of public peace; they have sought to do their work with money; at their behest, the people found bread; when they willed it otherwise, the bread was not available; they succeeded in inaugurating gatherings in front of the bakeshops and in securing the leadership of bands of famished men. We are surrounded by their hired assassins and their spies. We know this, we witness it ourselves, and yet they live! The perfidious emissaries who address us, who flatter us—these are the brothers, the accomplices, the bodyguard of those who destroy our crops, who threaten our cities, massacre our brothers, cut down our prisoners. They are all looking for a leader, even among us. Their chief interest is to incite us to enmity among ourselves * * * We shall continue to make war, war against England, against the Austrians, against all their allies. Our only possible answer to their pamphlets and lies is to destroy them. And we shall know how to hate the enemies of our country.

It is not in the hearts of the poor and the patriots that the fear of terror must dwell, but there in the midst of the camp of the foreign brigands, who would bargain for our skin, who would drink the blood of the French people.

The Committee of Public Safety has recognized that the law does not punish the great criminals with the necessary swiftness. Foreigners, well-known agents of the allied kings, generals besmirched with the blood of Frenchmen * * * have long been in custody and are yet not executed.

The conspirators are very numerous. It is far less necessary to punish a hundred unknown, obscure wretches, than to seize and put to death a single leader of the conspirators.

* * * We propose to you that the Committee of Public Safety be entrusted with the task of introducing a number of innovations in this connection, with the purpose of strengthening and accelerating the hand of justice in its procedure against intrigues. You have already commissioned the Committee, in a decree, to this effect. We propose that you create the means by which its judgments may be accelerated against foreigners and against generals conspiring with the tyrants.

Questions

1. How does a revolutionary government differ from a constitutional government?

2. What does Robespierre view as the most serious dangers to the French republic?

3. How do Robespierre's views compare with those expressed in the *Declaration of the Rights of Man* (see *Declaration of the Rights of Man*, in this chapter)?

Olaudah Equiano, The Case against the Slave Trade (1789)

Questions about the legitimacy of slavery increased in number and intensity throughout the Atlantic world in the eighteenth century. The British abolition movement—which sought to end the slave trade, not emancipate existing slaves—found a passionate and informed voice in Olaudah Equiano, a formerly enslaved African who labored in North America before finding passage to England. Purchased by a naval officer, Equiano traveled widely around the Atlantic. He converted to Christianity in 1759 and was baptized while in England. He was sold again to a Quaker merchant who helped him master reading and writing and allowed him to trade on his own account—a means by which Equiano earned enough money to buy his freedom. Uncomfortable as a free black in North America, Equiano moved to London where he became involved in the abolitionist movement.

Equiano wrote the *Interesting Narrative* in English. Upon its first publication in 1789, it quickly achieved widespread recognition. The book remains in print and is an important source for understanding the experiences of those enslaved, since most slaves had neither the education nor time to write. Note Equiano's facility with English rhetorical style, and his adept use of both Enlightenment and Christian thought to make his case. Where seventeenth-century observers such as Thomas Phillips (see Thomas Phillips, Buying Slaves at Whydah, in Chapter 13) and Richard Ligon (see Richard Ligon, *A True and Exact History of the Island of Barbadoes*, in Chapter 13) brought up the humanity of slaves in the context of describing them as either commodities or labor, in this passage Equiano takes the shared humanity of slaves and Britons for granted, and instead argues the economic benefits of abolition.

———

I hope to have the satisfaction of seeing the renovation of liberty and justice, resting on the British government, to vindicate the

SOURCE: Olaudah Equiano, *The Interesting Narrative of the Life of Olaudah Equiano or Gustavus Vassa, the African*, 9th ed. (London, 1794), pp. 353–58. Text modernized by Norton authors for this edition.

honor of our common nature. These are concerns which do not perhaps belong to any particular office: but, to speak more seriously, to every man of sentiment, actions like these are the just and sure foundations of future fame; a reversion, though remote, is coveted by some noble minds as a substantial good. It is upon these grounds that I hope and expect the attention of gentlemen in power. These are designs consonant to the elevation of their rank, and the dignity of their stations; they are ends suitable to the nature of a free and generous government; and, connected with views of empire and dominion, suited to the benevolence and solid merit of the legislature. It is a pursuit of substantial greatness. May the time come—at least the speculation to me is pleasing—when the sable people shall gratefully commemorate the auspicious era of extensive freedom: then shall those persons particularly be named with praise and honor, who generously proposed and stood forth in the cause of humanity, liberty, and good policy; and brought to the ear of the legislature designs worthy of royal patronage and adoption. May Heaven make the British senators the dispersers of light, liberty and science, to the uttermost parts of the earth: then will be glory to God in the highest, on earth peace, and goodwill to men—Glory, honor, peace, etc. to every soul of man that worketh good; to the Britons first (because to them the gospel is preached), and also to the nations. "Those that honor their Maker, have mercy on the poor." "It is righteousness exalteth a nation, but sin is a reproach to any people: destruction shall be to the workers of iniquity, and the wicked shall fall by their own wickedness." May the blessings of the Lord be upon the heads of all those who commiserated the cases of the oppressed Negroes, and the fear of God prolong their days; and may their expectations be filled with gladness! "The liberal devise liberal things, and by liberal things shall stand" (Isaiah 22:8). They can say with pious Job, "Did I not weep for him that was in trouble; Was not my soul grieved for the poor?" (Job 30:25).

As the inhuman traffic of slavery is now taken into the consideration of the British legislature, I doubt not, if a system of commerce was established in Africa, the demand for manufactures would most rapidly augment, as the native inhabitants would insensibly adopt the British fashions, manners, customs, etc. In proportion to the civilization, so will be the consumption of British manufactures.

The wear and tear of a continent, nearly twice as large as Europe, and rich in vegetable and mineral productions, is much easier conceived than calculated.

A case in point—It cost the Aborigines of Britain little or nothing in clothing, etc. The difference between their forefathers and the present generation, in point of consumption, is literally infinite. The supposition is most obvious. It will be equally immense in Africa— The same cause, *viz.* civilization, will ever have the same effect.

It is trading upon safe grounds. A commercial intercourse with Africa opens an inexhaustible source of wealth to the manufacturing interest of Great Britain, and to all which the slave trade is an objection.

If I am not misinformed, the manufacturing interest is equal, if not superior to the landed interests, as to the value, for reasons which will soon appear. The abolition of slavery, so diabolical, will give a most rapid extension of manufactures, which is totally and diametrically opposite to what some interested people assert.

The manufactures of this country must and will, in their nature and reason of things, have a full and constant employ, by supplying the African markets.

Population, the bowels and surface of Africa, abound in valuable and useful returns; the hidden treasures of centuries will be brought to light and into circulation. Industry, enterprise, and mining, will have their full scope, proportionably as they civilize. In a word, it lays open an endless field of commerce to the British manufacturers and merchant adventurer. The manufacturing interest and the general interests are synonymous. The abolition of slavery would be in reality a universal good.

Tortures, murder, and every other imaginable barbarity and iniquity, are practiced upon the poor slaves with impunity. I hope the slave trade will be abolished. I pray it may be an event at hand. The great body of manufacturers, uniting in their cause, will considerably facilitate and expedite it; and, as I have already stated, it is most substantially their interest and advantage, and as such the nation's at large (except those persons concerned in the manufacturing

[of] neck-yokes, collars, chains, handcuffs, leg-bolts, drags, thumb-screws, iron-muzzles, and coffins; cats, scourges, and other instru-ments of torture used in the slave trade). In a short time one sentiment alone will prevail, from motives of interest as well as justice and humanity. Europe contains one hundred and twenty millions of inhabitants. Query—How many millions doth Africa contain? Sup-posing the Africans, collectively and individually, to expend 5£ a head in raiment [clothing] and furniture yearly when civilized, etc. an immensity beyond the reach of imagination!

This I conceive to be a theory founded upon facts, and there-fore an infallible one. If the blacks were permitted to remain in their own country, they would double themselves every fifteen years. In proportion to such increase will be the demand for manufactures. Cotton and indigo grow spontaneously in most parts of Africa; a consideration this of no small consequence to the manufactur-ing towns of Great Britain. It opens a most immense, glorious, and happy prospect—the clothing, etc. of a continent ten thousand miles in circumference, and immensely rich in productions of every denomination in return for manufactures.

Questions

1. Who was Equiano's intended audience?

2. Equiano makes both moral and economic arguments against slavery. Which arguments would have been more persuasive with his intended audience?

3. Compare the economic benefits of abolition as presented by Equiano to the economic role of slaves as presented by Phillips (see Thomas Phillips, Buying Slaves at Whydah, in Chapter 13) and Ligon (see Richard Ligon, *A True and Exact History of the Island of Barbadoes*, in Chapter 13).

George Valentia, Calcutta (1809)

George Annesley (1770–1844), Viscount Valentia (and later Earl of Mountnorris), was an English aristocrat. He served briefly in the army and for four years in Parliament. Between 1802 and 1806—at the height of worldwide struggles between the British and Napoleonic empires—he traveled in Asia and Africa, later publishing a heavily illustrated three-volume account: *Voyages and Travels to India, Ceylon, the Red Sea, Abyssinia, and Egypt, in the Years 1802, 1803, 1804, 1805, and 1806.*

These were years of impressive expansion for the British Empire, but also of intense anxiety about security and the basis of social order—due both to the military conflicts accompanying expansion and to questions raised by the French Revolution. (Valentia was in France when the revolution broke out, but left quickly.) In the passage below, he moves quickly back and forth between describing the comfortable life of the British elite in Calcutta and concerns about how they might undermine their own position: either through fathering (and employing) mixed-blood children, or by unsettling society through the promotion of Christianity. It is worth bearing in mind as you read this that there were almost no European women in Calcutta at this time, and very large income differences between elite Europeans and ordinary clerks, soldiers, etc., among the British. Spelling has been updated in the following excerpt to reflect modern orthography.

It was formerly the fashion for gentlemen to dress in white jackets on all occasions, which were well suited to the country; but being thought too much an undress for public occasions, they are now laid aside for English cloth. The architecture of all the houses is Grecian, which I think by no means the best adapted to the country, as the pillars, which are generally used in the verandahs, require too great an elevation to keep out the sun, during the greater part of the morning and evening, although the heat is excessive at both

SOURCE: George Valentia, *Voyages and Travels to India, Ceylon, the Red Sea, Abyssinia, and Egypt* (London: William Miller, 1809), vol. 1, pp. 240–43, 250.

those periods. In the rainy season it is still worse, as the wet beats in, and renders them totally useless. The more confined Hindu or Gothic architecture, would surely be preferable.

On Lord Wellesley's first arrival in this country, he set his face decidedly against horse-racing, and every other species of gambling; yet at the end of November, 1803, there were three day's races at a small distance from Calcutta. Very large sums were betted, and of course were lost by the inexperienced. There are a few steady and practised gamblers, who encourage every species of play among the young servants of the [East India] Company, and make a considerable profit by their imprudence. As those are marked characters, I wonder they are not sent away.

The most rapidly accumulating evil of Bengal is the increase of half caste children. They are forming the first step to colonization, by creating a link of union between the English and the natives. In every country where this intermediate caste has been permitted to rise, it has ultimately tended to the ruin of that country. Spanish America and St. Domingo are examples of this fact. Their increase in India is beyond calculation; and though possibly there may be nothing to fear from the sloth of the Hindus, and the rapidly declining consequence of the Muslims, yet it may be justly apprehended that this tribe may hereafter become too powerful for control. Although they are not permitted to hold offices under the Company, yet they act as clerks in almost every mercantile house, and many of them are annually sent to England to receive the benefit of an European education. With numbers in their favour, with a close relationship to the natives, and without an equal proportion of that pusillanimity and indolence which is natural to them, what may not in time be dreaded from them? I have no hesitation in saying that the evil ought to be stopt; and I know no other way of effecting this object, than by obliging every father of half caste children, to send them to Europe, prohibiting their return in any capacity whatsoever. The expense that would thus attend upon children, would certainly operate as a check to the extension of zenanas [women's quarters in a large house], which are now but too common among the Europeans; and this would be a benefit to the country, no less in a moral, than in a political view.

After making these observations, I turn with much satisfaction to the brighter parts of the character of my Eastern countrymen. I can truly affirm, that they are hospitable in the highest degree, and that their generosity is unbounded. When an officer of respectability dies, in either the civil or military service, leaving a widow or children, a subscription is immediately set on foot, which in every instance has proved liberal, and not unfrequently has conferred on the parties a degree of affluence, that the life of the husband or parent could not for years have insured them. The hearts of the British in this country seem expanded by opulence: they do every thing upon a princely scale; and consequently do not save half the money that might be done with a narrower economy. The beginning, however, of a fortune being once made, it collects as rapidly as a snow ball. In seven years, or less, a capital is doubled; so that ten thousand rupees given to a child at birth, is a handsome independence by the time it arrives at the age of twenty one.

* * * Is it not [more] reasonable to suppose that there are insurmountable obstacles in the habits, laws, and religious prejudices of the inhabitants, that have prevented the pure doctrines of Christianity from having the same force over the minds of the Indians that they acquired over the Japanese, Chinese, and other nations? Has not the Muslim religion met with the same resistance from its first appearance, through the plenitude of its power, to its present decay? The Sultans found they could destroy their subjects, they could raze their temples, but they could not convert them; not from any antipathy to the religion of their masters, but from an attachment to their own. Yet we should remember, that the Sultans had advantages that we have not; they had a real, a physical power in the country, which rendered them superior to any risk of rebellion.

Very little encouragement is afforded therefore by past experience to expect that the future exertions of Missionaries should prove successful in converting the Hindus from a religion to which they are so bigottedly attached, and which is interwoven with their whole civil polity; while the danger of such attempts, if apparently favoured by the British Government, is manifest and urgent.

I cannot forbear expressing my dissent from an opinion supported by Dr. Buchanan and other advocates for conversion that if the Hindus were to become Christians, they would be better subjects to the British dominion. I have no doubt that should this point be attained, they would presently cease to be subjects altogether. At present the Hindu is irrevocably bound by the law of castes, to continue in that situation in life to which he is born, and no exertion of talent can raise him one step beyond it: he therefore looks with perfect apathy on the political intrigues of the higher orders, and dreads a revolution as productive of great personal distress, and as putting to hazard his life and little property. But were the path of ambition laid open to him by that equalization which would be the consequence of the destruction of castes, and the general reception of Christianity; talents would have their free career, and every man of spirit would consider himself as the establisher of his own fortune. Is it credible, then, that in such an event, so many millions of natives would submit to be governed by a few thousand Europeans, to whom they could feel no natural attachment, or obligation of allegiance?

Upon the whole, I am fully persuaded that the first step to be taken is that of rendering our own religion respectable in the eyes of our Indian subjects, by an establishment of greater splendour and dignity, and especially by a better choice and more vigilant inspection of the regular clergy; and that Government should studiously avoid interesting itself in the conversion of the natives, since it is impossible that they should not connect in their minds the zeal of proselyting, exerted by those in power, with a plan of coercion and intolerance. If placing in the hands of the Hindus translations of the Scriptures into the languages of the country, will not induce them to make unfavourable comparisons between our lives and our doctrines, and consequently expose us to contempt, no objection can be made to such a dissemination of the principles of true religion. To its silent operation the cause of Christianity should be left, and who will not rejoice in its success?

Questions

1. What does Valentia see as the positive and negative points of British society in Calcutta? What tensions are evident within it?

2. Why is Valentia so worried about half-caste children? How does he contrast them with the other inhabitants of Calcutta?

3. Why does Valentia think that Christian missionary work in India is likely to be futile? Why does he think it could be dangerous?

Testimony for the Factory Act (1833)

Debates in England around factory working conditions highlighted growing tensions about whether or not a modern government should regulate economic relations to serve human needs. The centrality of textile production, especially cotton fabric, to the British economy meant that industry (along with mining) received a great deal of scrutiny. Starting in 1802, Parliament passed various factory acts—reforms aimed at improving the health and safety of workers. (Such acts still regulate the workplace today.)

The implementation of factory production required a major change in schedules from seasonal, agrarian work cycles and introduced new concepts of work discipline. The reforming impulse behind the early factory acts did not challenge this discipline; it just sought to reduce the number of hours that workers were subjected to it.

The following passage provides three perspectives on factory labor considered in the proceedings leading up to the 1833 act—the medical examiners, a worker, and a mill owner. A central question was the desirability of a ten-hour work day. The final act stipulated that children fourteen to eighteen years old could not work longer than twelve hours without a lunch break, children nine to thirteen years old could not work longer than eight hours without a break, and children under age nine could not work in the textile industry.

TESTIMONY OF THE COMMISSION OF MEDICAL EXAMINERS

The account of the physical condition of the manufacturing population in the large towns in the North-eastern District of England is

---

SOURCE: *Second Report by Factories Inquiry Commission* (London: House of Commons, 1833), pp. 5, 26–28.

less favourable. It is of this district that the Commissioners state, "We have found undoubted instances of children five years old sent to work thirteen hours a day; and frequently of children nine, ten, and eleven consigned to labour for fourteen and fifteen hours." The effects ascertained by the Commissioners in many cases are, "deformity," and in still more "stunted growth, relaxed muscles, and slender conformation:" "twisting of the ends of the long bones, relaxation of the ligaments of the knees, ankles, and the like." "The representation that these effects are so common and universal as to enable some persons invariably to distinguish factory children from other children is, I have no hesitation in saying, an exaggerated and unfaithful picture of their general condition; at the same time it must be said, that the individual instances in which some one or other of those effects of severe labour are discernible are rather frequent than rare. * * * "Upon the whole, there remains no doubt upon my mind, that under the system pursued in many of the factories, the children of the labouring classes stand in need of, and ought to have, legislative protection against the conspiracy insensibly formed between their masters and parents, to tax them to a degree of toil beyond their strength."

"In conclusion, I think it has been clearly proved that children have been worked a most unreasonable and cruel length of time daily, and that even adults have been expected to do a certain quantity of labour which scarcely any human being is able to endure. I am of opinion no child under fourteen years of age should work in a factory of any description for more than eight hours a day. From fourteen upwards I would recommend that no individual should, under any circumstances, work more than twelve hours a day; although if practicable, as a physician, I would prefer the limitation of ten hours, for all persons who earn their bread by their industry."

✳ ✳ ✳

TESTIMONY OF JOHN WRIGHT

How long have you been employed in a silk-mill?—More than thirty years.

Did you enter it as a child?—Yes, betwixt five and six.

How many hours a day did you work then?—The same thirty years ago as now.

What are those hours?—Eleven hours per day and two over-hours: over-hours are working after six in the evening till eight. The regular hours are from six in the morning to six in the evening, and two others are two over-hours: about fifty years ago they began working over-hours.

*   *   *

Why, then, are those employed in them said to be in such a wretched condition?—In the first place, the great number of hands congregated together, in some rooms forty, in some fifty, in some sixty, and I have known some as many as 100, which must be injurious to both health and growing. In the second place, the privy is in the factory, which frequently emits an unwholesome smell; and it would be worth while to notice in the future erection of mills, that there be betwixt the privy door and the factory wall a kind of a lobby of cage-work. 3dly, The tediousness and the everlasting sameness in the first process preys much on the spirits, and makes the hands spiritless. 4thly, the extravagant number of hours a child is compelled to labour and confinement, which for one week is seventy-six hours. * * * 5thly, About six months in the year we are obliged to use either gas, candles, or lamps, for the longest portion of that time, nearly six hours a day, being obliged to work amid the smoke and soot of the same; and also a large portion of oil and grease is used in the mills.

What are the effects of the present system of labour?—From my earliest recollections, I have found the effects to be awfully detrimental to the well-being of the operative; I have observed frequently children carried to factories, unable to walk, and that entirely owing to excessive labour and confinement. The degradation of the workpeople baffles all description: frequently have two of my sisters been obliged to be assisted to the factory and home again, until by-and-by they could go no longer, being totally crippled in their legs. And in the next place, I remember some ten or twelve years ago working in one of the largest firms in Macclesfield, (Messrs. Baker and Pearson,) with about twenty-five men, where they were scarce one half fit for His Majesty's service. Those that are straight in their limbs are stunted in their growth; much inferior to their fathers in point of strength. 3dly, Through excessive labour and confinement there is often a total loss of appetite; a kind of langour steals over the whole frame—enters to the very core—saps the foundation of the best constitution—and lays our strength prostrate in the dust. In the 4th place, by protracted labour there is an alarming increase of cripples in various parts of this town, which has come under my own observation and knowledge.

* * *

Are all these cripples made in the silk factories?—Yes, they are, I believe.

* * *

TESTIMONY OF WILLIAM HARTER

What effect would it have on your manufacture to reduce the hours of labour to ten?—It would instantly much reduce the value of my mill and machinery, and consequently of far prejudice my manufacture.

How so?—They are calculated to produce a certain quantity of work in a given time. Every machine is valuable in proportion to the quantity of work which it will turn off in a given time. It is impossible that the machinery could produce as much work in ten hours as in twelve. If the tending of the machines were a laborious occupation, the difference in the quantity of work might not always be in exact proportion to the difference of working time; but in my mill, and silk-mills in general, the work requires the least imaginable labour; therefore it is perfectly impossible that the machines could produce as much work in ten hours as in twelve. The produce would vary in about the same ratio as the working time.

Questions

1. The medical examiners directly linked child labor to poor physical health. What conditions did they cite as particularly harmful, and what remedy did they propose?

2. John Wright did not directly challenge the length of the work day. What complaints about workplace conditions did he raise? Would a reduction in work hours have improved the consequences of those conditions? Why or why not?

3. How did William Harter justify a twelve-hour workday? What can you infer about the government's sympathies from the provisions of the 1833 act?

Domingo Sarmiento, Life in the Argentine Republic in the Days of the Tyrants (1845)

Domingo Faustino Sarmiento (1811–1888) grew up in rural Argentina during the often turbulent years following independence. His early activities ranged from founding a newspaper to creating a secular high school for girls. After participating in a failed rebellion, he fled to Chile, where he worked as an educator and journalist, publishing *Life in the Argentine Republic in the Days of the Tyrants*. He said at the time that his greatest ambition was to lift Argentina up from "barbarism" by "teaching the masses to read."

Sarmiento visited various European countries, but rejected them as models for Argentina because they were too aristocratic. He then turned to the United States, becoming very interested in its local government, public libraries, and especially public schools. After a successful rebellion in Argentina, Sarmiento returned and served as president from 1868 to 1874. He instituted various social and educational reforms, but ruled as an authoritarian.

As Europe industrialized, it began to import large amounts of farm goods from overseas. This demand, plus improved transport, made it profitable to turn relatively remote areas, ideal for grazing herds, into more densely settled farmland. The changes that accompanied this transformation were often quite wrenching; urban elites, like Sarmiento, saw this as a necessary step in "civilizing" the frontiers, while people living on resource frontiers—cowboys, hunters and trappers, wildcat miners, etc.—often felt that their way of life was being destroyed by "progress."

Buenos Ayres is destined to be some day the most gigantic city of either America. Under a benignant climate, mistress of the navigation of a hundred rivers flowing past her feet, covering a vast area, and surrounded by inland provinces which know no other outlet for their products, she would ere now have become the Babylon of America, if the spirit of the Pampa had not breathed upon her, and left undeveloped the rich offerings which the rivers and provinces should unceasingly bring. She is the only city in the vast Argentine territory which is in communication with European nations; she alone can avail herself of the advantages of foreign commerce; she alone has power and revenue. Vainly have the provinces asked to receive through her, civilization, industry, and European population; a senseless colonial policy made her deaf to these cries. But the provinces had their revenge when they sent to her in [Juan Manuel de] Rosas [rancher, general, and Conservative political leader] the climax of their own barbarism.

* * *

The cities of Buenos Ayres and Cordova have succeeded better than the others in establishing about them subordinate towns to serve as new foci of civilization and municipal interests; a fact which deserves notice. The inhabitants of the city wear the European dress, live in a civilized manner, and possess laws, ideas of progress, means of instruction, some municipal organization, regular forms of government, etc. Beyond the precincts of the city everything assumes a new aspect; the country people wear a different dress, which I will call South American, as it is common to all districts; their habits of

SOURCE: Domingo Sarmiento, *Life in the Argentine Republic in the Days of the Tyrants* (New York: Hafner Press, 1960), pp. 5, 14–16, 18. Originally published in 1868.

life are different, their wants peculiar and limited. The people composing these two distinct forms of society, do not seem to belong to the same nation. Moreover, the countryman, far from attempting to imitate the customs of the city, rejects with disdain its luxury and refinement; and it is unsafe for the costume of the city people, their coats, their cloaks, their saddles, or anything European, to show themselves in the country. Everything civilized which the city contains is blockaded there, proscribed beyond its limits; and any one who should dare to appear in the rural districts in a frock-coat, for example, or mounted on an English saddle, would bring ridicule and brutal assaults upon himself.

The whole remaining population inhabit the open country, which, whether wooded or destitute of the larger plants, is generally level, and almost everywhere occupied by pastures, in some places of such abundance and excellence, that the grass of an artificial meadow would not surpass them. * * * [T]he means of subsistence of the inhabitants—for we cannot call it their occupation—is stock-raising. Pastoral life reminds us of the Asiatic plains, which imagination covers with Kalmuck, Cossack, or Arab tents. The primitive life of nations—a life essentially barbarous and unprogressive—the life of Abraham, which is that of the Bedouin of to-day, prevails in the Argentine plains, although modified in a peculiar manner by civilization. * * *

Nomad tribes do not exist in the Argentine plains; the stock-raiser is a proprietor, living upon his own land; but this condition renders association impossible, and tends to scatter separate families over an immense extent of surface. Imagine an expanse of two thousand square leagues, inhabited throughout, but where the dwellings are usually four or even eight leagues apart, and two leagues, at least, separate the nearest neighbors. The production of movable property is not impossible, the enjoyments of luxury are not wholly incompatible with this isolation; wealth can raise a superb edifice in the desert. But the incentive is wanting; no example is near; the inducements for making a great display which exist in a city, are not known in that isolation and solitude. Inevitable privations justify natural indolence; a dearth of all the amenities of life induces all the externals of barbarism. Society has altogether disappeared. There is but the isolated self-concentrated feudal family. Since there is no collected society, no government is possible; there is neither municipal nor executive power, and civil justice has no means of reaching criminals. I doubt if the modern world presents any other form of association so monstrous as this.

* * *

Moral progress, and the cultivation of the intellect, are here not only neglected, as in the Arab or Tartar tribe, but impossible. Where can a school be placed for the instruction of children living ten leagues apart in all directions? Thus, consequently, civilization can in no way be brought about. Barbarism is the normal condition, and it is fortunate if domestic customs preserve a small germ of morality. Religion feels the consequences of this want of social organization. The offices of the pastor are nominal, the pulpit has no audience, the priest flees from the deserted chapel, or allows his character to deteriorate in inactivity and solitude.

Questions

1. Why does Sarmiento think it is a big problem that the people in the countryside "disdain [the city's] luxury and refinement"?

2. How do Sarmiento's various comparisons make rural people seem as if they belong to another time or another place?

3. What does "civilization" mean to Sarmiento? What are the main obstacles it faces in Argentina?

Chapter 16

ALTERNATIVE VISIONS
OF THE NINETEENTH
CENTURY

Honda Toshiaki, A Secret Plan of Government (1798)

Honda Toshiaki (1744–1822) was born in the provinces, but traveled to Edo (now Tokyo) at age eighteen to study mathematics. Within a few years he was a renowned mathematician with his own school. Dissatisfied with Japanese mathematics, he traveled to Nagasaki (Japan's one semi-open port) to learn Dutch, and through Dutch, European math, astronomy, and physics. Subsequently, Honda became even more interested in practical issues connected to navigation, shipping, commerce, economics, and government reform. Whenever possible, he tried to analyze these matters quantitatively; he would have been very much at home among some of his western European contemporaries who described their studies as "political arithmetic." And—again like some contemporaries, in both Europe and China—Honda became concerned that Japan's increasing population would soon put an intolerable strain on the society's resources. For this reason he became a strong advocate of both commercial and territorial expansion, and of technologies that would facilitate such expansion. His policy recommendations were not adopted and remained little known during his lifetime, but attracted greater attention in the nineteenth century. In his 1798 book, Toshiaki discussed why Japan needed to think about competition with other powers and learn European ways to compete successfully.

The book was more influential after his death than at its original publication.

It is because of the danger of such occurrences that in Europe a king governs his subjects with solicitude. It is considered to be the appointed duty of a king to save his people from hunger and cold by shipping and trading. This is the reason why there are no bandits in Europe. Such measures are especially applicable to Japan, which is a maritime nation, and it is obvious that transport and trade are essential functions of the government.

Ships which are at present engaged in transport do not leave coastal waters and put out to sea. They always have to skirt along the shore, and can navigate only by using as landmarks mountains or islands within visible range. Sometimes, as it inevitably happens, they are blown out to sea by a storm and lose their way. Then, when they are so far away from their familiar landmarks that they can no longer discern them, they drift about with no knowledge of their location. This is because they are ignorant of astronomy and mathematics, and because they do not possess the rules of navigation. Countless ships are thereby lost every year. Not only does this represent an enormous annual waste of produce, but valuable subjects also perish. If the methods of navigation were developed, the loss at sea of rice and other food products would be reduced, thus effecting a great saving. This would not only increase the wealth of the nation, but would help stabilise the prices of rice and other produce throughout Japan. The people, finding that they are treated equally irrespective of occupation and that the methods of government are fair, would no longer harbour any resentment, but would raise their voices in unison to pray for the prosperity of the rulers. By saving the lives of those subjects who would otherwise be lost at sea every

---

SOURCE: Donald Keene, *The Japanese Discovery of Europe: Honda Toshiaki and Other Discoverers, 1720–1798* (London: Routledge and Kegan Paul, 1952), pp. 169–72, 178.

year, we shall also be able to make up for our past shame, and will keep foreign nations from learning about weak spots in the institutions of Japan from Japanese sailors shipwrecked on their shores. Because of these and numerous other benefits to be derived from shipping, I have termed it [an] imperative need.

* * *

If the islands near Japan were colonised they would make highly desirable places. By such colonisation numerous possessions—some sixty or more—would be created, which would serve not only as military outposts for Japan, but would also produce in abundance metals, grain and fruit, as well as various other products, thus greatly adding to Japan's strength. I presume that run-of-the-mill officials must be thinking that colonisation could be effected only at the expense of the ruler, and the authorities are not in the least inclined to spend any government money on developing farmland. This is the way mediocre minds always react.

The order to be followed in colonising territories is as follows: First, ships are despatched to ascertain the location of the islands to be taken, and to measure their extent. The natural products of the islands are investigated, and the native population estimated. Then, when it is known about how many provinces the islands would make if colonised, the actual work is begun. If the natives are still living in caves, they are taught about houses. A house should be built for the tribal chief. Those natives without implements or utensils should be supplied with them. By helping the natives and giving them everything they desire, one will inspire a feeling of affection and obedience in them, like the love of children for their parents. This is true because they are moved by the same feelings that pervade the rest of the world, barbarians though they may be considered.

The way to compensate for the expenses involved in colonisation lies in taking the natural products of the islands and shipping them to Japan. Trading marks a beginning of compensation for those expenses. Even barbarians do not expect to ask favours and give nothing in return. The products they offer represent a commencement of taxation. Since every island has wooded areas, there will always be some value in the lumber which can be taken from the islands, even after a great many years. The value of other products besides lumber would be too great to calculate. It is the task of the ruler-father to direct and educate the natives in such a manner that there will not be a single one of them who will spend even one unprofitable day. This matter should not be put off for another moment; it is a vital state duty.

At this point we must discuss the foundation of colonisation— the sciences of astronomy and mathematics. In Japan these sciences are not as yet fully known, and there are few men who understand their significance. Even in China the principles of astronomy and mathematics have roughly been understood since the arrival of a number of Europeans late in the seventeenth century. If, in connection with colonisation projects, ships cross the seas without reference to the principles of astronomy and mathematics, there is no way to tell how much easier sea travel is than land travel. The name of the book in which the natural laws behind these principles are contained is *Schatkamer*, a European work. One may learn from the latitude of a particular island what its climate is like throughout the year. Or, without actually visiting an island, one can predict in this way whether it will prove fertile. This may be done with certainty; false tales need not be believed.

The key to colonisation is to establish a system with long-range objectives as to future profit and loss. By encouraging the good customs of the natives and eliminating their bad ones, it is possible to have them maintain human dignity. They should never be permitted to forget the generosity of the Japanese ruler. This is how colonisation should be set about, but Japan persists in her bad habit of imitating old Chinese usages. Very few of the government authorities possess any real knowledge of astronomy or mathematics, and it is because of their ignorance that whenever there is talk of colonising the northern territories, as occasionally happens, the project is never carried through. It is Japan's misfortune that her officials are misled by foolish tales about these great countries, which are actually far superior to Japan, and consequently do not take advantage of great opportunities for profitable ventures. This is a matter of especial regret because there have been Russian officials in the islands inhabited by the Ainu since about 1765. They have displayed such diligence in their colonisation efforts that eighteen or nineteen Kurile islands and the great land of Kamchatka have already been occupied. Forts are said to have been built at various places and a central administration established, the staff of which is regularly changed, and which rules the natives with benevolence. I have heard that the natives trust them as they would their own parents.

In Japan, on the other hand, this system is as yet not followed. It is forbidden to carry from the country seeds for the five cereals or edged tools for use in building houses. It is forbidden to teach Japanese to any natives. These are supplemented by a host of other prohibitions. It is a most lamentable system which has as its object keeping barbarians forever in their present condition. Since the Russians operate under a system which provides that their own subjects are sent out to live among the natives, it is only to be expected that the Ainu look up to the Russian officials as gods and worship them.

*　　*　　*

It is clear * * * that when the Ezo islands are colonised they will make worthwhile places which will yield several times as much produce as Japan does today. Although there are other islands both to the east and west which should also be Japanese possessions, I shall not discuss them for the moment. At this crucial time when the Ezo islands are being seized by Russia, we are faced with an emergency within an emergency. When, as now, Japan does not have any system for colonising her island possessions, there is no way of telling whether they will be seized by foreign countries or remain safe. This is not the moment for neglect; such actions by foreign powers may lead to the destruction of our national defence. With the establishment of a system of colonisation, a knowledge of navigation will naturally develop among Japanese, but if navigation, shipping and trade continue to be considered the occupation of merchants, the natives of our island possessions are doomed to an eternal want of civilisation. The fact that the Ainu are living in a state of barbarity has been regarded by Russia as affording a fine opportunity for her to devote her energies to the colonisation of the islands, a timely undertaking. The lack of a colonisation system has kept Japanese rule from the island, and has meant that the natives are unaware of the goodness of the ruler of Japan. Because of this ignorance they have been quick to become subject to Russia.

So important is colonisation that I have termed it [an] imperative need.

Questions

1. How does Honda try to persuade Japanese rulers—who generally saw agriculture as the main foundation of prosperity, and thus the chief focus of a government's economic policy—that they should pay more attention to shipping and commerce?

2. What does Honda see as the main benefits that would come from colonization of islands North of Japan?

3. How does Honda compare Russian and Japanese policies toward the lands of the northern Pacific? How do the indigenous Ainu people figure in his understanding of what frontier policy should be?

'Abd–Allah ibn 'Abd al–Wahhab, Wahhabi Reformers in Mecca (1803)

One of the most important developments in early modern Islam was the founding of Wahhabism, the dominant form of Islam in modern Saudi Arabia. Its founder was Muhammad ibn 'Abd al-Wahhab (1703–1792). He was offended by the laxity of his fellow Muslims and by many of the religious practices of his day, such as Sufi mysticism, prayers to saints, and pilgrimages to their tombs. These he regarded as little better than polytheism. 'Abd al-Wahhab's reform movement emphasized the uniqueness of God and called for a return to what he regarded as the early simplicity of an Islam based on the Quran and Sunnah (the tradition of the prophet Muhammad). He formed an alliance with a local ruler, Muhammad ibn Sa'ud, who married his daughter. They gradually extended their power over the Arabian Peninsula. In the state they founded, al-Wahhab served as the religious authority while members of the al-Sa'ud family, known as *amirs* and *imams*, handled political affairs. Al-Wahhab was succeeded by his grandson 'Abd-Allah, who participated in the short-lived Saudi seizure of Mecca from the Ottoman Empire in 1803. The following passage is 'Abd-Allah's description of this event, which was translated into English in 1874. Spelling has been updated in the following excerpt to reflect modern orthography.

In the name of God, the Compassionate and Merciful!

* * * Now I was engaged in the holy war, carried on by those who truly believe in the Unity of God, when God, praised be He, graciously permitted us to enter Mecca, the holy, the exalted, at midday, on the 6th day of the week on the 8th of the month (Muharram), 1218, Hijrí [1803]. Before this, Sa'ud, our leader in the holy war, whom the Lord protect, had summoned the nobles, the divines, and the common people of Mecca; for indeed the leaders of the pilgrims and the rulers of Mecca had resolved on battle, and had risen up against us in the holy place (haram), to exclude us from the house of God. But when the army of the true believers advanced, the Lord filled their hearts with terror, and they fled hither and thither. Then our commander gave protection to every one within the holy place, while we, with shaven heads and hair cut short, entered with safety, crying "Labbaika" [the invocation made by pilgrims when they enter the state of ritual taboo on pilgrimage to Mecca] without fear of any created being, and only of the Lord God. Now, though we were more numerous, better armed and disciplined than the people of Mecca, yet we did not cut down their trees, neither did we hunt, nor shed any blood except the blood of victims, and of those four-footed beasts which the Lord has made lawful by his commands.

When our pilgrimage was over, we gathered the people together on the forenoon of the first day of the week, and our leader, whom the Lord save, explained to the divines what we required of the people, [namely,] a pure belief in the Unity of God Almighty. * * *

SOURCE: *Journal of the Asiatic Society of Bengal* (Calcutta: C. B. Lewis, Baptist Mission Press, 1874), vol. 43, part 1, pp. 68–70, 73–76, 81.

He added that to [show] the significance of "shirk" [polytheism], the prophet (may he be blessed!) had put people to death on account of it; that he had continued to call upon them to believe in the Unity of God for some time after he became inspired, and that he had abandoned shirk before the Lord had declared to him the remaining four pillars of Islam. * * *

Then they jointly and severally admitted that our belief was best, and promised the Amir to be guided by the Quran and the Sunnah. * * * They then acknowledged our belief, and there was not one amongst them who doubted or hesitated to believe that that for which we condemned men to death, was the truth pure and unsullied. And they swore a binding oath, although we had not asked them, that their hearts had been opened and their doubts removed, and that they were convinced whoever said, "Oh prophet of God!" or "Oh Ibn 'Abbás!" or "Oh 'Abdul Qádir!" or called on any other created being, thus entreating him to turn away evil or grant what is good, (where the power belongs to God alone,) such as recovery from sickness, or victory over enemies, or protection from temptation, &c. ; he is a "Mushrik" [polytheist], his blood shall be shed and property confiscated. Nor is it any excuse that he believes the effective first cause in the movements of the universe is God, and only supplicates those mortals * * * to intercede for him or bring him nearer the presence of God, so that he may obtain what he requires from Him through them or through their intercession. Again, the tombs which had been erected over the remains of the pious, had become in these times as it were idols whither the people went to pray for what they required, they humbled themselves before them, and called upon those lying in them, in their distress, just as did those who were in darkness before the coming of Muhammad.

* * *

When this was over, we razed all the large tombs in the city which the people generally worshipped and believed in, and by which they hoped to obtain benefits or ward off evil, so that there did not remain an idol to be adored in that pure city, for which God be praised. Then the taxes and customs we abolished, all the different kinds of instruments for using tobacco we destroyed, and tobacco itself we proclaimed forbidden. Next we burned the dwellings of those selling *hashish*, and living in open wickedness, and issued a proclamation, directing the people to constantly exercise themselves in prayer.

*　*　*

We believe that good and evil proceed from God, the exalted; that nothing happens in His kingdom, but what He commands; that created beings do not possess free will, and are not accountable for their own acts; but on the contrary they obtain rank and spiritual reward, merely as an act of grace, and suffer punishment justly, for God is not bound to do anything for His slaves. We believe that the faithful will see Him in the end, but we do not know under what form, as it was beyond our comprehension. And in the same way we follow Imam Ahmad Ibn Hanbal [founder of the Hanbali school of jurisprudence] in matters of detail; but we do not reject any one who follows any of the four Imams [the founders of the four schools of Islamic jurisprudence], as we do the Shi'ahs, the Zaidiyyahs, and the Imamiyyahs, &c., who belong to no regular churches. Nor do we admit them in any way to act openly according to their vicious creeds; on the contrary, we compelled them to follow one of the four Imams. We do not claim to exercise our reason in all matters of religion, and none of our faith demand such a position, save that we follow our judgment where a point is clearly demonstrated to us in either the Quran or the Sunnah. *　*　*

We do not command the destruction of any writings except such as tend to cast people into infidelity to injure their faith, such as those on Logic, which have been prohibited by all Divines. But we are not very exacting with regard to books or documents of this nature, save if they appear to assist our opponents, we destroy them. *　*　* We do not consider it proper to make Arabs prisoners of war, nor have we done so, neither do we fight with other nations. Finally, we do not consider it lawful to kill women or children.

*　*　*

We believe that our prophet Muhammad *　*　* is more exalted by God than any other created being; that he is alive, lives in his grave a life quicker than that declared by revelation unto martyrs, and that he can hear the salutations of those who salute him. We consider pilgrimage is supported by legal custom, but it should not be undertaken except to a mosque, and for the purpose of praying in it. Therefore, whoever performs pilgrimage for this purpose, is not wrong, and doubtless those who spend the precious moments of their existence in invoking the Prophet, shall, according to the Hadith [accounts of what the Prophet Muhammad said or did], obtain happiness in this world and the next, and he will dispel their sorrows. We do not deny miraculous powers to the saints, but on the contrary allow them. They are under the guidance of the Lord, so long as they continue to follow the way pointed out in the laws and obey the prescribed rules. But whether alive or dead, they must not be made the object of any form of worship.

*   *   *

We prohibit those forms of Bid'ah [innovation] that affect religion or pious works. Thus drinking coffee, reciting poetry, praising kings, do not affect religion or pious works and are not prohibited. * * *

All games are lawful. Our prophet * * * allowed * * * play in his mosque. * * * So it is lawful to chide and punish persons in various ways; to train them in the use of different weapons; or to use anything which tends to encourage warriors in battle, such as a war-drum. But it must not be accompanied with musical instruments. These are forbidden, and indeed the difference between them and a war drum is clear.

Questions

1. According to 'Abd al-Wahhab, what makes someone who professes belief in Islam actually a "polytheist"?

2. For 'Abd al-Wahhab, what is the relationship between the believer and God?

3. What do the Wahhabis regard as forbidden, and what is permitted? Can they be regarded as puritanical?

Nathaniel Isaacs, Descriptions of Shaka and the Zulu Military (1836)

Nathaniel Isaacs (1808–1872) was an English merchant and adventurer who accompanied an expedition to southeastern Africa in 1825 in search of two shipwrecked Englishmen, Francis Farewell and Francis Fynn. The fact that the rescue party found Farewell and Fynn suggests that the region was not a wilderness, but rather populated by people with regular communication. Isaacs spent several years living in KwaZulu. As a foreigner, he had some access to Shaka's court and he fought alongside Zulu troops. He learned to speak Zulu and earned favor with Shaka, who granted him land. Isaacs, Farewell, and Fynn founded the town of Port Natal, which became Durban. His written account of his experiences was clearly intended to appeal to a British audience keen for adventure and sympathetic to the idea of an expanding British Empire. Isaacs's account is among the earliest written sources on the Zulu kingdom, and undoubtedly based on eyewitness observation. It is also full of exaggerations and plays to stereotypes of violent savagery. (Bear in mind that Britain still practiced judicial executions, and that pickpockets faced the death penalty until 1808.) Nevertheless, the account provides insights into Shaka's court and his military command, showing a hierarchical structure administered with absolute authority by the king. Spelling has been updated in the following excerpt to reflect modern orthography.

We now reached the head of the kraal [settlement or household], where a multitude of the natives had congregated and were seated in the form of a half circle. Shaka sat by himself on a large mat rolled up. Our natives saluted him after their manner, and I did the same, according to our European custom, and then took my seat among his people about twenty yards off. He desired me to approach him, which I did, when he immediately asked me how Mr. Farewell was, whose people we were, and if I had any knowledge of the Portuguese, mentioning that he had a Portuguese with him; at my express-

---

SOURCE: Nathaniel Isaacs, *Travels and Adventures in Eastern Africa* (London: Edward Churton, 1836), vol. 1, pp. 70–71, 75, 343–48.

ing a wish to see him, Shaka sent for the individual, and I was soon most agreeably surprised to see a European in this wild and unfrequented place.

* * *

On a sudden a profound silence ensued, when his majesty uttered one or two words, at which some of the warriors immediately rose and seized three of the people, one of whom sat near me. The poor fellows made no resistance, but were calm and resigned, waiting their fate with apparently stoical indifference. The sanguinary chief was silent; but from some sign he gave the executioners, they took the criminals, laying one hand on the crown and the other on the chin, and by a sudden wrench appeared to dislocate the head. The victims were then dragged away and beaten as they proceeded to the bush, about a mile from the kraal, where a stick was inhumanly forced up the fundament of each, and they were left as food for the wild beasts of the forest, and those carnivorous birds that hover near the habitations of the natives.

* * *

Thus the eve of going to war was always the period of brutal and inhuman murders, in which he [Shaka] seemed to indulge with as much savage delight as the tiger with his prey. When he once had determined on a sanguinary display of his power, nothing could restrain his ferocity; his eyes evinced his pleasure, his iron heart exulted, his whole frame seemed as if it felt a joyous impulse at seeing the blood of innocent creatures flowing at his feet; his hands grasped, his herculean and muscular limbs exhibiting by their motion a desire to aid in the execution of the victims of his vengeance: in short, he seemed a being in a human form, with more than the physical capabilities of a man; a giant without reason, a monster created with more than ordinary power and disposition for doing mischief, and from whom we recoil as we would at the serpent's hiss or the lion's growl.

It was an invariable rule of war with him never to give his troops more cattle or provisions than would barely suffice to support them till they arrived in the country of their enemy. They had strict injunctions to fight or die, to quarter on their enemy, and not return but as victors, bringing with them the fruits of their triumph.

He was exceedingly wary, and used great precaution in concealing even from his generals or chiefs, the power or tribe with whom he designed combating; nor until the eve of marching did he make known to them the object of their expedition. By this he evinced some discretion, and precluded the possibility of his enemy being apprised of his intentions. In this particular, Shaka showed a judgment not common with the native chiefs, and peculiarly his own.

When all was ready for entering upon their march, he confided to one general his design, and to him he entrusted the command, should he not head his army in person. He, however, never confided in one man but on one occasion; upon no occasion whatever did he repeat such confidence. * * *

Shaka always kept up a system of espionnage, by which he knew at all times the condition and strength of every tribe around him, both independent and tributary; and these persons were always directed to make such observations on the passes to and from the country to which they were sent, as might be useful in leading the troops to the scene of action with the surest chance of arriving at their position, without being discovered on the one hand, or surprised on the other.

At the return of his warriors from an expedition, he was usually generous to them, it must be admitted, but that only occurred in the case of their having achieved a triumph over his enemies; in such cases he gave the captured spoils liberally amongst them, as an encouragement for future exertions and enterprise: but to return without having accomplished what he had anticipated, was a signal for a scene of woe and lamentation—a massacre of no measured description.

After an expedition his troops were permitted to retire to their respective kraals for a short period, to recover from their fatigue, whence in a short time, the chiefs were called to collect the people and hear the details of those operations in which the warriors had been engaged; at which time all who had evinced cowardice were selected, brought forth, received the fiat of their ferocious master, and were led off immediately to be impaled, as an atonement for their offence, and as an example to others who should feel disposed to pursue a similar conduct. Such warriors who distinguished themselves in battle were honoured with a *nom de guerre*, by which they were afterwards accosted.

* * *

He can hold secret councils, and have any member killed, not excepting even the principal chief, if he fancy him opposed to his schemes. He is generally at variance with one half his chiefs, who are members of this military tribunal, and prevents their meeting by having his regiments in opposite directions and at positions at some distance apart. Although meetings are not publicly prohibited, it is well known they create Shaka's wrath and suspicion, and that they terminate with death to such as assemble without his knowledge. All meetings of this military council are held at the gateway of the king's kraal, or in the cattle-pound, which is their council-room, unless the king be present, when they meet in the palace.

Shaka had an extreme aversion to any thing like commercial traffic, and forbade it among his people. Towards the Europeans he always expressed himself decidedly opposed to any intercourse, having for its object the establishment of a mercantile connection with his subjects. His whole soul was engrossed by war, and he conceived that any thing like commerce would enervate his people and unfit them for their military duties.

Questions

1. Shaka seized control of the Zulu kingdom shortly before Isaacs arrived. What evidence does Isaacs provide of a ruler consolidating his power? Why might Isaacs not explain this context of contested succession?

2. Can you identify passages that seem likely to be exaggerated? Can you suggest why?

3. Isaacs describes the region as "wild and unfrequented," yet the conversation he reports with Shaka at the beginning of the excerpt suggests a ruler who is aware of the wider world, familiar with the Portuguese

based in Mozambique, and able to connect Isaacs to Farewell. How can you account for this discrepancy?

Maulvi Syed Kutb Shah Sahib, Call for Hindu–Muslim Unity (1858)

Originally written in Urdu by a Muslim leader, this letter is both a call to action and a list of specific grievances against expanding British rule in South Asia. The letter seeks to capitalize on the anti-British sentiment violently expressed in the Indian Rebellion the year before and to change the local political landscape. With a history of both religious strife and periods of significant tolerance in India, there was political and cultural precedent behind Maulvi Syed Kutb Shah Sahib's plea for concerted cooperation between Hindus and Muslims against British rule. He made the case that British policies sought to undermine both Hindus and Muslims by challenging religious belief and social practices. Note that Maulvi Syed provides examples of British affronts to both Muslims and Hindus, including references to popular belief that the British intentionally broke food taboos (pork for Muslims, all meat or animal fat for Hindus) in order to challenge people's faith. He was critical of Christian missionary efforts as well as government policies that eroded local choice in matters such as inheritance of property and political titles (in 1856 the British extended their rule in Lucknow and the province of Oudh by using English inheritance rules to overrule local practice) and social/religious practice such as *Sati* (widow burning) which the British sought to restrict although the practice was not widespread. Spelling has been updated in the following excerpt to reflect modern orthography.

---

* * * The English are people who overthrow all religions. You should understand well the object of destroying the religions of

---

SOURCE: *Accounts and Papers, East Indies. Mutiny, King Delhim Oude Proclamation* (1859), vol. 18, pp. 110–11.

Hindustan; they have for a long time been causing books to be written and circulated throughout the country by the hands of their priests, and, exercising their authority, have brought out numbers of preachers to spread their own tenets: this has been learned from one of their own trusted agents. Consider, then, what systematic contrivances they have adopted to destroy our religions. For instance, first, when a woman became a widow they ordered her to make a second marriage. Secondly, the self-immolation of wives on the funeral pyres of their deceased husbands was an ancient religious custom; the English had it discontinued, and enacted their own regulations prohibiting it. Thirdly, they told people it was their wish that they (the people) should adopt their faith, promising that if they did so they would be respected by Government; and further required them to attend churches, and hear the tenets preached there. Moreover, they decided and told the rajahs that such only as were born of their wives would inherit the government and property, and that adopted heirs would not be allowed to succeed, although, according to your Scriptures, ten different sorts of heirs are allowed shares in the inheritance. By this contrivance they will rob you of your governments and possessions, as they have already done with Nagpur and Lucknow.

Consider now another of their designing plans: they resolved on compelling prisoners, with the forcible exercise of their authority, to eat their bread. Numbers died of starvation, but did not eat it; others eat it, and sacrificed their faith. They now perceived that this expedient did not succeed well, and accordingly determined on having bones ground and mixed with flour and sugar, so that people might unsuspectingly eat them in this way. They had, moreover, bones and flesh broken small and mixed with rice, which they caused to be placed in the markets for sale, and tried, besides, every other possible plan to destroy our religions. At last some Bengali, after due reflection, said that if the troops would accede to the wishes of the English in this matter, all the Bengalis would also conform to them. The English, hearing this, approved of it, and said, "Certainly this is an excellent idea," never imagining they would be themselves exterminated. They accordingly now ordered the Brahmans and others of their army to bite cartridges, in the making up of which fat had been used. The Muslim soldiers perceived that by this expedient the religion of the Brahmans and Hindus only was in danger, but nevertheless they also refused to bite them. On this the English now resolved on ruining the faith of both, and blew away from guns all those soldiers who persisted in their refusal.

Seeing this excessive tyranny, the soldiery now, in self-preservation, began killing the English, and slew them wherever they were found, and are now considering means for slaying the few still alive here and there. It is now my firm conviction that if these English continue in Hindustan they will kill every one in the country, and will utterly overthrow our religions; but there are some of my countrymen who have joined the English, and are now fighting on their side. I have reflected well on their case also, and have come to the conclusion that the English will not leave your religion to both you and them. You should understand this well. Under these circumstances, I would ask, what course have you decided on to protect your lives and faith? Were your views and mine the same, we might destroy them entirely with a very little trouble; and if we do so, we shall protect our religions and save the country. And as these ideas have been cherished and considered merely from a concern for the protection of the religions and lives of all you Hindus and Muslims of this country, this letter is printed for your information. All you Hindus are hereby solemnly adjured, by your faith in the Ganges, Tulsi, and Saligram; and all you Muslims, by your belief in God and the Quran, as these English are the common enemy of both, to unite in considering their slaughter extremely expedient, for by this alone will the lives and faith of both be saved. It is expedient, then, that you should coalesce and slay them.

The slaughter of kine [cows] is regarded by the Hindus as a great insult to their religion. To prevent this, a solemn compact and agreement has been entered into by all the Muslim chiefs of Hindustan, binding themselves, that if the Hindus will come forward to slay the English, the Muslims will from that very day put a stop to the slaughter of cows, and those of them who will not do so will be considered to have abjured the Quran, and such of them as will eat beef will be regarded as though they had eaten pork; but if the Hindus will not gird their loins to kill the English, but will try to save them, they will be as guilty in the sight of God as though they had committed the sins of killing cows and eating flesh.

Perhaps the English may, for their own ends, try to assure the Hindus that as the Muslims have consented to give up killing cows from respect for the Hindu religion, they will solemnly engage to do the same, and will ask the Hindus to join them against the Muslims; but no sensible man will be gulled by such deceit, for the solemn promises and professions of the English are always deceitful and interested. Once their ends are gained they will infringe their engagements, for deception has ever been habitual with them, and the treachery they have always practised on the people of Hindustan is known to rich and poor. Do not, therefore, give heed to what they may say. Be well assured you will never have such an opportunity again. We all know that writing a letter is equivalent to an advance half way towards fellowship. I trust you will all write answers approving of what has been proposed herein. This letter has been printed under the direction of Maulvi Syed Kutb Shah Sahib, at the Bahaduri press, in the city of Bareilly.

Questions

1. What justification does Maulvi Syed give for resisting British rule? Do you think any of his depictions of British intentions are exaggerated? Why or why not?

2. Some scholars have described this call for unity as an example of early Indian nationalist politics. What evidence supports this characterization? Do you think this is a nationalist document? Why or why not?

3. Why did Maulvi Syed argue that this was the most opportune moment for united action against the British?

Pierre-Joseph Proudhon, What Is Property? (1840)

Industrialization in Europe in the early nineteenth century occurred amid glaring inequalities of wealth, producing a new class of impoverished workers and a new class of wealthy employers. Socialist thinkers argued that Europe needed not only a political revolution, like that which had taken place in France, but also an economic revolution that would eliminate inequality. One of these thinkers was Pierre-Joseph Proudhon (1809–1865), a French printer, journalist, and politician. Although Proudhon famously declared that "Property is theft!," unlike some other socialists he opposed state ownership of the means of production. Instead he favored ownership by associations of workers, a variety of socialism he called mutualism. He was also one of the earliest advocates of anarchism, the belief that society can regulate itself without state authority. Although he corresponded with Karl Marx, Marx was a fervent critic of his work. Proudhon's most important publication was *What Is Property?*, written soon after he moved to Paris and engaged with socialist ideas circulating there.

———

If I were asked to answer the following question: *What is slavery?* and I should answer in one word, *It is murder*, my meaning would be understood at once. No extended argument would be required to show that the power to take from a man his thought, his will, his personality, is a power of life and death; and that to enslave a man is to kill him. Why, then, to this other question: *What is property?* may I not likewise answer, *It is robbery*, without the certainty of being misunderstood; the second proposition being no other than a transformation of the first?

* * *

Property is robbery! * * * What a revolution in human ideas! *Proprietor* and *robber* have been at all times expressions as contra-

SOURCE: P. J. Proudhon, *What Is Property?*, translated by Benjamin R. Tucker (Princeton, Mass., 1876), pp. 11–13, 42, 53, 82–83, 148–49.

dictory as the beings whom they designate are hostile. * * * On what authority, then, do you venture to attack universal consent, and give the lie to the human race? Who are you, that you should question the judgment of the nations and the ages?

Of what consequence to you, reader, is my obscure individuality? I live, like you, in a century in which reason submits only to fact and to evidence. My name, like yours, is TRUTH-SEEKER. My mission is written in these words of the law: *Speak without hatred and without fear; tell that which thou knowest!* The work of our race is to build the temple of science, and this science includes man and Nature. Now, truth reveals itself to all; to-day to Newton and Pascal, tomorrow to the herdsman in the valley and the journeyman in the shop. Each one contributes his stone to the edifice; and, his task accomplished, disappears. * * *

Disregard then, reader, my title and my character, and attend only to my arguments. * * * Have the courage to follow me; and, if your will is untrammelled, if your conscience is free, if your mind can unite two propositions and deduce a third therefrom, my ideas will inevitably become yours. * * * The things of which I am to speak are so simple and clear that you will be astonished at not having perceived them before, and you will say: "I have neglected to think."

* * *

The Roman law defined property as the right to use and abuse one's own within the limits of the law. * * * A justification of the word *abuse* has been attempted, on the ground that it signifies, not senseless and immoral abuse, but only absolute domain. Vain distinction! invented as an excuse for property, and powerless against the frenzy of possession, which it neither prevents nor represses. The proprietor may, if he choose, allow his crops to rot under foot; sow his field with salt; milk his cows on the sand; change his vineyard into a desert, and use his vegetable-garden as a park: do these things constitute abuse, or no? In the matter of property, use and abuse are necessarily indistinguishable.

* *

The titles on which they pretend to base the right of property are two in number: *occupation* and *labor*. * * * I remind the reader that, to whatever authority we appeal, * * * property, to be just and possible, must necessarily have equality for its condition.

* * *

Not only does occupation lead to equality, it *prevents* property. For, since every man, from the fact of his existence, has the right of occupation, and, in order to live, must have material for cultivation on which he may labor; and since, on the other hand, the number of occupants varies continually with the births and deaths,—it follows that the quantity of material which each laborer may claim varies with the number of occupants; consequently, that occupation is always subordinate to population. Finally, that, inasmuch as possession, in right, can never remain fixed, it is impossible, in fact, that it can ever become property.

Every occupant is, then, necessarily a possessor or usufructuary,—a function which excludes proprietorship. Now, this is the right of the usufructuary: he is responsible for the thing entrusted to him; he must use it in conformity with general utility, with a view to its preservation and development; he has no power to transform it, to diminish it, or to change its nature; he cannot so divide the usufruct that another shall perform the labor while he receives the product. In a word, the usufructuary is under the supervision of society, submitted to the condition of labor and the law of equality.

* * *

All have an equal right of occupancy.
The amount occupied being measured, not by the will, but by the variable conditions of space and number, property cannot exist.

* * *

But I hear the exclamations of the partisans of another system: "Labor, labor! that is the basis of property!"

Reader, do not be deceived. This new basis of property is worse than the first, and I shall soon have to ask your pardon for having demonstrated things clearer, and refuted pretensions more unjust, than any which we have yet considered.

*   *   *

The isolated man can supply but a very small portion of his wants; all his power lies in association, and in the intelligent combination of universal effort. The division and co-operation of labor multiply the quantity and the variety of products; the individuality of functions improves their quality.

There is not a man, then, but lives upon the products of several thousand different industries; not a laborer but receives from society at large the things which he consumes, and, with these, the power to reproduce. * * *

The various articles of consumption are given to each by all; consequently, the production of each involves the production of all. One product cannot exist without another; an isolated industry is an impossible thing. * * * All industries are united by mutual relations in a single group; all productions do reciprocal service as means and end; all varieties of talent are but a series of changes from the inferior to the superior.

Now, this undisputed and indisputable fact of the general participation in every species of product makes all individual productions common; so that every product, coming from the hands of the producer, is mortgaged in advance by society. The producer himself is entitled to only that portion of his product, which is expressed by a fraction whose denominator is equal to the number of individuals of which society is composed. It is true that in return this same producer has a share in all the products of others, so that he has a claim upon all, just as all have a claim upon him; but is it not clear that this reciprocity of mortgages, far from authorizing property, destroys even possession? The laborer is not even possessor of his product; scarcely has he finished it, when society claims it.

Questions

1. For Proudhon, what is the distinction between property and occupancy? Why is it important for his argument to make this distinction?

2. How does Proudhon argue that labor does not give rise to property?

3. Why does Proudhon believe that his readers will ultimately agree with his arguments?

Chapter 17

NATIONS AND EMPIRES, 1850–1914

Raja Rammohan Roy, Debate on the Practice of Burning Widows Alive (1820)

Raja Rammohan Roy (1774–1833) was born to an elite Brahmin landowning family. He had an atypical education for the period, studying first in the Muslim city of Patna, where he learned Arabic and Persian and became familiar with the Quran. He later went to study in Varanasi (Benares), a particularly holy city for Hindus, where he learned Sanskrit and studied ancient Hindu texts. He also traveled in South Asia and studied Buddhism. In 1803 Roy went to work for the British East India Company, and through this engaged with Christians. Roy sought to integrate Western culture with what he took to be the best features of India's traditions. In that spirit, Roy combined elements of many religions and developed Brahma Samaj, a universal religion that played a role in modernizing Indian society. He successfully campaigned against sati, the Hindu practice of burning widows; the British colonial government outlawed sati in 1829. Roy established a number of schools based on western educational models. In the following excerpt from an imagined dialogue between a supporter and a critic of sati, Roy sets up one argument in favor of sati that he is able to criticize quite sharply. Spelling has been updated in the following excerpt to reflect modern orthography.

Advocate.—I alluded * * * to the real reason for our anxiety to persuade widows to follow their husbands, and for our endeavours to burn them pressed down with ropes: viz. that women are by nature of inferior understanding, without resolution, unworthy of trust, subject to passions, and void of virtuous knowledge; they according to the precepts of the Sastra are not allowed to marry again after the demise of their husbands, and consequently despair at once of all worldly pleasure:—hence it is evident, that death to these unfortunate widows is preferable to existence; for the great difficulty which a widow may experience by living a purely ascetic life as prescribed by the Sastras is obvious; therefore if she do not perform Concremation, it is probable that she may be guilty of such acts as may bring disgrace upon her paternal and maternal relations, and those that may be connected with her husband. Under these circumstances we instruct them from their early life in the idea of Concremation, holding out to them heavenly enjoyments in company with their husbands, as well as the beatitude of their relations, both by birth and marriage, and their reputation in this world. From this many of them, on the death of their husbands, become desirous of accompanying them; but to remove every chance of their trying to escape from the blazing fire, in burning them we first tie them down to the pile.

Opponent. The reason you have now assigned for burning widows alive is indeed your true motive, as we are well aware; but the faults which you have imputed to women are not planted in their constitution by nature. It would be therefore grossly criminal to condemn that sex to death merely from precaution. By ascribing to them all sorts of improper conduct, you have indeed successfully persuaded the Hindu community to look down upon them as contemptible and mischievous creatures, whence they have been subjected to constant miseries. I have therefore to offer a few remarks on this head. Women are in general inferior to men in bodily strength and energy; consequently the male part of the community, taking advantage of their corporeal weakness, have denied to them those excellent merits that they are entitled to by nature, and afterwards they are apt to say that women are naturally incapable

SOURCE: Raja Rammohan Roy, *A Second Conference between an Advocate and an Opponent of the Practice of Burning Widows Alive* (Calcutta: Baptist Mission Press, 1820), pp. 44–50.

of acquiring those merits. But if we give the subject consideration, we may easily ascertain whether or not your accusation against them is consistent with justice. As to their inferiority in point of understanding, when did you ever afford them a fair opportunity of exhibiting their natural capacity? How then can you accuse them of want of understanding? If after instruction in knowledge and wisdom a person cannot comprehend or retain what has been taught him, we may consider him as deficient; but as you keep women generally void of education and acquirements, you cannot therefore in justice pronounce on their inferiority. On the contrary, Lilavati, Bhanumati (the wife of the Prince of Karnat) and that of Kalidasa, are celebrated for their thorough knowledge of all the Sastras: moreover in the Vrihadaranyaka Upanishad of the Yajur Veda it is clearly stated, that Yajnavalkya imparted divine knowledge of the most difficult nature to his wife Maitreyi, who was able to follow and completely attain it!

Secondly. You charge them with want of resolution, at which I feel exceedingly surprised. For we constantly perceive in a country where the name of death makes the male shudder, that the female from her firmness of mind offers to burn with the corpse of her deceased husband; and yet you accuse those women of deficiency in point of resolution.

Thirdly. With regard to their trustworthiness, let us look minutely into the conduct of both sexes, and we may be enabled to ascertain which of them is the most frequently guilty of betraying friends.—If we enumerate such women in each village or town as have been deceived by men, and such men as have been betrayed by women, I presume that the number of the deceived women would be found ten times greater than that of the betrayed men.—Men are in general able to read and write and manage public affairs, by which means they easily promulgate such faults as women occasionally commit, but never consider as criminal the misconduct of men towards women.—One fault they have, it must be acknowledged; which is, by considering others equally void of duplicity as themselves to give their confidence too readily, from which they suffer much misery, even so far that some of them are misled to suffer themselves to be burnt to death.

In the fourth place, with respect to their subjection to the passions, this may be judged of by the custom of marriage as to the respective sexes; for one man may marry two or three, sometimes even ten wives and upwards: while a woman, who marries but one husband, desires at his death to follow him, forsaking all worldly enjoyments, or to remain leading the austere life of an ascetic.

Fifthly. The accusation of their want of virtuous knowledge is an injustice.—Observe what pain, what slighting, what contempt, and what afflictions their virtue enables them to support! How many Kulin Brahmans are there who marry ten or fifteen wives for the sake of money, that never see the greater number of them after the day of marriage, and visit others only three or four times in the course of their life. Still amongst those women, most, even without seeing or receiving any support from their husbands, living dependent on their fathers or brothers, and suffering much distress, continue to preserve their virtue. And when Brahmans or those of other tribes bring their wives to live with them, what misery do the women not suffer? * * * As long as the husband is poor she suffers every kind of trouble, and when he becomes rich she is altogether heart-broken.—All this pain and affliction their virtue alone enables them to support.—Where a husband takes two or three wives to live with him, they are subjected to mental miseries and constant quarrels.—Even this distressed situation they virtuously endure.— Sometimes it happens that the husband, from a preference for one of his wives, behaves cruelly to another.—Amongst the lower classes, and those even of the better class who have not associated with good company, the wife on the slightest fault, or even on bare suspicion of her misconduct, is chastised as a thief.—Respect to virtue and their reputation generally makes them forgive even this treatment. If, unable to bear such cruel usage, a wife leaves her husband's house to live separately from him, then the influence of the husband with the magisterial authority is generally sufficient to place her again in his hands; when, in revenge for her quitting him, he seizes every pretext to torment her in various ways;—and sometimes even puts her privately to death. These are facts occurring every day, and not to be denied.—What I lament is, that seeing the women thus dependent and exposed to every misery, you feel for them no compassion, that might exempt them from being tied down and burnt to death.

Questions

1. What is the advocate's main reason for supporting "concremation"?

2. Why would Roy start with this argument rather than material arguments, such as the difficulty of supporting a widow after her husband's death?

3. Roy's rebuttal take two tracks: it defends women's intellectual abilities and virtues; it describes women's limited material choices. Is one of these sets of reasons more convincing? Why or why not?

Temple Wage (1877)

A severe El Niño event caused a major monsoon failure and terrible drought in parts of India from 1876 to 1878. It also caused droughts in other places around the world. As food shortages became severe, arguments arose about what the British colonial government should do. Influenced by Malthusian ideas about famine correcting "over-population," by a belief that charity weakened people's character, and by pressure to keep government spending low (while continuing a war on the Afghan frontier), the authorities provided minimal relief, even refusing to reduce land taxes on farms with no harvest.

To receive what relief was available, people had to move to relief camps many miles away and do heavy labor on government projects. In return, they received one pound of rice per day. Since this was far below the amount of food needed to sustain heavy labor—even if people had been healthy when they arrived—and since poor sanitary conditions compounded the effects of malnutrition, death rates in these camps were extremely high.

In hard-hit Madras, the relief works were run by Richard Temple, and the ration became known as the "Temple wage." Ironically, Temple had led a more generous and successful famine relief effort in Bengal in

1873–1874, but was heavily criticized by his superiors and some British newspapers for this "extravagance." In Madras, he seems to have been determined to change his reputation.

A table, comparing the Temple wage to other rations and estimates of caloric needs, was compiled by Mike Davis, a contemporary American scholar and activist.

THE "TEMPLE WAGE" IN PERSPECTIVE

	Caloric Value	Activity Level
Basal metabolism (adult)	1500	No activity
Temple ration in Madras (1877)	1627	Heavy labor
Buchenwald ration (1944)	1750	Heavy labor
7-year-old child, approved diet (1981)	2050	Normal activity
Minimum war ration, Japan (1945)	2165	Moderate activity
Indian adult, subsistence (1985)	2400	Moderate activity
Temple ration in Bengal (1874)	2500	Heavy labor
Survey of Bengal laborers (1862)	2790	Heavy labor
Indian male, approved diet (1981)	3900	Heavy labor
Voit-Atwater standard (1895)	4200	Heavy labor

Source: Caloric value of Temple ration from Sumit Guha, *The Agrarian Economy of the Bombay Deccan, 1818–1941*, Delhi 1985, p. 186 fn35; Buchenwald ration from C. Richet, "Medicales sur le camp de Buchenwald en 1944–45," *Bulletin Academie Medicine* 129 (1945), pp. 377–88; recommended Indian adult subsistence diet from Asok Mitra, "The Nutrition Situation in India," in Margaret Biswas and Per Pinstrup-Andersen (eds.), *Nutrition and Development*, Oxford 1985, p. 149; basal metabolism from Philip Payne, "The Nature of Malnutrition," ibid., p. 7; child diet and recommended calories for Indian males performing heavy labor from C. Gapalan, "Undernutrition Measurement," in S. Osmani (ed.), *Nutrition and Poverty*, Oxford 1992, p. 2; Rev. James Long's 1862 study of Bengali diets in Greenough, *Prosperity and Misery in Modern Bengal*, Oxford 1982, p. 80 fn94; Voit-Atwater tables discussed in Elmer McCollom, *A History of Nutrition*, Boston 1958, pp. 191–2; and the Temple ration during the 1874 Bengal famine calculated on the basis of 1.5 pounds of rice per day with condiments and *dal* (see *Edinburgh Review*, July 1877).

SOURCE: Mike Davis, *Late Victorian Holocausts: El Niño, Famines and the Making of the Third World* (New York: Verso, 2001), Table 1.3, p. 39.

Questions

1. How did the Temple wage compare with other rations?

2. How much would the Temple wage have needed to be increased to avoid massive death rates in the camps?

3. Given the predictable result of such a diet combined with heavy labor, why do you think the relief camps were created at all?

Cecil Rhodes, Confession of Faith (1877)

Cecil Rhodes (1853–1902) was the fifth son of an English vicar whose formal education was cut short when he was sent to South Africa to improve his asthma. The climate suited his health and the colonial economy his entrepreneurial ambitions. Rhodes returned to England for one year to study at Oxford but preferred working in South Africa, never completing his degree. Rhodes was instrumental in consolidating individual diamond claims at Kimberly, forming the DeBeers conglomerate. He served as prime minister of the Cape Colony. He was an ardent supporter of the British Empire and famously dreamed of connecting the Cape to Cairo under the British flag. Rhodes never married, so there were no heirs to his great fortune. His will established the Rhodes Scholarship at Oxford, supporting his commitment to train young men in the service of empire.

He drafted the following essay in 1877 while at Oxford. The spelling and grammatical errors are in the original. While explicit on some points, the essay blurs distinctions between ideas about religion, social hierarchy, and political authority. Rhodes's visions of power are decidedly male; despite his interests in expanding English society and racial reproduction, women are completely absent.

It often strikes a man to inquire what is the chief good in life; to one the thought comes that it is a happy marriage, to another great

---

SOURCE: Cecil Rhodes, "Confession of Faith," in John Flint, *Cecil Rhodes* (Boston: Little, Brown and Co., 1974), pp. 248–52.

wealth, and as each seizes on his idea, for that he more or less works for the rest of his existence. To myself thinking over the same question the wish came to render myself useful to my country. I then asked myself how could I and after reviewing the various methods I have felt that at the present day we are actually limiting our children and perhaps bringing into the world half the human beings we might owing to the lack of country for them to inhabit that if we had retained America there would at this moment be millions more of English living. I contend that we are the finest race in the world and that the more of the world we inhabit the better it is for the human race. Just fancy those parts that are at present inhabited by the most despicable specimens of human beings what an alteration there would be if they were brought under Anglo-Saxon influence, look again at the extra employment a new country added to our dominions gives. I contend that every acre added to our territory means in the future birth to some more of the English race who otherwise would not be brought into existence. Added to this the absorption of the greater portion of the world under our rule simply means the end of all wars, at this moment had we not lost America I believe we could have stopped the Russian-Turkish war [in the Balkans, 1877–1878] by merely refusing money and supplies. Having these ideas what scheme could we think of to forward this object. I look into history and I read the story of the Jesuits I see what they were able to do in a bad cause and I might say under bad leaders.

In the present day I become a member in the Masonic order I see the wealth and power they possess the influence they hold and I think over their ceremonies and I wonder that a large body of men can devote themselves to what at times appear the most ridiculous and absurd rites without an object and without an end.

The idea gleaming and dancing before ones eyes like a will-of-the-wisp at last frames itself into a plan. Why should we not form a secret society with but one object the furtherance of the British Empire and the bringing of the whole uncivilised world under British rule for the recovery of the United States for the making the Anglo-Saxon race but one Empire. What a dream, but yet it is probable, it is possible. I once heard it argued by a fellow in my own college [Oriel at Oxford]. I am sorry to own it by an Englishman, that it was a good thing for us that we have lost the United States. There are some subjects on which there can be no arguments, and to an Englishman this is one of them, but even from an American's point of view just picture what they have lost, look at their government, are not the frauds that yearly come before the public view a disgrace to any country and especially their's which is the finest in the world. Would they have occurred had they remained under English rule great as they have become how infinitely greater they would have been with the softening and elevating influences of English rule, think of those countless 000's of Englishmen that during the last 100 years would have crossed the Atlantic and settled and populated the United States. Would they have not made without any prejudice a finer country of it than the low class Irish and German emigrants? All this we have lost and that country loses owing to whom? Owing to two or three ignorant pig-headed statesmen of the last century, at their door lies the blame. Do you ever feel mad? do you ever feel murderous. I think I do with those men. I bring facts to prove my assertion. Does an English father when his sons wish to emigrate ever think of suggesting emigration to a country under another flag, never—it would seem a disgrace to suggest such a thing I think that we all think that poverty is better under our own flag than wealth under a foreign one.

Put your mind into another train of thought. Fancy Australia discovered and colonised under the French flag, what would it mean merely several millions of English unborn that at present exist we learn from the past and to form our future. We learn from having lost to cling to what we possess. We know the size of the world we know the total extent. Africa is still lying ready for us it is our duty to take it. It is our duty to seize every opportunity of acquiring more territory and we should keep this one idea steadily before our eyes that more territory simply means more of the Anglo-Saxon race more of the best the most human, most honourable race the world possesses.

To forward such a scheme what a splendid help a secret society would be a society not openly acknowledged but who would work in secret for such an object.

I contend that there are at the present moment numbers of the ablest men in the world who would devote their whole lives to it. I often think what a loss to the English nation in some respects the abolition of the Rotten Borough System has been. What thought strikes a man entering the house of commons, the assembly that rules the whole world? I think it is the mediocrity of the men but what is the cause. It is simply—an assembly of wealth of men whose lives have been spent in the accumulation of money and whose time has been too much engaged to be able to spare any for the study of past history. And yet in the hands of such men rest our destinies. Do men like the great Pitt, and Burke and Sheridan not now exist. I contend they do. There are men now living with I know no other term the μεγα χοχεγις [unrecognizable phrase] of Aristotle but there are not ways for enabling them to serve their Country. They live and die unused unemployed. What has been the main cause of the success of the Romish Church? The fact that every enthusiast, call it if you like every madman finds employment in it. Let us form the same kind of society a Church for the extension of the British Empire. A society which should have its members in every part of the British Empire working with one object and one idea we should have its members placed at our universities and our schools and should watch the English youth passing through their hands just one perhaps in every thousand would have the mind and feelings for such an object, he should be tried in every way, he should be tested whether he is endurant, possessed of eloquence, disregardful of the petty details of life, and if found to be such, then elected and bound by oath to serve for the rest of his life in his Country. He should then be supported if without means by the Society and sent to that part of the Empire where it was felt he was needed.

Take another case, let us fancy a man who finds himself his own master with ample means on attaining his majority whether he puts the question directly to himself or not, still like the old story of virtue and vice in the Memorabilia a fight goes on in him as to what he should do. Take if he plunges into dissipation there is nothing too reckless he does not attempt but after a time his life palls on him, he mentally says this is not good enough, he changes his life, he reforms, he travels, he thinks now I have found the chief good in life, the novelty wears off, and he tires, to change again, he goes into the far interior after the wild game he thinks at last I've found that in life of which I cannot tire, again he is disappointed. He returns he thinks is there nothing I can do in life? Here I am with means, with a good house, with everything that is to be envied and yet I am not happy I am tired of life he possesses within him a portion of the μεγα χοχεγις [unrecognizable term] of Aristotle but he knows it not, to such a man the Society should go, should test, and should finally show him the greatness of the scheme and list him as a member.

Take one more case of the younger son with high thoughts, high aspirations, endowed by nature with all the faculties to make a great man, and with the sole wish in life to serve his Country but he lacks two things the means and the opportunity, ever troubled by a sort of inward deity urging him on to high and noble deeds, he is compelled to pass his time in some occupation which furnishes him with mere existence, he lives unhappily and dies miserably. Such men as these the Society should search out and use for the further-ance of their object.

(In every Colonial legislature the Society should attempt to have its members prepared at all times to vote or speak and advocate the closer union of England and the colonies, to crush all disloyalty and every movement for the severance of our Empire. The Society should inspire and even own portions of the press for the press rules the mind of the people. The Society should always be searching for members who might by their position in the world by their energies or character forward the object but the ballot and test for admit-tance should be severe)

Once make it common and it fails. Take a man of great wealth who is bereft of his children perhaps having his mind soured by some bitter disappointment who shuts himself up separate from his neighbours and makes up his mind to a miserable existence. To such men as these the society should go gradually disclose the greatness of their scheme and entreat him to throw in his life and property with them for this object. I think that there are thousands now existing who would eagerly grasp at the opportunity. Such are the heads of my scheme.

For fear that death might cut me off before the time for attempting its development I leave all my worldly goods in trust to S. G. Shippard and the Secretary for the Colonies at the time of my death to try to form such a Society with such an object.

Questions

1. What two models of organization does Rhodes identify for his proposed transnational secret society? What is significant about his admiration for order set alongside explicit criticism of ritual?

2. Identify passages in which Rhodes justifies colonial rule based on national chauvinism. What is significant about Rhodes's appeal to nationalist sentiment rather than the religious, racial, or economic justifications that also circulated widely in nineteenth-century Europe?

3. Christian converts at colonial missions were encouraged to write narratives about their paths to salvation. Does thinking about this genre of personal writing help you understand Rhodes's essay? Why or why not?

Edmund D. Morel, The Black Man's Burden (1920)

Opposition to colonial expansion grew louder at the end of the nineteenth and into the twentieth century. Edmund Morel (1873–1924) worked as a clerk for a British shipping company that carried freight between the Congo Free State and Belgium. He noticed a trade imbalance; the value of goods going from Europe was below the value of resources coming from Africa. Active in socialist politics, Morel began to investigate and publish tracts in local newspapers. In 1904 he published a book, *King Leopold's Rule in Africa*, which among other critiques provides details about "red rubber" (named for the blood spilled in its extraction). Morel collaborated with Roger Casement (see Sir Roger Casement, Consul General's Report to Sir Edward Grey, in Casebook: Rubber and the World Economy, following Chapter 18) to show the widespread effects of colonial exploitation.

Leopold II of Belgium ran the Congo Free State as private enterprise from 1885 to 1908, when the Belgian government assumed administrative control and proclaimed Congo a colony.

Morel's "The Black Man's Burden" title for the following 1920 essay

responds to Rudyard Kipling's 1899 poem, "The White Man's Burden,"
intended to encourage the United States to colonize the Philippines.

It is with the peoples of Africa, then, that our inquiry is concerned. It is they who carry the "Black man's" burden. They have
not withered away before the white man's *occupation.* Indeed, if
the scope of this volume permitted, there would be no difficulty in
showing that Africa has ultimately absorbed within itself every
Caucasian and, for that matter, every Semitic invader too. In hew-
ing out for himself a fixed abode in Africa, the white man has mas-
sacred the African in heaps. The African has survived, and it is
well for the white settlers that he has.

In the process of imposing his political dominion over the African, the white man has carved broad and bloody avenues from one
end of Africa to the other. The African has resisted, and persisted.

*　*　*

But what the partial occupation of his soil by the white man has
failed to do; what the mapping out of European political "spheres of
influence" has failed to do; what the maxim [the first machine gun,
1884] and the rifle, the slave gang, labour in the bowels of the earth
and the lash, have failed to do; what imported measles, smallpox and
syphilis have failed to do; what even the oversea slave trade failed to
do, the power of modern capitalistic exploitation, assisted by modern engines of destruction, may yet succeed in accomplishing.

For from the evils of the latter, scientifically applied and
enforced, there is no escape for the African. Its destructive effects
are not spasmodic: they are permanent. In its permanence resides
its fatal consequences. It kills not the body merely, but the soul. It
breaks the spirit. It attacks the African at every turn, from every
point of vantage. It wrecks his polity, uproots him from the land,

---

SOURCE: Edmund D. Morel, *The Black Man's Burden* (New York: B. W.
Huebsch, 1920), pp. 7–9.

invades his family life, destroys his natural pursuits and occupations, claims his whole time, enslaves him in his own home.

Economic bondage and wage slavery, the grinding pressure of a life of toil, the incessant demands of industrial capitalism—these things a landless European proletariat physically endures, though hardly. It endures—as a * * * population. The recuperative forces of a temperate climate are there to arrest the ravages. * * * But in Africa, especially in tropical Africa, which a capitalistic imperialism threatens and has, in part, already devastated, man is incapable of reacting against unnatural conditions. In those regions man is engaged in a perpetual struggle against disease and an exhausting climate, which tells heavily upon child-bearing; and there is no scientific machinery for salving the weaker members of the community. The African of the tropics is capable of tremendous physical labours. But he cannot accommodate himself to the European system of monotonous, uninterrupted labour, with its long and regular hours, involving, moreover, as it frequently does, severance from natural surroundings and nostalgia, the condition of melancholy resulting from separation from home. * * * Climatic conditions forbid it. When the system is forced upon him, the tropical African droops and dies.

Nor is violent physical opposition to abuse and injustice henceforth possible for the African in any part of Africa. His chances of effective resistance have been steadily dwindling with the increasing perfectibility in the killing power of modern armament. Gunpowder broke the effectiveness of his resistance to the slave trade, although he continued to struggle. He has forced and, on rare occasions and in exceptional circumstances beaten, in turn the old-fashioned musket, the elephant gun, the seven-pounder, and even the repeating rifle and the gatling gun. He has been known to charge right down repeatedly, foot and horse, upon the square, swept on all sides with the pitiless and continuous hail of maxims. But against the latest inventions, physical bravery, though associated with a perfect knowledge of the country, can do nothing. The African cannot face the high explosive shell and the bomb dropping aeroplane. * * *

Thus the African is really helpless against the material gods of the white man, as embodied in the trinity of imperialism, capitalistic-exploitation, and militarism. If the white man retains these gods and if he insists upon making the African worship them as assiduously as he has done himself, the African will go the way of the Red Indian, the Amerindian, the Carib, the Guanche, the aboriginal Australian, and many more. And this would be at once a crime of enormous magnitude, and a world disaster.

Questions

1. Morel differentiates among colonial occupation, administration, and assertion of economic control. Which does he argue poses the greatest challenge to Africans' survival? Why?

2. Why does Morel think that capitalist labor regimes are even harder on African workers than on Europeans? Do you agree with his argument? Why or why not?

3. What transnational comparisons does Morel invoke to support his argument? Can you identify the influence of socialist principles in Morel's choice of examples? How do the transnational comparisons Morel finds important differ from those invoked by Cecil Rhodes (see Cecil Rhodes, *Confession of Faith,* in this chapter).

Criminal Tribes Act (1871)

The Criminal Tribes Act of 1871 established a presumption that members of certain tribes or castes were professional criminals. It required all members of these groups throughout India to register with the police, and placed a legal obligation on all village headmen to report the comings and goings of any such people. The authorities could arrest such people without warrants, confine them to specified living areas, and insist that they work on government projects—clearing forests, draining swamps, etc.—or work for specified private employers. Among other things, this created pools of landless laborers in some places where they had not previously existed, and deprived them of any bargaining power.

British authorities frequently justified these measures by comparing the groups in question to the *thugee*, large and long-standing groups of bandits whom the British had suppressed in the 1830s. (Scholars differ as to how much the *thugee* were really a hereditary group sharing a common religion and illegal profession, as the British claimed.) A number of the groups classified under the 1871 act were nomadic peoples, whom the British saw as "vagrants" because their lifestyles were deemed incompatible with civilized life. (Many European states were also cracking down on vagrants and habitual criminals at home during this period, and debating to what extent such behavior might be inherited.) In some cases, the migratory routes of these people also crossed lands which the British believed should be private property. Others were seen as rebellious or otherwise undesirable.

The Criminal Tribes Act was extended and amended various times; at the time of Indian independence in 1947, it covered 13 million people. Similar acts were created for some of the British colonies in Africa.

PART I. CRIMINAL TRIBES

2. Local Government to report what tribes should be declared criminal.

3. Report to contain certain particulars.

4. Occupation of wandering tribe to be stated; also proposed residence and means of livelihood.

5. Notification declaring tribe to be criminal.

6. Bar of jurisdiction of Courts in questions relating to notification.

7. Register of members of such tribes.

8. Procedure in making register.

9. Penalties for failing to appear, refusing or giving false information.

10. Charge of register. Reporting desirable alterations.

11. By whom alterations to be made. Notice to persons affected.

12. Complaints of entries in register.

13. Settlement of tribe in place prescribed by Local Government.

14. Removal to other place.

SOURCE: *The Bengal Code*, edited by F. G. Wigley (Calcutta, India: Office of the Superintendant of Government Printing, 1905), vol. 1, pp. 240–48.

*   *   *

ACT 27 OF 1871

An Act for the Registration of Criminal Tribes and Eunuchs. Whereas it is expedient to provide for the registration, surveillance and control of certain criminal tribes and eunuchs; It is hereby enacted as follows:—

1. This Act may be called the Criminal Tribes Act, 1871. This section and section 20 extend to the whole of British India.

*   *   *

2. If the Local Government has reason to believe that any tribe, gang or class of persons is addicted to the systematic commission of non-bailable offences, it may report the case to the Governor General in Council, and may request his permission to declare such tribe, gang or class to be a criminal tribe.

3. The report shall state the reasons why such tribe, gang or class is considered to be addicted to the systematic commission of non-bailable offences, and, as far as possible, the nature and the

circumstances of the offences in which the members of the tribe are supposed to have been concerned; and shall describe the manner in which it is proposed that such tribe, gang or class shall earn its living when the provisions hereinafter contained have been applied to it.

4. If such tribe, gang or class has no fixed place of residence, the report shall state whether such tribe, gang or class follows any lawful occupation, and whether such occupation is, in the opinion of the Local Government, the real occupation of such tribe, gang or class, or a pretence for the purpose of facilitating the commission of crimes, and shall set forth the grounds on which such opinion is based; and the report shall also specify the place of residence in which such wandering tribe, gang or class is to be settled under the provisions hereinafter contained, and the arrangements which were proposed to be made for enabling it to earn its living therein.

5. If, upon the consideration of any such report, the Governor General in Council is satisfied that the tribe, gang or class to which it relates ought to be declared criminal, and that the means by which it is proposed that such tribe, gang or class shall earn its living are adequate, he may authorize the Local Government to publish in the local Gazette a notification declaring that such tribe, gang or class is a criminal tribe, and thereupon the provisions of this Act shall become applicable to such tribe, gang or class.

6. No Court of Justice shall question the validity of any such notification on the ground that the provisions hereinbefore contained, or any of them, have not been complied with, or entertain in any form whatever the question whether they have been complied with; but every such notification shall be conclusive proof that the provisions of this Act are applicable to the tribe, gang or class specified therein.

7. When the notification mentioned in section 5 has been published, the Local Government may direct the Magistrate of any district in which such tribe, gang or class, or any part thereof, is at the time resident, to make a register of the members of such tribe, gang or class, or of any part thereof.

The declaration of the Local Government that any such tribe, gang or class, or any part of it, is resident in any district shall be conclusive proof of such residence.

8. Upon receiving such direction the said Magistrate shall publish a notice in the place where the register is to be made, calling upon all the members of such tribe, gang or class, or of such portion thereof as is directed to be registered, to appear, at a time and place therein specified, before such persons as he appoints, and to give those persons such information as may be necessary to enable them to make the register.

9. Any member of any such tribe, gang or class, who, without lawful excuse, the [burden] of proving which shall lie upon him,—

shall fail to appear according to such notice,

or who shall intentionally omit to furnish such information,

or who shall furnish, as true, information on the subject which he knows or has reason to believe to be false,

shall be deemed guilty of an offence under the first parts of section 174, or 176, or 177 of the Indian Penal Code, respectively, as the case may be.

10. The register, when made, shall be kept by the District Superintendent of Police, who shall, from time to time, report to the said Magistrate any alterations which ought to be made therein, either by way of addition or erasure.

* * *

13. Any tribe, gang or class, which has been declared to be criminal, and which has no fixed place of residence, may be settled in a place of residence prescribed by the Local Government.

14. Any tribe, gang or class which has been declared to be criminal, or any part thereof, may, by order of the Local Government, be removed to any other place of residence.

15. No tribe, gang or class shall be settled or removed under the provisions of this Act until such arrangements as the Local Government shall, with the concurrence of the Governor General in Council, consider suitable, have been made for enabling such tribe, gang or class, or such part thereof as is to be so settled or removed, to earn a living in the place in or to which it is to be settled or removed.

16. When the removal of any persons has been ordered under this Act, the register of such persons' names shall be transferred to the District Superintendent of Police of the district to which such persons are removed, and the Magistrate of the said district and the Commissioner of the division in which it is situated shall thereupon be empowered to exercise respectively the powers provided in sections 11 and 12.

17. The Local Government may, with the sanction of the Governor General in Council, place any tribe, gang or class, which has been declared to be criminal, or any part thereof, in a reformatory settlement.

* * *

18. The Local Government may, with the previous consent of the Governor General in Council, make rules to prescribe—

* * *

(5) conditions as to holding passes under which such persons may be permitted to leave the said limits [of the area to which they have been confined];

(6) conditions to be inserted in any such pass as to—
   (a) the places where the holder of the pass may go or reside;
   (b) the officers before whom, from time to time, he shall be bound to present himself;
   (c) and the time during which he may absent himself;

(7) conditions as to answering at roll-call or otherwise, in order to satisfy the said Magistrate, or persons authorized by him, that the persons whose names are on the register are actually present at given times within the said limits;

(8) the inspection of the residences and villages of any such tribe, gang or class, and the prevention or removal of contrivances for enabling the residents therein to conceal stolen property, or to leave their place or residence without leave;

(9) the terms upon which registered persons may be discharged from the operation of this Act;

(10) the mode in which criminal tribes shall be settled and removed;

(11) the control and supervision of reformatory settlements;

(12) the works on which, and the hours during which, persons placed in a reformatory settlement shall be employed, the rates at which they shall be paid, and the disposal, for the benefit of such persons, of the surplus proceeds of their labour after defraying the whole or such part of the expenses of their supervision and control as to the Local Government shall seem fit;

(13) the discipline to which persons endeavouring to escape from any such settlement, or otherwise offending against the rules for the time being in force, shall be submitted; the periodical visitation of such settlement, and the removal from it of such persons as it shall seem expedient to remove;

(14) and generally to carry out the purposes of this Act.

* * *

19. * * * (2) Any person being a member of a proclaimed tribe violating a rule made under any other clause of section 18 shall be punishable with rigorous imprisonment for a term which may extend to six months, or with fine, or with whipping, or with all or any two of those punishments; and, on any subsequent conviction for a breach of any such rule, with rigorous imprisonment for a term which may extend to one year, or with fine, or with whipping, or with all or any two of those punishments.

* * *

20. Any person registered under the provisions of this Act, who is found in any part of British India, beyond the limits so pre-scribed for his residence, without such pass as may be required by the said rules, or in a place or at a time not permitted by the conditions of his pass, or who escapes from a reformatory settlement, may be arrested without warrant by any police-officer or village-watchman and taken before a Magistrate, who, on proof of the facts, shall order him to be removed to the district in which he ought to have resided, or to the reformatory settlement from which he has escaped (as the case may be), there to be dealt with according to the rules under this Act for the time being in force.

* * *

21. It shall be the duty of every village-headman and village-watchman in a village in which any persons belonging to a tribe, class or gang which has been declared criminal reside, and of every owner or occupier of land on which any such persons reside, to give the earliest information in his power at the nearest police-station of—

(1) the failure of any such person to appear and give information as directed in section 8;

(2) the departure of any such person from such village or from such land (as the case may be).

And it shall be the duty of every village-headman and village-watchman in a village, and of every owner or occupier of land, to give the earliest information in his power at the nearest police-station of the arrival at such village or on such land (as the case may be) of any persons who may reasonably be suspected of belonging to any such tribe, class or gang.

22. Any village-headman, village-watchman, owner or occupier of land, who shall fail to comply with the requirements of section 21, shall be deemed to have committed an offence under the first part of section 176 of the Indian Penal Code.

Questions

1. What is the procedure by which a group is classified as a criminal tribe? What recourse do such groups or individuals in the groups have against such proceedings?

2. What are the consequences of being a criminal tribe?

3. Who is supposed to supervise criminal tribes and how? What burdens and/or opportunities might this create for them?

Eugene Lyons, Revolt against Ugliness (1937)

Eugene Lyons (1898–1985) was born to Jewish parents in the Ukraine. He grew up in New York's Lower East Side ghetto, and became a socialist at a young age. In the 1920s, he became well-known as a radical journalist and author. From 1928 to 1934 he was United Press International's first Moscow correspondent, and wrote quite favorably about the Soviet Union. By 1937, when he published the autobiographical *Assignment in Utopia*, he had become very critical of the U.S.S.R., though from a generally leftist perspective. Later in life, he became much more conservative, writing for *Reader's Digest*, *National Review*, and *Human Events*.

The "Revolt against Ugliness" selection below comes from Lyons's description of growing up, and mixes general reflections on the immigrant experience in the United States with an explanation of why he gravitated to writing and radical politics rather than the career as a doctor or lawyer that his parents hoped he would pursue.

In America we still romanticize the glories of a hard, poverty-ridden youth. Our rags-to-riches legends and literature overlook the fact that Tony the Bootblack ends up as a hod-carrier or a gangster more often than a millionaire. They overlook the more vital fact that when he does achieve wealth he generally carries the scars of the unequal struggle on his mind and spirit forever. He can rarely attain the mellow quality of the full, cultured existence of those whose rise was more orderly, less desperate. Our up-from-the-gutter type of true, or nearly true, story is written by the few who did creep out of the quagmires of want and its endless degradations. The many who were swallowed up, or who emerged broken in body and spirit, do not write autobiographies or make after-dinner speeches.

On the East Side of New York, where I grew up, we knew hardship and fear in their less romantic guises. Our streets teemed with

SOURCE: Eugene Lyons, *Assignment in Utopia* (New York: Harcourt, Brace and Company, 1937), pp. 3–8.

crowded, chaotic life like the underside of a moss-grown stone. Our tenements were odoriferous garbage heaps where the same over-abundant life proliferated. We knew coarseness, vermin, want, so intimately that they became routine commonplaces. The affluence, the ease, the glimpse of ordered beauty were distant and unreal, like stories in books. Only the ugliness and sweat and unrelenting tussle were close and terribly familiar.

The idealization of poverty as "the university of hard knocks" seemed to me insult added to injury as early as I was able to think at all. The be-furred ladies who came into the social settlements of our slums to assure us patronizingly of the blessings we were enjoying infuriated me. They fascinated me too, with suggestions of incredible far-off splendors in their sleekness.

I was presiding at a Boy Scout meeting at the Educational Alliance one evening when just such a lady, trailing clouds of radiance from her up-town world, came into the room. Her intrusion offended some vague sense of fitness in me, so that when she asked me an innocent question I ordered her sharply not to interrupt our meeting. The reward of my impertinence was an invitation, several days later, to call on her at a West End Avenue address. I had never seen such elegance at close range (though it was only an ordinary apartment), and passed through the interview in numb bewilderment. I remember the softness of the rugs, like lush grass, and the loveliness of a little boy who called my hostess "mother"—the word "mother" somehow did not jibe in my experience with glossy, care-free, nicely-upholstered women; it had always meant harassed, overworked and slovenly women. But what I carried away chiefly was a burning humiliation because the lining of the overcoat I gave up to the valet was in tatters. In my confusion, when I retrieved the coat, I slipped my arm into the torn lining instead of the sleeve, and the glamorous lady herself helped me to extricate myself. The shame of it rankled for months.

Poverty was only half of our routine ordeal. The other half was an acute awareness of being aliens and intruders in a nation of Americans. Between the world of our text-books and movies and newspapers and the other world of our homes and parents there was a deep gulf: different interests, preoccupations, ideals, languages.

On the threshhold of your home you removed your American self like an overcoat, and you put it on once more when you left home. We lived this double existence so continuously that the idea of an integrated life, in which home and out-of-home activities were part of the same pattern, was beyond our imagination.

The school principal, Dr. Kottman, talked casually in my hearing one day about playing baseball with his son. The implication of a father who talked the same language and played the same games as his son, I can still recall, struck me as bizarre.

No American with deep roots in the American soil can understand the nostalgic homelessness of immigrant children, the pathos of second-generation aliens. *Land where our fathers died, land of the Pilgrims' pride*—sung in the assembly hall by several thousand Jewish, Russian, Italian, other foreign boys and girls whose fathers had never heard of the Pilgrims. We were "Americanized" about as gently as horses are broken in. In the whole crude process, we sensed a disrespect for the alien traditions in our homes and came unconsciously to resent and despise those traditions, good and bad alike, because they seemed insuperable barriers between ourselves and the adopted land.

We were caught and tangled in a mass of people for the most part resigned to their fate, sodden with hopelessness, and in a stupor of physical exhaustion. For the average boy it was easier to burrow deeper into the heap, taking the aroma and the drabness of the East Side into his soul, than to attempt the Gargantuan job of escaping. The Americanism that he acquired and dragged into the writhing heap was the loud, vulgar, surface—the slang, the sporting page, the crude success ideals of the movies and yellow journals—and nothing of the grandeur at the core of America.

But when the urge to escape does enter into the blood of a slum denizen, it is a feverish thing that drives him with whips of fire. "Success" is never a pale beckoning star. It is a flaming ball that blots out nearly everything else in the boy's firmament. Elsewhere it may be mere self-fulfillment. On our East Side it was that and more—a species of defiance and revenge against the clinging squalors and the smugness of the lucky ones and, above all, against the social system that breeds such plague spots.

Whatever the expression of that pitiless ambition, it is always shot through with hatred for the *status quo*. Sometimes it is openly defiant of restraints and carries the jungle law of dog-eat-dog competition to its logical conclusion in crime, gangsterism. At other times, the predatory technique is kept within the safer bounds of legality. Whether the exceptional boy revolting against putrescent surroundings turns into an unprincipled criminal or an unprincipled businessman is often simply a question of the proportions of courage and cleverness in his make-up.

And occasionally, as in my own case, the clamoring protest transcends the personal. The driving ambition widens out to embrace all the disinherited and exploited. It becomes a conscious protest against ugliness and injustice as such, and embraces passionately whatever formula of social revolt is closest to hand. There is a vast and unbridgeable difference between the radicalism that is accepted at second-hand, from the outside, through the mind, and the revolt that is nurtured in one's very bones. Those of us who were—or thought ourselves—"socialists" instinctively, through spontaneous hatred for the reality as we savored it, could never quite get over a certain distrust of "converts" to the cause from other social strata.

* * *

I thought myself a "socialist" almost as soon as I thought at all and years before I had heard of the *Communist Manifesto*. * * *

My memory can conjure up no one moment of thunderous illumination when the rightness and certainty of the socialist future of eternal justice and equality were revealed to me. In our multifarious world of dreams and ugliness, a boy soaked up a social faith, if he was built that way, as naturally and imperceptibly as his schoolmates and blockmates soaked up the tough-guy philosophy or the success-at-any-price philosophy. By a sort of social osmosis.

As a child, down in a stinking steerage hole full of vermin and vomit, in one of the foul ships which, at that time, dumped cargoes of bewildered immigrants on the American shores, I treasured a vision of the fairyland called America. I shut my eyes and saw it clearly—the glittering streets, the happy faces, the new shiny land stocked with beauty. That lovely vision broke sickeningly on the

garbage cans of the Corlears Hook section of New York. The spec-
ters of "slack" seasons, of strikes for a living wage, of illness that
cut off all earnings for a large family—the sight of my father's
cadaverous face after a long day at the machine (it was a curiously
handsome and sensitive face under the mask of bottomless
fatigue)—these were less horrible when viewed as aspects of the
perpetual class hostilities and as prelude to an ineffable triumph.

Our ant-heap was infested with street gangs. But I found myself
somehow enrolled in a "Socialist Sunday School" on East Broad-
way, run by the Workmen's Circle. The hymns we chanted were
Arise, ye prisoners of starvation, Arise, ye wretched of the earth!, and
The people's flag is deepest red.

*   *   *

From the Socialist Sunday School I graduated naturally into
the "Yipsels," the Young People's Socialist League, where we
debated weighty questions and took courses in Marx and Spencer
and distributed leaflets for socialist candidates without the slightest hope of their election.

The highest reach of anxious parental hope in homes like mine
was to turn sons into doctors and lawyers and to marry off daughters to doctors and lawyers. In affectionate moments, proud relatives, impressed by my seriousness and report cards, tried the prefix
"Dr." before my name, and, miraculously, it always fitted nicely.
The sacrifice involved in sending me to high school, and then to
college, rather than into the factory, practically made my eventual
emergence as a physician or lawyer a duty—a very onerous duty.
The fact that neither calling stirred me to enthusiasm made me
feel a good deal of an ingrate towards my parents and towards my
elder brother, who, since the age of thirteen, had been among the
sweated legions bending over sewing machines. But I had no stom-
ach for the professional respectability to which they aspired for me.
Ostensibly I was being primed for the law. But my dreams were of
writing, not as a means of making a living, but as a weapon on my
side of the class war.

My parents' sacrifices consisted in dispensing with my potential
contribution to the family income and in providing me with food,

clothing and shelter. But it could not easily be extended to include bugaboo items of carfares and occasional expenses. By working after school hours, I managed to earn these myself. At one tragic juncture, internal politics ousted me from a night job at the Educational Alliance and the lack of a single dollar a week threatened to cut short my high school career. That sum, advanced for ten weeks running by Adolph Nash, my Scoutmaster, helped a little to patch up the faith in social work which the ouster had shattered.

By the end of the ten weeks, I was earning three dollars a week as "assistant professor" to a teacher of English in the hurry-up preparatory schools for adults. My function was chiefly the correction of examination papers on literary subjects about which I knew precisely nothing. * * *

Questions

1. In what ways does Lyons think Americans romanticize poverty? What manifestations of this attitude did he find particularly annoying in his youth?

2. Why does Lyons describe young immigrants like himself as leading a "double existence"? What characteristics and attitudes does he think this tends to develop in young people? Why?

3. How, in Lyons's case, did these attitudes and circumstances lead him to political and social radicalism?

Chapter 18

AN UNSETTLED WORLD, 1890–1914

Denton J. Snider, World's Fair Studies (1893)

Denton J. Snider (1841–1925) belonged to a group of Midwestern intellectuals who sought to popularize European high culture (including Greek and Latin) among middle- and working-class Americans, including immigrants. Though largely forgotten today, he had a large following at the time.

The Chicago World's Fair, celebrating the 400th anniversary of Columbus's voyages, announced the emergence of the United States as a world power. Such fairs also allowed visitors (27 million at Chicago, in six months) to "explore" other countries at a time before television and cheap travel. Snider's immensely popular guide—parts of which were also printed in the influential *Atlantic Monthly*—told them how to interpret the spectacles on offer. In the excerpt below, he explains how the fair's layout reflects the ranking (by Social Darwinist criteria) of national and ethnic groups.

We may repeat, therefore, that the Plaisance is a voyage round the World and down Time; it is a living museum of humanity, not a dead collection of curiosities. Probably the best presentation of himself that man has ever looked upon is this, showing him in his totality; a universal human soul is present, if we can but look

SOURCE: Denton J. Snider, *World's Fair Studies: The Four Domes* (Chicago: Chicago Kindergarten College, 1895), pp. 237–38, 255–57.

through the outer body and commune with the spirit of the place. The world-man is here and at work, differentiated, it is true, into many individuals of many nations; still the world-man is he, quite as he has come down through the ages and has spread out over the globe. Call the whole a grand temple of humanity, intricate labyrinthine; can we seize its clew in thought and not get lost in its mazy compartments?

Let us note the first external fact concerning the Plaisance: it is a strip of land about one mile long and 600 feet wide, through the middle of which runs a broad street or highway leading to the World's Fair, or leading out of the same, just as the visitor chooses. On each side of the street are arranged the contents of the Plaisance—its shows, booths, eating-houses, drinking places, villages, peoples. Thus it is like a gallery of paintings or statues; truly a world-gallery, which is to be viewed on both sides of the passage.

* * *

But the most important of these regressive movements in the Plaisance is the ethnical, the dropping back through the various races which represent stages of man's culture. Here one can live rearwards in time and in human development; he can follow the lapse of the soul down, down through every phase of humanity, European, Asiatic, African, till he reaches the animal in Hagenbeck's menagerie, or even the plant in the nursery exhibit, in both of which the lower orders of nature have been trained till they throw out gleams of their former state before the mighty fall of a world. Such is the Oriental view, that of a great original lapse from the Divine, by which the curse has come upon us with all its consequent misery. Now, as we are entering the Orient, its world-view can well be followed, for a time at least, by the sympathetic visitor.

Nearest to us are the various phases of European and Christian peoples, represented by the Teuton and the Celt, in the two German and the two Irish villages. To these we may add the Laplander, a Turanian, to which race the Turk also belongs. With the Turk we pass out of Europe and Christendom into Western Asia, which is the great Mohammedan world, mainly Semitic. Observe that the center of the Plaisance is Mohammedan, and that the Moslem faith really dominates it, as is strikingly shown even at a distance by mosque and minaret. From Western we move to Eastern Asia, in which the authority of Mohammed ceases, the borderland being Hindostan, and the chief countries being China and Japan, inhabited by the Mongolian race with another world-religion. Next we cross into the Indian and Pacific Oceans, where lies Polynesia, chief abode of Malay peoples, which are well represented in the Plaisance. At last we descend to the savage races, the African of Dahomey and the North American Indian, each of which has its place in this grand sliding-scale of humanity. Now we are ready to go to the Zoological Arena to see the ancestral monkeys, or enter the Street of Cairo to observe old Egypt's sacred crocodiles. Perchance, however, we would prefer to vanish into leaves and flowers, which also are here awaiting us, in many attractive shapes.

Thus we have, in the Plaisance, fallen back to the beginning of human culture, which finds its culmination in the Exposition proper. Undoubtedly the best way of looking at these races is to behold them in the ascending scale, in the progressive movement; thus we can march forward with them, starting with the lowest specimens of humanity, and reaching continually upward to the highest stage. In that way we move in harmony with the thought of evolution, and not with that of the lapse or fall.

Herein the Orient differs deeply from the Occident. There is generally in Oriental thought and in Oriental religion the idea of the lapse, of the descent of the soul from the highest to the lowest, even to the animal. As already stated, the mind of the East conceives man as a fallen being, down he has been hurled from Heaven by God, and has become what he is, a sinful spirit. This is the trend of the great Semitic Sin-Mythus, which we of the Occident have received through the Hebrew Bible, but it seems to have been the common property of the Orient in one form or other at a very early date, being found on the old monuments of Egypt. The West has naturally the reverse process in spite of inherited doctrines; it believes in the rise rather than in the fall, in ascent more than descent; that is, the idea of development is the germinal idea of the Occident. Its migration indicates a continued new conquest of the world, the triumph over the unknown; its civilization is one of progress, inner and outer, spiritual and material.

Questions

1. According to Snider, what is the "Oriental" view of history and evolution? How does it differ from the "Occidental" view?

2. How does Snider rank order the various "races"?

3. What lesson does he want his (mostly American) readers to draw from the layout of the fair about their place in the world?

Fitter Families Display (1926)

Displays, such as the 1926 "Burden" one shown here, traveled the United States in the 1910s and 1920s. Often they were exhibits at state fairs in an era when such events were the major social and cultural gathering point for many rural communities. The fairs were also venues for other forms of popular education, so discussion of human reproduction and family formation was situated in a context where audiences expected practical instruction. Such displays sometimes accompanied fitter family contests, where parents and their children were evaluated, scored, and offered prizes. In the "Burden" photograph the flyer in the middle of the bottom row explains how visitors to the Eastern States Exposition could enter the local contest. It should not be surprising that families with the most northwestern European traits scored highest. The Fitter Families movement spread to forty states before World War I. The American Eugenics Society's Committee on Popular Education supported expansion of the program throughout the 1920s.

This light flashes every 15 seconds

Every 15 seconds 100 of your money
goes for the care of persons with bad
heredity such as the insane, feeble-
minded, criminals & other defectives

Some people are born to
be a burden on the rest.

This light flashes every 16 seconds

Every 16 seconds
a person is born in the
United States.

Fitter Families
CONTEST

EASTERN STATES EXPOSITION

This light flashes every 7½ minutes

Every 7½ minutes a high grade person
is born in the United States who will
have ability to do creative work &
be fit for leadership. About 4% of
all Americans come within this class

"Burden" flashing light display

Questions

1. This display makes a fairly unsophisticated economic argument in favor of eugenics. What is the argument? Why might it have resonated with American audiences of the 1910s and 1920s?

2. This display relies on text—short declarative statements. Why would a display method of communication have been more effective than print alone—in a flyer or a newspaper advertisement, for example?

3. According to this display, what happens to the 96 percent of Americans not born for creative work or leadership?

Source: "Burden" flashing light sign, 1926 photograph, Collection of the American Philosophical Society.

G. C. K. Gwassa, Interviews with Maji-Maji Revolt Survivors (1967)

In an effort to extract more profit from its East African colony of Tanganyika, the German government instituted head taxes on all adult men and conscripted labor to cultivate cotton for export. The need for people to shift to wage labor in order to earn cash to pay taxes, labor conscription, and the effects of land allocated away from food crops to cotton created economic hardship and social change. The material and social consequences of colonial exploitation led to a millenarian response in East Africa, as it did with the 1890 Ghost Dance in the United States, the 1856–1857 Xhosa Cattle Killing in South Africa, and the 1900 Boxer Uprising in China, among others.

In 1905 Kinjikitile Ngwale experienced a spirit possession. Word spread quickly that those who went to see him would receive war medicine that could turn German bullets to water (*maji* in KiSwahili). The ensuing Maji-Maji Revolt (1905–1907) was brutally suppressed by the German colonial military. Some scholars assert the famine that followed was partly engineered by colonial officials to keep an unruly populace from recovering (compare Temple Wage, in Chapter 17).

After independence in 1961, Tanzanian historian G. C. K. Gwassa began asking elders about their memories of Maji-Maji. From the fragments of information collected from people in various locations a narrative of events is reconstructed.

Mzee Nduli Njimbwi of Mtumbei Kipatimu. Interviewed September 24, 1967

During the [cotton] cultivation there was much suffering. We, the labour conscripts, stayed in the front line cultivating. Then behind us was an overseer whose work it was to whip us. Behind the overseer there was a jumbe [official], and every jumbe stood behind his fifty men. Behind the line of jumbes stood Bwana Kinoo [a Ger-

---

Source: *Records of the Maji Maji Uprising, Part 1*, edited by G. C. K. Gwassa and John Iliffe (Nairobi: East African Publishing House, 1967), pp. 5, 8–12.

man settler named Steinhagen] himself. Then, behold death there! And then as you till the land from beginning to end your footprints must not be seen save those of the jumbe. And that Selemani, the overseer, had a whip, and he was extremely cruel. His work was to whip the conscripts if they rose up or tried to rest, or if they left a trail of their footprints behind them. Ah, brothers, God is great— that we have lived like this is God's Providence! And on the other side Bwana Kinoo had a bamboo stick. If the men of a certain jumbe left their footprints behind them, that jumbe would be boxed on the ears and Kinoo would beat him with the bamboo stick using both hands, while at the same time Selemani lashed out at us labourers.

* * *

MZEE ELISE: SIMBANIMOTO OF NANDETE. INTERVIEWED SEPTEMBER 4, 1967

They [the people] waited for a long period because they were afraid. How could one clan face the Germans alone and not be wiped out? There had to be many.

BW. SEBASTIAN UPUNDA OF NANDETE. INTERVIEWED SEPTEMBER 5, 1967

It is true they were ruled for a very long time before they rose in arms against the Germans. The problem was how to beat him really well. Who would start? Thus they waited for a long time because there was no plan or knowledge. Truly his practices were bad. But while there were no superior weapons should the people not fear? Everywhere elders were busy thinking, "What should we do?"

* * *

MZEE NDUNDULE MANGAYA OF KIPATIMU. INTERVIEWED AUGUST 7, 1967

* * * The message in Njwiywila [secret communication] was like this: "This year is a year of war, for there is a man at Ngarambe [Kinjikitile] who has been possessed. * * * Why? Because we are suffering like this and because * * * we are oppressed. * * * We work without payment. * * * It [the Njwiywila message] spread quickly throughout Matumbi country and beyond. In the message of Njwiywila was also the information that those who went to Ngarambe would see their dead ancestors. Then people began going to Ngarambe to see for themselves.

* * *

MZEE MOHAMEND NGANOGA OF NGARAMBE RUHINGO.
INTERVIEWED AUGUST 31, 1967

It was like a wedding procession, I tell you! People were singing, dancing, and ululating throughout. When they arrived at Ngarambe they slept there and danced likinda, everyone in his own group. The following morning they received medicine and returned to their homes.

* * *

BW. SEBASTIAN UPUNDE OF NANDETE. INTERVIEWED
SEPTEMBER 5, 1967

The song of Mpokosi [a representative of Kinjikitile] during likinda was in the Ngindo language. He used to take his fly-whisk and his calabash container for medicine, and he went around sprinkling them with medicine. It was like military drilling with muzzle-loaders, and under very strict discipline. Thus Mpokosi would say:

"Attention!"
"We are at attention."
"What are you carrying?"
"We are carrying peas."
"Peas? Peas of what type?"
"Creeping peas."
"Creeping?"
"Creeping."

And so on as they marched, until Mpokosi ordered:

"Attention!"

"We are at attention."

"Turn towards Donde country [inland]."

(The warriors turned.)

"Turn towards the black water [the ocean]."

(They obeyed.)

"Destroy the red earth?"

"Destroy!"

"Destroy?"

"Destroy!"

And so on as they advanced as if to shoot.

During that time they were dressed in their military attire called Ngumbalyo. Further, each one was told where to go or the day to start drilling. Thus all gathered at Nandete for this type of likinda. The song was entirely in riddles. Thus the question "what are you carrying?" meant "what do you want to do?" The answer "we are carrying peas" meant "we are carrying bullets", and they used peas in their guns during drilling. "Creeping peas" are those that creep, and it meant that they were marching to the battlefield. "Creeping, creeping"—that was walking, that is military marching. "Destroy the red earth"—that meant tear the European apart or destroy him.

Questions

1. What kept colonial subjects from resisting the harsh working conditions described by Mzee Nduli Njimbwi?

2. Identify elements of the *likinda* dance that evoke precolonial African practices, and those of a colonial military. What might explain the combination of these elements in a secret, anticolonial movement?

3. Why would the *likinda* dialogue have been spoken in riddles? Why would Bw. Sebastian Upunda explain the riddles in 1967?

4. What are some of the benefits—and some of the drawbacks—to understanding history through the memories of many individuals?

W. E. B. Du Bois, The Negro Problems (1915)

Born five years after emancipation in the United States, W. E. B. Du Bois (1868–1963) was a tireless advocate for civil rights. The first African American graduate of Harvard University, Du Bois earned a Ph.D. in history, was a professor at Atlanta University, and founded the National Association for the Advancement of Colored People (NAACP). His work as a scholar, activist, and journalist was directed at challenging racial stereotypes and dismantling race-based inequalities. A founder of the Pan-Africanist movement to unite peoples of the continent and diaspora, Du Bois was also profoundly engaged with the conditions of life for people of color in the United States. A prolific writer, he authored over 4,000 essays, articles, and books. His books *The Souls of Black Folk* (1903) and *The Negro* (1915) are still widely read. The following excerpts come from the final chapter of *The Negro*, a wide-ranging history that includes discussions of precolonial Zimbabwe, Ghana, and Songhai that continue to stand up to modern scrutiny.

What is to be the future relation of the Negro race to the rest of the world? The visitor from Altruria [a fictional utopian island] might see here no peculiar problem. He would expect the Negro race to develop along the lines of other human races. In Africa his economic and political development would restore and eventually outrun the ancient glories of Egypt, Ethiopia, and Yoruba; overseas the West Indies would become a new and nobler Africa, built in the very pathway of the new highway of commerce between East and West—the real sea route to India; while in the United States a large part of its citizenship (showing for perhaps centuries their dark descent, but nevertheless equal sharers of and contributors to the civilization of the West) would be the descendants of the wretched victims of the seventeenth, eighteenth, and nineteenth century slave trade.

SOURCE: W. E. B. Du Bois, *The Negro* (Oxford: Oxford University Press, 2007), pp. 105–8, 110.

This natural assumption of a stranger finds, however, lodging in the minds of few present-day thinkers. On the contrary, such an outcome is usually dismissed summarily. Most persons have accepted that tacit but clear modern philosophy which assigns to the white race alone the hegemony of the world and assumes that other races, and particularly the Negro race, will either be content to serve the interests of the whites or die out before their all-conquering march. This philosophy is the child of the African slave trade and of the expansion of Europe during the nineteenth century.

* * *

As the emancipation of millions of dark workers took place in the West Indies, North and South America, and parts of Africa at this time, it was natural to assume that the uplift of this working class lay along the same paths with that of European and American whites. This was the *first* suggested solution of the Negro problem. Consequently these Negroes received partial enfranchisement, the beginnings of education, and some of the elementary rights of wage earners and property holders, while the independence of Liberia and [Haiti] was recognized. However, long before they were strong enough to assert the rights thus granted or to gather intelligence enough for proper group leadership, the new colonialism of the later nineteenth and twentieth centuries began to dawn. The new colonial theory transferred the reign of commercial privilege and extraordinary profit from the exploitation of the European working class to the exploitation of backward races under the political domination of Europe. For the purpose of carrying out this idea the European and white American working class was practically invited to share in this new exploitation, and particularly were flattered by popular appeals to their inherent superiority to "Dagoes," "Chinks," "Japs," and "Niggers."

This tendency was strengthened by the fact that the new colonial expansion centered in Africa. Thus in 1875 something less than one-tenth of Africa was under nominal European control, but the Franco-Prussian War and the exploration of the Congo led to new and fateful things. Germany desired economic expansion and, being shut out from America by the Monroe Doctrine, turned to

Africa. France, humiliated in war, dreamed of an African empire from the Atlantic to the Red Sea. Italy became ambitious for Tripoli and Abyssinia. Great Britain began to take new interest in her African realm, but found herself largely checkmated by the jealousy of all Europe. Portugal sought to make good her ancient claim to the larger part of the whole southern peninsula. It was Leopold of Belgium who started to make the exploration and civilization of Africa an international movement. This project failed, and the Congo Free State became in time simply a Belgian colony. While the project was under discussion, the international scramble for Africa began. * * *

This partition of Africa brought revision of the ideas of Negro uplift. Why was it necessary, the European investors argued, to push a continent of black workers along the paths of social uplift by education, trades-unionism, property holding, and the electoral franchise when the workers desired no change, and the rate of European profit would suffer?

There quickly arose then the *second* suggestion for settling the Negro problem. It called for the virtual enslavement of natives in certain industries, as rubber and ivory collecting in the Belgian Congo, cocoa raising in Portuguese Angola, and diamond mining in South Africa. This new slavery or "forced" labor was stoutly defended as a necessary foundation for implanting modern industry in a barbarous land; but its likeness to slavery was too clear and it has been modified, but not wholly abolished.

The *third* attempted solution of the Negro sought the result of the *second* by less direct methods. Negroes in Africa, the West Indies, and America were to be forced to work by land monopoly, taxation, and little or no education. In this way a docile industrial class working for low wages, and not intelligent enough to unite in labor unions, was to be developed. The peonage systems in parts of the United States and the labor systems of many of the African colonies of Great Britain and Germany illustrate this phase of solution. It is also illustrated in many of the West Indian islands where we have a predominant Negro population, and this population freed from slavery and partially enfranchised. Land and capital, however, have for the most part been so managed and monopolized that the black peasantry have been reduced to straits to earn a living in one of the richest parts of the world. The problem is now going to be intensified when the world's commerce begins to sweep through the Panama Canal.

All these solutions and methods, however, run directly counter to modern philanthropy, and have to be carried on with a certain concealment and half-hypocrisy which is not only distasteful in itself, but always liable to be discovered and exposed by some liberal or religious movement of the masses of men and suddenly overthrown. These solutions are, therefore, gradually merging into a *fourth* solution, which is to-day very popular. This solution says: Negroes differ from whites in their inherent genius and stage of development. Their development must not, therefore, be sought along European lines, but along their own native lines. Consequently the effort is made to-day in British Nigeria, in the French Congo and Sudan, in Uganda and Rhodesia to leave so far as possible the outward structure of native life intact; the king or chief reigns, the popular assemblies meet and act, the native courts adjudicate, and native social and family life and religion prevail. All this, however, is subject to the veto and command of a European magistracy supported by a native army with European officers. The advantage of this method is that on its face it carries no clue to its real working. Indeed it can always point to certain undoubted advantages: the abolition of the slave trade, the suppression of war and feud, the encouragement of peaceful industry. On the other hand, back of practically all these experiments stands the economic motive—the determination to use the organization, the land, and the people, not for their own benefit, but for the benefit of white Europe. For this reason education is seldom encouraged, modern religious ideas are carefully limited, sound political development is sternly frowned upon, and industry is degraded and changed to the demands of European markets. The most ruthless class of white mercantile exploiters is allowed large liberty, if not a free hand, and protected by a concerted attempt to deify white men as such in the eyes of the native and in their own imagination.

White missionary societies are spending perhaps as much as five million dollars a year in Africa and accomplishing much good, but at the same time white merchants are sending at least twenty million dollars' worth of European liquor into Africa each year, and the debauchery of the almost unrestricted rum traffic goes far to neutralize missionary effort.

Under this last mentioned solution of the Negro problems we may put the attempts at the segregation of Negroes and mulattoes in the United States and to some extent in the West Indies. Ostensibly this is "separation" of the races in society, civil rights, etc. In practice it is the subordination of colored people of all grades under white tutelage, and their separation as far as possible from contact with civilization in dwelling place, in education, and in public life.

On the other hand the economic significance of the Negro to-day is tremendous. Black Africa to-day exports annually nearly two hundred million dollars' worth of goods, and its economic development has scarcely begun. The black West Indies export nearly one hundred million dollars' worth of goods; to this must be added the labor value of Negroes in South Africa, Egypt, the West Indies, North, Central, and South America, where the result is blended in the common output of many races. The economic foundation of the Negro problem can easily be seen to be a matter of many hundreds of millions to-day, and ready to rise to the billions tomorrow.

* * *

What do Negroes themselves think of these their problems and the attitude of the world toward them? First and most significant, they are thinking. There is as yet no great single centralizing of thought or unification of opinion, but there are centers which are growing larger and larger and touching edges. The most significant centers of this new thinking are, perhaps naturally, outside Africa and in America: in the United States and in the West Indies; this is followed by South Africa and West Africa and then, more vaguely, by South America, with faint beginnings in East Central Africa, Nigeria, and the Sudan.

The Pan-African movement when it comes will not, however, be merely a narrow racial propaganda. Already the more far-seeing Negroes sense the coming unities: a unity of the working classes everywhere, a unity of the colored races, a new unity of men. The proposed economic solution of the Negro problem in Africa and America has turned the thoughts of Negroes toward a realization of the fact that the modern white laborer of Europe and America has the key to the serfdom of black folk, in his support of militarism and colonial expansion. He is beginning to say to these workingmen that, so long as black laborers are slaves, white laborers cannot be free. Already there are signs in South Africa and the United States of the beginning of understanding between the two classes.

In a conscious sense of unity among colored races there is to-day only a growing interest. There is slowly arising not only a curiously strong brotherhood of Negro blood throughout the world, but the common cause of the darker races against the intolerable assumptions and insults of Europeans has already found expression. Most men in this world are colored. A belief in humanity means a belief in colored men. The future world will, in all reasonable probability, be what colored men make it. In order for this colored world to come into its heritage, must the earth again be drenched in the blood of fighting, snarling human beasts, or will Reason and Good Will prevail? That such may be true, the character of the Negro race is the best and greatest hope; for in its normal condition it is at once the strongest and gentlest of the races of men: "Semper novi quid ex Africa!" [There is always something new coming out of Africa!]

Questions

1. What are the "Negro problems" that Du Bois identifies? What is their connection to slavery and colonialism?

2. What solutions to the Negro problems have been suggested by white thinkers, governments, and business?

3. What solutions does Du Bois see in Pan-Africanism? Why does he think these solutions offer more hope of success?

V. I. Lenin, The Transition from Capitalism to Communism (1917)

One of the most momentous events of the twentieth century was the 1917 October Revolution which led to the founding of the Soviet Union. A leading architect of the revolution was Vladimir Illich Lenin (real name Ulyanov, 1870–1924). Lenin was not only a political leader, he was also the author of many works that had a decisive role in shaping the Soviet Union's political regime. The execution of Lenin's brother in 1887 for his part in a failed attempt on the life of the Russian tsar, Alexander III, pushed Lenin into revolutionary politics. For many years he lived in exile, organizing the Bolshevik wing of the Russian Social-Democratic Workers' Party, which evolved into the Communist Party. When a revolution overthrew the tsarist government and installed a provisional government in February 1917, Lenin returned to Russia and took part in the October Revolution that in turn overthrew the provisional government. As chair of the Council of People's Commissars, he led the newly formed Soviet Union through a civil war that lasted until 1920. In his writings Lenin argued that the Russian working class could not bring about a revolution by itself. Revolution was only possible if it was led by a party of professional, full-time revolutionaries. Once in power this party would establish a "dictatorship of the proletariat," suppress the revolution's enemies and lead the masses into socialism. Lenin wrote *The State and Revolution* when he was hiding from arrest by the provisional government in 1917. In it, he sets forth many of his ideas, including "The Transition from Capitalism to Communism," excerpted below.

Marx [states]: "Between capitalist and communist society lies the period of the revolutionary transformation of the one into the other. Corresponding to this is also a political transition period in which the state can be nothing but *the revolutionary dictatorship of the proletariat*." Marx bases this conclusion on an analysis of the role played by the proletariat in modern capitalist society, on the data concerning the development of this society, and on the irrec-

SOURCE: *The Lenin Anthology*, edited by Robert C. Tucker (New York: Norton, 1975), pp. 371–75.

oncilability of the antagonistic interests of the proletariat and the bourgeoisie.

Previously the question was put as follows: to achieve its emancipation, the proletariat must overthrow the bourgeoisie, win political power and establish its revolutionary dictatorship.

Now the question is put somewhat differently: the transition from capitalist society—which is developing towards communism—to communist society is impossible without a "political transition period," and the state in this period can only be the revolutionary dictatorship of the proletariat.

What, then, is the relation of this dictatorship to democracy?

* * *

In capitalist society, providing it develops under the most favourable conditions, we have a more or less complete democracy in the democratic republic. But this democracy is always hemmed in by the narrow limits set by capitalist exploitation, and consequently always remains, in effect, a democracy for the minority, only for the propertied classes, only for the rich. Freedom in capitalist society always remains about the same as it was in the ancient Greek republics: freedom for the slave-owners. Owing to the conditions of capitalist exploitation, the modern wage slaves are so crushed by want and poverty that "they cannot be bothered with democracy," "cannot be bothered with politics"; in the ordinary, peaceful course of events, the majority of the population is debarred from participation in public and political life.

* * *

Democracy for an insignificant minority, democracy for the rich—that is the democracy of capitalist society. If we look more closely into the machinery of capitalist democracy, we see everywhere, in the "petty"—supposedly petty—details of the suffrage (residential qualification, exclusion of women, etc.), in the technique of the representative institutions, in the actual obstacles to the right of assembly (public buildings are not for "paupers"!), in the purely capitalist organisation of the daily press, etc., etc.—we see restriction after restriction upon democracy. These restrictions, exceptions, exclusions, obstacles for the poor seem slight, especially in the eyes of one who has never known want himself and has never been in close contact with the oppressed classes in their mass life (and nine out of ten, if not ninety-nine out of a hundred, bourgeois publicists and politicians come under this category); but in their sum total these restrictions exclude and squeeze out the poor from politics, from active participation in democracy.

Marx grasped this *essence* of capitalist democracy splendidly when, in analysing the experience of the Commune, he said that the oppressed are allowed once every few years to decide which particular representatives of the oppressing class shall represent and repress them in parliament!

But from this capitalist democracy—that is inevitably narrow and stealthily pushes aside the poor, and is therefore hypocritical and false through and through—forward development does not proceed simply, directly and smoothly, towards "greater and greater democracy," as the liberal professors and petty-bourgeois opportunists would have us believe. No, forward development, i.e., development towards communism, proceeds through the dictatorship of the proletariat, and cannot do otherwise, for the *resistance* of the capitalist exploiters cannot be *broken* by anyone else or in any other way.

And the dictatorship of the proletariat, i.e., the organisation of the vanguard of the oppressed as the ruling class for the purpose of suppressing the oppressors, cannot result merely in an expansion of democracy. *Simultaneously* with an immense expansion of democracy, which *for the first time* becomes democracy for the poor, democracy for the people, and not democracy for the money-bags, the dictatorship of the proletariat imposes a series of restrictions on the freedom of the oppressors, the exploiters, the capitalists. We must suppress them in order to free humanity from wage slavery, their resistance must be crushed by force; it is clear that there is no freedom and no democracy where there is suppression and where there is violence.

* * *

Democracy for the vast majority of the people, and suppression by force, i.e., exclusion from democracy, of the exploiters and oppressors of the people—this is the change democracy undergoes during the *transition* from capitalism to communism.

Only in communist society, when the resistance of the capitalists has been completely crushed, when the capitalists have disappeared, when there are no classes (i.e., when there is no distinction between the members of society as regards their relation to the social means of production), *only* then "the state * * * ceases to exist," and "*it becomes possible to speak of freedom.*" Only then will a truly complete democracy become possible and be realised, a democracy without any exceptions whatever. And only then will democracy begin to *wither away*, owing to the simple fact that, freed from capitalist slavery, from the untold horrors, savagery, absurdities and infamies of capitalist exploitation, people will gradually *become accustomed* to observing the elementary rules of social intercourse that have been known for centuries and repeated for thousands of years in all copy-book maxims. They will become accustomed to observing them without force, without coercion, without subordination, *without the special apparatus* for coercion called the state.

The expression "the state *withers away*" is very well chosen, for it indicates both the gradual and the spontaneous nature of the process. Only habit can, and undoubtedly will, have such an effect; for we see around us on millions of occasions how readily people become accustomed to observing the necessary rules of social intercourse when there is no exploitation, when there is nothing that arouses indignation, evokes protest and revolts, and creates the need for *suppression*.

And so in capitalist society we have a democracy that is curtailed, wretched, false, a democracy only for the rich, for the minority. The dictatorship of the proletariat, the period of transition to communism, will for the first time create democracy for the people, for the majority, along with the necessary suppression of the exploiters, of the minority. Communism alone is capable of providing really complete democracy, and the more complete it is, the sooner it will become unnecessary and wither away of its own accord.

In other words, under capitalism we have the state in the proper sense of the word, that is, a special machine for the suppression of one class by another, and, what is more, of the majority by the minority. Naturally, to be successful, such an undertaking as the systematic suppression of the exploited majority by the exploiting minority calls for the utmost ferocity and savagery in the matter of suppressing, it calls for seas of blood, through which mankind is actually wading its way in slavery, serfdom and wage labour.

Furthermore, during the *transition* from capitalism to communism suppression is *still* necessary, but it is now the suppression of the exploiting minority by the exploited majority. A special apparatus, a special machine for suppression, the "state," is *still* necessary, but this is now a transitional state. It is no longer a state in the proper sense of the word; for the suppression of the minority of exploiters by the majority of the wage slaves of *yesterday* is comparatively so easy, simple and natural a task that it will entail far less bloodshed than the suppression of the risings of slaves, serfs or wage-labourers, and it will cost mankind far less. And it is compatible with the extension of democracy to such an overwhelming majority of the population that the need for a *special machine* of suppression will begin to disappear. Naturally, the exploiters are unable to suppress the people without a highly complex machine for performing this task, but *the people* can suppress the exploiters even with a very simple "machine," almost without a "machine," without a special apparatus, by the simple *organisation of the armed people* (such as the Soviets of Workers' and Soldiers' Deputies, we would remark, running ahead).

Lastly, only communism makes the state absolutely unnecessary, for there is *nobody* to be suppressed—"nobody" in the sense of a *class*, of a systematic struggle against a definite section of the population. We are not utopians, and do not in the least deny the possibility and inevitability of excesses on the part of *individual persons*, or the need to stop *such* excesses. In the first place, however, no special machine, no special apparatus of suppression, is needed for this; this will be done by the armed people themselves, as simply and as readily as any crowd of civilised people, even in modern society, interferes to put a stop to a scuffle or to prevent a woman from being assaulted. And, secondly, we know that the fundamental social cause of excesses, which consist in the violation of the rules of social intercourse, is the exploitation of the people, their want and their poverty. With the removal of this chief cause, excesses will inevitably begin to *"wither away."* We do not know how quickly and in what succession, but we do know they will wither away. With their withering away the state will also *wither away.*

Questions

1. Why, in a capitalist society, no matter how democratic, is democracy "only for the propertied classes; only for the rich"?

2. What is the purpose of the dictatorship of the proletariat? Why is it needed during the period of transition from capitalism to communism?

3. Why will the state "wither away" under communism? In the context of 1917, does the idea that the state eventually will wither away seem plausible?

Casebook

RUBBER AND THE
WORLD ECONOMY

The enormous industrial expansion of the last 200 years has had equally large effects on those who live by growing crops, tending animals, or extracting "natural resources" from the earth and sea. In hundreds of cases, new industrial processes created unprecedented demand for old goods, allowing vast fortunes to be made from previously humdrum products. Whether it was cultivators, landlords, merchants, industrialists, or others who would reap those profits was another matter, sometimes leading to fierce social conflict. The scramble to meet new demand often changed local work arrangements, created large migrations to places where the goods could be produced, and in some cases led to violence as older residents of resource frontiers were displaced, colonial powers struggled over borders, and smaller-scale claimants fought each other.

Meanwhile, these booms often moved people into uncharted territory, literally and figuratively. In some cases, local ecosystems were badly damaged by vastly more intensive and less varied kinds of production. In others, new kinds of production shifted demand from one kind of labor to another (male versus female, seasonal versus year-round, skilled versus unskilled, and so on), leading to major changes in family life, class relations, and other fundamental aspects of life. Often, export booms created a steady flow of easily taxed products—and/or a need to police quality in order to maintain market share—greatly strengthening states vis-à-vis local societies.

And very often, these booms disappeared as suddenly as they began. Temporary shortages might suddenly give way to gluts as old bottlenecks were resolved. For instance, millions of Egyptians, Indians, and Brazilians who began growing cotton for British mills when the U.S. Civil War cut those mills off from their main suppliers were then left stranded when U.S. production resumed. In other cases, the same technological innovation that created new uses for a product later created a substitute for it. For example, a worldwide boom in peanut oil, used to lubricate machinery during the 1910s and 1920s, crashed when cheaper petroleum-based lubricants became available. (One side effect was the spread of peanut butter, which created a new demand for huge stockpiles of now-unneeded peanuts.) In others, demand for a product remained strong, but first entrants into the market soon found themselves undercut by new areas that could produce the product more cheaply.

From among many possible case studies, we have chosen rubber. A tropical plant with virtually no economic uses in 1840, it became very important by 1900, and vastly more important a bit later, as ever more numerous cars, trucks, airplanes, tanks, and so on needed tires. Most varieties of natural rubber will only grow in the tropics, yet the major industrial powers were almost all in temperate zones. Therefore, issues related to rubber were particularly global from the very beginning.

Sir Roger Casement, Consul General's Report to Sir Edward Grey (1911)

Until about 1900, when rubber plantations became well-established in British Malaya, almost all production came from tapping wild trees, mostly in the Amazon basin. This was exhausting work, in tropical heat and humidity, and required knowing the forest well; it thus relied heavily on local gatherers, who had little incentive to maximize their output. Many rubber-gathering companies responded by setting production quotas for natives and threatening extreme violence if they did not comply. The most infamous cases, in the Congo domains of King Leopold II of Belgium, became a global scandal (see Edmund D. Morel, *The Black Man's Burden*, in Chapter 17). The death toll from Leopold's abuses ran into the millions, though not all of that is attributable to rubber gathering. But as the following excerpt shows, conditions in the Amazon were sometimes little better.

A Peruvian politician and entrepreneur, Julio Cesar Arana, began exporting large amounts of rubber from the Putumayo region of Colombia and Peru. He claimed ownership of an area almost the size of

Maryland that was home to roughly 50,000 Native Americans. He took the company public on the London Stock Exchange in 1907. Arana employed heavily armed middlemen—some Peruvian "white" people, some "black" men from Barbados (British colonial subjects), and assorted others—who were in charge of forcing the workers to provide rubber. These middlemen received various privileges, but were also forced to go into debt to the company; these debts could only be met by driving their subordinates relentlessly.

In 1909 a traveling American railroad worker, Walter Hardenburg, published articles about the abuses he had seen in Putumayo. The British government demanded an investigation; the resulting team including Roger Casement (1864–1916), an Irish-born British consular officer who had helped uncover Leopold's abuses in the Congo. (Casement later became an Irish nationalist, and was executed in 1916 for collaborating with the Germans.)

The atrocities revealed in Casement's 1911 report caused embarrassment, but had few lasting consequences. Arana liquidated his company in the 1920s (by which time he could no longer compete with Southeast Asian rubber anyway), and the firm's British directors were not punished. Armando Normand and a few other particularly abusive middlemen were arrested, but escaped from jail without trial.

The man Dyall, who had completed nearly six years' service when I met him at Chorrera on the 24th of September, appeared to be in debt to the company to the sum of 440 *soles* (say, £44) for goods nominally purchased from its stores. Some of this indebtedness was for indispensable articles of food or clothing, things that the working-man could not do without. These are all sold at prices representing often, I am convinced, 1,000 per cent over their cost prices or prime value. Much of the men's indebtedness to the company was also due to the fact that they were married—that is to say, that every so called civilised employee receives from the agent of the company, on arrival, an Indian woman to be his temporary wife. Sometimes the women are asked; sometimes, I should say from

SOURCE: W. E. Hardenburg, *The Putumayo: The Devil's Paradise*, edited by C. Reginald Enock (London: T. F. Unwin, 1912), pp. 283–84, 199–303.

what I observed, their wishes would not be consulted—they certainly would not be consulted in the case of a white man who desired a certain Indian woman. With the Barbados men it was, no doubt, a more or less voluntary contract on each side—that is to say, the agent of the company would ask one of the numerous Indian women kept in stock at each station whether she wished to live with the new arrival. This man Dyall told me, in the presence of the chief agent of the Peruvian Amazon Company at La Chorrera, that he had had nine different Indian women given to him as "wives" at different times and at the various stations at which he had served. When an employee so "married" leaves the station at which he is working to be transferred to some other district, he is sometimes allowed to take his Indian wife with him, but often not. It would depend entirely upon the goodwill or caprice of the agent in charge of that station. As a rule, if a man had a child by his Indian partner he would be allowed to take her and the child to his next post, but even this has been more than once refused. * * * These wives had to be fed and clothed, and if there were children, then all had to be provided for. To this source much of the prevailing indebtedness of the Barbados men was due. Another fruitful cause of debt was the unrestricted gambling that was openly carried on up to the period at which I visited the district. The employees at all the stations passed their time, when not hunting the Indians, either lying in their hammocks or in gambling. As there is no money in circulation, gambling debts can only be paid by writing an IOU, which the winner passes on to the chief agency at La Chorrera, where it is carried to the debit of the loser in the company's books.

* * *

Before my visit ended more than one Peruvian agent admitted to me that he had continually flogged Indians, and accused more than one of his fellow-agents by name of far greater crimes. In many cases the Indian rubber-worker—who knew roughly what quantity of rubber was expected of him—when he brought his load to be weighed, seeing that the needle of the balance did not touch the required spot, would throw himself face downwards on the ground, and in that posture await the inevitable blows. An individual who had often taken part in these floggings and who charged himself with two murders of Indians has thus left on record the manner of flogging the Indians at stations where he served. I quote this testimony, as this man's evidence, which was in my possession when I visited the region, was amply confirmed by one of the British subjects I examined, who had himself been charged in that evidence with flogging an Indian girl whom the man in question had then shot, when her back after that flogging had putrefied, so that it became "full of maggots." He states in his evidence—and the assertion was frequently borne out by others I met and questioned:—

"The Indian is so humble that as soon as he sees that the needle of the scale does not mark the 10 kilos he himself stretches out his hands and throws himself on the ground to receive the punishment. Then the chief or a subordinate advances, bends down, takes the Indian by the hair, strikes him, raises his head, drops it face downwards on the ground, and after the face is beaten and kicked and covered with blood the Indian is scourged."

This picture is true; detailed descriptions of floggings of this kind were again and again made to me by men who had been employed in the work. Indians were flogged, not only for shortage in rubber, but still more grievously if they dared to run away from their houses, and, by flight to a distant region, to escape altogether from the tasks laid upon them. Such flight as this was counted a capital offence, and the fugitives, if captured, were as often tortured and put to death as brutally flogged. Expeditions were fitted out and carefully planned to track down and recover the fugitives, however far the flight might have been. The undisputed territory of the neighbouring Republic of Colombia, lying to the north of the River Japurá (or Caquetá), was again and again violated in these pursuits, and the individuals captured were not always only Indians.

The crimes alleged against Armando Normand, dating from the end of the year 1904 up to the month of October, 1910, when I found him in charge of this station of Matanzas or Andokes, seem wellnigh incredible. They included innumerable murders and tortures of defenceless Indians—pouring kerosene oil on men and women and then setting fire to them, burning men at the stake, dashing the brains out of children, and again and again cutting off the arms and legs of Indians and leaving them to speedy death in this agony. These charges were not made to me alone by Barbados men who had served under Normand, but by some of his fellow-*racionales*. A Peruvian engineer in the company's service vouched to me for the dashing out of the brains of children, and the chief representative of the company, Señor Tizon, told me he believed Normand had committed "innumerable murders" of the Indians.

Westerman Leavine, whom Normand sought to bribe to withhold testimony from me, finally declared that he had again and again been an eyewitness of these deeds—that he had seen Indians burned alive more than once, and often their limbs eaten by the dogs kept by Normand at Matanzas. It was alleged, and I am convinced with truth, that during the period of close on six years Normand had controlled the Andokes Indians he had directly killed "many hundreds" of those Indians—men, women, and children. The indirect deaths due to starvation, floggings, exposure, and hardship of various kinds in collecting rubber or transferring it from Andokes down to Chorrera must have accounted for a still larger number. Señor Tizon told me that "hundreds" of Indians perished in the compulsory carriage of the rubber from the more distant sections down to La Chorrera. No food is given by the company to these unfortunate people on these forced marches, which, on an average, take place three times a year. I witnessed one such march, on a small scale, when I accompanied a caravan of some two hundred Andokes and Boras Indians (men, women, and children) that left Matanzas station on the 19th of October to carry their rubber that had been collected by them during the four or five preceding months down to a place on the banks of the Igaraparaná. * * * The path to be followed was one of the worst imaginable—a fatiguing route for a good walker quite unburdened.

For two days—that is to say, from Matanzas to Entre Rios—I marched along with this caravan of very unhappy individuals, men with huge loads of rubber weighing, I believe, sometimes up to 70 kilos each, accompanied by their wives, also loaded with rubber, and their sons and daughters, down to quite tiny things that could do no more than carry a little cassava-bread (prepared by the mothers before leaving their forest home), to serve as food for parents and children on this trying march. Armed *muchachos*, with Winchesters, were scattered through the long column, and at the rear one of the *racionales* of Matanzas, a man named Adan Negrete, beat up the stragglers. Behind all, following a day later, came Señor Normand himself, with more armed *racionales*, to see that none fell out or slipped home, having shed their burdens of rubber on the way. On the second day I reached Entre Rios in the early afternoon, the bulk of the Indians having that morning started at 5.15. * * * At 5.15 that evening they arrived with Negrete and the armed *muchachos* at Entre Rios, where I had determined to stay for some days. Instead of allowing these half-starved and weary people, after twelve hours' march, staggering under crushing loads, to rest in this comparatively comfortable station of the company, where a large rest-house and even food were available, Negrete drove them on into the forest beyond, where they were ordered to spend the night under guard of the *muchachos*. This was done in order that a member of the company's commission (Mr. Walter Fox), who was at Entre Rios at the time along with myself, should not have an opportunity of seeing too closely the condition of these people.

Questions

1. How was violence used to keep the people who actually gathered the rubber under control? How does Casement say that they responded to their treatment?

2. What seems to have motivated the middlemen who served as enforcers in this scheme?

3. What role did race and gender play in this system of exploitation? Explain.

Rubber Prices (1900–1940)

The graph shown here records average spot prices of rubber on the London exchange from 1900 to 1940. Because these are London prices, not the prices paid at the farm, they include certain relatively constant costs for things like shipping and insurance; consequently they actually *understate* the fluctuations experienced by the producers. This is true for other, technical, reasons as well—at the very bottom in 1932, rubber actually cost about 1/200th of what it cost at its 1910 peak. Prices rose again during World War II and the Korean War but never to the levels of the early twentieth century.

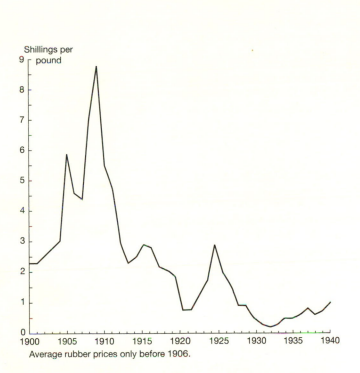

Average rubber prices only before 1906.

Average Annual Spot Prices (Buyers') of Rubber in London, 1900–1940

SOURCE: Rubber Research Institute of Ceylon, Agalawatta. Colin Barlow and John Drabble, "Government and the Emerging Rubber Industries in Indonesia and Malaya, 1900–1940." In Anne Booth et al., eds., *Indonesia Economic History in the Dutch Colonial Era* (New Haven, Conn.: Yale University Southeast Asia Studies, 1990), p. 191.

Questions

1. A well-tended rubber tree is likely to keep yielding rubber for twenty years or so. Pick various dates at which somebody could have begun growing rubber trees (perhaps sensing opportunity when prices were high) and try to figure out what would have happened to his or her earnings over the next twenty years.

2. What global events seem to be reflected in this graph? Are there any that you might expect to show up, but do not? Why might that be?

3. In 1920, when British Malaya and the Dutch East Indies were by far the largest rubber producers in the world, the Dutch and British entered into a deal to try to stabilize global rubber prices at a level acceptable to both growers and industrial users. How successful were they?

Fordlandia (1927–1942)

Ford Motor Company was one of the world's largest purchasers of rubber. In the 1920s and 1930s, most global rubber production was located within the Dutch and British empires in Southeast Asia. Seeking a reliable and cheaper source of rubber, Henry Ford purchased roughly 2.5 million acres (almost the size of Connecticut) in Brazil's Amazon jungle in 1927–1928. Ford also hoped Fordlandia would be a model plantation, where high efficiency would make it possible to offer workers decent wages (as Ford did in his automobile plants) and living arrangements would encourage moral lifestyles. He banned alcohol and tobacco. (For treatment of rubber tappers elsewhere, see Edmund D. Morel, *The Black Man's Burden*, in Chapter 17; and Sir Roger Casement, Consul General's Report to Sir Edward Grey, in this casebook.) The first photo below shows houses intended to be occupied by workers.

However, Fordlandia became a complete disaster. There were many reasons, but probably the biggest was ecological. Naturally occurring rubber trees are interspersed with much other vegetation. Rubber tappers in the jungle thus spent time walking from one tree to the other. It was also harder to supervise the spread out workers. On plantations in Southeast Asia and Africa, on the other hand, areas were cleared of other vegetation, and rubber trees were planted in straight rows as close to each other as possible. This approximated an outdoor assembly line and allowed much higher labor productivity. This system could not be duplicated in Brazil; unless the rubber trees were spaced far apart, insects and micro-organisms moved easily among them, spreading uncontrollable epidemics. These predators were native to the Amazon, having co-evolved with the rubber tree. This problem did not occur on plantations elsewhere. Ford Motor Company gave up in 1942, selling the land at a substantial loss in 1945.

Worker homes in Fordlandia

SOURCE: From the Collections of the Henry Ford Museum and Archive.

Fordlandia ruins

SOURCE: From the Collections of the Henry Ford Museum and Archive; this version is cropped down from the original image width.

Questions

1. What do the houses look like? What kind of community does the developer seem to envision? What might be the obstacles to creating such a community in this setting?

2. What does the plantation look like at the time of its abandonment? How does this probably differ from what it had previously looked like?

Kenneth Pomeranz, Trying to Get a Grip: Natural Rubber's Century of Ups and Downs (2006)

Unlike most documents in this book, this one was written by a historian, but not for a scholarly audience. It comes from a book of short articles, most of them originally written for a business magazine. It goes with another article in that book, which describes the first Amazon rubber boom—during which some Brazilian landlords became so rich that they sent their clothes out to be cleaned and pressed in London—and British efforts to transplant the rubber tree to some place where they could better control production. Kenneth Pomeranz's article picks up the story after that effort succeeded, and just as the rise of the automobile was sending demand for rubber through the roof.

As we all know, motor vehicles made the twentieth century the century of oil—but as we sometimes forget, cars also made it the century of rubber. Rubber tires allowed cars to go over fifteen miles an hour without the ride being painfully jarring, thus helping them become popular; but the rubber business has taken people on a wild ride indeed.

The first rubber boom occurred in the late nineteenth-century Amazon rainforest, where *Hevea brasiliensis,* the most usable of

SOURCE: Kenneth Pomeranz and Steven Topik, *The World That Trade Created: Society, Culture, and the World Economy, 1400 to the Present,* 2nd ed. (Armonk, N.Y.: M. E. Sharpe, 2006), pp. 138–40.

various latex-producing plants, grew naturally. But big rubber consumers soon found importing from the Amazon unsatisfactory. It was hard to make rubber-tapping "efficient" in the wildly diverse rainforest—in many areas, they averaged fewer than one per acre, so tappers spent a huge amount of time going from tree to tree. This made it hard to raise productivity, and as demand soared, so did prices: even in nominal dollars, natural rubber cost roughly 10 times as much at its all-time peak in 1910 ($12.00 per kilo) as it does today.

The major consuming countries—all the industrial powers of the day—could not grow *Hevea* at home: it's a tropical plant, and they were all in the temperate zone. Britain quickly worked on transplanting rubber trees to its tropical colony in Malaya (now Malaysia), where they could not only have political control, but could clear indigenous rainforests and create plantations with nothing but rubber trees, neatly spaced as close as they could get. This eliminated the time "wasted" on walking from tree to tree in the Amazon and allowed workers to be kept constantly at work. The Dutch did the same in the Dutch East Indies (now Indonesia) with help from American investment. The workers—mostly imported Tamils from South India and Fujianese from South China—did not thrive. Among other things, clearing the forest canopy let more sunlight reach pools of water on the ground, creating ideal breeding conditions for malaria mosquitoes (previously rare in the area). Diseases, bad food and medical care, and often brutal discipline produced horrific death rates in the early decades—5 percent of workers each year on most estates, and close to 20 percent in the worst cases. (Health legislation and unionization later did much to improve this.) Nor did the land thrive: depleted by monoculture, it soon needed huge amounts of fertilizers. But the trees prospered, producing far better than they had in Brazil itself. Smallholders in both colonies soon followed the plantations' lead (though they never planted just rubber): these two colonies soon produced two-thirds of the world's natural rubber and continued to do so until recently. In fact, they did almost too well. Once rubber trees reached maturity, it cost very little to keep them producing for many years, so heavy planting soon generated gluts: prices had dropped to

$2.00 per kilo by 1913. Producers have tried periodically to restrict supply ever since.

Other powers lacked this colonial option. The United States, which by the 1920s had 85 percent of the world's automobiles and bought 75 percent of its rubber, had one tropical colony—the Philippines—but its legislature refused to waive limits on land-ownership to facilitate giant rubber plantations. When the British and Dutch collaborated in a price-fixing scheme in the early 1920s, tire magnate Harvey Firestone turned to Liberia, the West African republic ruled by descendants of former American slaves. There he leased a million acres (almost the size of Delaware), built infra-structure, and refinanced the government's foreign debt. The gov-ernment in turn assigned tribal chiefs in the interior quotas to recruit a certain number of laborers; their methods led to charges of slavery, affirmed by a League of Nations commission in 1930. Plenty of rubber was produced, but not nearly enough to sate American appetites. Meanwhile, Firestone's friend Henry Ford returned to Brazil, buying 2.5 million acres in 1927. But his "Ford-landia" plantation was a disaster. It turned out there was a reason why *Hevea* trees were rarely found close together in nature: this prevented a variety of pests from moving from one tree to the next. (These pests did not exist in Liberia or Southeast Asia, allowing successful plantations there.) Fordlandia turned into a feast for caterpillars and was abandoned in 1942. Rubber hunger had mean-while induced other American entrepreneurs to try planting *Kok saghyz* a dandelion-like rubber producer that would grow outside the tropics, in Southern California; they gave up amidst low yield and Depression-era prices in 1931. (Rubber hit bottom at $.06 per kilo in 1932.) The USSR, also without tropics, even more con-cerned about self-sufficiency, and unconstrained by unprofitability, continued planting *Kok saghyz* in Central Asia for decades.

The rubber plant's natural limits also encouraged experiments with synthetic rubber. Germans took the early lead, rightly fearing that in the event of war, Britain's Royal Navy would cut them off from any tropical imports; Germans achieved partial success during World War I and improved the product further during the 1930s. (Despite a looming war, Germany's I.G. Farben shared this know-how with

DuPont and Standard Oil of New Jersey; through the same deal, they later helped Farben manufacture improved airplane fuel.) But in addition to being more expensive, synthetic rubber was inferior, especially for tires that must bear a lot of weight. (Even today, when synthetic rubber has been improved further and makes up most of the average automobile tire, truck tires use mostly natural rubber.) This made it a poor choice for things like airplane tires or tank treads and left generals still craving natural rubber.

There was one more approach to a rubber shortage. Lacking both tropical colonies and top-notch chemical labs in the 1930s, Japan's leaders decided that their "security" amidst competing power blocs required seizing Indonesia and Malaya from their Dutch and British colonial masters—even though this was bound to mean war with the United States.

World War II proved to be the last time that war isolated major rubber producers and consumers from each other. For a time, it seemed that steadily improving oil-based synthetics would eventually squeeze out most natural rubber, but when oil prices jumped in the 1970s, natural rubber bounced back; it has had roughly one-third of the global market ever since. Today's industrial and military titans probably lose little sleep over *Hevea brasiliensis*; but ever-more of us have a lot riding on that quirky perennial.

Questions

1. What are the main geographical and botanical realities that underlie the story told here?

2. How did plantation production in Southeast Asia differ from the situation in Latin America (see also Sir Roger Casement, Consul General's Report to Sir Edward Grey, in this casebook; and Fordlandia, in this casebook) and in West Africa? What did these differences mean for workers and for investors, respectively?

3. What problems did the rubber-consuming countries face in the first half of the twentieth century? How did different countries approach this? How successful were they?

Chapter 19

OF MASSES AND VISIONS OF THE MODERN, 1910–1939

British Army's Form A. 2042 (1914–1918)

During World War I (1914–1918) letters written by British troops to those at home were generally full of understatements and clichés. Soldiers knew that their letters would be censored. More important, they did not want to alarm their friends and family. If a soldier did not write a letter of his own, he could send a preprinted postcard, known as Form A. 2042, shown below. Millions were mailed. British soldiers referred to them as "Whizz-bangs" (slang for an artillery shell that traveled faster than sound so that one heard the whiz of the shell passing overhead before the bang of the gun) or "Quick-Firers" (also slang, denoting an artillery piece that could be fired rapidly without re-aiming). Soldiers devised codes to convey more information than the form allowed. The mother of Wilfred Owen (one of whose poems is reprinted in this chapter; see Wilfred Owen, *Dulce et Decorum Est*), knew that if she received a card from her son with "I am being sent down to base" crossed out with two lines, he was on the frontlines.

NOTHING is to be written on this side except
the date and signature of the sender. Sentences
not required may be erased. If anything else is
added the post card will be destroyed.

[Postage must be prepaid on any letter or post card
addressed to the sender of this card.]

I am quite well.

I have been admitted into hospital
{ *sick* } *and am going on well.*
{ *wounded* } *and hope to be discharged soon.*

I am being sent down to the base.

I have received your { *letter dated* _____
{ *telegram „* _____
{ *parcel „* _____

Letter follows at first opportunity.

I have received no letter from you
{ *lately*
{ *for a long time.*

Signature }
only }

Date _____
Wt.W65—P.P.948. 8000m. 5-18. C. & Co., Grange Mills, S.W.

Form A. 2042

Questions

1. What types of information *cannot* be communicated with this
   postcard?

2. What is the general tone of the postcard? What picture does it give of
   the state of mind of the soldier sending it?

SOURCE: Imperial War Museum, London.

3. Literary critic Paul Fussell said of these postcards, "As the first widely
   known example of dehumanized, automated communication, the post
   card popularized a mode of rhetoric indispensable to the conduct of
   later wars fought by great faceless conscripted armies" (Paul Fussell,
   The Great War and Modern Memory [New York: Oxford University
   Press, 1975], p. 186). What do you think this statement means? Does
   Form A. 2042 support this interpretation?

Wilfred Owen, Dulce et Decorum Est (1918)

World War I proved more devastating than almost anyone had imagined.
All the resources of industrialized society were employed to wage war.
Approximately 65 million men fought. Casualties were staggering. On the
first day of the Somme offensive, July 1, 1916, the British army lost
20,000 killed and 40,000 wounded. All told, around 8.5 million soldiers
died; another 21 million were wounded. Civilian casualties were also in
the millions. The scale of the slaughter horrified those who took part in
it and occasioned some of the most eloquent war poetry ever written.
Probably the greatest war poet was Wilfred Owen (1893–1918). A devout
Church of England member, he was teaching English in France when the
war began. Commissioned as an officer, he joined the fighting on the
Somme in 1917. After harrowing experiences, he was diagnosed with
"shell-shock" and sent to a mental hospital in Scotland. Eventually judged
fit for duty he returned to the front in September 1918. He was killed on
November 4, one week before the end of the war. "Dulce et Decorum Est"
is his most famous work. The title and the last two lines are taken from
the Roman poet Horace and mean "Sweet and fitting it is to die for one's
country." In 1913 the poem was inscribed on the walls of the Royal Military
College at Sandhurst. In the first draft of the poem, Owen dedicated it to
Jessie Pope, who had published enthusiastic, patriotic poetry about the war.

Bent double, like old beggars under sacks,
Knock-kneed, coughing like hags, we cursed through sludge,
Till on the haunting flares we turned our backs,

SOURCE: Wilfred Owen, *Poems* (New York: The Viking Press, 1921), p. 15.

And towards our distant rest began to trudge.
Men marched asleep. Many had lost their boots,
But limped on, blood-shod. All went lame, all blind;
Drunk with fatigue; deaf even to the hoots
Of gas-shells dropping softly behind.

Gas! GAS! Quick, boys!—An ecstasy of fumbling
Fitting the clumsy helmets just in time,
But someone still was yelling out and stumbling
And flound'ring like a man in fire or lime.—
Dim through the misty panes and thick green light,
As under a green sea, I saw him drowning.

In all my dreams before my helpless sight
He plunges at me, guttering, choking, drowning.

If in some smothering dreams, you too could pace
Behind the wagon that we flung him in,
And watch the white eyes writhing in his face,
His hanging face, like a devil's sick of sin,
If you could hear, at every jolt, the blood
Come gargling from the froth-corrupted lungs
Bitten as the cud
Of vile, incurable sores on innocent tongues,—
My friend, you would not tell with such high zest
To children ardent for some desperate glory,
The old Lie: *Dulce et decorum est*
Pro patria mori.

Questions

1. Why is "Dulce et decorum est pro patria mori" the "old Lie"?

2. The poem alternates between realistic description and dreamlike experiences. What is Owen trying to communicate with this device?

3. Do courage, loyalty, duty, or patriotism play any role in the universe conjured up by the poem? Why or why not?

Sol Plaatje, The Mote and the Beam: An Epic on Sex-Relationship 'twixt White and Black in British South Africa (1921)

Born in colonial South Africa, Sol Plaatje (pronounced ply-kee) (1875–1932) studied at the Berlin mission in Pniel, since missions were the only possible education for blacks. Accomplished in English, Dutch, Tswana, arithmetic, scripture, singing, and handwork, he went to work as a postman in Kimberly and studied privately for his Cape Civil Service certificate. Once qualified, he served as a court interpreter and magistrate's clerk, which made good use of his fluency in eight languages. In 1902 he founded a Tswana-English newspaper, placing him among the pioneers of journalism in South Africa. In 1912 he served as secretary-general to the newly founded African National Congress. He traveled with a deputation of five Africans on a failed lobby to urge the British government to veto the 1913 Natives Land Act, which severely restricted African access to land. (Post-1994 legislation considers illegal seizure of black-owned land as far back as the 1913 act.) Plaatje waited out World War I in England, and later traveled to the United States and Canada, where he wrote a long pamphlet, *The Mote and the Beam* in 1921. The pamphlet responds to an increase in the prosecution of black men for sexual violence against white women, known as the "Black Peril." His searing critiques of white settler actions and hypocritical morality would have landed him in jail if published during South Africa's apartheid era (1948–1994).

By "Black Peril" the South African whites mean "assaults by black men upon white women." It is an unsavoury subject. I do not wish to write about it, but the importance attached to it by white contributors to the daily press, who usually give only one side, impel me to give the other side of the same picture. It is such a painful subject to deal with that, through fear of wounding the susceptibilities of the more sensitive of my readers, I will refrain from telling all I know about it.

SOURCE: *Sol Plaatje: Selected Writings*, edited by Brian Willan (Athens: Ohio University Press, 1997), pp. 274–76, 278–79.

SANCTIMONIOUS WHITE SOUTH AFRICANS

History does not condemn Christianity because some of its adherents were criminals, nor the Puritans because some of them burned witches. But white writers on this subject are apt to condemn us all for the sins of a few; and, in doing so, they forget that before the European invasion there were no prostitutes in South Africa. Again, they forget that members of their own favoured race whom white juries refused to convict, have saddled hundreds of Native women with nameless babies and we do not blame clean-living white men for the sins of the erring few. Moreover, they are too apt to overlook the fact that fancy salaries, free education and preferential treatment have not succeeded in keeping white people's fingers off other people's goods.

I do not for a moment deny the existence of a criminal class among Natives, especially along the Witwatersrand gold reef. Every race in the world has its criminals, and no human effort has yet succeeded in ridding society of crime; but, in South Africa, thousands of Natives have been sent to prison with hard labour for such innocuous peccadilloes as "walking on the pavement," "visiting their parents for longer than forty-eight hours" while on a month's leave of absence, "looking at the shop windows," "riding in the ordinary railway carriages" instead of in the Native compartment—which is not always found in the train. All these are artificial crimes manufactured by the authorities, with the result of herding innocent Natives into prison, and bringing them in contact with real criminals.

It is a miracle that in the circumstances the bulk of the Native population has managed to keep out of gaol. I know my white fellow-countrymen as well as I know my black kinsmen, and that knowledge leads me to say without fear of contradiction that if the laws and by-laws at present applicable to Natives were applied to white men, for only six months, ninety per cent of the white population would at the end of that period be gaol-birds. But "they bind heavy burdens and grievous to be borne, and lay them on men's shoulders; but they themselves will not move them with one of their fingers" [Matthew 23.4].

Twentieth-Century Pharisees

In regard to the sexual relations that exist between white and black people in South Africa, there are some white men who are never so happy as when descanting upon the moral decadence of the South African Natives; that is to say, they demand for the Native a higher ethical standard than they themselves practise. Their habit of domineering over Natives in South Africa is now leading them to dogmatize on a subject upon which they might well keep silence whenever they cross the seas. I will refer to one such instance, by no means isolated but one of the most recent and fairly typical.

A colonial girl, not long ago, landed in Great Britain and heralded her presence by airing the following extraordinary views in the columns of an evening paper: "I was amazed when I came to England and saw for the first time in my life white girls courting black men." The action of these girls, she complained, created "an impression of equality between the whites and the blacks," and when they return "to the kraals [African homesteads] of the Transvaal," these black men will "become discontented and make the other Natives dissatisfied" by telling them "stories of the good time they had with English girls in Europe."

Now, when I read this article, I had been travelling for seven months in Great Britain, and I can confidently say that, with the exception of a few dozen Natives returning home from war service in Europe, there were no Transvaal Natives for English girls to pay court to. The hundreds of black men that I have spoken to at different centres in England came from other parts of the globe, and had no desire to go and share our serfdom in "the kraals of Transvaal."

Profiting on the Labour of Others

The trouble about many of my white fellow-countrymen and countrywomen is that they think the whole world is within the boundaries of Transvaal, wherein, they presume, their domination is unquestioned. Their self-esteem may perhaps be attributable to the fact that during the great war they exploited all the benefits, but did for the cause of empire proportionately less than, for instance, the little island of Jamaica or that of Trinidad, who, by means of annual levies, are still helping the mother country to bear the cost of the great war. But it is consistent with the South African paradox to which we are accustomed that, whereas Trinidad and Bermuda got nothing for their pains, South Africa alone has annexed the diamond fields and cattle ranches of German South West Africa. It was done under a different name, of course, but the fact remains that it is annexation pure and simple.

Grown wealthy on the proceeds of ill-requited black labour, by profiteering on wool and other commodities, also the product of black-sweated labour, white South Africans now cast aspersions on their fellow-whites in other lands and boast of visionary virtues "in Transvaal where," the same writer said (with a pen whose facility seemed to have been untrammelled by such trifles as facts), "black and white unions are prohibited." One wonders if she always closed her eyes when she passed through such places as Doornfontein, Roodepoort and Maraisburg? For white and black unions are not only prevalent in the above Transvaal city slums and suburbs, but also in such country places as Korsten, Magatespruit and Mara, up in the Zoutpansbergen of the Transvaal, where white and black parents cohabit and procreate children that are neither white nor black.

* * *

Not All Tarred with the Same Brush

It may be explained that those Transvaal Natives who are enamoured of white girls almost invariably take their white lovers across the border and marry them there, then return the next day to live with their white wives in Transvaal without the interference of the law. In justice to the whites (and lest it be supposed that all the children of mixed blood are illegitimate) I must add that some white men who are allowed by the Transvaal laws to cohabit illegally with black women, and who are debarred by the same law from marrying them in Transvaal, have nevertheless taken similar steps to legalize their unions beyond the provincial boundaries, and have returned to live in the Transvaal with their lawfully wedded black wives; so that only a Pharisee and a hypocrite could, after spending a lifetime in Transvaal, declare to have seen such unions "for the first time in England."

THE NATIVES' SHINING ETHICAL STANDARD

It is not at all necessary for me to dwell upon the moral code of the South African Natives before the advent of the whites, for white pioneers have writen about it sufficiently. Under it there were no mothers of unwanted babies, no orphanages because there were no stray children. The Natives had little or no insanity; they had neither cancer nor syphilis and no venereal disease because they had no prostitutes. It differed entirely from that of the Christian dispensation, but it was seraphic compared with the diabolical white man's law of Transvaal which prevents men from marrying their wives and forces them—sometimes against their wish—to make harlots of good mothers, adulteresses of potential housewives and bastards of children born of true parental love. And the white race—capable of enacting and enforcing such a law—the white race which, by the aid of regular and irregular alliances with black women, have become progenitors of the three-quarters of a million mulattos in South Africa, a race that has introduced lung-sickness and venereal disease into South Africa should have been the very last to talk of racial purity.

It is just possible that we are hopelessly blind; but it must be confessed that we cannot see the disgrace in a white family and a black living a mile apart on the same farm, while it is apparently no disgrace for a white man to sleep in the same house or share a railway compartment with a black man, if the latter be a servant, as laid down by the South African laws.

If it be a disgrace for a white man and a black to live in the same street or a European to ride in the same tram with a black passenger (as laid down in the South African municipal and traffic regulations) our myopic reasoning cannot see the propriety of his sharing the same blanket with, and sleeping in the same bed as, and in the bare arms of, a black woman.

Here the reader may justly ask: "Your book claims to be a record of your own personal observations. Did you personally see these mixed couples in bed?" My answer to that would be: "Certainly not. But I have seen black mothers nursing half-caste babies; I have seen the white fathers of some of these babies; and some of them know that I know them."

There was a time when it was an abomination for Basuto to have social intercourse with Shangaans, and when Bechuana custom forbade intermarriage with Matebele. They carried their prejudice to its logical conclusion and allowed no exceptions in favour of illegitimate unions with Shangaan or Matebele girls. But a white South African apparently finds no paradox in procreating illegitimate half-castes with the girls of a race he looks down upon.

I think white people from the Transvaal would create a better impression, if they made an effort to preach and practise at home the standards of morality they preach to white girls of other countries. Under present circumstances the English girls so severely criticised could justifiably say to their lecturer, "Physician, heal thyself."

WHERE LAW ABETS IMMORALITY

Those of us who are simple "Natives" of this country, and who cannot claim the arrogant designation of "white South Africans," must surely be very ignorant, for we simply cannot understand how the squint-eyed policy embodied in the marriage laws of the Transvaal is anything to feel proud of.

Questions

1. Does Plaatje think accusations of African sexual impropriety are justified? Why or why not?

2. How do existing marriage laws in Transvaal force people into illegal relationships? How do individuals seek to circumvent these legal challenges?

3. Consider Plaatje's tone, word choice, and examples. Do you think Plaatje is writing for an international or a South African audience? Why?

Mohandas K. Gandhi,
Second Letter to Lord Irwin (1930)

In this letter to the head of the British colonial government in India, Mohandas Gandhi (1869–1948) makes a political claim for British recognition of Indian self-determination as he announces his intentions to continue to challenge the legitimacy of the colonial state. An outspoken critic of the British raj, Gandhi advocated for Indian self-reliance and the practice of *satyagraha* (nonviolent protest) to achieve political change. Salt had been regulated by the English East India Company, a privilege that the British government maintained when it assumed control of Indian territories. The 1882 Salt Act enforced a government monopoly on salt collection and manufacturing—making individual salt collection at the seaside illegal. Gandhi made the contentious salt tax the target of *satyagraha*; in March 1930 he and seventy-eight followers walked 390 kilometers (240 miles) to Dandi, Gujarat, to collect salt from the ocean without paying the tax. The march attracted thousands of followers and international media attention, placing the colonial government in a bad light. Newsreels showed audiences around the world scenes of Gandhi's march and other protests. Gandhi was arrested on May 5, 1930, the day after he wrote the letter to Lord Irwin announcing plans for a second salt march.

Dear Friend

God willing, it is my intention * * * to set out for Dharasana and reach there with my companions * * * and demand possession of the Salt Works. The public have been told that Dharasana is private property. This is mere camouflage. It is as effectively under Government control as the Viceroy's House. Not a pinch of salt can be removed without the previous sanction of the authorities.

It is possible for you to prevent this raid, as it has been playfully and mischievously called, in three ways:

SOURCE: *The Collected Works of Mahatma Gandhi*, 2nd ed. (New Delhi: Publications Division, Ministry of Information and Broadcasting Government of India, 2000), vol. 49, pp. 260–63.

1. by removing the salt tax;

2. by arresting me and my party unless the country can, as I hope it will, replace everyone taken away;

3. by sheer goondaism [thugishness] unless every head broken is replaced, as I hope it will.

It is not without hesitation that the step has been decided upon. I had hoped that the Government would fight the civil resisters in a civilized manner. I could have had nothing to say if in dealing with the civil resisters the Government had satisfied itself with applying the ordinary processes of law. Instead, whilst the known leaders have been dealt with more or less according to the legal formality, the rank and file has been often savagely and in some cases even indecently assaulted. Had these been isolated cases, they might have been overlooked. But accounts have come to me from Bengal, Bihar, Utkal, U.P. [Uttar Pradesh], Delhi and Bombay confirming the experiences of Gujarat of which I have ample evidence at my disposal. In Karachi, Peshawar and Madras the firing would appear to have been unprovoked and unnecessary. Bones have been broken, private parts have been squeezed for the purpose of making volunteers give up, to the Government valueless, to the volunteers precious salt. At Mathura an Assistant Magistrate is said to have snatched the national flag from a ten-year old boy. The crowd that demanded restoration of the flag thus illegally seized is reported to have been mercilessly beaten back. That the flag was subsequently restored betrayed a guilty conscience. In Bengal there seem to have been only a few prosecutions and assaults about salt, but unthinkable cruelties are said to have been practised in the act of snatching flags from volunteers. Paddy fields are reported to have been burnt, eatables forcibly taken. A vegetable market in Gujarat has been raided because the dealers would not sell vegetables to officials. These acts have taken place in front of crowds who, for the sake of Congress mandate have submitted without retaliation. I ask you to believe the accounts given by men pledged to truth. Repudiation even by high officials has, as in the Bardoli case [site of the 1928 *satyagraha*], often proved false. The officials,

I regret to have to say, have not hesitated to publish falsehoods to the people even during the last five weeks. I take the following samples from Government notices issued from Collectors' offices in Gujarat:

1. Adults use five pounds of salt per year, therefore pay three annas per year as tax. * * * If Government removed the monopoly people will have to pay higher prices and in addition make good to the Government the loss sustained by the removal of the monopoly. * * * The salt you take from the seashore is not eatable, therefore the Government destroys it.

2. Mr. Gandhi says that Government has destroyed hand-spinning in this country, whereas everybody knows that this is not true, because throughout the country, there is not a village where hand-spinning of cotton is not going on. Moreover in every province cotton spinners are shown superior methods and are provided with better instruments at less price and are thus helped by Government.

3. Out of every five rupees of the debt that the Government has incurred rupees four have been beneficially spent.

I have taken these three sets of statements from three different leaflets. I venture to suggest that every one of these statements is demonstrably false. The daily consumption of salt by an adult is three times the amount stated and therefore the poll tax that the salt tax undoubtedly is at least 9 annas per head per year. And this tax is levied from man, woman, child and domestic cattle irrespective of age and health.

It is a wicked falsehood to say that every village has a spinning-wheel, and that the spinning movement is in any shape or form encouraged or supported by the Government. Financiers can better dispose of the falsehood that four out of every five rupees of the public debt is used for the benefit of the public. But those falsehoods are mere samples of what people know is going on in everyday contact with the Government. Only the other day a Gujarati poet, a brave man, was convicted on perjured official evidence in spite of his emphatic statement that at the time mentioned he was sleeping soundly in another place.

Now for instances of official inactivities. Liquor dealers have assaulted pickets admitted by officials to have been peaceful and sold liquor in contravention of regulations. The officials have taken no notice either of the assaults or the illegal sales of liquor. As to the assaults, though they are known to everybody, they may take shelter under the plea that they have received no complaints.

And now you have sprung upon the country a Press Ordinance surpassing any hitherto known in India. You have found a short cut through the law's delay in the matter of the trial of Bhagat Singh and others by doing away with the ordinary procedure. Is it any wonder if I call all these official activities and inactivities a veiled form of Martial Law? Yet this is only the fifth week of the struggle!

Before, then, the reign of terrorism that has just begun over-whelms India, I feel that I must take a bolder step, and if possible divert your wrath in a cleaner if more drastic channel. You may not know the things that I have described. You may not even now believe in them. I can but invite your serious attention to them.

Anyway I feel that it would be cowardly on my part not to invite you to disclose to the full the leonine paws of authority so that the people who are suffering tortures and destruction of their property may not feel that I, who had perhaps been the chief party inspiring them to action that has brought to light the Government in its true colours, had left any stone unturned to work out the satyagraha programme as fully as it was possible under given circumstances.

For, according to the science of satyagraha, the greater the repression and lawlessness on the part of authority, the greater should be the suffering courted by the victims. Success is the certain result of suffering of the extremest character, voluntarily undergone.

I know the dangers attendant upon the methods adopted by me. But the country is not likely to mistake my meaning. I say what I mean and think. And I have been saying for the last fifteen years in India and outside for twenty years more and repeat now that the only way to conquer violence is through non-violence pure and undefiled. I have said also that every violent act, word and even thought interferes with the progress of non-violent action. If in spite of such repeated warnings people will resort to violence, I must disown responsibility save such as inevitably attaches to every human being for the acts of every other human being. But the question of responsibility apart, I dare not postpone action on any cause whatsoever, if non-violence is the force the seers of the world have claimed it to be and if I am not to belie my own extensive experience of its working.

But I would fain avoid the further step. I would therefore ask you to remove the tax which many of your illustrious countrymen have condemned in unmeasured terms and which, as you could not have failed to observe, has evoked universal protest and resentment expressed in civil disobedience. You may condemn civil disobedience as much as you like. Will you prefer violent revolt to civil disobedience? If you say, as you have said, that the civil disobedience must end in violence, history will pronounce the verdict that the British Government, not bearing because not understanding non-violence, goaded human nature to violence which it could understand and deal with. But in spite of the goading I shall hope that God will give the people of India wisdom and strength to withstand every temptation and provocation to violence.

If, therefore, you cannot see your way to remove the salt tax, and remove the prohibition on private salt-making, I must reluctantly commence the march adumbrated in the opening paragraph of my letter.

Questions

1. What did Gandhi hope to achieve by alerting Lord Irwin to his plans?

2. How does Gandhi justify his intention to break the laws regarding salt collection?

3. What responsibility does Gandhi take for acts of violence related to protests against the colonial government? What responsibility for violence does he ascribe to Lord Irwin's government?

Advertising (1924, 1936)

Print advertisements from the interwar United States speak to the role of advertising in the modern economy. Improving efficiencies in industrial production meant that big-ticket items, such as cars, were becoming increasingly affordable for the middle class (though not yet truly mass-market purchases).

The 1924 Ford ad is one in a series targeting the "increasing number of women who prefer to drive their own cars" (language from another 1924 Ford ad). The image shows a woman alone in a bucolic setting. Dressed in leisure clothes, she needs neither guide nor chaperone to enjoy the freedom offered by owning a car. Her drive in the woods provides escape from the site of the car's industrial production and from the labor of an ordinary day—though a woman able to purchase a Model T would not likely have physically demanding work at home or in the workplace.

The female Ford owner's independence contrasts sharply to the image of forlorn women (and men) who populated Listerine ads a decade later. These ads told stories, typically about social interactions gone wrong for reasons that no one would tell the protagonist. The 1936 Listerine campaign created a specter of bad breath you'll never know about—and a job, date, or marriage you'll now never have. Hygiene products were among the most intensively advertised goods of the twentieth century, creating new demands in industrializing markets and helping to make claims about universal standards of cleanliness around the world (in terms set by Lever Brothers and other manufacturers). Listerine, originally made for cleaning wounds, invented "halitosis" as a named condition that then required a treatment. Almost unknown in 1920, mouthwash was ubiquitous by 1930.

These ads—one for a high-end product and one for a daily, mass-market item—reveal tensions in American ideas about womanhood during this period. Questions about appropriate degrees of female independence, social relationships, and women's purchasing power were debated in the United States. Through the advertisement of American products in other markets these issues became part and parcel of globalization in the twentieth century.

FREEDOM To own a Ford car is to be free to venture into new and
for the woman untried places. It is to answer every challenge of Nature's
who owns a Ford charms, safely, surely and without fatigue. ⟨ Where a narrow
lane invites or a steep hill promises a surprise beyond, a
Ford will take you there and back, in comfort, trouble-free.
⟨ Off and away in this obedient, ever-ready car, women may "re-
charge the batteries" of tired bodies, newly inspired for the day's work.
FORD MOTOR COMPANY, DETROIT, MICHIGAN

"Freedom for the woman who owns a Ford" advertisement, 1924

SOURCE: From the Collections of the Henry Ford Museum and Archive,
Ad No. F. M. 66, 1924. Printed advertisement originally appeared in the
October 1924 issues of *Delineator, Designer,* and *Pictorial Review.*

MAY 1936

3

Often a bridesmaid but never a bride

EDNA'S case was really a pathetic one. Like every woman, her primary ambition was to marry. Most of the girls of her set were married—or about to be. Yet not one possessed more grace or charm or loveliness than she.

And as her birthdays crept gradually toward that tragic thirty-mark, marriage seemed farther from her life than ever.

She was often a bridesmaid but never a bride.

* * *

That's the insidious thing about halitosis (unpleasant breath). You, yourself, rarely know when you have it. And even your closest friends won't tell you.

Sometimes, of course, halitosis comes from some deep-seated organic disorder that requires professional advice. But usually—and fortunately—halitosis is only a local condition that yields to the regular use of Listerine as a mouth wash and gargle. It is an interesting thing that this well-known antiseptic that has been in use for years for surgical dressings, possesses these unusual properties as a breath deodorant.

It halts food fermentation in the mouth and leaves the breath sweet, fresh and clean. Not by substituting some other odor but by really removing the old one. The Listerine odor itself quickly disappears. So the systematic use of Listerine puts you on the safe and polite side.

Your druggist will supply you with Listerine. He sells lots of it. It has dozens of different uses as a safe antiseptic and has been trusted as such for half a century. Remember, Listerine is as safe as it is effective. Lambert Pharmacal Company, St. Louis, Mo.

This smart Moire Cosmetic Bag **FREE** → THE HIT OF PALM BEACH
Fits into purse, keeps powder, lipstick and other cosmetics in one place.

WITH PURCHASE OF LARGE SIZE **LISTERINE** *At your druggist's while they last*
This offer good in U.S.A. only

"Often a bridesmaid but never a bride" Listerine advertisement, 1936

SOURCE: From the Advertising Archives, UK. Originally appeared in the May 1936 issue of *Ladies' Home Journal*.

Questions

1. How did Ford try to generate demand for its product? Does this ad appear to be directed at a wide segment of the market in 1924?

2. The Ford ad creates a positive, aspirational image, while the Listerine ad is based on the consumer avoiding a negative perception. Both strategies rely on a shared understanding of social norms. What can these ads tell you about the idealized role of women in interwar America?

3. The Listerine ad says that friends and relatives won't tell you the hard truth about your breath or appearance. Who are the readers then encouraged to turn to for such personal information?

4. What can you infer about the presumed social class of the target audiences for these ads?

Chapter 20

THE THREE-WORLD
ORDER, 1940–1975

Yamagata Aritomo, The Coming Race War
(1914–1915)

By 1914 Yamagata Aritomo (1838–1922) had theoretically retired from politics, but behind the scenes he was one of the most powerful men in Japan. An important leader of the Meiji Restoration he served twice as prime minister, but probably had even greater influence through his role in shaping the army and navy. He modeled their internal organization and discipline along Prussian lines. He also made it almost impossible for civilian politicians to get control of the military.

The first excerpt is from a letter Yamagata wrote to Premier Ōkuma in August 1914. At this time the recently established Republic of China was experiencing serious political and financial difficulties. With the European powers preoccupied elsewhere, and their banks tied up financing the war, Japanese leaders saw—and took advantage of—the moment to increase their influence in China. In January 1915 Japan presented the Chinese government with the so-called "Twenty-One Demands," which would have severely compromised Chinese sovereignty; ultimately the Chinese accepted thirteen of them. The second excerpt below is Yamagata's record of a private conversation in his home on May 14, 1915.

The recent international situation points to an increasing intensity in racial rivalry from year to year. It is a striking fact that the Turkish and Balkan wars of former years and the Austro-Serbian and the Russo-German wars of today all had their inception in racial rivalry and hatred. The anti-Japanese movement in the state of California in the United States, and the discrimination against Hindus in British Africa are also manifestations of the same racial problem. Thus, the possibility of the rivalry between the white and colored races henceforth growing in intensity and leading eventually to a clash between them cannot be ruled out entirely. * * *

Now among the colored peoples of the Orient, Japan and China are the only two countries that have the semblance of an independent state. True, India compares favorably with China in its expansive territory and teeming population, but she has long since lost her independence, and there seems to be no reason today to believe that she will recover it. Thus, if the colored races of the Orient hope to compete with the so-called culturally advanced white races and maintain friendly relations with them while retaining their own cultural identity and independence, China and Japan, which are culturally and racially alike, must become friendly and promote each other's interests. China in the past has been invaded by other races and even subjugated by them. Thus, it is not difficult to understand why China, in the rivalry with white races, is not as deeply sensitive as Japan is in this regard. But the Chinese ought to know that China in her four thousand years of history has never been under the yoke of the white man. And thus, if she is approached with reason it will not be entirely hopeless to make her change her attitude and to instill in her the feeling of trust and reliance in our empire.

*   *   *

I have explained above the prevailing trend of racial problems and my premonitions of a bitter clash in the future between the white and colored peoples. However, I consider it more prudent, as far as China is concerned, not to raise the issue of a league of colored peoples. Our empire is now in alliance with England; it has agreements with Russia and France; and we are mutually striving

SOURCE: *Sources of Japanese Tradition*, compiled by Ryūsaku Tsunoda, Wm. Theodore de Bary, and Donald Keene (New York: Columbia University Press, 1958), pp. 714–17.

to promote both the peace of the Orient and the independence of China. But we must also realize the need to negotiate with America. Our politicians must be sternly warned against raising the issue of racialism which would hurt the feelings of other countries and impair their friendship for us. The crux of the matter is that China must be won over by hints and suggestions, and only gradually, before we can realize our plans in the future.

* * *

What I should like to explain to Yuan [Shikai, the president of China] is that the cause of war in various parts of the world today is, in general, racial in character. A recent example is the conflict between Turkey and Italy. The current European war is also basically a manifestation of the racial problem. The racial problem is likewise the key to the solution of the Asia problem. Now, are not Japan and China the only true states in Asia? Is it not true that other than these two countries there is no other which can control all of Asia? In short, we must attempt the solution of our myriad problems on the premise of "Asia for the Asians." However, Japan is an island country. She is a small, narrow island country which cannot hope to support within its island confines any further increase in population. Thus, she has no alternative but to expand into Manchuria or elsewhere. That is, as Asians the Japanese must of necessity live in Asia. China may object to the Japanese setting foot in Manchuria, but had not Japan fought and repelled Russia from Manchuria, even Peking might not be Chinese territory today. Thus, while the expansion of Japan into Manchuria may be a move for her own betterment and that of her people, it would also be a necessary move for the self-protection of Asians and for the co-existence and co-prosperity of China and Japan.

Questions

1. What evidence does Yamagata cite to show that "racial rivalry" is steadily increasing? What implications does he think this has for Japanese foreign policy?

2. Why does he think the Chinese should welcome increased influence in their country? Why might they not?

3. Is Yamagata's vision of "Asia for the Asians" imperialist, anti-imperialist, or both? Is his rhetoric of Japanese-Chinese solidarity just a smoke-screen for advancing Japanese power, or does it have real significance? Explain.

Adolf Hitler, Mein Kampf (1925)

Adolf Hitler (1889–1945) was one of the most feared and brutal dictators of the twentieth century. Master of Germany from 1933, he was largely responsible for World War II, the largest and most destructive war in history, costing the lives of at least 50 million people, including the murder of 6 million Jewish civilians. Hitler was born in Austria but fought in the German army on the Western front during World War I. In 1919, still in the army, he was ordered to report on political groups in Munich. One of these, which eventually became the Nazi party, he first joined and then led. In 1923 his effort to overthrow the government of Bavaria failed and he was sentenced to five years in prison for treason. During his nine-month incarceration, he wrote the first volume of *Mein Kampf* ("My Struggle"), published in 1925 (the second volume appeared in 1926). He set forth his ideology and his plans for a Nazi state. Hitler subscribed to the pseudo-scientific body of ideas known as "scientific racism," which held that races were real and distinct biological entities and that race determined culture. Hitler further believed that the Aryan race was superior to all others and was responsible for all advances in human civilization. He saw Jews as a "race" that was uniquely destructive and bent on the annihilation of the Aryan race. One of the topics he touched on was the need of the German people for *Lebensraum*, or "living space," which he planned to acquire by expanding into eastern Europe and Russia, inhabited by the Slavs, whom he regarded as another inferior race.

EASTERN ORIENTATION OR EASTERN POLICY

There are two reasons which induce me to submit to a special examination the relation of Germany to Russia:

1. Here perhaps we are dealing with the most decisive concern of all German foreign affairs; and

2. This question is also the touchstone for the political capacity of the young National Socialist movements to think clearly and to act correctly.

* * *

As National Socialists we can, furthermore, establish the following principle. * * *

The foreign policy of the folkish state must safeguard the existence on this planet of the race embodied in the state, by creating a healthy, viable natural relation between the nation's population and growth on the one hand and the quantity and quality of its soil on the other hand.

* * *

Only an adequately large space on this earth assures a nation of freedom of existence.

Moreover, the necessary size of the territory to be settled cannot be judged exclusively on the basis of present requirements, not even in fact on the basis of the yield of the soil compared to the population. For, * * * *in addition to its importance as a direct source of a people's food, another significance, that is, a military and political one, must be attributed to the area of a state.* If a nation's sustenance as such is assured by the amount of its soil, the safeguarding of the existing soil itself must also be borne in mind. This lies in the general power-political strength of the state, which in turn to no small extent is determined by geo-military considerations.

SOURCE: Adolf Hitler, *Mein Kampf*, translated by Ralph Manheim (Boston: Houghton Mifflin Company, 1971), pp. 641–46, 651, 654–55, 660–63.

Hence, the German nation can defend its future only as a world power.

* * *

In an era when the earth is gradually being divided up among states, some of which embrace almost entire continents, we cannot speak of a world power in connection with a formation whose political mother country is limited to the absurd area of five hundred thousand square kilometers.

From the purely territorial point of view, the area of the German Reich vanishes completely as compared with that of the so-called world powers. * * * England in reality is merely the great capital of the British world empire which calls nearly a quarter of the earth's surface its own. In addition, we must regard as giant states, first of all the American Union, then Russia and China. All are spatial formations having in part an area more than ten times greater than the present German Reich.

* * *

We must bear this bitter truth coolly and soberly in mind.

* * *

The National Socialist movement must strive to eliminate the disproportion between our population and our area. * * * And in this it must remain aware that we, as guardians of the highest humanity on this earth, are bound by the highest obligation, and the more it strives to bring the German people to racial awareness * * * the more it will be able to meet this obligation.

* * *

Today it is not princes and princes' mistresses who haggle and bargain over state borders; it is the inexorable Jew who struggles for his domination over the nations. No nation can remove this hand from its throat except by the sword. Only the assembled and concentrated might of a national passion rearing up in its strength can defy the international enslavement of peoples. Such a process is and remains a bloody one.

If, however, we harbor the conviction that the German future, regardless what happens, demands the supreme sacrifice, quite aside from all considerations of political expediency as such, we must set up an aim worthy of this sacrifice and fight for it.

The boundaries of the year 1914 mean nothing at all for the German future. Neither did they provide a defense of the past, nor would they contain any strength for the future. Through them the German nation will neither achieve its inner integrity, nor will its sustenance be safeguarded by them, nor do these boundaries, viewed from the military standpoint, seem expedient or even satisfactory, nor finally can they improve the relation in which we at present find ourselves toward the other world powers, or, better expressed, the real world powers.

$*$ $*$ $*$

And so we National Socialists consciously draw a line beneath the foreign policy tendency of our pre-War period. We take up where we broke off six hundred years ago. We stop the endless German movement to the south and west, and turn our gaze toward the land in the east. At long last we break off the colonial and commercial policy of the pre-War period and shift to the soil policy of the future.

If we speak of soil in Europe today, we can primarily have in mind only *Russia* and her vassal border states.

Here Fate itself seems desirous of giving us a sign. By handing Russia to Bolshevism, it robbed the Russian nation of that intelligentsia which previously brought about and guaranteed its existence as a state. For the organization of a Russian state formation was not the result of the political abilities of the Slavs in Russia, but only a wonderful example of the state-forming efficacity of the German element in an inferior race. $*$ $*$ $*$ For centuries Russia drew nourishment from this Germanic nucleus of its upper leading strata. Today it can be regarded as almost totally exterminated and extinguished. It has been replaced by the Jew. Impossible as it is for the Russian by himself to shake off the yoke of the Jew by his own resources, it is equally impossible for the Jew to maintain the mighty empire forever. He himself is no element of organization, but a ferment of decomposition. * * * And the end of Jewish rule in Russia will also be the end of Russia as a state. We have been chosen by Fate as witnesses of a catastrophe which will be the mightiest confirmation of the soundness of the folkish theory.

* * *

On top of this there is the following:

1. *The present rulers of Russia have no idea of honorably entering into an alliance, let alone observing one.*

Never forget that the rulers of present-day Russia are common blood-stained criminals; that they are the scum of humanity which, favored by circumstances, overran a great state in a tragic hour, slaughtered and wiped out thousands of her leading intelligentsia in wild blood lust, and now for almost ten years have been carrying on the most cruel and tyrannical régime of all time. Furthermore, do not forget that these rulers belong to a race which combines, in a rare mixture, bestial cruelty and an inconceivable gift for lying, and which today more than ever is conscious of a mission to impose its bloody oppression on the whole world. Do not forget that the international Jew who completely dominates Russia today regards Germany, not as an ally, but as a state destined to the same fate. * * *

2. *The danger to which Russia succumbed is always present for Germany.* * * * [T]his is an instinctive process; that is, the striving of the Jewish people for world domination, a process which is just as natural as the urge of the Anglo-Saxon to seize domination of the earth. And just as the Anglo-Saxon pursues this course in his own way and carries on the fight with his own weapons, likewise the Jew. He goes his way, the way of sneaking in among the nations and boring from within, and he fights with his weapons, with lies and slander, poison and corruption, intensifying the struggle to the point of bloodily exterminating his hated foes. *In Russian Bolshevism we must see the attempt undertaken by the Jews in the twentieth century to achieve world domination.* * * * And so he [the Jew] advances on his fatal road until another force comes forth to oppose him, and in a mighty struggle hurls the heaven-stormer back to Lucifer.

* * *

The hand of the world clock * * * is loudly striking the hour in which the destiny of our nation must be decided in one way or another. The process of consolidation in which the great states of the earth are involved at the moment is for us the last warning signal to stop and search our hearts, to lead our people out of the dream world back to hard reality, and show them the way to the future which alone will lead the old Reich to a new golden age.

Questions

1. For Hitler, what is the relationship between the "state" and "race"? What threatens the German state? Why was prerevolutionary Russia able to maintain a state? Why must the Bolshevik state inevitably fail?

2. Why must Germany expand into Russia?

3. How does Hitler conceptualize the relationship between states?

Hanna Lévy-Hass, Diary of Bergen-Belsen (1944–1945)

Bergen-Belsen was nowhere near the worst of the Nazi concentration camps. It had no gas chambers and included some groups the Nazis hoped to exchange for prisoners held by the Allies. Therefore its prisoners were treated less badly than others elsewhere. Still, food was inadequate, sanitation was terrible, and brutality was rampant. For some types of inhabitants, this was effectively an extermination camp even in its earlier form. Probably 18,000 of the 20,000 Soviet prisoners of war held at the camp between summer 1941 and spring 1942 died. Death rates were then relatively low until 1944.

Circumstances worsened dramatically in late 1944. As Soviet armies neared the Nazi camps in the East, thousands of prisoners were moved to Bergen-Belsen; its population rose from 7,300 in July 1944 to 60,000 in April 1945. Food rations became even more inadequate, and the minimal sanitary facilities were overwhelmed. Tens of thousands died during these last months, and 13,000 more died shortly afterward from diseases contracted in the camp. Ultimately, British soldiers burned the facility to prevent the spread of typhus.

Hanna Lévy-Hass (1913–2001) was a Jewish schoolteacher in Yugoslavia who joined the resistance when the Nazis invaded. At one point she considered joining other partisan fighters in the hills, but decided not to for fear that the Nazis would kill all the other Jews in her village in retaliation. Deported to Bergen-Belsen, she managed to survive, and to keep a secret diary, excerpted below. She returned briefly to Yugoslavia after the war, but lived most of her remaining life in Israel.

December 1944

Starvation is everywhere; each of us is nothing more than a shadow. The food we receive gets scarcer each day. For three days we haven't seen a piece of bread. Some people have saved theirs and now they open up their miserable provisions and everything is moldy. Bread is gold. You can get anything with bread; you will risk everything for bread. And there are more and more thieves, especially at night. Someone suggested we take turns staying up and keeping watch so we could catch them. The hunt lasted two nights in the densest darkness. It was very dramatic, very noisy. No one slept and the results were nil.

Anyone who has a little bit of bread keeps it under his pillow or rather makes a pillow out of it. That way they feel more secure when they sleep. The mothers, especially, resort to this method to ensure a few mouthfuls for their children. As for the workers who are out working all day, they're forced to lug their entire stock with them everywhere in their bag. And their entire stock means six days' rations, at most, which is about half a loaf. The temptation is strong. Everyone ends up at some point eating the entire six days' worth in one day.

SOURCE: Hanna Lévy-Hass, *Diary of Bergen-Belsen*, translated by Sophie Hand (Chicago: Haymarket Books, 2009), pp. 93–101, 104, 119–21.

* * *

In order to mobilize the maximum number of internees possible for all kinds of work, the Germans have multiplied their terror tenfold. Each day, before dawn, at four o'clock in the morning, everyone must be up. We feel hunted. A feverish coming and going, marked by anguish and terror. * * * It's the middle of winter; it's bitterly cold. At five o'clock, the human columns must already be in perfect order in the *Appellplatz*. This is the first *Appell* of the day (*Arbeitsappell*—roll call for work). It's still completely dark out, we stand for at least two hours waiting for the officer in charge who has to count us and send us off to work. Frozen, extremely weakened, famished, we feel our strength abandon us. But no leaving the square, no moving, even.

Due to the icy cold and starvation, many faint and collapse to the ground. Twice, I myself became violently dizzy and nearly succumbed. * * * But I managed to gather myself one more time. Falling ill here is not a good thing. No one and nothing in the world can help us. We die, and that's it.

The German officer finally deigns to count us at seven or seven thirty. He begins with a hearty volley of insults and cursing directed at everyone, he starts to let fly, kicking people for no reason, randomly. Afterwards, he chooses his victims, those who dare to explain why they can't work. These are the ones he "sets right." Systematically, he lunges at them, gives them a back-breaking beating, drags them on the ground, and tramples them—after which he forces them to stand up and take their place in the ranks.

December 1944

The camp commander was just dismissed. Kramer was appointed in his place. Kramer, however, is the former commander of Auschwitz. Ominous reminder. All commentary is useless. * * * The camp regime gets more atrocious by the day. Beatings are commonplace; punishments that in the past were given to individuals and meant depriving one person of bread or of food are now collective measures meted out to the camp as a whole. What difference does it make if there are small children and sick people among us? * * *

An atrocious fright has gripped all of our hearts. We feel that there will be no one to look after us anymore. We are completely at the mercy of the new commander, a villain and avowed anti-Semite. Absolute Master of the camp, he is subordinate to no one. No authority exists for us, except him. God Himself is powerless here.

Kramer does what he likes. Endless transports keep pouring in. Processions of strange creatures move constantly between the blocks and the barbed wire. Pitiful, their terrifying appearance so unlike that of human beings. Ghosts. They look at us with fright and we look at them the same way. * * * We change places every day, each time more tightly squeezed together. Finally, they give the order that we are to sleep two to a bed, so the three-tiered bunks now contain six people. The space between the bunks is even narrower than before. This is how we emptied half of our barracks to make room for new arrivals.

*   *   *

What is important to us at the moment is Kramer and his band. He has imposed a new command on us, composed of Aryans, common criminals (the *Häftlinge*) of German, Polish, or French nationality. They are well-fed types, big and strong as bulls. They continually strut among us with clubs, beating whomever they wish. They wear convicts' clothes, those striped pants and long shirts with large numbers marked on the back. But the most tragic thing is that by their very nature, they are criminals in the worst sense of the word. Their body and soul sold to the devil—to Kramer—they have nothing of humanity left in them. Cynical, cruel, sadistic. You should see the perverse joy they take in beating people. I've noticed it clearly. They are wild animals disguised as men. This is what the Germans have done, what they have reduced them to. And it seems that it is on us that they intend to take their revenge.

These hardened criminals are our masters from this moment on, free to dispose of our lives, our souls, our children. We are enslaved under these vile serfs. What an infernal scheme! The Nazi brute is never short of ideas when it comes to finding a way to humiliate man better, to crush him better. The new command, these new *Kapos* attack the male internees especially. * * * There is a place called the *Stuppenkommando*. It's the death commando. In the evening, after work, not one of the men who have worked there returns unscathed. There they are beaten to the point of being broken, bloody, and swollen. Yesterday, December 30, two men died under their bludgeons. The same day, two others were brought back to the camp on stretchers carried by their comrades. The "kapos" also strike the women or, worse yet, succeed in prostituting them.

January 1945

I succeeded in talking to some of the women from the transport that came from Auschwitz. Most of them are Jewish women from Poland, Greece, or Hungary. They tell us what they've experienced at Auschwitz. In 1943 and 1944 alone, during the time they were there, hundreds of thousands of people were exterminated. They are among the few hundred who miraculously managed to get out of there.

"There are no words to describe what we went through," they tell us. And they tell us of mass murders, by gas, of 99 percent of the detainees who were eliminated in this way, of their executioners' depraved behavior. They tell us all this while scrutinizing us to see if we believe them; because, they say, they are beginning themselves to doubt the truth of what they say. They fear that no one will ever believe them, that their words will be taken as those of aberrant, demented people. Only a few hundred women remain alive out of all those who were deported to Auschwitz. The men and the children were immediately eliminated, as were the elderly and the weak. A Jewish woman from Greece tells me that out of seventy thousand Greek Jews interned at Auschwitz with her, only three hundred women are still alive. She herself saw her parents and her entire family disappear in smoke.

It's strange. These women who have escaped from hell and who worked in the kitchens, in the depots, in the orchestra, even, seem relatively healthy. They're all robust, well preserved. It's bizarre, when you compare them to our own bodies. They tell us: Back there, in Auschwitz, people got enough to eat. On top of that, the internees themselves had organized a sort of mutual assistance program and made arrangements to procure what they needed. In general, they didn't suffer from hunger. On the other hand, the risk of death hovered over everyone, each person knew he was under constant threat of a sudden, irrevocable death, as each one imagined himself already consumed by the flames. * * *

The death factory functioned at full capacity every day. Columns of men, of women, several hundreds and sometimes even one or two thousand per day, waited their turn at the entrance to the gas showers. The crematory smoked right before their eyes, and they just watched, knowing exactly what it meant. The smoke spoke to them of the fire where their loved ones had burned and where they themselves would soon end their existence. No, they weren't hungry there, our companions from Auschwitz tell us, dismayed by our tales of the methodical hunger we are subjected to. All this just shows that the goal is the same, only the means vary. Back there, a brutal and cynical process, mass assassinations by gassing; here, a slow extermination, calculated in a cowardly way through hunger, violence, terror, consciously sustained epidemics.

January 1945

Death has moved in to stay. It's our most loyal tenant. Always and ever present. Men die en masse due to vile treatment, hunger, humiliation, dysentery, and vermin. They fall, they collapse. Their number diminishes rapidly. Many of my acquaintances ended their lives in this manner. Every morning we find one or two corpses in the beds. One, two, three, four. * * * We end up confusing the living and the dead. Because in essence the difference between them is minimal; we are skeletons who still possess some capacity to move, they are immobile skeletons.

There is yet a third category: those who still breathe a little but remain lying down, unable to move. We wait for them to pass, to make room for others. It's not surprising that we confuse them with the dead and that we lose count.

April 1945

I am terribly ashamed to have lived through all this. Men are rotting and decomposing in the mud. There are reports that in one of the neighboring blocks acts of cannibalism have arisen. According to a personal statement by a German doctor who finally came to our block to take stock of the "progress" of mass deaths— according to his statement, then, over the past two months, February and March, more than seventeen thousand internees per month died—that is to say, thirty-five thousand out of forty-five thousand internees.

If only they had been simple, humane deaths. * * * Ah, no, I don't want to die like this. I don't want to! It would be better to die right away, as quickly as possible * * * like a human being. What? Allow your body and soul to putrefy and to wallow in their own filth, to slowly but irrevocably disappear from total starvation, to sink into nothingness, devoured by pus and stench and going through all the stages of decomposition before rotting to death? Because that's exactly what it is: we don't die here, we rot to death. Why wait? That would be an affront to human dignity. What a disgrace, what an immense disgrace. * * *

I look at this gloomy barracks full of ghosts, humiliation, hatred, these motionless sick people reduced to total powerlessness, these living and already putrefied corpses * * * a dark abyss where an entire humanity founders. * * * Oh, no, as long as my brain can function normally, I will not allow myself to end like this. It is man's duty to die like a man, to avoid a death worse than all deaths, a death that isn't a death.

*   *   *

This darkest and most degrading slavery imaginable has made it so that life in this camp has nothing in common with life as humans conceive it.

It is indeed a cruel plan aiming to cause the systematic and certain end of thousands of human lives. Of that, *there is not the slightest doubt, not the slightest doubt.* It requires nothing but to see clearly and to follow attentively everything that goes on in order to deduce, with no hesitation: this camp is not made to hold civilian deportees or prisoners of war for a specific period of time, to temporarily deprive them of freedom for whatever political, diplomatic, or strategic reasons with the intention of holding them and releasing them alive before or after the cessation of hostilities. * * * No: this camp is consciously and knowingly organized and arranged in such a way as to methodically exterminate thousands of human beings according to a plan. If this continues for only one more month, it is highly doubtful that one single person among us will come through.

Questions

1. Who is in charge of the prisoners, and how do they behave?

2. How does Lévy-Hass compare the horrors of Bergen-Belsen with those of Auschwitz? What does she conclude about the goals of the Nazis?

3. What can you tell about Lévy-Hass's view of herself and her fellow prisoners? Explain.

E. B. Sledge, At Okinawa (1945)

World War II was the most destructive war in the history of mankind. At least 50 million people, soldiers and civilians, were killed. In the Pacific the most costly fighting was for the island of Okinawa. Between April and June 1945, 12,000 American soldiers, 110,000 Japanese soldiers, and perhaps as many as 150,000 civilians died. The following excerpt about Okinawa comes from the memoir of Eugene Bondurant Sledge (1923–2001). Born in Alabama, Sledge joined the Marine Corps in 1942. Although he was enrolled in officer candidate school at the Georgia Institute of Technology, he left the program to fight as an enlisted man. In 1944 he took part in the brutal campaign on the island of Peleliu and in 1945 on Okinawa. After the war he taught biology at the University of Montevallo in Alabama. He began writing *With the Old Breed* immediately after the fighting on Peleliu, but did not finish it until the late 1970s. The memoir was initially intended for his family members, but he was persuaded to publish it in 1981. With its unflinching description of combat, it has become one of the classic firsthand accounts of World War II.

By day the battlefield was a horrible scene, but by night it became the most terrible of nightmares. Star shells and flares illuminated the area throughout the nights but were interspersed with moments of chilling, frightening blackness.

Sleep was almost impossible in the mud and cold rain, but sometimes I wrapped my wet poncho around me and dozed off for brief periods while my foxhole mate was on watch and bailing out the hole. One usually had to attempt sleep while sitting or crouching in the foxhole.

As usual, we rarely ventured out of our foxholes at night unless to care for wounded or to get ammunition. When a flare or star shell lighted the area, everyone froze just as he was, then moved during the brief periods of darkness. When the area lighted up with that eerie greenish light, the big raindrops sparkled like silver shafts as they slanted downward. During a strong wind they looked as though they were being driven along almost horizontal to the deck. The light reflected off the dirty water in the craters and off the helmets and weapons of the living and the dead.

I catalogued in my mind the position of every feature on the surrounding terrain. There was no vegetation, so my list consisted of mounds and dips in the terrain, foxholes of my comrades, craters, corpses, and knocked-out tanks and amtracs. We had to know where everyone, living and dead, was located. If one of us fired at an enemy infiltrating or on a raid, he needed to know where his comrades were so as not to hit them. The position and posture of every corpse was important, because infiltrating Japanese also would freeze when illuminating shells lit up. So they might go unnoticed among the dead.

SOURCE: E. B. Sledge, *With the Old Breed: At Peleliu and Okinawa* (New York: Presidio Press, 2007), pp. 292–95.

The longer we stayed in the area, the more unending the nights seemed to become. I reached the state where I would awake abruptly from my semisleep, and if the area was lit up, note with confidence my buddy scanning the terrain for any hostle sign. I would glance about, particularly behind us, for trouble. Finally, before we left the area, I frequently jerked myself up into a state in which I was semiawake during periods between star shells.

I imagined Marine dead had risen up and were moving silently about the area. I suppose these were nightmares, and I must have been more asleep than awake, or just dumbfounded by fatigue. Possibly they were hallucinations, but they were strange and horrible. The pattern was always the same. The dead got up slowly out of their waterlogged craters or off the mud and, with stooped shoulders and dragging feet, wandered around aimlessly, their lips moving as though trying to tell me something. I struggled to hear what they were saying. They seemed agonized by pain and despair. I felt they were asking me for help. The most horrible thing was that I felt unable to aid them.

At that point I invariably became wide awake and felt sick and half-crazed by the horror of my dream. I would gaze out intently to see if the silent figures were still there, but saw nothing. When a flare lit up, all was stillness and desolation each corpse in its usual place.

Among the craters off the ridge to the west was a scattering of Marine corpses. Just beyond the right edge of the end foxhole, the ridge fell away steeply to the flat, muddy ground. Next to the base of the ridge, almost directly below me, was a partially flooded crater about three feet in diameter and probably three feet deep. In this crater was the body of a Marine whose grisly visage has remained disturbingly clear in my memory. If I close my eyes, he is as vivid as though I had seen him only yesterday.

The pathetic figure sat with his back toward the enemy and leaned against the south edge of the crater. His head was cocked, and his helmet rested against the side of the crater so that his face, or what remained of it, looked straight up at me. His knees were flexed and spread apart. Across his thighs, still clutched in his skeletal hands, was his rusting BAR [a light machine gun]. Canvas leggings were laced neatly along the sides of his calves and over his boondock-ers. His ankles were covered with muddy water, but the toes of his boondockers were visible above the surface. His dungarees, helmet, cover, and 782 gear [the field equipment of a Marine infantryman] appeared new. They were neither mud-spattered nor faded.

I was confident that he had been a new replacement. Every aspect of that big man looked much like a Marine "taking ten" on maneuvers before the order to move out again. He apparently had been killed early in the attacks against the Half Moon, before the rains began. Beneath his helmet brim I could see the visor of a green cotton fatigue cap. Under that cap were the most ghastly skeletal remains I had ever seen—and I had already seen too many.

Every time I looked over the edge of that foxhole down into that crater, that half-gone face leered up at me with a sardonic grin. It was as though he was mocking our pitiful efforts to hang on to life in the face of the constant violent death that had cut him down. Or maybe he was mocking the folly of the war itself: "I am the harvest of man's stupidity. I am the fruit of the holocaust. I prayed like you to survive, but look at me now. It is over for us who are dead, but you must struggle, and will carry the memories all your life. People back home will wonder why you can't forget."

During the day I sometimes watched big raindrops splashing into the crater around that corpse and remembered how as a child I had been fascinated by raindrops splashing around a large green frog as he sat in a ditch near home. My grandmother had told me that elves made little splashes like that, and they were called water babies. So I sat in my foxhole and watched the water babies splash-ing around the green-dungaree-clad corpse. What an unlikely com-bination. The war had turned the water babies into little ghouls that danced around the dead instead of little elves dancing around a peaceful bullfrog. A man had little to occupy his mind at Shuri—just sit in muddy misery and fear, tremble through the shellings, and let his imagination go where it would.

Questions

1. How does Sledge use childhood memories to comment on the fighting on Okinawa?

2. In this description, what are the most distressing aspects of combat for Sledge?

3. Why does he picture the dead Marine as saying, "It is over for us who are dead, but you must struggle, and will carry the memories all your life. People back home will wonder why you can't forget"?

George F. Kennan, Baghdad (1944)

George F. Kennan (1904–2005) was among the early applicants to the newly established Foreign Service in the State Department. He joined shortly after his 1925 graduation from Princeton and served until 1952, becoming a highly influential adviser. The architect of the U.S. policy of "containment," Kennan participated in major political transformations of the mid-twentieth century. He moved between posts in western and central Europe and Washington, D.C. Early in his career he received government-supported training in Russian language and history, developing into one of the State Department's top, professionally trained experts on the Soviet Union. Kennan spent most of World War II at diplomatic posts in Europe, including service in London as counselor of the U.S. delegation to the European Advisory Commission, coordinating Allied policy in Europe. The following passage from his memoirs recounts a short stay in Baghdad in June 1944 while en route to his new post as deputy chief of mission for the U.S. embassy in Moscow. This excerpt foreshadows a notable characteristic of Kennan's foreign policy: a clear cultural, ideological, and political distinction between the United States and other powers.

All day we were barricaded in the legation (where the temperature never fell below 90°) by the much fiercer heat outside. We might look out the windows (as one looks out the windows in zero weather in the north) and see the burning dusty wind tearing at the eucalyptus trees and the flat, bleached country enveloped in the colorless sunshine of the desert; a sunshine with no nuances, no shades, no shadows—a sunshine which does not even brown the skin, but only strikes and penetrates and dissolves with its unbending hostile power. Into this inferno of heat only "mad dogs and Englishmen," as Noel Coward used to sing, could dream of venturing. At night, it cooled off considerably, and we slept in reasonable comfort on the roof. But by that time the real mad dogs and the jackals had come in from the desert, and it was not safe to walk in the outlying district where the legation was situated. The only tolerable time of day, when it would have been possible to break out of the prison walls, was the early morning.

The dryness of the heat was nerve-racking. One had to keep drinking water from morning to night; and even then the kidneys had a tendency to cease working entirely.

In general, it was possible to keep healthy only by a very strict and scientifically conceived discipline and routine of private life.

So much for the handicaps; what of the possibilities of service in Baghdad? A country in which man's selfishness and stupidity have ruined almost all natural productivity, where vegetation can survive only along the banks of the great rivers which traverse its deserts, where climate has become unfavorable to human health and vigor.

A population unhygienic in its habits, sorely weakened and debilitated by disease, inclined to all manner of religious bigotry and fanaticism, condemned by the tenets of the most widespread faith to keep a full half of the population—namely, the feminine half—confined and excluded from the productive efforts of society by a system of indefinite house arrest, deeply affected—and bound to be affected—by the psychological habits of pastoral life, which have ever been at variance with the agricultural and industrial civilization.

This people has now come just enough into contact with Western life so that its upper class has a thirst for many things which

SOURCE: George Kennan, *Memoirs 1925–1950* (New York: Pantheon Books, 1967), pp. 184–85.

can be obtained only in the West. Suspicious and resentful of the British, they would be glad to obtain these things from us. They would be glad to use us as a foil for the British, as an escape from the restraints which the British place upon them.

If we give them these things, we can perhaps enjoy a momentary favor on the part of those interested in receiving them. But to the extent that we give them, we weaken British influence, and we acquire—whether we wish it or not—responsibility for the actions of the native politicians. If they then begin to do things which are not in our interests, which affect the world situation in ways unfavorable to our security, and if the British are unable to restrain them, we then have ourselves at least in part to blame and it is up to us to take the appropriate measures.

Are we willing to bear this responsibility? I know—and every realistic American knows—that we are not. Our government is technically incapable of conceiving and promulgating a long-term consistent policy toward areas remote from its own territory. Our actions in the field of foreign affairs are the convulsive reactions of politicians to an internal political life dominated by vocal minorities.

Those few Americans who remember something of the pioneer life of their own country will find it hard to view these deserts without a pang of interest and excitement at the possibilities for reclamation and economic development. If trees once grew here, could they not grow again? If rains once fell, could they not again be attracted from the inexhaustible resources of nature? Could not climate be altered, disease eradicated?

If they are seeking an escape from reality, such Americans may even pursue these dreams and enter upon the long and stony road which could lead to their fruition. But if they are willing to recall the sad state of soil conservation in their own country, the vast amount of social improvement to be accomplished at home, and the inevitable limitations on the efficacy of our type of democracy in the field of foreign affairs—then they will restrain their excitement at the silent, expectant possibilities in the Middle Eastern deserts, and will return, like disappointed but dutiful children, to the sad deficiencies and problems of their native land.

Questions

1. What did Kennan see as the possibilities to serve U.S. government interests in Baghdad?

2. Kennan's role as policy adviser did not mean he saw the world from an impersonal or dispassionate vantage point; locate passages where Kennan makes moral or value judgments about Iraq. What were the implications for U.S. policy that was informed by American—rather than Iraqi—cultural norms?

3. Why did Kennan think the United States could expand its influence in Iraq in 1944? Why did he think the United States was not ready to bear the responsibility for this effort?

George F. Kennan, The Long Telegram (1946)

After the cessation of hostilities in Europe, belligerent nations were faced with the challenge of rebuilding war-ravaged economies and societies. American leaders determined it was in the interest of the United States to assist its wartime allies in order to have peace-time trading partners and to help ensure political stability. George Kennan supported postwar reconstruction, helped to craft the Marshall Plan, and continued to argue that Soviet policy was intrinsically hostile to U.S. goals. Kennan wrote the "Long Telegram" when he was deputy chief of mission for the U.S. embassy in Moscow; it was a reply to the Treasury Department's request for an explanation of why the U.S.S.R. would not support proposals for the World Bank and the International Monetary Fund.

In 1947 Kennan anonymously published an article, "Sources of Soviet Conduct," that elaborated the arguments he laid out in the Long Telegram. The published version widely disseminated the opinions of the telegram and informed U.S. foreign policy throughout the cold war. Kennan went on to serve as the U.S. ambassador to the Soviet Union (1951–1952) and Yugoslavia (1961–1963). The following excerpt is less than half the original document, long indeed for a mid-century telegram.

[THE CHARGÉ IN THE SOVIET UNION TO THE SECRETARY OF STATE, FEBRUARY 22, (1946), 9 P.M.]

Answer to [inquiry from Treasury Department], Feb 3 involves questions so intricate, so delicate, so strange to our form of thought, and so important to analysis of our international environment that I cannot compress answers into single brief message without yielding to what I feel would be dangerous degree of over-simplification. I hope, therefore, Dept will bear with me if I submit in answer to this question five parts, subjects of which will be roughly as follows:

(One) Basic features of post-war Soviet outlook.

(Two) Background of this outlook.

(Three) Its projection in practical policy on official level.

(Four) Its projection on unofficial level.

(Five) Practical deductions from standpoint of US policy.

* * * PART ONE: BASIC FEATURES OF POST WAR SOVIET OUTLOOK, AS PUT FORWARD BY OFFICIAL PROPAGANDA MACHINE, ARE AS FOLLOWS:

(A) USSR still lives in antagonistic "capitalist encirclement" with which in the long run there call be no permanent peaceful coexistence. As stated by Stalin in 1927 to a delegation of American workers: "In course of further development of international revolution there will emerge two centers of world significance: a socialist center, drawing to itself the countries which tend toward socialism, and a capitalist center, drawing to itself the countries that incline toward capitalism. Battle between these two centers for command of world economy will decide fate of capitalism and of communism in entire world."

SOURCE: Telegram, George Kennan to George Marshall ["Long Telegram"], February 22, 1946, Harry S. Truman Administration File, Elsey Papers, Harry S. Truman Library and Museum, http://www.trumanlibrary.org/whistlestop/study_collections/coldwar/documents/index.php?documentdate=1946-02-22&documentid=6-6&studycollectionid=&pagenumber=1.

* * *

(C) Internal conflicts of capitalism inevitably generate wars. Wars thus generated may be of two kinds: intra-capitalist wars between two capitalist states, and wars of intervention against socialist world. Smart capitalists, vainly seeking escape from inner conflicts of capitalism, incline toward latter.

* * *

(G) Among negative elements of bourgeois-capitalist society, most dangerous of all are those whom Lenin called false friends of the people, namely moderate-socialist or social-democratic leaders (in other words, non-communist left-wing). * * *

So much for premises. To what deductions do they lead from standpoint of Soviet policy? To following:

* * *

(B) Soviet efforts, and those of Russia's friends abroad, must be directed toward deepening and exploiting of differences and conflicts between capitalist powers. If these eventually deepen into an "imperialist" war, this war must be turned into revolutionary upheavals within the various capitalist countries.

* * *

PART TWO: BACKGROUND OF OUTLOOK

Before examining ramifications of this party line in practice there are certain aspects of it to which I wish to draw attention.

First, it does not represent natural outlook of Russian people. Latter are, by and large, friendly to outside world, eager for experience of it, eager to measure against it talents they are conscious of possessing, eager above all to live in peace and enjoy fruits of their own labor. Party line only represents thesis which official propaganda machine puts forward with great skill and persistence to a public often remarkably resistant in the stronghold of its innermost thoughts. But party line is binding for outlook and conduct of people who make up apparatus of power—party, secret police and government—and it is exclusively with these that we have to deal.

Second, please note that premises on which this party line is based are for most part simply not true. Experience has shown that peaceful and mutually profitable coexistence of capitalist and socialist states is entirely possible. Basic internal conflicts in advanced countries are no longer primarily those arising out of capitalist ownership of means of production, but are ones arising from advanced urbanism and industrialism as such, which Russia had thus far been spared not by socialism but only by her own backwardness.

* * *

At bottom of Kremlin's neurotic view of world affairs is traditional and instinctive Russian sense of insecurity. Originally, this was insecurity of a peaceful agricultural people trying to live on vast exposed plain in neighborhood of fierce nomadic peoples. To this was added, as Russia came into contact with economically advanced west, fear of more competent more powerful, more highly organized societies in that area. But this latter type of insecurity was one which afflicted rather Russian rulers than Russian people; for Russian rulers have invariably sensed that their rule was relatively archaic in form, fragile and artificial in its psychological foundation, unable to stand comparison or contact with political systems of western countries. * * *

It was no coincidence that Marxism, which had smouldered ineffectively for half a century in Western Europe, caught hold and blazed for first time in Russia. Only in this land which had never known a friendly neighbor or indeed any tolerant equilibrium of separate powers, either internal or international, could a doctrine thrive which viewed economic conflicts of society as insoluble by peaceful means. After establishment of Bolshevist regime, Marxist dogma, rendered even more truculent and intolerant by Lenin's interpretation, became a perfect vehicle for sense of insecurity with which Bolsheviks, even more than previous Russian rulers, were afflicted. In this dogma, with its basic altruism of purpose, they found justification for their instinctive fear of outside world, for the dictatorship without which they did not know how to rule, for cruelties they did not dare not to inflict, for sacrifices they felt bound to demand. In the name of Marxism they sacrificed every single ethical value in their methods and tactics. Today they cannot dispense with it. It is fig leaf of their moral and intellectual respectability. Without it they would stand before history, at best, as only the last of that long succession of cruel and wasteful Russian rulers who have relentlessly forced country on to ever new heights of military power in order to guarantee external security of their internally weak regimes.

* * *

PART THREE: PROJECTION OF SOVIET OUTLOOK IN PRACTICAL POLICY ON OFFICIAL LEVEL

* * *

On official plane we must look for following:

* * *

(B) Wherever it is considered timely and promising, efforts will be made to advance official limits of Soviet power. For the moment, these efforts are restricted to certain neighboring points conceived of here as being of immediate strategic necessity, such as Northern Iran, Turkey, possibly Bornholm.

* * *

(D) Toward colonial areas and backward or dependent peoples, Soviet policy, even on official plane, will be directed toward weakening of power and influence and contacts of advanced western nations, on theory that in so far as this policy is successful, there will be created a vacuum which will favor communist-Soviet penetration.

* * *

(F) In international economic matters. Soviet policy will really be dominated by pursuit of autarchy: for Soviet Union and Soviet-dominated adjacent areas taken together.

* * *

PART FOUR: FOLLOWING MAY BE SAID AS TO WHAT WE MAY EXPECT BY WAY OF IMPLEMENTATION OF BASIC SOVIET POLICIES ON UNOFFI-

CIAL, OR SUBTERRANEAN PLANE, i.e. ON PLANE FOR WHICH SOVIET
GOVERNMENT ACCEPTS NO RESPONSIBILITY

Agencies utilized for promulgation of policies on this plane are
following:

One. Inner central core of communist parties in other countries. While many of persons who compose this category may also
appear and act in unrelated public capacities, they are in reality
working closely together as an underground operating directorate of
world communism, a concealed Comintern tightly coordinated and
directed by Moscow. It is important to remember that this inner core
is actually working on underground lines, despite legality of parties
with which it is associated.

* * *

Three. A wide variety of national associations or bodies which
can be dominated or influenced by such penetration. These
include: labor unions, youth leagues, womens organizations, racial
societies, religious societies, social organizations, cultural groups,
liberal magazines, publishing houses, etc.

* * *

[Seven.] (B) On unofficial plane particularly violent efforts will
be made to weaken power and influence of western powers [on]
colonial, backward, or dependent peoples. On this level, no holds
will be barred. Mistakes and weaknesses of western colonial administration will be mercilessly exposed and exploited. Liberal opinion
in western countries will be mobilized to weaken colonial policies.
Resentment among dependent peoples will be stimulated. And
while latter are being encouraged to seek independence of western
powers, Soviet dominated puppet political machines will be under-
going preparation to take over domestic power in respective colonial areas when independence is achieved.

* * *

PART FIVE PRACTICAL DEDUCTIONS FROM STANDPOINT OF U.S. POLICY:

In summary, we have here a political force committed fanati-
cally to the belief that with US there can be no permanent modus

vivendi, that it is desirable and necessary that the internal harmony of our society be disrupted, our traditional way of life be destroyed, the international authority of our state be broken, if Soviet power is to be secure. This political force has complete power of disposition over energies of one of world's greatest peoples and resources of world's richest national territory, and is borne along by deep and powerful currents of Russian nationalism. * * *

(One) Soviet power, unlike that of Hitlerite Germany, is neither schematic nor adventuristic. It does not work by fixed plans. It does not take unnecessary risks. Impervious to logic of reason, and it is highly sensitive to logic of force. For this reason it can easily with-draw—and usually does—when strong resistance is encountered at any point. Thus, if the adversary has sufficient force and makes clear his readiness to use it, he rarely has to do so. If situations are properly handled there need be no prestige engaging showdowns.

(Two) Gauged against western world as a whole, Soviets are still by far the weaker force. Thus, their success will really depend on degree of cohesion, firmess and vigor which western world can mus-ter. And this is factor which it is within our power to influence.

* * *

For these reasons I think we may approach calmly and with good heart problem of how to deal with Russia. As to how this approach should be made, I only wish to advance, by way of conclusion, fol-lowing comments:

* * *

(Two) We must see that our public is educated to realities of Russian situation. I cannot over-emphasize importance of this. * * * I am convinced that there would be far less hysterical anti-Sovietism in our country today if realities of this situation were better under-stood by our people. There is nothing as dangerous or as terrifying as the unknown. * * *

(Three) Much depends on health and vigor of our own society. World communism is like malignant parasite which feeds only on diseased tissue. This is point at which domestic and foreign poli-cies meet. Every courageous and incisive measure to solve internal problems of our own society, to improve self confidence, discipline, morale and community spirit of our own people, is a diplomatic victory over Moscow worth a thousand diplomatic notes and joint communiques. * * *

(Four) We must formulate and put forward for other nations a much more positive and constructive picture of sort of world we would like to see than we have put forward in past. It is not enough to urge people to develop political processes similar to our own. Many foreign peoples, in Europe at least, are tired and frightened by experiences of past, and are less interested in abstract freedom than in security. They are seeking guidance rather than responsibilities. We should be better able than Russians to give them this. And unless we do, Russians certainly will.

(Five) Finally we must have courage and self confidence to cling to our own methods and conceptions of human society. After all, the greatest danger that can befall us in coping with this problem of Soviet Communism, is that we shall allow ourselves to become like those with whom we are coping.

Questions

1. In "Sources of Soviet Conduct" Kennan said, "The main element of any United States policy toward the Soviet Union must be a long-term, patient but firm and vigilant containment of Russian expansive tendencies." What reasons does he give in the telegram to justify the policy of containment?

2. Kennan notes that Stalin anticipated direct military conflict with capitalist powers. Where did Kennan (accurately) predict these conflicts would occur? What does this tell you about the role of less powerful states in a bipolar world?

3. Kennan frequently used history to make arguments about current politics; how does Kennan's use of Russian history compare to a similar rhetorical strategy invoking Iraq's colonial past in his memoir (see George F. Kennan, Baghdad, in this chapter)?

Juan and Eva Perón, The Peróns Justify Their Regime (1944–1951)

Juan Domingo Perón (1895–1974) and wife Maria Eva Duarte de Perón (1919–1952), his mistress and later his wife, are among the most controversial figures in Latin American history. A military officer of Fascist sympathies, he was the authoritarian president of Argentina from 1945 to 1955. Deposed by a military coup, he went into exile, returned in 1973, and served again as president until his death. Perceived by some as a political rightist, by others as a leftist, his regime in Argentina tried to extend the economic benefits of industrialization to the working classes, without fundamentally altering the existing political and social system. His wife Eva played a significant role in his regime. Extremely popular with the poor, to whom she was known as the "Lady of Hope," she was an important liaison between her husband and urban workers. She also headed a wealthy private foundation that built hospitals, schools, and low-income housing. In 1947 she promoted a bill that gave Argentine women the right to vote. As head of the women's branch of the Peronista party, she helped deliver the bulk of the female vote to Perón during his election campaign of 1952. The first excerpts below are from speeches made by Juan Perón. With the exception of the last, they all come from the period when he was either vice president (1944) or president of Argentina. The last of his statements included here was made shortly after he had been overthrown in September 1955 by a military coup. The excerpt by Eva Perón comes from her autobiography, published shortly before her death in 1952.

JUAN DOMINGO PERÓN, *PERÓN EXPOUNDS HIS DOCTRINE*

The Ruling Class

An attempt has been made to lead the public to believe that the oligarchy, that untoward lodge of demagogues, represented the ruling class in the country, its élite, and as such was made up of wise, rich and good people. We must observe that "the wise are seldom rich, and the rich seldom good." Nor must we forget that neither the wise nor the good found a place among Argentine politicians.

October 15th, 1944

Objectives

From today onwards we shall industrialize the country so that our work may be done by Argentine workers and so that they may earn what foreign workers earned before. This is what industrialization means to us. To accomplish this cycle we shall complete and intensify the economic cycle of production and consumption, we shall produce more, and value that production in view of our own industrialization and commerce, avoiding exploitation and increasing the consumption. When this cycle is closed, we shall be able to provide our country with 80 or 90 per cent of our production and we shall only export 10 or 20 per cent, because it is necessary to convince ourselves that the money of a man from Catamarca or Santiago del Estero is worth as much as that of the English, Americans or Japanese. * * *

July 30th, 1947

Everything Should Be Argentine

Foundations have already been laid for the national tin-plate factory—an article of trade which is taking too long in getting to our country—in which the containers we need to export our production in will be manufactured. Due to the lack of a factory of tin-plate containers, the Republic has lost many thousands of millions of pesos; and we have not had any tin-plate factory before because certain foreigners that negotiated with our food production, objected to it. But in the future we shall have the containers that our production

---

SOURCE: Juan Domingo Perón, *Perón Expounds His Doctrine* (New York: AMS Press, 1973), pp. 49, 122–24. Juan Domingo Perón, *The Voice of Perón* (Buenos Aires: Subsecretaria de Informaciones de la Presidencia de la Nación Argentina, 1950), pp. 131–32. Juan Domingo Perón, *La Fuerza es el Derecho de las Bestias* (Mexico: Editorial Al Día, 1956), pp. 18–19, translated by Maura Elizabeth Cunningham for this edition. Eva Perón, *La Razón de Mi Vida y Otros Escritos* (Buenos Aires: Planeta, 1996), pp. 205–7, translated by Maura Elizabeth Cunningham for this edition.

requires, the ships necessary to transport it, and those who in previous times commanded here as if they were in their own land, will have to submit and receive our products canned by Argentine hands, transported by Argentine railways and taken to Europe by Argentine ships.

March 2nd, 1947

* * *

JUAN DOMINGO PERÓN, *THE VOICE OF PERÓN*

Another Social Service

It would never occur to anyone that the air, the sun, the light, and the water in the rivers were the exclusive heritage of a chosen few. The very idea seems absurd to us. The time will come when it will also seem absurd to us that culture and advantages of industrial civilization, petroleum, and sources of energy should be exploited by a privileged few.

In the same way, I understand that, with the passing of the years, the distribution of food supplies will become another social service, because proper nourishment is one of the most powerful sources of energy, and one which is most directly responsible for the development and perfecting of a community of human beings.

April 29th, 1949

Argentine Railways

We have reached our "coming of age" which enables us, to the same extent as anybody else, to estimate our true value and to govern our country by ourselves. For this reason it is of vital importance that basic industries should be national, sometimes controlled by the State and at others privately owned, but always in the hands of Argentines. In achieving this purpose and effecting this policy of recovery, it is of vital importance that the railways should be nationalised, to say nothing of reasons of sovereignty which are easy to understand.

September 17th, 1946

* * *

JUAN DOMINGO PERÓN, *FORCE IS THE RIGHT OF THE BEASTS*

When I came into the government, in my country there were people who earned twenty centavos per day and peons who got only ten or fifteen pesos per month. They were killed recklessly in the sugar mills and fields laboring under criminal working conditions. In a country that possessed 45 million cows, its inhabitants died of constitutional weakness [malnutrition]. It was a country of fat bulls and gaunt peons.

Social security was almost unknown, and insignificant pensions covered only public employees and officials of the armed forces. We established retirement pensions for all who worked, including the employers. We created pensions for the elderly and the invalid, banishing from the country the sad spectacle of misery amid abundance.

We legalized the existence of union organizations formerly declared illegal by Argentine law and promoted the formation of the General Confederation of Labor, with six million contributing members. * * *

We made possible absolutely free education for all those who desired to study, without distinction of class, creed, or religion, and in eight years we constructed eight thousand schools of all types.

Large dams and their power plants expanded the size of Argentine agriculture and more than 35,000 public works were completed solely through the effort of the first government five-year plan, among them a gas pipeline 1,800 kilometers long, the Pistarini Airport, the Eva Perón oil refinery (which the rebels want to bombard despite its cost of 400 million dollars and ten years of work), the exploitation of Río Turbio's coal and [construction of] its railroad, more than twenty large electric plants, etc., etc. * * *

Now I hope that the People will know how to defend what has been accomplished against the greed of their false liberators. * * *

Eva Perón, The Home or the Factory

Every day thousands of women abandon the feminine sphere and start to live like men.

They work almost like men. They prefer, like men, the street to the home. They are not resigned to being either mothers or wives.

They substitute for men everywhere.

Is this "feminism"? I think that it is more accurately the masculinization of our sex.

And I ask myself if all this change has solved our problem.

But no. All the old problems continue and other new ones, even, appear. The number of young women convinced that the worst bargain for them is to form a home is greater every day.

And all the same it is for this purpose that we are born.

Here is our greatest problem.

We feel that we are born for the home, and the home has become a weight too heavy for our shoulders.

We renounce the home and then * * * we go out to look for a solution * * * we think that the solution is to emancipate ourselves economically and work somewhere * * * but this work makes us equal to men * * * No! We are not like them * * * they can live alone * * * we cannot * * * we feel the need for company, for total companionship * * * we feel the need to give more than we receive * * * We cannot work for nothing more than to earn a salary like men can!

And on the other hand, if we renounce the work that liberates us and form a home * * * there we burn our ships once and for all.

No profession in the world has fewer possibilities for return than our profession of womanhood.

Even if we are chosen by a good man * * * our home will not always be like that which we dreamed of when we were single.

At the doorways of the home the entire nation ends and other laws and other rights begin * * * the law and the right of the man * * * who many times is only a master and at times is also * * * a dictator.

And nobody is able to intervene there.

The mother of the family is at the margin of all the security measures. She is the only worker in the world who does not know a salary, nor guaranteed respect, nor the limiting of working hours, nor Sunday, nor vacations, nor any sleep, nor indemnity against dismissal, nor strikes of any kind * * * All this—so we have learned since we were "girls"—belongs to the sphere of love * * * and the worst is that love oftentimes disappears quickly in the house * * * and therefore, everything becomes "forced work" * * * obligations without any rights! Free services in exchange for pain and sacrifice!

I do not say it is always like this. I should not have the right to say anything, because my home is happy * * * if I did not see every day the pain of all the women who live like this * * * without any horizon in sight, without any rights, without any hope.

For this reason every day there are fewer women to form homes * * *

True homes, united and happy! And in reality every day the world needs more homes, and, for them, more women willing to fulfill their destiny and their mission. For this reason the first objective of a feminine movement that wants to make things better for women * * * which does not aspire to change them into men, should be the home.

We are born to establish homes. We are not born for the street. Common sense shows us the solution. We must have in the home that which we go out to find: our own small economic independence * * * which would save us from becoming poor women without any outlook, without any rights, and without any hope!

Questions

1. What are Juan Perón's goals in industrializing Argentina? Why should "basic" industries be national? In the context of the world market in the 1940s and 1950s, do Perón's goals seem realistic?

2. What does Perón see as his most significant accomplishments? Some historians have seen Perón as pro-Fascist. Is this incompatible with his program of reforms?

3. For Eva Perón, what seems to be the difference between "feminism" and "masculinazation"? Why is choosing between the "home" and the "factory" difficult?

Isabel and David Crook, Chinese Revolution (1940s)

Isabel (b. 1915) and David (1910–2000) Crook traveled different routes to Ten Mile Inn, the village where they witnessed the Chinese revolution. Born to missionaries in Sichuan, Isabel was educated in Canada, returning to China in 1938 as an anthropologist. There she met David, a communist party operative and Spanish Civil War veteran from England. After joining the Allied armed forces during World War II, they returned to China in 1947, slipping through nationalist lines to reach communist-controlled territory. They stayed in China after 1949, teaching college English in Beijing. Both were persecuted during the Cultural Revolution (1966–1976).

The first excerpt here discusses land reform, which in this village occurred in stages, beginning with tax reform in 1943 and ending with final assignments of land in 1948. The second excerpt discusses Fu Gao-lin, an abusive communist leader; his misdeeds began in 1943, and the campaign against him described here took place in March 1948. The large number of bachelors among the poor stemmed from an imbalance of marriageable men and women in prerevolutionary China. Some elite men had a wife and a concubine. Girls died more often than boys, victims of inferior treatment or, sometimes, sex-selective infanticide.

TEN MILE INN

In 1937 before the beginning of the reforms, 70 percent of the people of the village lived in the most dire circumstances. For much of the year they subsisted on husks, wild herbs, and watery gruel "so thin you could see the reflection of the moon in it." In terms of an economically advanced country, there were no wealthy people in Ten Mile Inn. Landlords and peasants alike were pitifully poor. Nevertheless there was a profound difference between them. In time of famine, it was the members of the poor families who died or emigrated, who were forced by poverty to kill or sell children whom

SOURCE: Isabel and David Crook, *Ten Mile Inn: Mass Movement in a Chinese Village* (New York: Pantheon Books, 1979), pp. 8–11, 145–48.

they could not feed, who were driven by hunger to join the warlord armies, who were imprisoned for the nonpayment of taxes or lost their meager property by default for nonpayment of debts. But for the landlords and rich peasants, famine was a time for foreclosure on mortgages and for adding to their own landholdings.

In 1937 there were just over 1,400 people in Ten Mile Inn, and just under 700 acres of land. [H]alf an acre a head if it had been evenly divided [but] * * * [e]ight households of landlords and rich peasants owned 120 acres, and landlords living in other villages owned another 90 or so. There were 40 families of upper-middle peasants who had enough to get along on and could even put aside a little each year. The remaining 373 families had only 218 acres among them.

For every ten people in the village there was only one draft animal. But here again, the twenty richest families had two animals each; the remaining families averaged only "one leg each," as the peasants said when four of them shared a donkey. In fact, most of them owned "not even one hair of a donkey."

Poverty drove numerous peasants to leave Ten Mile Inn. * * * [M]any became itinerant brickmakers during the slack farming season. When they were lucky enough to find work, the brickmakers earned more in a month than a farmhand could make in a year. But the work was too irregular to afford a reliable income. * * * Without such secondary occupations, many of the poor-peasant families could not have survived.

* * *

Then, as the peasants say, "The sun arose in the West." Units of the Communist-led Eighth Route Army, driving eastward from their bases in the heart of the Taihang Mountains, organized the peasants to defend themselves.

* * *

Yet these initial steps took place in the cruelest of contexts. They lessened suffering, but they could not prevent it. People still went begging, sold their children, hanged themselves. In 49 of Ten Mile Inn's 400-odd families, 59 people starved to death.

* * * Not surprisingly, it was the poor and middle peasants who rallied most closely around the newly formed underground Communist Party. And it was mainly from them that new Communists were recruited during the Party's campaigns for successive reforms. In the early 1940s, after organizing against the famine and the Japanese invaders, the Party introduced a new taxation system. Taxes were now levied proportionately among the richest 30 percent of the families. Thus 70 percent of the villagers were freed from taxation. Never before had the peasants dreamed of such good fortune. For the first time, many villagers found that they had enough seed for sowing. Gone was the need to borrow at seeding time when grain prices were highest and to repay at harvest time when they were lowest. By this simple but sweeping reform, the cycle of peasant debt was frontally assaulted.

* * *

As a result of the Communist-led reforms, a new class emerged—the "new middle peasants." * * * [R]oughly one-third of all the families in the village had moved into it from the ranks of the poor peasants and hired laborers. Poor peasants still made up about one-third of the total number of families in the village, but now they all owned land. Although * * * they were far below the average in standard of living, their subsistence was at least guaranteed. And the threat of moneylenders', or landlords', bailiffs sweeping down on their homes to seize their few belongings—wooden doors, quilts, cooking pots, or pottery jars—was now at an end. Former landlords and rich peasants held only one-sixth the land they had had in the past.

* * *

Fu Gao-lin

At the grievance meeting to discuss Fu Gao-lin on the afternoon of March 19, no other topic received so much attention as his divorce and remarriage. Before the Eighth Route Army came, Fu Gao-lin had been a poor peasant who could barely eke out a living in spite of his hard work. And of course he had no wife, though he was tall and handsome. But he fanshenned [made himself economically and socially secure] when the army arrived and lost no time in finding one. She bore him several children, but none survived, and he finally bought a son from a starving poor peasant during the famine.

Fu Gao-lin prospered politically as well as economically, becoming in turn chairman of the peasant union and village head. Meanwhile he grew increasingly dissatisfied with the wife he had wed in his less prosperous days. In time he found a woman more suited to his taste and his new condition, even though she was already married. Her husband had neither a robust physique nor a forceful personality, and the wife had henpecked him even before Fu appeared on the scene.

* * * [Fu] worked untiringly to undermine his rival's marriage. With Fu's encouragement the wife subjected her wretched husband to a daily barrage of curses, refused to cook for him, and openly flaunted the fact that she slept with the village head. Finding life intolerable, the henpecked husband left home and soon afterwards conveniently died. Fu Gao-lin immediately divorced his first wife and married the second. But as the sordid affair became common knowledge, village resentment increased until it "tied a knot in the hearts of the people."

* * * The last to speak [at a village grievance meeting] was the mother of the man who died. "Fu Gao-lin drove my son away so that he died far from home," she said. "Then he took all my boy's belongings. * * * Before my son left the village, he was afraid to go home to eat. He had been locked up by Fu Gao-lin several times, and many times he had tried to commit suicide. * * * "

Fu Gao-lin had also created a string of wrecked marriages in the village for purposes not of sentiment, but business. As prosperity spread, more and more poor peasants who had been bachelors from poverty became prosperous new middle peasants seeking wives. Women were scarce, and Fu Gao-lin let it be known that for a consideration he would do what he could to find wives for these men.

In the interests of his matchmaking business, Fu kept an eye out for unhappily married couples and promoted discord wherever he could. Then he approached the woman and suggested that in his official capacity he could arrange a divorce, provided she married the bachelor he recommended.

* * *

Not all the accusations concerned Fu's abilities as a marriage broker.

"When I was away from home peddling secondhand clothes," said one man, "he seized the key to my house and set up a bakery in one of the rooms. He burned all my chaff and wheat stalks and even sold some of my bricks. When I came back and protested, he tried to make me back down. In the end he said he'd get out in a month." During the famine Fu Gao-lin gave people bread from his bakery on credit. When they couldn't pay the debt, he demanded their labor or even their land, just as the landlords had done.

* * *

In 1944 when Fu lost his Party membership, he withdrew from village affairs and concentrated on farming. His misdeeds belonged to the past, and in many cases he had already made compensation to people he had harmed. He had not become a model character, of course.

* * *

[When a grievance meeting was called to deal with an old landlord named Wang Ke-bin it also took up the old complaints against Fu Gao-lin.] The consensus was that the question of referring Fu's case to the people's court should be delayed. * * * Meanwhile he was instructed to vacate any property which he had occupied against the owner's will. The general principle was that he should "cough up what he had swallowed" in graft and extortion.

But in addition, the militants proposed that Fu Gao-lin be separated immediately from his second wife. Some of them even wanted him to remarry his first wife, although she already had two children by her second husband in Three Princes Village. * * * [B]ut when Leng Bing asked for a show of hands on the proposal, only five went up.

A peasant then suggested that Fu Gao-lin be required to do some work for the soldiers' families, and there was general agreement.

"Maybe Wang Ke-bin should do that too," someone said, "instead of sweeping the streets. It's been raining every day, so sweeping is a waste of time."

"Wang Ke-bin would love that idea," said Li Bao-yu. "He'd rather work on the soldiers' families' fields for ten days than sweep the streets for three."

For that very reason, the people turned the proposal down. Their hatred for the tiger demanded a feudal punishment, even though the labor wasted in sweeping the muddy streets could have been put to good use.

Questions

1. What were the manifestations of poverty in prerevolutionary Ten Mile Inn? Of inequality? To what extent did land reform address each of these?

2. Describe the rise and fall of Fu Gao-lin.

3. Why do you think the peasants preferred "feudal" punishments for disgraced leaders over making them do more useful work? What might that say about how they perceived the injuries of inequality and poverty?

Nahum Goldmann and Fawaz Turki, Conflicting Perspectives on Israel/Palestine (1969, 1972)

The conflicting claims of Jews and Palestinians to the land of Israel/Palestine created one of the most intractable political problems of the period after 1948. In the late nineteenth century many Jews, mostly eastern European, beset by social and economic crises, oppressed by anti-Semitism and influenced by the growth of nationalist ideas, began to promote emigration to Israel. The Zionist Organization, founded in 1897, lobbied for the creation of a Jewish homeland in Palestine. The murder of 6 million Jews during World War II shocked world opinion and increased public sympathy for the establishment of a Jewish homeland. In November 1947 the UN General Assembly voted to recommend partition of Palestine into independent Jewish and Arab states. This led to a war in 1948–1949 that forced 700,000 Palestinians into exile and left Israel in control of most of Palestine. In subsequent wars Israel increased the Arab-inhabited lands under its control. About 4 million Palestinians now live under Israeli occupation. The following excerpts give the views of a Zionist and a Palestinian refugee. Nahum Goldmann (1895–1982), a Lithuanian Jew born in the Russian Empire, worked tirelessly for the establishment of a Zionist state. Despite becoming an Israeli citizen, he never lived there. In the last decades of his life he criticized Israel's reliance on military force in its dealings with the Arabs and called for a more conciliatory policy. Fawaz Turki (b. 1940) was born in Haifa. In 1948 his family fled to Lebanon.

NAHUM GOLDMANN

I spent several weeks in Tel Aviv, which then consisted of only a few streets, several more in Rishon le-Ziou and Rehovot, and a week in Rosh Pina in Galilee. But most of my time I spent in Jerusalem, where I rented, in what was then the Russian apartment-house complex, a romantic attic with a balcony. I used to sleep on the balcony when the weather got warm.

A detailed account of colonization in those days is beyond the scope of this [discussion], but it was all in quite a primitive stage, except for a few old-established settlements such as Petah Tiqva, Rishon le-Zion, and one or two others. I was especially impressed by kibbutzim, such as Deganyah and Kinneret, and by the type of young *halutz*, or pioneer, Zionists I encountered for the first time. In Jerusalem I tried to get to know the old *yishuv*, the pre-Zionist Orthodox Jewish community, as well as the new one and had some very impressive encounters with kabbalists and mystics in the Meah Shearim quarter of Jerusalem. * * *

SOURCE: *The Autobiography of Nahum Goldmann: Sixty Years of Jewish Life*, translated by Helen Sebba (New York: Holt, Rinehart, and Winston, 1969), pp. 39–42, 44, and Fawaz Turki, *The Disinherited: Journal of a Palestinian Exile* (New York: Monthly Review Press, 1972), pp. 45, 47–48, 53–54.

I often used to take long moonlight rides with friends and once, on our way back, we were surrounded by a Bedouin band. They would certainly have robbed us and left us naked on the road if one of my companions, who was familiar with the country, had not advised us to act naturally, to sing and occasionally pat our hip pockets as if we were carrying guns. Apparently this produced the desired effect. After riding along with us for about ten minutes, the Bedouin suddenly scattered. Another time I found myself in a precarious situation when my Arab guide in Jericho arranged for me to be a hidden spectator at an Arab wedding and at the bride's dancing—something forbidden to foreigners under Bedouin law. I had already watched several dances, unforgettable in their wild passion, when my guide rushed up to me, pale with fear, and said that one of the bride's relatives had noticed something and was looking for me. We disappeared as fast as we could and got back to the hotel before it was too late.

*   *   *

But even more than the people and the early achievements of Jewish colonization, the country itself impressed me. Never again was Palestine to have such an impact upon me. For one thing I was younger and more sensitive to such impressions and less distracted by other responsibilities than I was during later visits. The exceptional quality of this curious little territory, which has acquired a unique significance in human history not to be explained by its natural resources or geopolitical situation—what I would like to call its mystical meaning—was brought home to me then as never again. Later it became much more difficult to sense that special aura; one was too distracted by what was happening in and to the country. But at that time Palestine was still untouched. You felt the presence of the mountains without having to think about the settlements that would be established on them. You rode across the plains unmarred by buildings and highways. You traveled very slowly; there were no cars and only a few trains; you usually rode on horseback or in a cart. It took two days to get from Haifa to Jerusalem. One saw the country clearly as if emerging from thousands of years of enchantment. The clearness of the air, the brilliance of the starry sky, the mystery of the austere mountains, made it seem as though its history had grown out of the landscape. In those days it was an extraordinarily peaceful, idealistic country, absorbed in a reverie of its own unique past. In the atmosphere lingered something of the prophets and the great Talmudists, of Jesus and the Apostles, of the Safed kabbalists, and the singers of bygone centuries.

* * *

When I left Palestine my Zionism had been enriched by a momentous factor, the country itself. Until then Zionism had been an abstract idea to me, and I had no real conception of what the return of the Jews meant in any concrete sense. My visit gave me that feeling for the soil without which Zionism is bound to remain quite unsubstantial. From then on I began to understand what it means, not merely negatively in terms of leaving the Diaspora behind, but also positively, as a new beginning in a Jewish homeland.

* * *

Fawaz Turki

Man adapts. We adapted, the first few months, to life in a refugee camp. In the adaptation we were also reduced as men, as women, as children, as human beings. At times we dreamed. Reduced dreams. Distorted ambitions. One day, we hoped, our parents would succeed in buying two beds for me and my sister to save us the agonies of asthma, intensified from sleeping on blankets on the cold floor. One day, we hoped, there would be enough to buy a few pounds of pears or apples as we had done on those special occasions when we fought and sulked and complained because one of us was given a smaller piece of fruit than the others. One day soon, we hoped, it would be the end of the month when the UNRWA [United Nations Relief and Works Agency for Palestine Refugees in the Near East] rations arrived and there was enough to eat for a week. One day soon, we argued, we would be back in our homeland.

* * *

The days stretched into months and those into a year and yet another. Kids would play in the mud of the winters and the dust of the summers, while "our problem" was debated at the UN and moths died around the kerosene lamps. A job had been found for me in a factory not far from the camp, where I worked for six months. I felt pride in the fact that I was a bread earner and was thus eligible to throw my weight around the house, legitimately demand an extra spoonful of sugar in my tea, and have my own money to spend on comic books and an occasional orange on the side. I had even started saving to buy my own bed, but I was fired soon after that.

A kid at work had called me a two-bit Palestinian and a fist fight ensued. The supervisor, an obese man with three chins and a green stubble that covered most of his face and reached under his eyes, came over to stop the fight. He decided I had started it all, slapped me hard twice, deducted three lira from my wages for causing trouble (I earned seven lira a week), paid me the rest, called me a two-bit Palestinian, and, pointing to my blond hair, suggested I had a whore mother and shoved me out the door.

I went to the river and sat on the grass to eat my lunch. I was shaken more by the two-bit-Palestinian epithet than by the plight of being unemployed. At home and around the camp, we had unconsciously learned to be proud of where we came from and to continue remembering that we were Palestinians. If this was stigmatic outside, there it was an identity to be known, perpetuated, embraced. My father, reproaching us for an ignoble offense of some kind, would say: "You are a Palestinian." He would mean: as a Palestinian one is not expected to stoop that low and betray his tradition. If we came home affecting a Lebanese accent, our mother would say: "Hey, what's wrong with your own accent? You're too good for your own people or something? You want to sound like a foreigner when we return to Haifa? What's wrong with you, hey?"

* * *

Our Palestinian consciousness, instead of dissipating, was enhanced and acquired a subtle nuance and a new dimension. It was buoyed by two concepts: the preservation of our memory of Palestine and our acquisition of education. We persisted in refusing the houses and monetary compensation offered by the UN to settle us in our host countries. We wanted nothing short of returning to our homeland. And from Syria, Lebanon, and Jordan, we would see, a few miles, a few yards, across the border, a land where we had been born, where we had lived, and where we felt the earth. "This is my land," we would shout, or cry, or sing, or plead, or reason. And to that land a people had come, a foreign community of colonizers, aided by a Western world in a hurry to rid itself of guilt and shame, demanding independence from history, from heaven, and from us.

Questions

1. What sort of contacts with "Bedouins" does Goldmann have? What is his opinion of them?

2. Writing about his 1913 experience, Goldmann thinks that Palestine is "untouched." Why? Do you think this characterization of the country is correct?

3. What aspects of life as a refugee in Lebanon does Turki find disturbing?

Frantz Fanon, The Wretched of the Earth (1961)

An activist, journalist, psychiatrist, and statesman, Frantz Fanon's (1925–1961) writings influenced anticolonial and civil rights movements around the world. Born to a middle-class family in the French colony of Martinique, Fanon attended the most prestigious high school on the island. The school, a French *lycée*, represented the French policy of assimilation: well-educated colonial subjects who assimilated to French culture would become part of the nation.

When World War II brought Vichy soldiers to the Caribbean, Fanon chose to serve in the French army; he was wounded in Europe and awarded the *Croix de Guerre*. After the war Fanon studied medicine and psychiatry in Lyon, France. During his wartime service and subsequent studies, Fanon confronted the realities of racism that were at odds with the philosophy of assimilation. He struggled with this identity crisis as he was studying radical innovations in psychology that gave attention to the previously overlooked role of culture in mental health. His first book, *Black Skin, White Masks* (1952), addresses the psychological costs of black colonial subjects who could never be fully integrated into French culture despite high levels of education and language fluency.

After completing his studies, Fanon went to Algeria, then a French colony, to practice at a government hospital. Soon after his arrival, anticolonial sentiments erupted into a war for independence. During the Algerian War (1954–1962) the French exercised brutal tactics to suppress opposition and deployed troops from other colonies against Algerian forces. Fanon resigned his post and joined the liberation movement. His observations of the psychological costs of colonial oppression and the inescapability of violence to end political and cultural domination were published in France in 1961 as *Les Damnés de la Terre* (in English, *The Wretched of the Earth*) with a foreword by Jean-Paul Sartre, a leading intellectual. Fanon died of leukemia later that year. The last section of the book is a series of cases that Fanon dealt with when he practiced at the government hospital. They provide examples of the very real human costs of violence and a culture of domination.

CASE NO 5. A EUROPEAN POLICE INSPECTOR WHO TORTURED HIS WIFE AND CHILDREN

R__, 30 years old. Came of his own accord to consult us. He was a police inspector and stated that for several weeks "things weren't working out." Married, had three children. He smoked a lot: five packets of cigarettes a day. He had lost his appetite and his sleep was frequently disturbed by nightmares. These nightmares had no special distinguishing features. What bothered him most were what he called "fits of madness." In the first place, he disliked being con-tradicted: "Can you give me an explanation for this, doctor: as soon as someone goes against me I want to hit him. Even outside my job, I feel I want to settle the fellows who get in my way, even for noth-ing at all. Look here, for example, suppose I go to the kiosk to buy the papers. There's a lot of people. Of course you have to wait. I

SOURCE: Frantz Fanon, *The Wretched of the Earth*, translated by Constance Farrington (New York: Grove Press, 1963), pp. 217–19.

hold out my hand (the chap who keeps the kiosk is a pal of mine) to take my papers. Someone in the queue gives me a challenging look and says 'Wait your turn.' Well, I feel I want to beat him up and I say to myself, 'If I had you for a few hours my fine fellow you wouldn't look so clever afterwards.'" The patient dislikes noise. At home he wants to hit everybody all the time. In fact, he does hit his children, even the baby of 20 months, with unaccustomed savagery.

But what really frightened him was one evening when his wife had criticised him particularly for hitting his children too much. (She had even said to him "My word, anyone'd think you were going mad.") He threw himself upon her, beat her and tied her to a chair, saying to himself "I'll teach her once and for all that I'm master in this house."

Fortunately his children began roaring and crying. He then realised the full gravity of his behaviour, untied his wife and the next day decided to consult a doctor, "a nerve specialist." He stated that "before, he wasn't like that"; he said that he very rarely punished his children and at all events never fought with his wife. The present phenomena had appeared "since the troubles." "The fact is," he said, "now-a-days we have to work like troopers. Last week, for example, we operated like as if we belonged to the army. Those gentlemen in the government say there's no war in Algeria and that the arm of the law, that's to say the police, ought to restore order. But there *is* a war going on in Algeria, and when they wake up to it it'll be too late. The thing that kills me most is the torture. You don't know what that is, do you? Sometimes I torture people for ten hours at a stretch * * * "

"What happens to you when you are torturing?"

"You may not realise, but it's very tiring * * * It's true we take it in turns, but the question is to know when to let the next chap have a go. Each one thinks he's going to get the information at any minute and takes good care not to let the bird go to the next chap after he's softened him up nicely, when of course the other chap would get the honour and glory of it. So sometimes we let them go; and sometimes we don't.

Sometimes we even offer the chap money, money out of our own pockets, to try to get him to talk. Our problem is as follows:

are you able to make this fellow talk? It's a question of personal success. You see, you're competing with the others. In the end your fists are ruined. So you call in the Senegalese. But either they hit too hard and destroy the creature or else they don't hit hard enough and it's no good. In fact, you have to be intelligent to make a success of that sort of work. You have to know when to lay it on and when to lay it off. You have to have a flair for it. When the chap is softened up, it's not worth your while going on hitting him. That's why you have to do the work yourself; you can judge better how you're getting on. I'm against the ones that have the chap dealt with by others and simply come to see every hour or so what state he's in. Above all, what you mustn't do is to give the chap the impression that he won't get away alive from you. Because then he wonders what's the use of talking if that won't save his life. In that case you'll have no chance at all of getting anything out of him. He must go on hoping; hope's the thing that'll make him talk.

But the thing that worries me most is this affair with my wife. It's certain that there's something wrong with me. You've got to cure me, doctor."

His superiors refused to give him sick leave, and since moreover the patient did not wish to have a psychiatrist's certificate, we tried to give him treatment "while working full-time." The weaknesses of such a procedure may easily be imagined. This man knew perfectly well that his disorders were directly caused by the kind of activity that went on inside the rooms where interrogations were carried out, even though he tried to throw the responsibility totally upon "present troubles." As he could not see his way to stopping torturing people (that made nonsense to him for in that case he would have to resign) he asked me without beating about the bush to help him to go on torturing Algerian patriots without any prickings of conscience, without any behaviour problems and with complete equanimity.

Questions

1. What does the police inspector want to achieve by seeking help from a pyschiatrist?

2. The police inspector describes two sites of violence in his life—his workplace and his home. Does he see a causal relationship between the two places of violence? If so, what is it?

3. Does Fanon think it is possible to keep these two spheres of the police inspector's life separate from one another?

Nelson Mandela, The Rivonia Trial (1964)

His face became one of the icons of the twentieth century, but for more than a quarter of it, Nelson Rolihlala Mandela's (born 1918) image was banned by the South African government. As a young lawyer, Mandela joined the African National Congress (ANC), which became increasingly active after the 1948 electoral victory of the National Party and the implementation of segregationist apartheid legislation. Mandela organized the nonviolent Defiance Campaign (1952) and was involved in the creation of the Freedom Charter (1955), which claims "South Africa belongs to all who live in it, black and white." Mandela was among those prosecuted in the Treason Trial (1956–1961): 156 people were charged with various anti-apartheid protests (all the defendants were found not guilty). Mandela then organized Umkhonto we Sizwe (Spear of the Nation), the armed wing of the ANC. In 1963 and 1964 Mandela and several co-defendants were tried in the Rivonia Trial—named for the suburb where some of them were arrested. They were charged with 221 acts of sabotage. Mandela was found guilty, sentenced to life in prison, and served twenty-seven years. Upon his release in 1990 he worked with President F. W. de Klerk and other political leaders to create a nonracial constitution and electoral system. Mandela and de Klerk shared the Nobel Peace Prize in 1993. A year later, Mandela won South Africa's first nonracial elections and served one five-year term.

In the following excerpt from the speech Mandela made to the court from the prisoner's box near the end of the Rivonia Trial, he appeals to the significance of local history and sets South Africa's political challenges in a global context. This was the last time his voice was heard publically until his release from prison.

I am the First Accused.

* * *

At the outset, I want to say that the suggestion made by the State in its opening that the struggle in South Africa is under the influence of foreigners or communists is wholly incorrect. I have done whatever I did, both as an individual and as a leader of my people, because of my experience in South Africa and my own proudly felt African background, and not because of what any outsider might have said.

In my youth * * * I listened to the elders of my tribe telling stories of the old days. Amongst the tales they related to me were those of wars fought by our ancestors in defence of the fatherland. * * * I hoped then that life might offer me the opportunity to serve my people and make my own humble contribution to their freedom struggle. This is what has motivated me in all that I have done in relation to the charges made against me in this case.

Having said this, I must deal immediately and at some length with the question of violence. Some of the things so far told to the Court are true and some are untrue. I do not, however, deny that I planned sabotage. I did not plan it in a spirit of recklessness, nor because I have any love of violence. I planned it as a result of a calm and sober assessment of the political situation that had arisen after many years of tyranny, exploitation, and oppression of my people by the Whites.

I admit immediately that I was one of the persons who helped to form Umkhonto we Sizwe, and that I played a prominent role in its affairs until I was arrested in August 1962.

In the statement which I am about to make I shall correct certain false impressions which have been created by State witnesses.

* * *

SOURCE: Nelson Mandela, *No Easy Walk to Freedom* (Oxford: Heinemann, 1965), pp. 162–65, 182, 184–85, 187–89.

I have already mentioned that I was one of the persons who helped to form Umkhonto. I, and the others who started the organization, did so for two reasons. Firstly, we believed that as a result of Government policy, violence by the African people had become inevitable, and that unless responsible leadership was given to canalize and control the feelings of our people, there would be outbreaks of terrorism which would produce an intensity of bitterness and hostility between the various races of this country which is not produced even by war. Secondly, we felt that without violence there would be no way open to the African people to succeed in their struggle against the principle of White supremacy. All lawful modes of expressing opposition to this principle had been closed by legislation, and we were placed in a position in which we had either to accept a permanent state of inferiority, or to defy the Government. We chose to defy the law. We first broke the law in a way which avoided any recourse to violence; when this form was legislated against, and then the Government resorted to a show of force to crush opposition to its policies, only then did we decide to answer violence with violence.

But the violence which we chose to adopt was not terrorism. We who formed Umkhonto were all members of the African National Congress, and had behind us the ANC tradition of non-violence and negotiation as a means of solving political disputes. We believe that South Africa belonged to all the people who lived in it, and not to one group, be it Black or White. We did not want an interracial war, and tried to avoid it to the last minute. * * *

The African National Congress was formed in 1912 to defend the rights of the African people which had been seriously curtailed by the South Africa Act, and which were then being threatened by the Native Land Act. For thirty-seven years—that is until 1949—it adhered strictly to a constitutional struggle. * * * But White Governments remained unmoved, and the rights of Africans became less instead of becoming greater. In the words of my leader, Chief Lutuli, who became President of the ANC in 1952, and who was later awarded the Nobel Peace Prize:

who will deny that thirty years of my life have been spent knocking in vain, patiently, moderately, and modestly at a closed and barred door? What have been the fruits of moderation? The past thirty years have seen the greatest number of laws restricting our rights and progress, until today we have reached a stage where we have almost no rights at all.

Even after 1949, the ANC remained determined to avoid violence. At this time, however, there was a change from the strictly constitutional means of protest which had been employed in the past. The change was embodied in a decision which was taken to protest against apartheid legislation by peaceful, but unlawful, demonstrations against certain laws. Pursuant to this policy the ANC launched the Defiance Campaign, in which I was placed in charge of volunteers. This campaign was based on the principles of passive resistance. More than 8,500 people defied apartheid laws and went to jail. Yet there was not a single instance of violence in the course of this campaign on the part of any defier.

* * *

I think that in the circumstances I am obliged to state exactly what my political beliefs are.

I have always regarded myself, in the first place, as an African patriot. * * *

Today I am attracted by the idea of a classless society, an attraction which springs in part from Marxist reading and, in part, from my admiration of the structure and organization of early African societies in this country. The land, then the main means of production, belonged to the tribe. There were no rich or poor and there was no exploitation.

It is true, * * * that I have been influenced by Marxist thought. But this is also true of many of the leaders of the new independent States. Such widely different persons as Gandhi, Nehru, Nkrumah, and Nasser all acknowledge this fact. We all accept the need for some form of socialism to enable our people to catch up with the advanced countries of this world and to overcome their legacy of extreme poverty. But this does not mean we are Marxists.

* * *

Our fight is against real, and not imaginary, hardships or, to use the language of the State Prosecutor, "so-called hardships." Basically, we fight against two features which are the hallmarks of African life in South Africa and which are entrenched by legislation which we seek to have repealed. These features are poverty and lack of human dignity, and we do not need communists or so-called "agitators" to teach us about these things.

South Africa is the richest country in Africa, and could be one of the richest countries in the world. But it is a land of extremes and remarkable contrasts. The Whites enjoy what may well be the highest standard of living in the world, whilst Africans live in poverty and misery. Forty per cent of the Africans live in hopelessly overcrowded and, in some cases, drought-stricken Reserves, where soil erosion and the overworking of the soil makes it impossible for them to live properly off the land. Thirty per cent are labourers, labour tenants, and squatters on White farms and work and live under conditions similar to those of the serfs of the Middle Ages. The other 30 per cent live in towns where they have developed economic and social habits which bring them closer in many respects to White standards. Yet most Africans, even in this group, are impoverished by low incomes and high cost of living.

* * *

The complaint of Africans, however, is not only that they are poor and the Whites are rich, but that the laws which are made by the Whites are designed to preserve this situation. There are two ways to break out of poverty. The first is by formal education, and the second is by the worker acquiring a greater skill at his work and thus higher wages. As far as Africans are concerned, both these avenues of advancement are deliberately curtailed by legislation.

* * *

The Government often answers its critics by saying that Africans in South Africa are economically better off than the inhabitants of the other countries in Africa. I do not know whether this statement is true and doubt whether any comparison can be made without having regard to the cost-of-living index in such countries. But even if it is true, as far as the African people are concerned it is irrelevant. Our complaint is not that we are poor by comparison with people in other countries, but that we are poor by comparison with the White people in our own country, and that we are prevented by legislation from altering this imbalance.

The lack of human dignity experienced by Africans is the direct result of the policy of White supremacy. White supremacy implies Black inferiority. Legislation designed to preserve White supremacy entrenches this notion.

* * *

Africans want to be paid a living wage. Africans want to perform work which they are capable of doing, and not work which the Government declares them to be capable of. Africans want to be allowed to live where they obtain work, and not be endorsed out of an area because they were not born there. Africans want to be allowed to own land in places where they work, and not to be obliged to live in rented houses which they can never call their own. Africans want to be part of the general population, and not confined to living in their own ghettoes. African men want to have their wives and children to live with them where they work, and not be forced into an unnatural existence in men's hostels. African women want to be with their menfolk and not be left permanently widowed in the Reserves. Africans want to be allowed out after eleven o'clock at night and not to be confined to their rooms like little children. Africans want to be allowed to travel in their own country and to seek work where they want to and not where the Labour Bureau tells them to. Africans want a just share in the whole of South Africa; they want security and a stake in society.

Above all, we want equal political rights, because without them our disabilities will be permanent. I know this sounds revolutionary to the Whites in this country, because the majority of voters will be Africans. This makes the White man fear democracy.

But this fear cannot be allowed to stand in the way of the only solution which will guarantee racial harmony and freedom for all.

It is not true that the enfranchisement of all will result in racial domination. Political division, based on colour, is entirely artificial and, when it disappears, so will the domination of one colour group by another. The ANC has spent half a century fighting against racialism. When it triumphs it will not change that policy.

This then is what the ANC is fighting. Their struggle is a truly national one. It is a struggle of the African people, inspired by their own suffering and their own experience. It is a struggle for the right to live.

During my lifetime I have dedicated myself to this struggle of the African people. I have fought against White domination, and I have fought against Black domination. I have cherished the ideal of a democratic and free society in which all persons live together in harmony and with equal opportunities. It is an ideal which I hope to live for and to achieve. But if needs be, it is an ideal for which I am prepared to die.

Questions

1. Mandela makes pointed appeals to African nationalism. What are they, and why would they have been important to his audience?

2. How does Mandela justify the ANC's turn to sabotage? Is the argument convincing?

3. Mandela's speech justifies violence, but does not condone it. Frantz Fanon (see Frantz Fanon, *The Wretched of the Earth*, in this chapter) argues, in contrast, that violence is necessary to break the hierarchies of colonial oppression. What might account for Mandela's more conservative position?

Simone de Beauvoir, The Second Sex (1949)

Although she wrote many novels, plays, and essays, Simone de Beauvoir (1908–1986) is best known internationally for her book *The Second Sex* (1949), which is a philosophical manifesto, a rallying cry, and a detailed analysis of women's oppression. Beauvoir was an exceptional student; in

1929 she was the youngest to have earned *agrégation* (competitive qualification for secondary and some university-level teaching) in philosophy. She met fellow student Jean-Paul Sartre at the Sorbonne. The two had a life-long sexual relationship, though they never married and both also had other relationships.

Beauvoir's philosophy of feminist existentialism posits that one is not born a woman, but rather one becomes a woman through social context and expectations. She argues "existence precedes essence"—the fact of existing does not determine the contours of that existence. Beauvoir also deployed the Hegelian concept of "the Other," an important element of self-consciousness in which the self is defined in relation to differences with "the Other." Beauvoir extended this line of thinking to argue that modern French society understood masculine perspectives as the baseline from which others deviated—making the perspective of women (and by implication also racial minorities) not normal. She thus critiqued previous feminists for aspiring to emulate masculine ideals, rather than seeking independence and equality in their own terms.

The innumerable conflicts that set men and women against each other stem from the fact that neither sex assumes all the consequences of this situation that one proposes and the other undergoes: this problematic notion of "equality in inequality" that one uses to hide his despotism and the other her cowardice does not withstand the test of experience: in their exchanges, woman counts on the abstract equality she was guaranteed, and man the concrete inequality he observes. From there ensues the endless debate on the ambiguity of the words *give* and *take* in all relationships: she complains of giving everything, he protests that she takes everything from him. The woman has to understand that an exchange—a basic law of political economy—is negotiated according to the value the proposed

SOURCE: Simone de Beauvoir, *The Second Sex*, translated by Constance Borde and Sheila Malovany-Chevallier (London: Jonathan Cape, 2009), pp. 774, 777–78, 780, 782.

merchandise has for the buyer and not for the seller: she was duped by being persuaded she was priceless; in reality she is merely a distraction, a pleasure, company, an inessential article for the man; for her he is the meaning, the justification of her existence; the two objects exchanged are thus not of the same quality. * * *

But is it enough to change laws, institutions, customs, public opinion and the whole social context for men and women to really become peers? "Women will always be women," say the sceptics; other seers prophesy that in shedding their femininity they will not succeed in changing into men and will become monsters. This would mean that today's woman is nature's creation; it must be repeated again that within the human collectivity nothing is natural, and woman, among others, is a product developed by civilisation; the intervention of others in her destiny is originary: if this process were driven in another way, it would produce a very different result. Woman is defined neither by her hormones nor by mysterious instincts but by the way she grasps, through foreign consciousnesses, her body and her relation to the world; the abyss that separates adolescent girls from adolescent boys was purposely dug out from early infancy; later, it would be impossible to keep woman from being what she *was made*, and she will always trail this past behind her; if the weight of this past is accurately measured, it is obvious that her destiny is not fixed in eternity. One must certainly not think that modifying her economic situation is enough to transform woman: this factor has been and remains the primordial factor of her development, but until it brings about the moral, social and cultural, etc. consequences it heralds and requires, the new woman cannot appear; as of now, these consequences have been realised nowhere: in the USSR no more than in France or the USA; and this is why today's woman is torn between the past and the present; most often, she appears as a "real woman" disguised as a man, and she feels as awkward in her woman's body as in her masculine garb. She has to shed her old skin and cut her own clothes. She will only be able to do this if there is a collective change. No one teacher can today shape a "female human being" that would be an exact homologue to the "male human being": if raised like a boy, the girl feels she is an exception and that subjects her to a new kind of specification. * * * But if we suppose, by contrast, a society where sexual equality is concretely realised, this equality would newly assert itself in each individual.

If, from the earliest age, the little girl were raised with the same demands and honours, the same severity and freedom as her brothers, taking part in the same studies and games, promised the same future, surrounded by women and men who are unambiguously equal to her, the meanings of the "castration complex" and "Oedipus complex" would be profoundly modified. The mother would enjoy the same lasting prestige as the father if she assumed equal material and moral responsibility for the couple; the child would feel an androgynous world around her and not a masculine world.

* * *

People will say that all these considerations are merely utopian because to "remake woman" society would have had to have already made her *really* man's equal; conservatives have never missed the chance to denounce this vicious circle in all analogous circumstances: yet history does not go round in circles. Without a doubt, if a caste is maintained in an inferior position, it remains inferior: but freedom can break the circle; let blacks vote and they become worthy of the vote; give woman responsibilities and she knows how to assume them; the fact is, one would not think of expecting gratuitous generosity from oppressors; but the revolt of the oppressed at times and changes in the privileged caste at other times create new situations; and this is how men, in their own interest, have been led to partially emancipate women: women need only pursue their rise and the success they obtain encourages them; it seems most certain that they will sooner or later attain perfect economic and social equality, which will bring about an inner metamorphosis.

* * *

To emancipate woman is to refuse to enclose her in the relations she sustains with man, but not to deny them; while she posits herself for herself she will nonetheless continue to exist for him *as well*: recognising each other as subject, each will remain an *other* for the other; reciprocity in their relations will not do away with the miracles that the division of human beings into two separate categories engenders: desire, possession, love, dreams, adventure; and the words that move us: to give, to conquer, and to unite will keep their meaning; on the contrary, it is when the slavery of half of humanity is abolished and with it the whole hypocritical system it implies that the "division" of humanity will reveal its authentic meaning and the human couple will discover its true form.

Questions

1. Beauvoir identifies legal, economic, social, and sexual norms which subordinate women. In her view, what role do women play in perpetuating this subordination?

2. What changes does she advocate as necessary for a more equal relationship between men and women?

3. What does Beauvoir's more equal future look like? What criticisms of this vision does she acknowledge?

Hermann Muller, One Hundred Years without Darwinism Are Enough (1959)

Hermann Muller (1890–1967) won the 1946 Nobel Prize in Medicine for work on genes, radiation, and mutations. Politics also played a big role in his life—sometimes involuntarily. His work in the 1920s suggested that humans could be genetically improved; however, Muller opposed policies such as immigration restrictions favored by many eugenicists. In 1932, under FBI investigation for involvement with a socialist newspaper, Muller joined a German lab, leaving shortly after Hitler took power. Three years in Moscow followed; he was forced out for opposing T. D. Lysenko's anti-Darwinian theories, which Stalin supported. After returning to the United States, Muller played a small role in the Manhattan Project, won the Nobel Prize, and became active in efforts to limit nuclear weapons. In "One Hundred Years without Darwinism Are Enough," he emphasizes his opposition to Soviet communism, but also criticizes both religious and commercial aspects of American society that he feels interfere with the technical, social, and spiritual progress science offers.

One hundred years ago, on July 1, 1858, Charles Darwin and Alfred Russell Wallace made their joint announcement of the theory of evolution by natural selection. * * * Since that time, the whole matter has been subjected to the most copious and exacting criticism, and to ever more searching exploration and testing. The result has been that this principle of living nature now stands as one of the most firmly established generalizations of science and that far more is now understood about the manner by which evolution operates than was even imagined a century ago.

* * *

It ill befits our great people, four generations after Darwin and Wallace published their epochal discovery of evolution by natural selection, to turn our backs on it, to pretend that it is unimportant or uncertain, to adopt euphemistic expressions to hide and soften its impact, to teach it only as one alternative theory, to leave it for advanced courses where the multitudes cannot encounter it, or, if it is dealt with at all in a school or high school biology course, to present it as unobtusively and near the end of the course as possible, so that the student will fail to appreciate how every other feature and principle found in living things is in reality an outgrowth of its universal operation.

Are we teachers in whose hands lies the responsibility of bringing to the next generation a true and modern view of the nature of things, as gained by the devoted efforts of the world community of critical scientific minds, not deeply ashamed that we have been so remiss in our task of awakening in that developing generation an adequate realization of the most basic forces of life and of how

---

SOURCE: Hermann Muller, "One Hundred Years without Darwinism Are Enough," *School Science and Mathematics* 59 (April 1959): 305–14.

these forces have worked and are still working to give rise to all life's outer manifestations? * * *

We need, in these decisive days of world tension, when free men will stand or fall according to how fully they recognize and act upon the most honest views of the truth that they can glean, to execute a complete about-face in this critical area of education. We dare not leave it to the Soviets alone to offer men the inspiration that is to be gained from the wonderful world view opened up by Darwin and other Western biologists. This view, founded so solidly upon the discoveries of modern science, is, when fully incorporated into men's personalities, the source of the profoundest idealism and hope. * * * [I]t shows how the most essential properties of living things have led to their perpetual reaching out, self-transformation, progression, and conquest of the rest of nature. * * * But * * * noting the millions of species that have fallen by the way, this view of things also points to the practical dangers, and leads us to seek ways of avoiding the pitfalls and the insidious deflections of course that would otherwise cause disaster again.

Boys and girls in grade and high school are by no means too young for such lessons. * * * I well remember the deep impression made on me when at the age of seven or eight I saw the series of fossil horses' legs at the Natural History Museum and listened to my father explain how they had come about as a result of the ever speedier variants escaping better from the carnivores generation after generation. The essential basis of natural selection, given in this form, is easily grasped by any child and * * * applied to case after case as these cases are encountered.

*　*　*

The text called "Modern Biology" which has been assigned in many high school classes in Indiana and elsewhere fails to contain the word evolution in the index or anywhere else. It does, however, in its next-to-the-last chapter have a moderately acceptable discussion of evolution, without using the word. This treatment, unfortunately, comes at too late a point to allow consideration of all other parts of biology as manifestations of evolution, Moreover, the words *"racial development"* are given, in heavy print * * * as the term by which this principle of nature is known! What better expression could be devised for veiling from one's view the awe inspiring pattern by which primeval life progressively and divergently flowered out into all kinds of living beings, including ourselves!

*   *   *

A study published in 1942 by the Commission on the Teaching of Biology of the Union of American Biological Societies showed that even then less than half of the high school teachers of biology taught evolution as the principle underlying the development of all living things. * * * With the passage of time, this ostrich policy has become, if anything, even more firmly fixed, despite the fact, or rather, *because* of the fact, that this field is so pregnant in its implications for everyone. Thus do we fail our youth.

*   *   *

We have no more right to starve the masses of our people intellectually and emotionally because of the objections of the uninformed than we have a right to allow people to keep their children from being vaccinated and thus to endanger the whole community physically. Fortunately, leaders of important religious groups are coming to realize their obligations in this matter.

*   *   *

Since the first successful Russian sputnik was launched, we have been hearing on all sides clamors for better and more effective teaching of science and mathematics in our schools. The President's committee, to our shame, reported last year that the Russians, whose population is not much greater than ours and who forty years ago were in large measure an illiterate people with a very weakly developed technology, already have more scientists and engineers than we do and are turning out more than twice as many science and engineering graduates per year as we do.

*   *   *

In the field of biology and of biological evolution in particular we have at present a more concrete advantage over the Russians, if we will but use it. * * * For it happens that the political powers in the Soviet Union have for more than twenty years exerted an especially destructive influence through their dictatorial policies in the field of genetics, the field that provides the most direct evidence concerning the way evolution works. In this crucial area of biology the Russian system of absolute authoritarianism has in fact proved fatal. It has literally killed off their great leaders in genetics, deprived their rank and file geneticists of the opportunity of doing further researches along their own lines, expurgated their curricula, textbooks and periodicals of any treatments of the subject, and brought up a whole generation on totally false biological doctrines. Central to these falsehoods is the doctrine of the inheritance of acquired characters and its corollary, that this is the means by which evolution works.

Only for the past year and a half have geneticists in Soviet countries been allowed to work and speak out somewhat more freely again. * * * In this field, then, a field basic to the understanding of biological evolution and of everything that has resulted therefrom, we have a potential advantage of many years if only we will give this subject its due place in the education of our own youth. * * *

It would in many ways be a grievous step backward if the Soviet system, with its authoritarianism and its perversion of biological as well as social progress, were to win out in the struggle for the minds, hearts and bodies of men. We have in our own ways of life much more inspiring possibilities, if only we will grant them adequate opportunities for development in the hearts of our younger generation. At present we do not. Our youth are now being allowed to fall into the decadence of the commercialized hoopla that is carried to them over television and radio, in stadia and other public gatherings, and they are being on all sides encouraged in their rush to exploit privately and capriciously the opportunities of their high-powered automobiles and their increased allowances. * * *

For beings who have been endowed by evolution with the social and moral natures of men, individual freedom soon turns into caprice, disillusionment, and decadence unless the individual sees himself as an integral part of a greater whole, working with others in the pursuit of the higher freedoms of his community. In our modern age with its shrinkage of distances, this community now means the whole of mankind. This is the deepest lesson that the study of evolution, especially in its human aspects, can bring to the individual.

* * *

The work of reconstruction of our biology teaching should go on at all levels. The most immediate need is for the preparation and adoption of high-quality texts that give evolution its due axial position and deal with it outspokenly and adequately. The author of one of our most widely used high school biology texts has informed me that if he had insisted on this policy his book would have been rejected by the publishers. A representative of the publishers has next asserted that the fault was not theirs, since if they had been on the level with the children (an expression not used by him!) the book would have been rejected in Southern states in which the teaching of evolution is still illegal and by many textbook commissions and school boards in other parts of the United States as well, and that in that case they, the publishers, could not have afforded to publish the book. So the passing of the buck (*whose buck?*) will go on until the vicious circle is broken somewhere, by means of determined, concerted action.

Questions

1. Why, according to Muller, do American science curricula de-emphasize evolution? Why are anti-evolutionists so influential?

2. What benefits does Muller claim would result from more teaching of evolution? Why?

3. Rhetorically, Muller is in a tricky position—he wants to promote evolution, but he thinks it has social implications much of his society would oppose. How does he handle this?

Chapter *21*

GLOBALIZATION, 1970–2000

World Energy (1850–2000)

As the world energy graph shows, human energy use has increased more than twentyfold since 1850—when it was already much higher than 100 years earlier. In per capita terms, this represents more than a fourfold increase. These global averages mask differences among countries that were already large in 1850, and are even larger today. In 2005, an average U.S. citizen used 45 times as much energy as a Bangladeshi, and the average Qatari over 100 times as much. Bangladeshi consumption even in 2005 was barely one-third of what world per capita consumption had been in 1850.

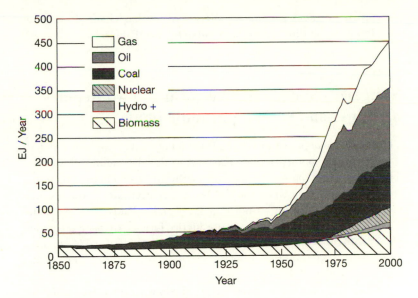

Graph of World Energy, 1850–2000

Questions

1. Which periods have seen the most dramatic changes in total energy use? What changes in energy sources have been associated with those periods?

2. The first commercial oil well was drilled in 1859; it also produced natural gas. How long thereafter did it take for each of these energy sources to become important on a global scale?

3. On average the carbon emissions for each megawatt of electricity made with natural gas are 1.0–1.7 (depending on the technology used), that for oil is 2.5, for coal a bit over 3, and for wood (biomass) about 4.3. (1.0 ≈ 250 pounds.) For hydroelectric and nuclear it can be negligible once the plants are constructed (though under some circumstances, dams can have high carbon emissions). What does this suggest about how the

SOURCE: Redrawn from Alfred W. Crosby, *Children of the Sun* (New York: Norton, 2006), p. 162.

carbon emissions per unit of energy we use has changed over time? How does this differ from the trend in total emissions?

Sean Daily and Daniel Zwerdling, Two Reports on Water and Farming in India (2009)

The two documents that follow highlight a national example of a global problem: contemporary farming uses unsustainable amounts of water. Though there are many problems in wealthy areas—including Australia, the American Great Plains, and California's central valley—the resulting social problems are most serious in parts of India, Pakistan, and North China. Densely populated, highly productive farms have been created in places with limited and unreliable rainfall. About half of Pakistan, for instance, gets less rain than Phoenix, Arizona; 80 percent of the country gets less rain than Tel Aviv.

Major irrigation works, pioneered in the late nineteenth century (especially in India, Egypt, Australia, and the western United States), were an obvious way of raising agricultural output to meet soaring demand as populations increased. Early projects mostly diverted surface water from lakes and rivers. As cheap, powerful motors proliferated, irrigators increasingly tapped underground aquifers. Worldwide, irrigated acreage increased by 600 percent in the twentieth century; half of that growth came after 1960.

Spectacular output gains followed. New lands became arable, droughts were reduced, and plentiful, reliable water allowed farmers to use highly productive new seeds and fertilizers. In most countries, government policies made the water cheap. But these same developments—often exacerbated by pollution—have drastically depleted both surface and underground water resources. Farming accounts for 70 percent of worldwide freshwater use.

Every proposed solution also raises questions. Various technical solutions—genetically engineered drought-tolerant plants, more efficient water delivery, desalinization—are possible, but uncertain; many are also likely to be expensive and/or to have further unforeseen environmental effects. Raising water prices can reduce waste, but can also devastate the poor. And with global population still rising—and climate change (see Intergovernmental Panel on Climate Change, *Summary for Policymakers*, in this chapter) likely to create new drought zones—reducing farm output implies tragedy.

Mass Farmer Suicide Sobering Reminder of Consequences of Water Shortages

In one of the more tragic stories related to water shortage in recent history, some 1,500 farmers in India's agricultural state of Chhattisgarh committed mass suicide in response to the devastating effects of water shortages on their crop production.

The story * * * underscores the potentially devastating effects of water shortages to agriculture-centric regions of the globe, and to those who rely on water for not only their financial livelihoods and health, but for their hope. "The water level has gone down below 250 feet here. It used to be at 40 feet a few years ago," said Shatrughan Sahu, a villager local from a Chhattisgarh district, to India's *Down To Earth* magazine. The district has been particularly devastated by farmer suicides in recent years, having recorded 206 in the past year alone. District police records indicate that many of the deaths occur due to distress over financial debt related to crop failures. In the Chhattisgarh region, water levels in the area have been reported to have been in major decline during recent years primarily due to drought, which has all but destroyed agricultural efforts in the region.

However, farmer suicides, including those committed en masse, have a tragic history in India beyond Chhattisgarh state itself.

Source: Sean Daily, "Mass Farmer Suicide Sobering Reminder of Consequences of Water Shortages," Blue Living Ideas (blog), 2009, http:// bluelivingideas.com/topics/water-availability/mass-farmer-suicide-sobering -reminder-of-consequences-of-water-shortages/, and Daniel Zwerdling, "India's Farming 'Revolution' Heading for Collapse," National Public Radio (USA), April 13, 2009, www.npr.org/templates/story/story.php?storyId= 102893816.

According to the statistics of National Crime Records Bureau, some 200,000 farmers have committed suicide during the past 12 years. The BBC, citing another government report, reported in 2007 that "about 12 per cent of marginal and small farmers have left farming" during the past several years.

India is by no means the only region experiencing such dramatic levels of drought and resulting threat to agricultural production and farmer livelihood. For example, some Australian farmers are experiencing similar financial hardships as a result of water shortages due to drought, and which are exacerbated by loan conditions that make it difficult for farmers to manage their debt. Many believe that though such regions today serve as flashpoints for the water crisis, they are actually harbingers of problems destined to face many other regions of the globe in coming years.

In addition to putting a sobering exclamation point on the present state of global water availability, the story also serves as a further reminder of how farmers and agricultural nations stand at the forefront of the world water crisis and are presently suffering the most immediate and dramatic of its effects. Recent documentary films such as Sam Bozzo's indy water documentary *Blue Gold: World Water Wars* and Irena Salina's *FLOW* include stories of the plight of farmers in relation to drought, regional politics, and economically driven multinational water interests.

India's Farming "Revolution" Heading for Collapse

Farmers in the village of Chotia Khurd in northern India don't realize it, but they symbolize a growing problem that could become a global crisis.

They gathered on a recent morning in a stone-paved courtyard—a circle of Sikhs with brightly colored turbans and big, bushy beards—to explain why the famed "bread basket" of India is heading toward collapse.

Their comparatively small region, Punjab, grows far more wheat and rice for India than any other region. But now these farmers are running out of groundwater.

They have to buy three times as much fertilizer as they did 30 years ago to grow the same amount of crops. They blitz their crops with pesticides, but insects have become so resistant that they still often destroy large portions of crops.

The state's agriculture "has become unsustainable and non-profitable," according to a recent report by the Punjab State Council for Science and Technology. Some experts say the decline could happen rapidly, over the next decade or so.

One of the best-known names in India's farming industry puts it in even starker terms. If farmers in Punjab don't dramatically change the way they grow India's food, says G. S. Kalkat, chairman of the Punjab State Farmers Commission, they could trigger a modern Dust Bowl. That American disaster in the 1930s laid waste to millions of acres of farmland and forced hundreds of thousands of people out of their homes.

The "Green Revolution"

The story begins in the 1960s, when parents in America's well-fed suburbs would admonish ungrateful children to "think about the starving people in India." Occasional news reports told wrenching stories about Indians subsisting on grass and leaves. The country survived on imports, like a beggar.

The public concern prompted a loose coalition of scientists, government officials and philanthropists—spurred and funded, in part, by the Rockefeller Foundation—to launch a "Green Revolution."

In the context of the times, "green" did not refer to what it means today—organic, pesticide-free farming methods. To the contrary, India's farmers were persuaded to abandon their traditional methods and grow crops the modern, American way.

For example, the advisers told farmers to stop growing old-fashioned grains, beans and vegetables and switch to new, high-yield varieties of wheat, rice and cotton. Farmers began using chemical fertilizers instead of cow dung. They plowed with tractors instead of bulls.

The "Green Revolution" of the 1960s and 1970s meant that if farmers embraced chemicals and high-yield seeds, their fields would turn lush green with crops. (An official at the U.S. State Department, William Gaud, apparently coined the term in 1968.)

During the Cold War, the term also implied that if countries like India could stamp out hunger, the population would be less likely to foment a violent revolution and go communist.

A *Temporary Fix*

In India, ground zero for the Green Revolution was the state of Punjab, which borders Pakistan and the foothills of the Himalayas. And the system seemed to work miracles—for a while.

The United States sent money and technical support, including advisers from one of America's most prestigious agriculture universities. India's government showered Punjab with low-cost chemicals and seeds—and they paid the farmers, in effect, to use them by guaranteeing minimum prices for Green Revolution crops.

It helped India transform itself from a nation that depends on imports and food aid to a budding superpower that often exports grains.

Villages like Chotia Khurd were harvesting three to four times as much grain per acre as they did before.

Many of the farmers and the local government were flush with money. They paved their dirt roads. The farmers replaced their mud houses with bricks and cement. They bought American tractors for a small fortune.

Just about everybody in Chotia Khurd bought cell phones, with a wide variety of ring tones—so it's hard to chat with a farmer without getting interrupted by electronic versions of Sikh chants or theme songs from Bollywood hits.

But government reports and farmers themselves say that era is over—and today, the Green Revolution system of farming is heading toward collapse.

"Farmers Are Committing a Kind of Suicide"

To show why, the district director of the Punjab Agriculture Department, Palwinder Singh, leads the way up a narrow dirt road into wheat fields that encircle the village.

On the surface, they look robust. The countryside is electric green in every direction.

But Singh points to a large contraption rising above the crop, like a steel praying mantis. The machine is blanketing the country-side with a percussive, deafening roar.

"That's part of our most serious problem," he says. It's a drilling rig. A young farmer in a purple turban, Sandeep Singh, is standing next to the rig, looking unhappy. (The two men are not related—according to tradition, all Sikh men share the last name "Singh," which means "lion.")

When farmers switched from growing a variety of traditional crops to high-yield wheat and rice, they also had to make other changes. There wasn't enough rainwater to grow thirsty "miracle" seeds, so farmers had to start irrigating with groundwater. They hired drilling companies to dig wells, and they started pumping groundwater onto the fields.

But Sandeep says he has been forced to hire the drilling com-pany again, because the groundwater under his fields has been sinking as much as 3 feet every year.

Government surveys confirm it. In fact, his family and other farmers have had to deepen their wells every few years—from 10 feet to 20 feet to 40 feet, and now to more than 200 feet—because the precious water table keeps dropping below their reach.

Nobody was surprised when environmental activists started warning years ago that the Green Revolution was heading toward disaster. But they were astonished as government officials started to agree.

"Farmers are committing a kind of suicide," warns Kalkat, the director of the Punjab State Farmers Commission. "It's like a sui-cide, en masse."

Kalkat offers an unsettling prediction in a nation whose popu-lation is growing faster than any other on Earth: If farmers don't drastically revamp the system of farming, the heartland of India's agriculture could be barren in 10 to 15 years.

Questions

1. How do the tone and the focus of these two reports differ? Do they imply different approaches to the problem, or not?

2. How does Zwerdling's analysis (broadcast on public radio in the United States) explain the origins of Punjab's water crisis?

3. Since farming uses more water per dollar of output than manufacturing or services, some development planners argue that countries like China and India can best alleviate their water crises through even more rapid urbanization. What pros and cons can you see in this approach?

Voice of Bangladeshi Bloggers, Bangladeshi Workers in Kuwait (2008)

Since 1970 the world economy has become increasingly globalized. The end of the cold war and the last vestiges of European colonial rule removed many of the most important barriers to the free flow of capital and labor. World trade increased dramatically and national economies became ever more dependent on resources from and access to foreign markets. Great masses of people moved across the globe, usually from poorer countries to richer ones in search of better wages. Some were legal migrants; many were not. This labor migration posed difficult questions of how these guest workers would fit into the political, economic, and cultural structures of their host societies. The following excerpt comes from Deshi Voice, a blog established by Bangladeshis. It discusses the problems faced by Bangladeshi workers in Kuwait, one of the world's major exporters of oil. These workers have migrated for construction, oil field, and domestic service jobs.

BANGLADESHI WORKERS IN KUWAIT

The US based National Labor Committee [NCL] has recently published an investigative report on the plight of the Bangladeshi laborers in Kuwait. These workers were trafficked to Kuwait and forced to a sub-human living standard. The report says,

> Hundreds of thousands of foreign guest workers—among them 240,000 Bangladeshis—have been trafficked to Kuwait, where they are immediately stripped of their passports. Many work seven days a week for wages of just 14 to 36 cents an hour, which means they are being cheated of up to 84 percent of the 90-cent-an-hour wage they were guaranteed when they purchased their three-year contracts to work in Kuwait. Workers who ask for their proper wages are beaten and threatened with arrest and forcible deportation. The workers are housed in squalid, overcrowded dorms with eight workers sharing each small 10-by-10-foot room, sleeping on narrow, double-level metal bunk beds.

Kuwaiti companies have cheated these poor laborers and denied them of basic human rights. Kuwaiti Government kept their blind eyes and neglected to address these inhuman conditions of these poor workers. But is Kuwait a poor country? No, not at all. The NCL report adds,

> Kuwait is not poor. Quite the opposite: It is the world's seventh largest oil exporter. Kuwait's GDP is expected to grow 6.8 percent this year to $172.4 billion. Kuwait's trade surplus is running at $84 billion this year. Government revenues for the current fiscal year (April 1, 2008 through March 31, 2009) are also projected to grow by 40 percent, to reach approximately $129 billion. Even after all conceivable expenses, the Kuwait government should end the year with a fiscal surplus of $66.21 billion.
>
> Kuwait does not need to exploit desperately poor foreign guest workers. They have the money to treat all workers in Kuwait with a modicum of dignity.

SOURCE: "Bangladeshi Workers in Kuwait," Voice of Bangladeshi Bloggers, August 31, 2008, http://deshivoice.blogspot.com/2008/08/bangladeshi-workers-in-kuwait.html.

Ninety percent of Kuwait's private sector workers are non-Kuwaiti. Sixty-three percent—or 2.3 million people out of a total population of 3.4 million—are expatriates. Hundreds of thousands of foreign guest workers have been trafficked to Kuwait from Bangladesh, India, Sri Lanka, Egypt, Sudan, Pakistan, Indonesia and the Philippines.

In 2007, Ambassador Mark Lagon and the U.S. State Department's Office to Monitor and Combat Trafficking in Persons demoted Kuwait to "Tier 3"—the lowest level, for being among those countries doing the least to prevent the trafficking of human beings.

The government of Kuwait however, does take care of its own people. When inflation skyrocketed in 2008—(it's expected to reach 13.5 percent by year's end)—the government moved quickly. In June 2008, any Kuwaiti public sector employee who was earning $45,000 a year or less, received a $188 a month wage increase. For those who had been earning $45,000 a year, this meant receiving a $2,257 increase, bringing their new annual wage to $47,397. The government was well aware that Kuwaitis earning just $45,000 were struggling in the face of inflation, especially given the soaring food costs.

However, when it came to the foreign guest workers in Kuwait, who were earning an average of just $903 a year and who were surely suffering due to the soaring cost of food, there was no similar concern by the government, despite the fact that the guest workers were earning less than two percent of what "low income" Kuwaitis were earning. The compounded inflation rate between 2006 and the end of 2008 is expected to reach 23.3 percent, and is causing the guest workers tremendous hardship".

The NCL urges everyone to SEND A LETTER TO SECRETARY OF STATE CONDOLEEZA RICE URGING HER TO TAKE ACTION FOR GUEST WORKERS AT CAMP ARIFJAN. Here is a draft of the letter that you can send:

The Honorable Condoleezza Rice
Secretary of State
Department of State
2201 C St., NW
Washington, DC 20520

Dear Secretary Rice:

I urge you to call upon the Government of Kuwait to end the trafficking of hundreds of thousands of foreign guest workers to Kuwait, where they are stripped of their passports, forced to work long hours, often seven days a week, while being cheated of half their wages. The workers are housed in squalid dorms. Some of these victims of human trafficking are actually working on a U.S. military base in Kuwait.

As you are well aware, Operation Desert Storm to liberate Kuwait cost the lives of 294 U.S. troops, with another 458 wounded. Moreover, 183,000 veterans of the Gulf War are now permanently disabled! This was a very heavy price to pay. The U.S. also has a defense pact with Kuwait to guarantee the security of the Kuwaiti people and government. This gives the Government of United States a very powerful voice, which the Kuwaiti Government must take seriously. I urge you again to call upon the Government of Kuwait to end the heinous practice of human trafficking, to assure that all guest worker passports are returned to them and to finally guarantee that the legal rights of these hundreds of thousands of guest workers be respected.

These workers, including those working on U.S. military bases, should also be made whole again and paid the back wages of which they were cheated.

Thank you for your concern and efforts to end human trafficking.

Questions

1. Why does the author of the blog post say that Bangladeshi workers were "trafficked" to Kuwait? Why not use another term?

2. What are the chief grievances of the blogger about the condition of Bangladeshi laborers in Kuwait?

3. What does this post tell us about information networks and the economic aspects of globalization in the first decade of the twenty-first century?

Intergovernmental Panel on Climate Change, Summary for Policymakers (2007)

The Intergovernmental Panel on Climate Change (IPCC) was established in 1988 by the World Meteorological Organization and the United Nations Environmental Program. It is a scientific body of leading researchers that synthesizes current findings. It does not undertake its own research. The IPCC's work supports the UN Framework Convention on Climate Change, the basic treaty that led to the 1997 Kyoto Protocol to reduce worldwide emissions of greenhouse gasses. The panel's work is regarded as authoritative by almost all climate scientists around the world. The IPCC shared the 2007 Nobel Peace Prize with former U.S. vice president Al Gore in recognition of efforts to call attention to the effects of human actions on the environment.

The following chart comes from an executive summary of four lengthy volumes that comprise the IPCC's Fourth Assessment Report: "The Physical Science Basis," "Impacts, Adaptation, and Vulnerability," "Mitigation of Climate Change," and "The AR Synthesis Report." The full text of the report is available online at www.ipcc.ch/.

Phenomenon and direction of bend	Likelihood of future trends based on projections for 21st century using SRES scenarios	Examples of major projected impacts by sector			
		Agriculture, forestry and ecosystems	Water resources	Human health	Industry, settlement and society
Over most land areas, warmer and fewer cold days and nights, warmer and more frequent hot days and nights	Virtually certain	Increased yields in colder environments; decreased yields in warmer environments: increased insect outbreaks	Effects on water resources relying on snow melt; effects on some water supplies	Reduced human mortality from decreased cold exposure	Reduced energy demand for heating; increased demand for cooling; declining air quality in cities; reduced disruption to transport due to snow; ice; effects on winter tourism
Warm spells/heat waves. Frequency increases over most land areas	Very likely	Reduced yields in warmer regions due to heat stress; increased danger of wildfire	Increased water demand; water quality problems, e.g., algal blooms	Increased risk of heat-related mortality, especially for the elderly, chronically sick, very young and socially isolated	Reduction in quality of life for people in warm areas without appropriate housing; impacts on the elderly, very young and poor
Heavy precipitation events. Frequency increases over most areas	Very likely	Damage to crops; soil erosion, inability to cultivate land due to waterlogging of soils	Adverse effects on quality of surface and groundwater; contamination of water supply; water scarcity may be relieved	Increased risk of deaths, injuries and infectious, respiratory and skin diseases	Disruption of settlements, commerce, transport and societies due to flooding; pressures on urban and rural infrastructures; loss of property

Phenomenon and direction of bend	Likelihood of future trends based on projections for 21st century using SRES scenarios	Examples of major projected impacts by sector			
		Agriculture, forestry and ecosystems	Water resources	Human health	Industry, settlement and society
Area affected by drought increases	Likely	Land degradation; lower yields/crop damage and failure; increased livestock deaths; increased risk of wildfire	More widespread water stress	Increased risk of food and water shortage; increased risk of malnutrition; increased risk of water- and food-borne diseases	Water shortages for settlements, industry and societies; reduced hydropower generation potentials; potential for population migration
Intense tropical cyclone activity increases	Likely	Damage to crops: windthrow (uprooting) of trees; damage to coral reefs	Power outages causing disruption of public water supply	Increased risk of deaths, injuries, water- and food-borne diseases; post-traumatic stress disorders	Disruption by flood and high winds; withdrawal of risk coverage in vulnerable areas by private insurers, potential for population migrations, loss of property
Increased incidence of extreme high sea level (excludes tsunamis)	Likely	Salinisation of irrigation water, estuaries and freshwater systems	Decreased freshwater availability due to saltwater intrusion	Increased risk of deaths and injuries by drowning in floods; migration-related health effects	Costs of coastal protection versus costs of land-use relocation; potential for movement of populations and infrastructure; also see tropical cyclones above

SRES, Special Report on Emissions Scenario

Questions

1. What message do the report authors want policymakers to understand?

2. According to this chart, what are the most noticeable effects of climate change on the earth's ecosystems? For human activities?

3. Why would the authors have created a chart to include in the summary to a four-volume scientific study? What is gained—and what is lost—by presenting information in this format?

SOURCE: *Climate Change 2007: Impacts, Adaptation and Vulnerability. Contribution of Working Group II to the Fourth Assessment Report of the Intergovernmental Panel on Climate Change*, ed. by M. L. Parry, O. F. Canziani, J. P. Palutikof, P. J. van der Linden, and C. E. Hanson (Cambridge, Eng.: Cambridge University Press, 2007), p. 18, Table SPM.1.

Text Permissions